Airdrie
Marigold Library System

D0248853

Airdrie
Marigold Library System

A
FURIOUS SKY

OTHER BOOKS BY

ERIC JAY DOLIN

Black Flags, Blue Waters:
The Epic History of America's
Most Notorious Pirates

Brilliant Beacons:
A History of the
American Lighthouse

When America First Met China:
An Exotic History of Tea,
Drugs, and Money
in the Age of Sail

Fur, Fortune, and Empire:
The Epic History of the
Fur Trade in America

Leviathan:
The History of Whaling
in America

Political Waters

Snakehead: A Fish Out of Water

Smithsonian Book of
National Wildlife Refuges

A
FURIOUS SKY

....

The Five-Hundred-Year History of America's Hurricanes

....

ERIC JAY DOLIN

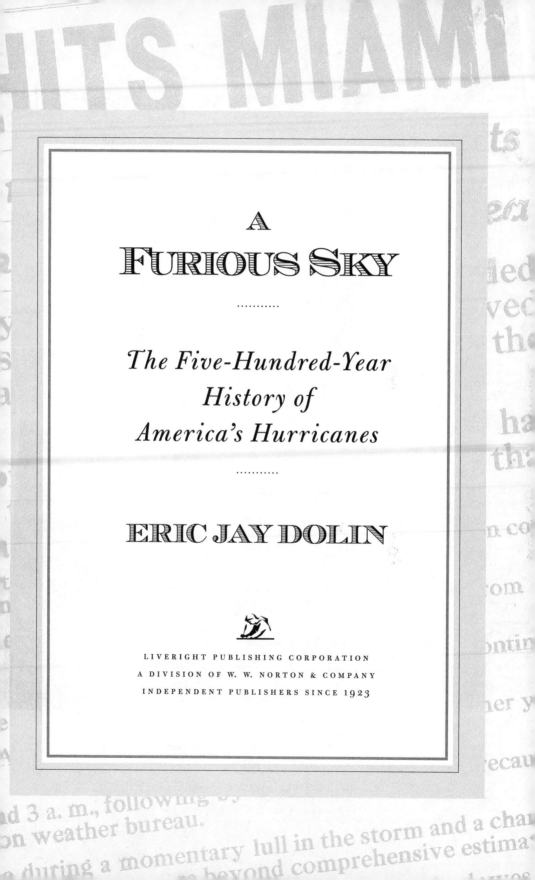

LIVERIGHT PUBLISHING CORPORATION
A DIVISION OF W. W. NORTON & COMPANY
INDEPENDENT PUBLISHERS SINCE 1923

Copyright © 2020 by Eric Jay Dolin

All rights reserved
Printed in the United States of America
First Edition

For information about permission to reproduce selections from this book, write to
Permissions, Liveright Publishing Corporation, a division of W. W. Norton & Company, Inc.,
500 Fifth Avenue, New York, NY 10110

For information about special discounts for bulk purchases, please contact
W. W. Norton Special Sales at specialsales@wwnorton.com or 800-233-4830

Manufacturing by LSC Communications, Harrisonburg
Book design by Barbara M. Bachman
Production manager: Anna Oler

ISBN 978-1-63149-527-4

Liveright Publishing Corporation, 500 Fifth Avenue, New York, N.Y. 10110
www.wwnorton.com

W. W. Norton & Company Ltd., 15 Carlisle Street, London W1D 3BS

1 2 3 4 5 6 7 8 9 0

To Jennifer,
who always believes in me

Contents

Extracts

(Supplied by a Sub-Sub-Librarian)*

Out of the south cometh the whirlwind.

JOB 37:9

Good God! What horror and destruction. . . .
It seemed as if a total dissolution of nature was taking
place. The roaring of the sea and wind, fiery meteors
flying about it in the air, the prodigious glare of almost
perpetual lightning, the crash of the falling houses,
and the ear-piercing shrieks of the distressed,
were sufficient to strike astonishment into angels.

—A TEENAGE ALEXANDER HAMILTON, WRITING
TO HIS FATHER, DESCRIBING A HURRICANE
THAT BARRELED INTO HIS HOME ISLAND
OF ST. CROIX IN LATE AUGUST 1772

Reader, persons who have never witnessed a hurricane,
such as not infrequently desolates the sultry climates

---

* With a nod to Herman Melville, whose classic *Moby-Dick* and, in particular, its prefatory materials with the same title gave me this idea.

*of the south, can scarcely form an idea of their terrific
grandeur. . . . Like a scythe of the destroying angel, it
cuts everything by the roots . . . when at last its frightful
blasts have ceased, nature, weeping and disconsolate,
is left bereaved of her beautiful offspring.*

—JOHN JAMES AUDUBON (1834)

*There is probably no feature of nature more
interesting to study than a hurricane, though feelings of
the observer may sometimes be diverted by
thoughts of personal safety.*

—F. H. BIGELOW (1898)

*Remember to get the weather in your god
damned book—weather is very important.*

—ERNEST HEMINGWAY TO JOHN DOS PASSOS (1932)

*All the thousands of hurricane stories boil down to this,
that even with all modern scientific developments,
a man and his family can be alone in a hurricane,
as cut off by extreme peril from any human help as the
first naked Indian who ever died in one.*

—MARJORY STONEMAN DOUGLAS (1958)

AUTHOR'S NOTES

THE COST OR DAMAGE ESTIMATES FOR THE HURRICANES listed in the text are the costs as they were tallied in the year the hurricane occurred. Many people are also interested in how much the damage from past hurricanes would amount to in current dollars. Rather than clutter up the text with those amounts, I've added two tables at the end of the book that cover the most expensive hurricanes in modern history. One table lists the hurricanes that caused at least $1 billion of damage in the year they occurred. The other table ranks the most expensive hurricanes according to the 2019 Consumer Price Index adjusted cost. Note that not all hurricanes mentioned in the text are in those tables. By the same token, many hurricanes in those tables are not discussed in the text.

FOR THE HURRICANES DISCUSSED in this book, death tolls are given. Before the 1980s, virtually all of the hurricane-related deaths tallied by officials were *direct* deaths. A direct death is more immediate and occurs during the storm. Examples include drowning, being hit by a flying object, or being crushed by a collapsing building. Since the 1980s, better records and methodologies have enabled people to track *indirect* deaths as well. Indirect deaths occur after the storm has passed. Examples might include being killed in a car accident because the electricity is out and there are no traffic lights; dying as a result of a preexisting health condition that is exacerbated by the stress or strain of the storm, or because your medicine runs out; being electrocuted days after the storm by a downed wire; or dropping dead of a heart attack while cleaning up debris.

The distinction between direct and indirect deaths is not always clear, and the time frame for counting deaths indirectly related to a given storm varies depending on who is doing the counting. For example, some might count only deaths that occur in the days and weeks after the storm, while others would include deaths taking place many months or even years later. Still, delineating between direct and indirect deaths is useful. Therefore, the death tolls reported in the text for hurricanes before the 1980s include direct fatalities only. For later hurricanes, numbers are presented for both direct and indirect deaths when available. Bear in mind, then, that the death tolls for hurricanes before the 1980s would be considerably higher if indirect deaths were also accounted for.

THE HISTORY OF EVERY hurricane has four basic components: the time leading up to landfall, the impact of the storm, the immediate response, and the long-term recovery. This book will focus on the first three, since the fourth component, or the long tail of every hurricane, may span decades and is a complex political and bureaucratic story that can't be adequately told or even summarized within the confines of a single book that covers so many hurricanes.

Introduction

Lithograph by Nathaniel Currier, depicting the clipper ship
Comet *struggling through a hurricane off the coast of Bermuda,*
during its 1852 voyage from New York to San Francisco.

THE CRAWFISH KNEW IT WAS COMING. ON WEDNESDAY, JUNE 26, 1957, battalions of the crustaceans left their watery abodes along the southwestern coast of Louisiana and headed farther inland across streets and highways to escape the approaching storm. The locals knew it was coming too. Throughout the day, television and radio broadcasters, relying on the federal weather forecasts for guidance, warned area residents that Hurricane Audrey was on the way and advised those in low-lying areas to evacuate to higher ground. But since the warnings also said the hurricane wouldn't arrive until late Thursday afternoon, nobody evacuated right away, instead delaying their departure until the last possible moment.

Around midnight on Wednesday, however, with the hurricane only about 170 miles from the coast, the situation changed dramatically. Strengthened by the warm Gulf of Mexico waters, Audrey transformed into a much stronger storm overnight, and started speeding toward the Louisiana shore. Most people were asleep when the new and much more alarming forecast was issued at 1:00 a.m., and they had no idea the hurricane was almost upon them.

Audrey zeroed in on Cameron Parish, Louisiana, near the mouth of the Sabine River, where Texas and Louisiana meet. Eighty percent of the rural parish consists of coastal marshes, while the remaining dry land averages only 4 feet above sea level. In the wee hours of Thursday, the outer edge of the hurricane roared in. As the whipping winds shook their houses, and the boiling Gulf waters began rushing over the countryside, most of the roughly 6,000 parish residents, rudely jolted from their slumber, experienced the same reaction of stunned surprise. "How could the hurricane be here already?" they asked one another. The warnings said it wasn't supposed to arrive until much later in the day. Their surprise was quickly replaced with an entirely different emotion: fear. And with fear came a determination to survive. Unfortunately, many would not.

EARLY THAT MORNING, DR. CECIL CLARK and his wife, Sybil, were sitting on the couch in their four-bedroom brick ranch house about 5 miles to the east of Cameron, the parish seat. The gusting winds and rain made it difficult to sleep, and they were already up when the phone rang. It was one of Dr. Clark's nurses calling from his twelve-bed clinic in Cameron. The strain registered in her voice as she told him, "Water is seeping into the hospital from under the doors."

Cecil and Sybil, who was a nurse and served as manager of the clinic, decided to drive there immediately to help take care of their six patients. They roused their housekeeper, Zulmae Dubois, and asked her to watch over their three youngest children. The Clarks' two older boys, eight-year-old John and seven-year-old Joe, were at their grandparents' house 15 miles away.

The Clarks' car ground to a halt just three blocks from the clinic. The water was too high to proceed, so they turned around and raced back home. Still anxious about their patients, the Clarks decided to split up. Cecil would head back to the clinic, while Sybil would stay behind and get the kids ready to evacuate once Cecil returned.

Cecil enlisted the help of his neighbor, James Derouen, who had a truck. Cecil's plan was to follow the truck for as long as he could and then, when the water got too deep, abandon his car and ride in the truck the rest of the way. If the car ended up near the clinic, Cecil thought he could use it to rush home before the hurricane struck full force. In the meantime, he hoped that he and his nurses would be able to transport his patients to the Cameron courthouse, the largest and sturdiest building in the parish. Sybil watched her husband and James drive off, and then she and Zulmae woke the kids and got them dressed.

The doctor's plan failed. Fast-rising waters forced the truck to turn around, and Cecil and James headed back home. But surging waters hurled Cecil's car off the road into a ditch. James, unaware that his neighbor was no longer following him, continued driving. Cecil jumped into the raging, waist-deep waters and sought shelter with a family in a nearby house. As dawn was breaking, everyone in the house climbed to the attic, where they huddled together for warmth. Occasionally, Cecil peered out into the lightening gloom only to see nearby houses crumble under the assault of 145-mph winds and a 12-foot storm surge,* upon which 10- to 15-foot waves tumbled and crashed. A couple of hours later, the hurricane made landfall† just a few miles to the west.

Around 5:00 p.m. on Thursday, when the winds finally subsided, Cecil and the others ventured outside. A scene of utter devastation greeted them: homes obliterated, mighty trees washed away, and water, receding toward the Gulf, covering the land in every direction. Slowly, storm refugees gathered around. This being a close-knit community, they all knew the doctor. They told him that many of the injured were being taken to Cameron's courthouse and pleaded with him to go there to provide medical treatment.

---

* *Storm surge* is the abnormal rise in seawater level during a storm, measured as the height of the water above the normal predicted astronomical tide.

† *Landfall* is the point at which the center, or eye, of the hurricane intersects with the coastline.

Cecil was torn. In one direction was his family, hopefully alive, and possibly in need of his help. In the other direction were his fellow citizens and his patients, whom he had taken an oath to serve. Placing his medical obligation over his personal concerns, as he knew Sybil would have done under the same circumstances, Cecil began the long walk to the courthouse. He arrived there at 7:00 p.m.

WHILE CECIL WAS COPING with the storm, Sybil was enduring her own ordeal. "When I saw the water rising," Sybil later recalled, "I knew Cecil couldn't make it home. And I knew we were trapped."

Since the attic was too small to crawl into, Sybil and Zulmae retreated to the kitchen. They placed the children on the counter and barricaded the door with a chest of drawers, hoping to keep the wind and surging waters at bay. For hours, the house was under siege, trembling in the maelstrom. As the water seeped under the door and crept ever higher, Sybil and Zulmae joined the children atop the counter and clutched them tight, hoping to give them some sense of security.

Around 8:00 a.m., the house collapsed, and Sybil was temporarily knocked out. When she came to, she frantically searched for her children and Zulmae, but they were nowhere to be found. Carried along in the debris-laden water, Sybil was repeatedly submerged, only to claw her way back to the surface. Finally, she found refuge in a neighbor's house, climbing in through a hole in its roof. But that house, too, was soon demolished by the storm.

Throughout the day and into the following morning, Sybil—bruised, battered, and chilled to the bone—drifted on a remnant of the roof. Finally, at noon on Friday, a small boat picked her up and took her to Lake Charles, a city about 30 miles from Cameron.

MEANWHILE, AT THE COURTHOUSE, Cecil ministered to the sick and injured, including his patients from the clinic who had been brought there Thursday morning. Whenever someone new entered the building, Cecil would ask whether they had heard anything about his family or Zulmae. Each time, he got the same soul-crushing response: no. Despite his mounting grief, Cecil continued his rounds, a steely commitment to his work keeping him from emotionally and physically breaking down.

At 7:00 p.m. on Friday, Cameron Parish's state representative, Alvin Dyson, was in the courthouse radio room, speaking with the operator from Lake Charles, trying to get the latest information on recovery efforts. As soon as the operator told him that Sybil and the two oldest Clark boys, John and Joe, were alive and in Lake Charles, Alvin dropped the receiver and dashed through the building, searching for Cecil. When he found the doctor and shared the news, Cecil didn't believe it. "It must be a mistake. The two boys were with my mother. They must mean my *mother* and the two boys."

Cecil asked Alvin to get the operator back on the line to confirm what he had heard. A few minutes later Alvin reported that there was no mistake. Cecil's wife and two sons were alive, as were his parents. Soon, Cecil was on a helicopter heading for Lake Charles, where he was reunited with Sybil and the boys, who had ridden out the hurricane alongside their grandparents, tied together with rope to the crook of an old oak tree. The reunion, however, was heart-wrenchingly bittersweet, for although Sybil and the two eldest boys had survived, the three youngest Clark children, and Zulmae, had perished.

After spending some time with his family, Cecil dutifully answered reporters' questions about conditions in Cameron, before going to sleep for the first time in nearly three days. Just a few hours later he was up again, headed for the local air base to catch a helicopter ride back to Cameron to continue caring for those who needed his help.

In the ensuing months, Cecil would be showered with local and national awards, honoring his selfless heroism in tending to the sick and injured in the aftermath of the hurricane. But all the adulation made him a bit uncomfortable. "I did what was necessary for me to do as a doctor," he said. "That's just the way it was."

THIS HARROWING AND TRAGIC story is just one of thousands that played out that day. Hurricane Audrey destroyed nearly every building in Cameron Parish, leaving 5,000 people homeless and causing $150–$200 million in damage. Roughly 500 people died, the vast majority coming from the parish seat, Cameron, which lost more than a third of its population. In the immediate aftermath, area residents wandered about in a daze, shell-shocked by the experience. Some could be heard muttering to themselves, "Everything's gone."

WHILE HURRICANE AUDREY IS unique in its particulars, from a broader perspective it is an all-too-familiar narrative. Hurricanes are—have always been—an integral, inevitable, and painful part of the American experience. Just as we can count on the sun rising and setting each day, so, too, can we expect hurricanes to periodically visit our shores. These days, their arrival is heralded by an annual ritual that is an ominous portent of potential danger on the horizon.

In the spring, after the computer models have been run and scientists have scrutinized the numbers, government, academic, and private organizations issue their outlooks for the upcoming hurricane season, which officially runs from June 1 through November 30. The news is trumpeted in the press and eagerly consumed by a weather-obsessed culture. These reports are just predictions, a range of possibilities that offer no guarantees of where, when, or whether a hurricane might crash ashore, but they incite anxiety. If you are among the many tens of millions of people inhabiting the East Coast, Gulf Coast, or the Caribbean, hurricanes are looming threats that might invade your life, and there is nothing you can do to prevent their strike.[*]

In an average year, six hurricanes dance over the Atlantic, three of which are major hurricanes, defined as having sustained winds[†] of at least 111 mph. The number of hurricanes varies from year to year. Fortunately, few of these storms actually make landfall. Typically, two hurricanes hit the United States annually, and a major one pummels us only about once every two years.

---

[*] Although hurricanes do hit Hawaii, they are extremely rare there. Nevertheless, Hawaii's worst hurricane, Iniki, is discussed in Chapter 8. As for the West Coast, the only documented case of a hurricane striking that region was one in 1858 that plowed into San Diego. Hurricanes spare the West Coast for two reasons: the prevailing winds tend to push storms offshore, and the waters are generally too cold to sustain such massive storms.

[†] Winds are considered *sustained* when they maintain a measured or estimated average speed for one minute at a height of 30 feet aboveground.

There have also been years when not a single hurricane visited American shores, or those that did had minimal impact. During such relatively quiet times, memories fade and the fear of hurricanes begins to diminish. Former National Hurricane Center director Max Mayfield called this dangerous tendency to forget the lessons of the past "hurricane amnesia." Only the old-timers who have the hard-earned wisdom of age know what every meteorologist knows: if you live in a place that hurricanes have visited before, they will, one day, come again. Even if your slice of the coast has never been struck by a hurricane, or has received only glancing blows, your time, too, will likely come. But hurricanes are not equal-opportunity offenders. While twenty-one coastal states have been hit by hurricanes, certain states are particularly prone to be afflicted by these massive storms. Residents of Florida, Texas, North Carolina, Louisiana, and South Carolina—in that order—take the brunt of the punishment, with Florida alone accounting for roughly 40 percent of all hurricane strikes.

Hurricanes, however, are not merely coastal events. After making landfall, they typically head inland. Although they eventually fade away, as they degrade and weaken they can still leave a trail of calamity in their wake. And no matter where you reside in the United States, even if hurricanes or their remnants never reach you, they can still significantly impact your life in the form of economic dislocation, harm to friends and relatives, and the use of federal funds for relief instead of other public purposes.

Hurricanes have been churning up ocean waters and slamming into land for all of recorded history, and almost certainly much farther back into the recesses of time. Every society tormented by hurricanes bears the scars of these encounters, including the native populations of the Americas, the European settlers who came after them, and the American colonists, as well as the nation they created.

Coursing through the centuries like brawlers bobbing and weaving and slugging anyone or anything that stands in their way, hurricanes have left an indelible mark on American history. Since 1980 they have accounted for roughly 50 percent of the cost of all the natural disasters in the United States that exceeded $1 billion in damage. And going back to the late 1800s, hurricanes have killed nearly 30,000 people. Of course, hurricanes will continue to make history, and there are strong indications that the blows they land will only become more powerful and more destructive in the future.

A Furious Sky is the history of the American hurricane or, more specifically, the hurricanes that have hit what is today the United States. Given that there have been hundreds, if not more than a thousand, such hurricanes in the past five centuries, *A Furious Sky* must understandably be selective, focusing mainly on storms that have, arguably, had the most impact on the nation's long history. Before the discussion goes any further, however, a key term must be defined: What is a *hurricane?*

THIS IS A SURPRISINGLY complex question. But by way of introduction, a basic definition will do. Simply put, hurricanes are violent, swirling storms with sustained winds of at least 74 mph. They generally form where the ocean's upper layer—down to about 150 feet—reaches the trigger temperature of at least 80 degrees Fahrenheit, thereby providing the massive amounts of heat energy needed to fuel them. Two other conditions necessary for a hurricane to thrive are low vertical wind shear,* which keeps the hurricane from being ripped apart, and an abundance of warm, moist air that evaporates from the ocean surface. When that moist air rises, it cools and condenses, forming clouds and releasing the heat that powers the storm.

Hurricanes can be anywhere from tens of miles in diameter to more than a thousand, and over 50,000 feet high, reaching from the ocean's surface all the way up to the top of the troposphere. These behemoths rotate in a counterclockwise direction in the Northern Hemisphere and clockwise in the Southern. But wherever and however they spin, hurricanes are characterized by extremely low pressure and a relatively calm center called the eye, with the most ferocious winds occurring in the eyewall and decreasing in intensity as one travels outward from the core. Hurricanes whip up the seas, generate gargantuan waves and mammoth storm surges, and pour down such diluvial quantities of water that they seem to presage the end of time.

Hurricanes also discharge vast quantities of energy. Considering only the wind, an average hurricane produces the equivalent of half of the world's electrical generating capacity. But hurricanes produce even more energy when water vapor condenses to form clouds—a type of energy

---

* *Vertical wind shear* is a change of wind speed or direction with a change in altitude.

known as the latent heat of condensation. By this measure, an average hurricane produces the equivalent of two hundred times the world's generating capacity. To put it another way, an ordinary hurricane releases the same amount of energy as 10,000 nuclear bombs. For a major hurricane the number is higher still.

Of all the hurricane's astounding features, the most curious and startling is the eye, which is typically 20–40 miles wide. While the hurricane rages all around it, creating the meteorological equivalent of a temper tantrum on steroids, the eye is comparatively tranquil. Here the winds fall away to gentle, warm breezes, and the skies open up to let in the sun's streaming rays or the ethereal glow of stars and planets. In some eyes, the core is virtually clear, but even when swirling clouds remain, there is a serene aspect to the sky. And as the spiraling clouds of the eyewall ascend, they tilt back, forming a massive and undeniably grand amphitheater miles high.

The eye is experienced quite differently, depending on whether one is on land or at sea. On the ocean, despite the dying of the winds and transformation of the sky, the power of the hurricane is still evident in the waves and swells that race in all different directions, smashing into one another, generating a jumbled landscape where mountains of water merge and diverge, and rise and fall in an erratic way. One mariner in the 1860s, whose ship spent thirty minutes in the eye of a hurricane off the coast of New York, described the sea as a "number of huge watery cones . . . that were dancing an infernal reel, played by some necromancer." But on land, as the eye passes overhead it is as if the hurricane has departed. In fact, there are more than a few examples when people thought this was the case and walked about in the eye, confident the worst was over, only to be caught in the open when the eye moved on, leaving them to confront the fury of the storm's other side.

Most of the hurricanes in the North Atlantic originate not over the water, as some may think, but over the southern flanks of the Sahara desert. There, a convergence of arid, scorching desert air and the moist air winging in off the Indian Ocean from the east, and coming from the Gulf of Guinea coast to the south, creates areas of low pressure. These low-pressure pockets are accompanied by intense thunderstorms that extend into the upper atmosphere and are steered to the west by the prevailing easterly winds. This mass of unstable air, called an African easterly wave, leaves the continent roughly every three to four days and is swept out over the Atlantic.

Fortunately, these systems usually fizzle out or fall apart. But every fourth or fifth wave continues its westward journey, wafting past the Cape Verde Islands, where trouble can brew. Under the favorable conditions mentioned earlier, these waves can strengthen into a *tropical depression*, a system with organized circulation but sustained winds of 38 mph or less. If such conditions persist, these depressions can grow into *tropical storms*, with sustained winds ranging from 39 mph to as high as 73 mph. Only a fraction of African easterly waves, however, ever ascend the weather ladder, evolving from tropical depression to tropical storm to a full-fledged hurricane that travels across the Atlantic.

Since these hurricanes begin to take shape in the vicinity of the Cape Verde Islands, they are often called Cape Verde hurricanes. While about 60 percent of the hurricanes in the North Atlantic are Cape Verde hurricanes, they account for roughly 85 percent of all *major* hurricanes. Many other hurricanes, which require the same favorable environment to thrive, are born in the Caribbean Sea or the Gulf of Mexico as tropical depressions, and rather than barreling across the Atlantic from east to west, they often travel roughly from south to north. In addition, a significant number of hurricanes form in the mid- or western Atlantic.

Whether they come from the east across the Atlantic, or arise in the Caribbean or the Gulf of Mexico and come up from the south, hurricanes typically travel over the ocean at a rather leisurely pace of between 10 and 25 mph. However, a few are veritable speed demons that have reached speeds as high as 60 mph. Exactly when and where a hurricane will make landfall can remain a mystery up until it is about to roar ashore. Even with the most sophisticated technology tracking their whereabouts and forecasting their course, these storms are somewhat unpredictable.

Hurricanes share many characteristics, including powerful winds, torrential rain, plummeting pressure, and the magisterial eye. They often follow similar paths, are of similar size, and cause similar damage. Nevertheless, no two hurricanes are identical. Each one has its distinctive meteorological history, written in the sky and on the land.

HURRICANES GO BY DIFFERENT names in different parts of the world. For example, they are *cyclones* in the Indian Ocean, and in the northwestern Pacific Ocean they are called *typhoons*, a term derived from the

Chinese *tai fung*, meaning "great [or big] wind." Some Australians refer to hurricanes as "cockeyed Bobs" or "willy-willys." In the Atlantic, the Caribbean, and the Gulf of Mexico—the regions that are the main focus of this book—hurricanes are called just that, *hurricanes*, a word that has its origins in the languages of the Caribbean basin, where native cultures attributed the region's wild weather to the work of gods. The Mayans named their god of storms or destruction *hunraken*, and the Quiche and the Arawak called theirs *hurakan*, while the Taíno peoples called theirs *juracán*. Over the centuries of European colonization, one or more of these names ultimately morphed into *huracán*, *ouragan*, *orkaan*, *orkanen*, and *hurricane*, in Spanish, French, Dutch, Danish, and English, respectively.

Hurricane is not a monolithic designation. There are gradations within the umbrella term. According to the Saffir-Simpson Hurricane Wind Scale, there are five categories of hurricanes, ranked from 1 to 5—the higher the number, the more intense the hurricane. Winds in Category 1 hurricanes range from 74 to 95 mph; in Category 2, from 96 to 110 mph; in Category 3, from 111 to 129 mph; in Category 4, from 130 to 156 mph; and for the ultimate Category 5 hurricanes, winds equal or exceed 157 mph. Category 3 and higher hurricanes are classified as major hurricanes, the ones that are typically the most damaging and feared, even though less powerful hurricanes can also cause tremendous harm.

While a Category 1 hurricane can rip shingles and vinyl siding off a building, topple small trees, and down power lines, a Category 5 storm will result in catastrophic damage, leaving impacted areas virtually uninhabitable for days, or even months, and in some cases creating such apocalyptic conditions that people choose to relocate rather than rebuild. As one climbs the hurricane category hierarchy, the force of the winds does not increase in a linear fashion; instead, it jumps. For example, a relatively anemic Category 1 hurricane with winds of a mere 74 mph could launch a two-by-four into the air with such force that it is capable of being driven clear through a thin, nonreinforced concrete block. Doubling the wind speed to 148 mph (a strong Category 4) does not double the force, but rather quadruples it, making the storm four times as powerful as a Category 1. At that wind speed, a flying two-by-four would likely go through almost anything it hit.

The Saffir-Simpson scale came into being only at the tail end of the twentieth century. Before that, back to the early 1800s, hurricanes were typically defined by the Beaufort scale as force-12 storms, having winds so strong that "no canvas could withstand them." (Much later, when speed was added to the Beaufort scale, force-12 storms were defined as those having sustained winds higher than 74 mph.) Going back further in time, when humans' ability to accurately measure wind speed was meager or nonexistent, the hurricane label was applied subjectively to storms of immense violence that were deemed to be worthy of such a designation. Thus, in this book, hurricanes will be identified by their Saffir-Simpson category when data allows, but will be called only hurricanes when it does not.*

While the Saffir-Simpson and Beaufort scales both focus on wind speed, water poses a far greater threat to human life. The massive storm surges and torrential rains that accompany hurricanes are the real killers. Together, these two elemental forces account for roughly nine out of every ten direct hurricane-related fatalities. Each cubic yard of water weighs about 1,700 pounds. That is why the walls of water generated by a hurricane—especially when full of storm wreckage—become battering rams that can level any structure in their way, strip the landscape bare, and swallow people whole. Because of this immense capacity for destruction, meteorologists and emergency managers are fond of saying that when confronting a hurricane, it is best to "hide from the wind, run from the water."

Even after the hurricane has passed, the water left behind remains a serious hazard. By destroying what humans have built, hurricanes liberate a host of toxins into the environment. Oil, gas, cleaning chemicals, and waste from livestock pens, as well as overflow from landfills, sewage systems, and hazardous waste sites, can be swept into the turbulent waters; and decomposing animal carcasses and human corpses are often added to the churning mix. The longer the waters remain, the more dangerous this potentially deadly concoction becomes, acting as an incubator and transmitter of disease. And for those structures that are able to withstand the hurricane's winds, waves, and deluge from the sky, the peril is just

---

* The Hurricane Research Division of the National Oceanic and Atmospheric Administration (NOAA) has analyzed the historical records and, for hurricanes dating back to 1851, has assigned each one a Saffir-Simpson category level based on the available information, such as pressure and wind speed. Those are the category designations used in this book.

beginning. The standing water gives mold spores the boost they need to germinate, quickly transforming buildings into biological war zones.

Regardless of the category and the amount of water that surges in or rains down, hurricanes have the humbling ability to strip away the trappings of modern society and return us, if only temporarily, to a time when electricity, clean water, sanitation, and even a roof over one's head were unimaginable luxuries. By leaving behind the detritus of civilization—mangled buildings and torn landscapes—hurricanes redefine reality and fracture people's lives.

A FURIOUS SKY WEAVES together a great range of captivating themes. There is the intriguing and, at times, rather nasty history of meteorology, with advances attributable to gifted amateurs and skilled experts alike. The death, destruction, and despair caused by hurricanes are on full display, as are stories of charity, kindness, humor, and resilience. The influence of hurricanes on the course of empire, the outcomes of war, and the fortunes of individuals adds to the story. Critical innovations in communication, aviation, computer, and satellite technology play an important part, as does the women's movement and its role in the naming of hurricanes. In the end, the history of America's hurricanes forces us to confront thorny questions of how we can learn to survive and adapt to the continued barrage that is sure to come from the greatest storms on Earth.

Seen from space, hurricanes are one of the most beautiful and mesmerizing features in the world. Racing around the globe like downy, spinning pinwheels floating silently above the Earth, their very magnificence belies their dreadful impact on American history. But however painful that history is, it is also enthralling, and, much like hurricanes, it reveals the brilliance and drama of the planet we call home.

A
FURIOUS SKY

CHAPTER

1

A New and Violent World

*A 1594 engraving, by Theodor de Bry, of a hurricane
striking Hispaniola in the early sixteenth century, causing
Spanish soldiers and native Americans to flee.*

CHRISTOPHER COLUMBUS, THE FIFTY-ONE-YEAR-OLD, REGALLY anointed "Grand Admiral of the Ocean Sea" was in dire straits. In early May 1502, he set out with four small ships and a crew of 135 men and boys from the Spanish port of Cádiz. They sailed across the Atlantic to the Caribbean, where Columbus hoped to finally find the holy grail he had long sought: the fabled western route to the Indies and the unimaginable riches of the Far East. Now, in early July, his little flotilla was bobbing in the water just off the Spanish city of Santo Domingo in Hispaniola,* and he desperately needed help. One of his ships was in bad shape, and Columbus feared that if it weren't replaced, the lives of its crew might be endangered. His only chance, he thought, was to send an emissary to ask the governor of Hispaniola, Nicolás de Ovando, for permission to enter the port to acquire a new vessel. But Columbus had another potent reason for wanting to enter the port: he was convinced a great storm was brewing, and he hoped that the harbor's sheltering embrace would protect him and his men from its rage.

Ovando flatly refused the request, and although this response greatly angered Columbus, he could hardly have been surprised. After all, he was persona non grata in Hispaniola. This was his fourth trip to the New World, his voyages there reaching back to the first and by far most famous one in 1492. It was during that groundbreaking voyage that he supposedly "discovered" the New World of the Americas, when in fact it had already been "discovered" by the Vikings five centuries earlier, and by the native peoples who had lived there for thousands of years. King Ferdinand and Queen Isabella of Spain had sponsored the first three voyages, which fell far short of their expectations. Not only did Columbus fail to find the much-sought route to the Indies; he also did a miserable job in his tenure as governor of Hispaniola. In fact, he had been forcibly ousted from that position and sent back to Spain in chains in late 1500.

Despite his precipitous fall from grace, Columbus somehow managed to yet again obtain the favor of the monarchs, who agreed to sponsor his fourth and final attempt to locate the watery highway to the Orient. Mindful of his troubled history in Hispaniola, Ferdinand and Isabella prudently ordered Columbus to steer clear of Santo Domingo on this voyage. And even though Ovando, who the king and queen had selected to replace Columbus as governor, was unaware of this restrictive order, it was public knowledge that he disliked and distrusted his predecessor, and therefore was not about to welcome him with open arms.

---

* The island of Hispaniola is today split between the Dominican Republic and Haiti.

At the same time that Columbus was trying unsuccessfully to gain access to the harbor in Santo Domingo, he issued Ovando a warning. Having learned that a homeward-bound fleet was finishing preparations for its trip back to Spain, Columbus begged the governor to forbid them from sailing "for eight days because of the great danger" posed by the looming storm. Columbus was particularly insistent that Ovando heed his warning for purely selfish reasons. One of the fleet's twenty-eight vessels was the diminutive and delicate *Aguja* ("Needle"), which carried the gold that the king and queen had promised to Columbus as compensation for his earlier service to the crown. If the *Aguja* sank, all of Columbus's treasure would be lost. Ovando, derisively labeling Columbus "as a prophet and sooth-sayer," ignored him. That dismissal of Columbus's warning turned out to be a huge mistake. Columbus was correct; a hurricane was on its way.

Christopher Columbus's landfall in the New World, as depicted in a 1594 engraving by Theodor de Bry. A group of Europeans are greeted by Native Americans who offer treasure in the form of jewelry, shells, and boxes. Three ships stand at anchor while European soldiers raise a cross. Other Native Americans flee in the background.

———

WHEN COLUMBUS FIRST ARRIVED in the New World in 1492, he, like all Europeans, knew nothing about hurricanes. While Europe certainly had terrific and destructive storms, it was not visited by massive, swirling, meteorological behemoths worthy of being called hurricanes.* And even during his first voyage to the New World, Columbus remained largely ignorant of these monstrous tempests because he experienced nothing like them. In fact, the conditions he encountered were so pleasant that Columbus—still under the illusion that he had arrived in the Far East—wrote to a friend, "In all the Indies, I have always found weather like May."

In 1493, during Columbus's second voyage to the New World, he discovered that Caribbean weather could be far from benign. He and his men rode out a few very powerful storms, and he saw evidence of even greater storms far away. Some historians have claimed that the storms that battered Columbus's ships were, in fact, hurricanes. But the historical record is sketchy on their nature and violence, and it appears more likely that they were either powerful tropical storms or even relatively rare tornadoes. Columbus's third voyage to the New World (1498–1500), was, like the first, relatively uneventful, meteorologically speaking.

In the course of his first three voyages, the Taíno Indians, who lived on the islands comprising the Greater Antilles, told Columbus about hurricanes and the warning signs that often attended them, including large swells, high wispy clouds, and an ominous red sky in the morning; and he had witnessed some of these omens himself. Now, during his fourth voyage, as his small fleet lay maddeningly close to the shelter of Santo Domingo, Columbus observed these portents and surmised that a hurricane was in the offing. His anger at Ovando's rejection notwithstanding, Columbus spent little time lamenting his situation; instead, he took action. His ships sailed westward, hugging the coast of Hispaniola until they came upon a secluded harbor. Dropping their anchors and battening down the hatches, Columbus and his men braced themselves for the storm.

———

* The remnants of many hurricanes throughout history traveled across the Atlantic, making their way to Europe, but virtually all of them weakened considerably and were no longer hurricanes by the time they arrived. Recently, however, some massive winter storms have pelted parts of Europe with hurricane-force winds.

Meanwhile, the homeward-bound fleet embarked from Santo Domingo. As they rounded the eastern tip of Hispaniola on July 10, heading into the Mona Passage, the hurricane struck with awesome fury. Mountainous waves battered the ships, whipping winds shredded their sails, masts splintered, and twenty-four of the ships sank, killing all the men on board except for the few who managed to swim to shore. One of those who perished was Francisco de Bobadilla, the special prosecutor that Ferdinand and Isabella had dispatched to Hispaniola to investigate the numerous complaints against Columbus's tenure as governor, and the man who had sent Columbus back to Spain in chains. Of the remaining ships, three limped back to Santo Domingo, informing the horrified Ovando of the disaster. Only one ship, the *Aguja*, with

Painting purporting to be of Christopher Columbus, by Italian painter Sebastiano del Piombo (Sebastiano Luciani), from 1519. The painting was done thirteen years after Columbus's death in 1506, and it is not certain that it is, in fact, Columbus, since no paintings or drawings of him from life are known to exist. According to the Metropolitan Museum of Art, however, this painting is considered to be the "authoritative likeness" of the mariner.

Columbus's stash safely stowed in the hold, survived the hurricane and made it home to Spain.

A few hours after sinking the bulk of the fleet headed for Spain, the hurricane plowed into Columbus and his men. As he later recounted, "The storm was terrible and on that night the ships [having torn from their anchorages] were parted from me. Each one of them was reduced to an extremity, expecting nothing save death." As he struggled to survive the hurricane, Columbus railed against the great injustice that Ovando and, by extension, the king and queen had done to him. "For, in such weather, when it was for my safety and for that of my son, my brother, and my friends, I was forbidden [to enter] the land and harbors which, by the will of God, I, sweating blood, gained for Spain." In the end, Columbus's ships made it through without the loss of a single man, and the following day they rendezvoused in the harbor of Azua on Hispaniola's southern coast.

In the aftermath of the catastrophe, Columbus was accused of practicing sorcery, on account of his prescient prediction of the hurricane's arrival.* Columbus's "enemies," his son Ferdinand observed, "charged that by his magic arts he had raised that storm to take revenge on Bobadilla and others" who had stood against him, while at the same time protecting his own ships. It was not witchcraft, however, that did in Columbus's adversaries and saved him, his men, and his treasure, but rather an all-too-common hurricane, and a master mariner's skill at learning from the natives, reading the signs, and seeking shelter.

THIS METEOROLOGICAL BAPTISM BY fire was a most appropriate prologue to European settlement of the New World. Over the next few centuries, hurricanes would continue to plague settlers, including those who came to North America. In the mid-1500s, for example, two separate hurricanes played a critical role in Florida's early colonial history.

Ever since Columbus's first voyage, Spain had claimed rights to an enormous swath of the New World, largely on the basis of the Treaty of Tordesillas, an agreement signed in 1494 between Spain and Portugal.

---

* This prediction can lay claim to being the first weather forecast in the New World issued by a European, and a correct one at that!

The heart of this treaty was a geographic line of demarcation drawn on the world map by Pope Alexander VI that ran north to south. Spain was given the right to all lands lying to the west of that line that weren't already controlled by a Christian ruler, while Portugal had rights to similar lands to the east of the line. This agreement essentially gave everything in North and South America, minus part of eastern Brazil, to Spain.

Spain capitalized on this territorial windfall by ruthlessly conquering native cultures, including the Aztecs and the Incas, and by colonizing many areas of Central, South, and North America. Florida—then broadly defined by the Spanish as including not only modern-day Florida but much of the Southeast, all the way up to South Carolina—certainly fell within Spain's ambitions. As a result, Spain launched a number of attempts to colonize the area in the second half of the sixteenth century. One of the most impressive efforts was led by Don Tristán de Luna y Arellano, who set out in June 1559 from the port of Veracruz in modern-day Mexico. He was at the head of an imposing fleet of eleven ships, carrying 1,000 colonists and servants, and 500 soldiers.

In mid-August, the fleet entered modern-day Pensacola Bay and debarked in the heart of what is now the city of Pensacola. While one of the ships returned to Mexico to tell the viceroy there of the expedition's arrival, Luna prepared to settle in. But his high hopes for the nascent colony were almost immediately dashed. Having assumed that he would be able to trade with the local Indians for food to supplement his limited stores, Luna was deeply distressed to find that, in fact, there were few natives in the area. His situation became far more dire when a powerful hurricane smashed into the coast. Only three of his ships survived; six sank in the bay, along with most of the expedition's supplies, while another was driven high onto the shore by the wind and surging waters. Many colonists and soldiers died, and, making matters worse, the food that had already been off-loaded was ruined by the drenching rain.

Facing starvation, the colonists desperately struggled to endure. But despite multiple relief missions from Mexico, endeavors to establish outposts farther inland, and various attempts to obtain or steal food from frightened and at times hostile Indians, the Spaniards were unable to hang on. Roughly two years into this colonial experiment, the settlement finally disappeared into the mists of history, as the last of the colonists sailed from Pensacola Bay.

JUST A FEW YEARS after the collapse of the Luna colony, another hurricane affected the course of Florida's history, as well as the imperial designs of ancient rivals Spain and France. Like many European countries that didn't accept the validity of the Treaty of Tordesillas, France believed it had every right to colonize those portions of the New World that it could possess. As a result of earlier explorations, France had already claimed an extensive part of North America called New France, which many Frenchmen assumed included Florida. Acting on this understanding, in February 1562 French admiral Gaspard de Coligny dispatched a small fleet under the command of Jean Ribaut to Florida to lay the groundwork for a colony

Detail of a map of Florida by Jacques le Moyne de Morgues, a French painter who was part of Jean Ribaut's expedition to the New World in 1564. Directly to the west of the ship, along the coast, are the May River and Fort Caroline. The roundish body of water farther to the west and a little to the south is what later came to be known as Lake Okeechobee.

where Huguenot refugees could settle to escape religious persecution in Catholic France.

Ribaut arrived a few months later on the coast of Florida, at the mouth of what is now the St. John's River in Jacksonville, which he christened the May River and claimed for France. Instead of settling there, he continued up the coast to modern-day Parris Island in Port Royal, South Carolina. There he built a small fort, and then he sailed back to France, leaving thirty of his men behind. Soon thereafter, as was the destiny of many fledgling settlements in the New World, the fort was abandoned.

Having failed once to establish a colony in Florida, Coligny launched another expedition with the same goal in 1564, led by René Goulaine de Laudonnière. Laudonnière's fleet of three ships, with 300 colonists and a small contingent of soldiers, arrived at the mouth of the May River at the end of June, and the group built Fort Caroline atop the adjoining bluffs.

Spain, well aware of both of the French expeditions to Florida, was furious at these encroachments upon its domain. It was even angrier at reports that Ribaut was readying another fleet to sail to Fort Caroline and use it as a base to launch attacks on Spain's treasure ships that transported silver and gold from the mines of South and Central America back

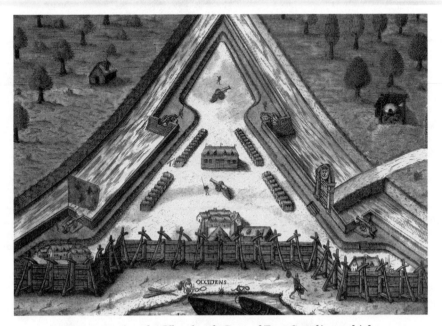

A 1591 engraving, by Theodor de Bry, of Fort Caroline, which was built by the French at the mouth of the May River in 1564.

home. In response, King Philip II, who reigned over Spain from 1556 to 1598, prepared his own fleet. Under the leadership of Pedro Menéndez de Avilés, the Spanish fleet set sail for Florida to destroy the French fleet and the French settlement at Fort Caroline, and to establish a Spanish colony in its stead.

But Philip's intelligence was faulty. Ribaut's goal was not to launch attacks against the treasure fleets, but rather to resupply and strengthen the fledgling French colony at Fort Caroline, which was on the verge of falling apart because of mutinous infighting, rapidly diminishing stores, and the constant threat of Indian attack. Nevertheless, the die had been cast, and in the summer of 1565, two powerful fleets—one French, the other Spanish—were sailing across the Atlantic on a collision course.

Engraving, circa 1791, of Pedro Menéndez de Avilés.

Ribaut's flotilla arrived first at Fort Caroline, on August 28, but the Spanish were close behind, steadily making their way up from Cape

Canaveral, about 120 miles south of the fort. Ten days later, Menéndez arrived at the mouth of the May River, where he sighted the French fleet moored in the distance. An inconclusive skirmish ensued, after which Menéndez retreated about 40 miles down the coast, coming ashore at an excellent harbor he had first seen earlier, on August 28. Because the day of that sighting was the official Spanish holiday known as St. Augustine's Day, Menéndez christened the landing place St. Augustine and claimed it in the name of the Spanish king.

Three French ships had pursued Menéndez down to St. Augustine, but they didn't strike. Instead, they hovered offshore and then returned to Fort Caroline to inform Ribaut of the Spaniard's location. As soon as the French ships departed, Menéndez and his men began fortifying the area, preparing for the attack they presumed was coming.

The Spanish presence precipitated a heated debate among the French, with some wanting to raid St. Augustine, and others preferring to reinforce Fort Caroline and wait for the Spanish to arrive. Ribaut was in the former camp, and being the person in command, his decision carried the day. Four ships and eight pinnaces* were readied for battle, and in mid-September they headed down the coast, their decks crowded with more than 400 soldiers and roughly 200 sailors.

Two days later, Ribaut was off the coast of St. Augustine. He could clearly see the Spanish ships in the harbor and men on the shore frantically preparing their defenses. Rather than attacking, he demanded that Menéndez surrender. But before the opposing forces could resolve the standoff, Mother Nature intervened. According to Laudonnière, who had remained behind at Fort Caroline, "There rose so great a tempest accompanied with such storms, that the Indians themselves assured me that it was the worst weather that ever was seen on the coast." The hurricane swept the French ships southward to Cape Canaveral, where they crashed in the shallows. More than half of the Frenchmen survived and struggled onto land, while the rest perished in the furious seas.

Menéndez didn't know what had happened to the French ships, but given the violence of the hurricane and the direction the wind was blowing, he conjectured that they couldn't have returned to Fort Caroline, and he rightly concluded that they had been wrecked. Thus, he surmised that

---

* A *pinnace* is a small boat with sails, typically used as a tender to a larger vessel.

the fort must be largely unprotected, and that now was the best time to attack. Rallying 500 of his men, Menéndez set off in the midst of the hurricane, hoping to gain the element of surprise. After a 40-mile overland slog north, through marshes and scrubland, across rain-swollen rivers, and over sandy plains, the Spaniards reached Fort Caroline on the evening of September 19.

Wasting no time, Menéndez attacked at dawn the following day. Many Frenchmen fled into the surrounding woods, but most of them were captured, and 130 were mercilessly slaughtered by the Spaniards. (It is worth noting, though, that fifty individuals were spared—women, infants, and boys under the age of fifteen.) Menéndez then turned his sights on the three French ships in the harbor. He managed to sink one, using the fort's armaments, but the other two escaped. Some days later, the ships returned to the area to collect the Frenchmen who had scattered into the woods, and then they sailed for France, not knowing what had happened to Ribaut's expedition but assuming the worst.

Fearing that if Ribaut and his men had survived the hurricane they might attack St. Augustine, Menéndez led a detachment of his men south back down the coast. Over the next few weeks, they captured about 400 Frenchmen, the remnants of Ribaut's forces. In another merciless display of utter hatred for his enemies, Menéndez put 300 of the Frenchmen to death by sword, including Ribaut, *after* they had surrendered, laid down their arms, and had their hands tied behind their backs. The rest were spared and taken as prisoners.

Although French forces briefly retook Fort Caroline (then called San Mateo) a few years later and murdered the Spaniards within, Menéndez's brutal routing of Ribaut's forces effectively put an end to France's ambitions of colonizing Florida. It remained under Spanish control until it was traded to Great Britain in 1763 in exchange for the return of Havana, Cuba, which the British had taken during the Seven Years' War. During the American Revolution, Spain regained control of Florida, only to relinquish it to the United States in 1821. Despite these shifts in ownership, St. Augustine persisted, earning it the honor of being the oldest continuously occupied city in the United States.

The destiny of the American continent might have shifted substantially, had the hurricane in 1559 not hit Pensacola, and the one in 1565 not slammed into Florida's east coast. For one, if the hurricane had spared the

*Engraving, circa 1706, showing a French soldier, perhaps
Jean Ribaut himself, kneeling before Pedro Menéndez de Avilés, who
captured the French forces after their ships foundered in the hurricane.
The French were taken in groups of thirty to be questioned as to whether
they were Catholic. If they were not, they were brought outside and
executed. In the background, Spanish soldiers can be seen
chopping off the heads of French soldiers.*

Luna expedition, the bulk of its food and supplies wouldn't have been lost, and more soldiers and colonists would have survived. That might have been enough for the colony to thrive, giving the Spanish their first secure foothold on the American mainland, from which they could have extended their reach farther west, east, and north into the heart of the continent. Similarly, had Ribaut's fleet not been wrecked by a hurricane, the French might have vanquished the Spanish, and Florida would have fallen into France's orbit.

AS SPAIN AND FRANCE wrestled with hurricanes, England, too, had to contend with them as it tried to settle the American continent. The first one, in the summer of 1609, affected Jamestown, Virginia, England's earliest permanent settlement in the New World.

Founded on May 14, 1607, by the Virginia Company of London, Jamestown was a poorly planned, miserably executed endeavor. Too many of the earliest settlers were "gentlemen" who were either unwilling or seemingly incapable of doing a hard day's work, and expected things to be done for them—not exactly a recipe for success in an alien and unforgiving environment, which the settlers dubbed the "Savage Kingdom." Spending much of their energy pursuing the chimerical goal of finding gold in Virginia's soil, the settlers neglected more practical things such as growing food and building their defenses. Exacerbating their problems were constant infighting, fractured leadership, and an inability to maintain friendly relations with the native population, which led to skirmishes and limited opportunities for trading. In addition to these largely self-inflicted wounds, the settlers suffered from a massive fire that destroyed much of their fort, and from miserable timing, having arrived during a severe drought that depressed food production throughout the region.

Despite these obstacles, the colony survived its first few years because of periodic lifelines thrown from England. In early 1608, and again later in the same year, supply missions brought new people and food, each pulling the colony back from the brink of extinction. A third supply effort, comprising nine ships and roughly 500 colonists, left England in early June 1609. Leading this flotilla was the 300-ton *Sea Venture*, carrying roughly 150 passengers, including Sir George Somers (the fleet's admiral) and Sir Thomas Gates, who was slated to become Virginia's new governor. Also on board was John Rolfe, who would later gain fame for taking Pocahontas as his second wife and for spearheading the first successful commercial cultivation of tobacco in America. For seven weeks the fleet kept close company as it made its way across the relatively calm Atlantic, until late July, when the weather turned ominous.

In the evening of July 24, when the fleet was barely a week away from Jamestown, dark clouds filled the sky and the winds began to gust with escalating violence. The next day it was as if the world had exploded. William Strachey, a budding poet and playwright, and one of the *Sea Venture*'s passengers, captured the scene. "A dreadful and hideous storm began to blow from out the Northeast, which, swelling and roaring as it were by fits, some hours with more violence than others, at length did beat all light from heaven, which like a hell of darkness, turned black upon us." Scattered by the hurricane, each ship struggled to stay afloat. Seven of them ultimately made it to Jamestown in the coming weeks, while another ship and all of its passengers were lost to the storm. An English gentleman named William Box, who was on one of the surviving ships, described how "some [of them] lost their masts, some their sails blown from their yards. The seas so overtaking our ships much of our provision was spoiled, . . . and our men sick, and many died, and in this miserable estate we arrived in Virginia." As for the *Sea Venture*, it had the most terrifying and amazing ordeal of all.

For twenty-four hours, the hurricane blew with ever-increasing intensity, and just when the passengers thought it couldn't get any worse, it did, with "fury added to fury." The sound was so deafening that none could hear any other speak, even when shrieking at the top of their lungs. All sails were lowered because the ferocious winds would have torn them asunder, or short of that, knocked the ship on its beam-ends. "It could not be said to rain," Strachey observed, for "the waters like whole rivers did flood in the air."

The pounding of the waves shook oakum—the tarred, twisted rope used to caulk ships—from the seams between the hull's wood planking, opening numerous gaps that let the ocean rush in. Desperate men broke open the hogsheads of dried beef and shoved the meat into the breaches, but it failed to hold back the flood. At one point, a massive wave broke over the ship, covering it "from stern to stem like a garment or a vast cloud," only adding to the deluge. Manning the pumps and passing the buckets around the clock, every man and woman on board did their part to keep the ship from sinking. Strachey had been in powerful storms before in the Mediterranean, "yet all that I had ever suffered gathered together might not hold comparison with this," he wrote. "There was not a moment in which the sudden splitting or instant oversetting of the ship was not expected."

Even after the hurricane passed, gale-force winds and pummeling seas continued to tear at the *Sea Venture*, which was riding very low, its hold almost filled with 10 feet of violently sloshing water. For three more days the ship, without using so much as a patch of sail to catch the wind, scudded over the waves at a tremendous clip, while those on board, bereft of food and sleep, feared that every moment would be their last. Finally, four days after the hurricane hit, as the winds finally began to die down, Admiral Somers spied land in the distance.

It was the largest island among those of the Bermuda archipelago, which were called the "Devil's Islands" by European sailors on account of their jagged reefs that had wrecked many ships, as well as the "wicked spirits" that were said to haunt them. Devil or no, the island was Somers's only hope for salvation, so he sailed for it. But when it was still nearly a mile off, soundings showed that the bottom was rising fast, and it became clear that the *Sea Venture* would not be able to make it past the encircling reefs to shore. Instead, Somers expertly steered the ship toward two large rocks peeking out above the water, and solidly wedged it in between them.

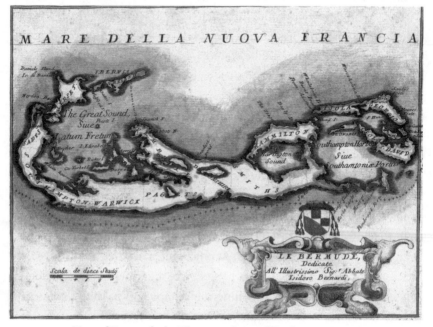

Map of Bermuda by Vincenzo Coronelli, circa 1692–94.

Far from being devil's islands, Bermuda turned out to be a genuine paradise, with lush vegetation, tasty fruits, plentiful fish that were "very fat and sweet," oysters that produced a "great store of pearl," fowl in great number, and numerous large and sturdy trees. The castaways remained on the island for nearly a year, during which time they built from the island's cedars and the *Sea Venture*'s carcass two small vessels, aptly named *Deliverance* and *Patience*, to take them on the last leg of their journey to Virginia.

Arriving in Jamestown on May 23, 1610, they were greeted by a horrific sight. The fort was in shambles, the palisades torn down, and most of the houses empty, their occupants having long since died. The little colony had barely survived the "starving time," during which the population had plummeted from around 500 to 60, the latter of which were mere shells of their former selves, veritable living skeletons. As the famine worsened, the dwindling few had resorted to eating their horses, followed by dogs, cats, mice, and snakes, as well as the leather from their boots and shoes. Then, clinging to the edge of life, some settlers even turned to cannibalism.

Not realizing that they would be encountering hell on Earth, the Bermuda castaways had brought only a couple of weeks of rations with them. Nevertheless, given the sorry state of the remaining colonists, the food on board the *Deliverance* and *Patience* was critical. "If God had not sent Sir Thomas Gates from the Bermudas," a contemporary pamphlet published in London opined, "within four days" those colonists would have all perished.

The meager rations, however, were not enough to sustain the colony, so Gates decided to abandon Jamestown. On June 7, everyone boarded the three remaining ships, and the pitiful fleet headed down the James River on its way back to England. After overnighting on shore just a few miles from the fort, they continued their journey and soon saw a small boat heading upriver with a lone Englishman on board. The man announced himself as Captain Edward Brewster. He handed Gates a letter from Thomas West, Lord De La Warr. Just two days earlier, De La Warr, leading the fourth supply mission, had arrived at the mouth of the river with three ships loaded with provisions and 150 new settlers. There, at Point Comfort, he had met a few men who were waiting to be picked up by Gates, and they told him about the colony's travails and the decision to leave. De La Warr was alarmed. He had with him a commission from the Virginia Company naming him the new governor of the colony, and he wasn't about to let the colony disband. In the letter he ordered Gates to return to Jamestown, and with that, the colony was saved.

As with the earlier hurricanes in Florida, the one that struck Jamestown's third supply mission in July 1609 left its mark on American history. It did so by depriving the colony of leadership and supplies during its most trying time, and by creating the circumstances that ultimately led to Gates's arrival from Bermuda nearly a year later, which provided the starving settlers with the lifeline that sustained them until the appearance of De La Warr. The hurricane also left its mark on literary history, since most scholars agree that William Shakespeare relied in part on Strachey's passionate account of the hurricane and its aftermath in penning his play *The Tempest*, the plot of which revolves around an extremely powerful storm and subsequent shipwreck on an island.

––––––

HURRICANES WOULD REMAIN AN inevitable part of American colonial life. Striking without warning, they upended lives and livelihoods. It must be added, though, that some people viewed hurricanes in a favorable light, arguing that they brought much-needed rains and the restoration of unhealthy air "to a salubrious state." Such an optimistic perspective, how-

Frontispiece illustration in Nicholas Rowe's edition of William Shakespeare's The Tempest, *published in 1709.*

ever, was a distinct minority. The overwhelming majority of colonists had a mortal fear of hurricanes and fervently prayed that they would stay away.

The list of colonial hurricanes is long, and many caused great destruction. But two of them are particularly noteworthy: the Great Colonial Hurricane of 1635 and the Treasure Fleet Hurricane of 1715.

THE GREAT COLONIAL HURRICANE of 1635 struck the Plymouth and Massachusetts Bay Colonies with a mighty wallop on August 15, leveling hundreds of thousands of trees, turning numerous houses into kindling, driving ships from their anchors, and killing many people, including eight Indians on the edge of Narragansett Bay, who were drowned "flying from their wigwams" when the waters surged ashore 14 feet higher than normal. According to William Bradford, governor of the Massachusetts Bay Colony, it "was such a mighty storm of wind and rain, as none living in these parts, either English or Indians, ever saw." The hurricane's story is best told through the tales of two vessels with very different fates.

Four days earlier, on the morning of August 11, Anthony Thacher and his cousin, the minister Joseph Avery, were standing on the wharf in Ipswich, Massachusetts, where the pinnace *Watch and Wait* was preparing to depart. Ministers were not easy to find in the Massachusetts Bay Colony, and the people of Marblehead, a small fishing village north of Boston, had persuaded Avery to be their pastor. They sent the *Watch and Wait* to pick him up, along with his cousin, who had also decided to move to Marblehead. While the master and his three crewmen readied the vessel for the trip, the passengers boarded. In addition to Avery and Thacher were both of their large families, two servants, and another gentleman. All told, there were twenty-three people.

For the first three days, with various lengthy stops along the way, the trip went well, but on August 14 "the Lord suddenly turned" the group's "cheerfulness into mourning and lamentations." At about 10:00 in the evening, the wind rose to a gale force, splitting the sails. The sailors refused to replace them on account of the dark, and instead anchored for the night. By dawn the gale had turned into a hurricane. The *Watch and Wait* began dragging its anchor; then the cable snapped, casting the vessel adrift in the turbulent seas. Thacher, Avery, and their families prayed and comforted one another as best they could, while expecting to be consigned to the deep at any moment.

The *Watch and Wait* was then thrown onto a large rock, where it was wedged in place and pummeled by the waves. As the cabin flooded and the vessel started breaking apart, the ocean began to claim its victims, almost one by one. The master and the crewmen were the first to be swept overboard. Rather than despair, Thacher held on to his faith. While peering out of the cabin into the roiling seas, he saw treetops in the distance. This discovery raised his hopes, and he told his cousin, "It hath pleased God to cast us here . . . the shore not far from us" (one has to wonder, though, whether Thacher questioned why God had not simply set the vessel *on* the shore). But Avery pleaded with him to stay so that they and their families could "die together" and be delivered to heaven.

No sooner had Thacher agreed to accept this fate than a thunderous wave surged into the cabin, washing him, his daughter, Avery, and Avery's eldest son out onto the rock. Clambering higher up, the four called to those still in the cabin to join them. The others apparently had frozen with fear, and only Thacher's wife responded. As she began crawling through a hatch to the quarterdeck, another wave smashed into the vessel, obliterating what was left of it and sending her and all the other occupants into the churning water. The force of the same wave also swept everyone from the rock, save Thacher, who managed tenaciously to cling to the rock face. Then, just as he was reaching out to grab a plank from the vessel, another wave dislodged him, and he, too, was pitched into the sea.

In the end, only Thacher and his wife survived what would become one of the most dramatic and fabled shipwrecks in Massachusetts Bay Colony history. Bruised, battered, and nearly naked, they washed up on a small, uninhabited island about a mile from the mainland of Cape Ann. They covered themselves with clothing from the wreck and survived on food that had also floated ashore. Five days passed before a boat came within hailing distance and rescued them.

The disaster quickly became the talk of New England, where many shared the deep sorrow felt by the Thachers. In September 1635 the Massachusetts legislature awarded Thacher "forty marks," or about twenty-six British pounds, to help compensate him for "his great losses"; and a year later it gave him the island "upon which he was preserved from shipwreck, as his proper inheritance." Thacher named the island "Thacher's Woe," but it is known today as Thacher Island, which is part of the town of Rockport.

At the same time that Thacher and company were succumbing to the hurricane's wrath, the ship *James* was fighting its own battle against the elements while anchored off the Isle of Shoals, located about 6 miles from the point along the coast where Maine and New Hampshire meet. The ship was carrying a group of 100 Puritan settlers who were leaving England to escape religious persecution and thus were part of the great Puritan migration of the 1620s and 1630s that sent roughly 20,000 dissenters from the Church of England to New England's shores. The *James's* most prominent passenger was Puritan minister Richard Mather, who was traveling with his wife and four sons to the town of Dorchester, just south of Boston, where he planned to preach at First Church.

The hurricane struck in the early-morning hours on August 15. "The Lord sent forth a most terrible storm of rain and easterly wind," Mather later recounted, "whereby we were in as much danger as I think ever people were." The *James's* three large anchors were useless in the face of the mounting winds and waves. Two of the anchor chains parted, and the

Richard Mather, in the frontispiece of John Foster's
The Life and Death of That Reverend Man of God,
Mr. Richard Mather, Teacher of the Church of
Dorchester in New England, *circa 1670.*

third was cut by "the seamen in extremity and distress, to save the ship and their own lives." When that last cable was severed, the *James* was set adrift, perilously close to the nine rocky islands that make up the Isle of Shoals. The sails were also no match for the storm, being "rent asunder and split in pieces, as if they had been but rotten rags."

Mather and his fellow puritans "cried unto the Lord" to be saved, and, by their telling, the Lord "was pleased to have compassion and pity upon us, for by his overruling providence and his own immediate good hand, he guided the ship past the rock[s], assuaged the violence of the sea, and the wind and rain, and gave us a little respite." (They had undoubtedly entered the eye of the hurricane.) During the calm, the crew hung new sails. When winds rapidly picked up again, they pushed the *James* toward the increasingly calmer waters off Cape Ann. "It was a day much to be remembered," Mather said, "because on that day the Lord granted us as wonderful a deliverance as I think ever people had, out of as apparent [a] danger as I think people ever felt." Mather and his family ultimately made it safely to Dorchester, where he quickly rose to become one of New England's most prominent preachers.

There is a strange asymmetry between these two accounts. Both involve men of the cloth who fervently believed that God had a plan for them and was at the controls. Yet, for one of them a hurricane brought death and misery, while the other walked away unscathed. This disparity certainly supports what people often say, that God works in mysterious ways. As it happens, by surviving, Mather had a profound impact on American history. Not only was he an esteemed and influential preacher, but his son, Increase Mather, and his grandson, Cotton Mather, played pivotal roles in the religious and political life of New England for the better part of a century.

THE HURRICANE THAT STRUCK off of Florida in 1715 is notable less for the direct damage it caused than for its impact on the course of piracy in America. During the final years of the War of the Spanish Succession (1702–13), the traditional Spanish treasure fleets had been unable to make their annual journeys across the Atlantic, resulting in the accumulation of a vast backlog of money and goods sitting in warehouses at Spanish American ports. Further delays after the war meant that it was May 1715 before the long-awaited fleet of eleven ships, commanded by Captain-General Don Juan Esteban de Ubilla, finally sailed from Havana bound for Cádiz. On board these ships were jewels, coins, ingots, and exotic goods from the Orient worth an estimated 7 million "pieces of eight," or Spanish silver dollars. Accompanying the fleet was a lone French ship, *Le Grifon*, transporting cargo to Spain for Havana's governor.

Early on July 30 the fleet was hugging Florida's east coast, not far from modern-day Vero Beach, when the sun disappeared behind billowing black clouds, the wind started howling, and mounting waves began pitching the ships about like corks. As the hurricane intensified, according to one of the sailors who survived the tempest, "it was so violent that the water flew in the air like arrows, doing injury to all those it hit, and seamen who had ventured much said they had never seen the like before." By the following morning, the entire fleet had been destroyed, the ships' backs broken as they were dashed against the reefs or run ashore. Only *Le Grifon*, which had sailed farther out to sea, survived the tempest. More than a thousand men, roughly half of the entire complement, lost their lives, with the battered survivors struggling to swim ashore and haul themselves onto the beach. Wreckage from the fleet was strewn over 30 miles of ocean and sand.

News of the disaster quickly spread in ever-widening circles throughout the Atlantic. The image of gold, silver, and jewels carpeting the ocean floor fed thousands of fantasies and led to a rush of mariners sailing to the Florida coast to recover some of the booty. Despite Spain's herculean salvage efforts, some interlopers succeeded in extracting riches from the seafloor, or violently wresting them from Spanish salvagers. Whether successful or not, many erstwhile treasure hunters decided to continue their search for loot by becoming pirates. They contributed to the dramatic rise in piracy in the mid-1710s, which lasted until the mid-1720s. Those pirates, who were operating during the tail end of the so-called Golden Age of Piracy, terrorized merchant ships in the Atlantic and had a significant and deleterious impact on the life of the colonies and the mother country.

WHILE AMERICAN COLONISTS WERE quite familiar with hurricanes, either through direct experience or by reading about them in the ever-expanding colonial press, they knew nothing about the origins of these storms, the forces that governed their behavior, or how they were structured and progressed over time. The almost universally held theory began and ended with the belief that they were God's work and, as mentioned earlier, God worked in mysterious ways. Another widely held, but mistaken, belief was that most hurricanes developed and died in roughly the same location, and when they moved, they were carried along in the same direction as prevailing winds. The first person to advance the understanding of hurricanes in a substantive manner was America's founding scientist, Benjamin Franklin.

CHAPTER

2

The Law of Storms

*Late-eighteenth-century engraving of
Thomas Jefferson, who had a keen interest in
meteorology and the advancement of the field.*

ON THE EVENING OF OCTOBER 21, 1743, THE THIRTY-SEVEN-year-old Benjamin Franklin craned his neck to look up at the Philadelphia sky, hoping to observe the predicted eclipse of the moon. Already a rising star in the colonies, lauded for publishing the wildly successful *Poor Richard's Almanack* and for clever inventions, such as his eponymous stove,

Franklin was sorely disappointed. Heavy cloud cover occluded his view, and then a hurricane sent him scurrying inside.

Since the hurricane's winds were rushing in from the northeast, Franklin assumed the storm had come from that direction. Thus, he was quite surprised when he learned from newspaper accounts and correspondence that the fair people of Boston, including his brother John, had witnessed the eclipse under clear skies, but that soon thereafter a violent storm with winds from the northeast similarly blocked their view. Franklin concluded that what had at first seemed like two storms was in fact the same storm, and that it had moved from the vicinity of Philadelphia to the northeast, where it hit Boston a few hours later. This conclusion was bolstered by reports that the same hurricane had passed over New York and Newport, Rhode Island, on its way to Boston. Thus, Franklin became the first person to realize that hurricanes had forward movement, and that a hurricane's winds could blow contrary to the direction in which it was moving. Although Franklin didn't understand the reason why (hurricanes are

Mid-nineteenth-century lithograph of an oil painting of
Benjamin Franklin by Joseph-Siffred Duplessis in 1779,
done while Franklin was in Paris trying to garner support
for the American war effort.

whirlwinds that swirl in a counterclockwise direction, and he was on the left side of the hurricane's eye as it passed), his observation was an important first step forward in deciphering the mysteries of hurricane behavior.

Franklin's insight was not the only meteorological first related to the so-called Eclipse Hurricane of 1743. On the day of the hurricane, John Winthrop, the great-great-grandson of the Massachusetts governor of the same name, was at work in his lab at Harvard University, where he was a professor of mathematics and philosophy. Just the year prior, he had begun keeping a "Meteorologie Diary," in which he recorded a great range of measurements, including temperature, precipitation, and pressure. This last item was quite unusual. Italian physicist and mathematician Evangelista Torricelli invented the mercury barometer in 1643, but this ingenious instrument for measuring atmospheric pressure didn't make its way to the American colonies until 1717, when one was brought to Philadelphia; and only ten years later did Winthrop procure his device.

As the hurricane bore down on Cambridge, Winthrop kept checking his barometer as it dropped; it reached its lowest point of 29.35 inches of mercury at 2:00 p.m. Since a normal barometric reading at sea level is 29.92 inches,* Winthrop's reading was not particularly low, indicating a fairly weak hurricane, but then again he was located a bit inland and his barometer might have been poorly calibrated. Nevertheless, his observation made Winthrop the first person ever to measure the barometric pressure of a hurricane—a piece of data that would ultimately become a critical element in determining the intensity of such storms.

Franklin and Winthrop had begun a process of scientific inquiry that would help unlock the secrets of hurricanes. But it was just a rudimentary beginning, and one that would not be built upon in any substantive way until the middle of the next century. This long period of stagnation with respect to hurricane science is quite surprising, given the inquisitiveness that characterized the times.

FRANKLIN AND WINTHROP LIVED in the midst of the Age of Enlightenment, or the Age of Reason as it was often called, which began in the late 1600s and lasted until the early 1800s. It was an intellectually exciting

---

* 29.92 inches is the equivalent of 14.7 pounds per square inch.

time of ferment and change, during which rational thought and experimentation were celebrated as a means of better understanding the world and improving the human condition by solving problems that had long vexed society. In the realm of science and natural history, it was a period of great discoveries, many of which helped explain, categorize, quantify, and make sense of the laws, forces, and elements that affected life on Earth.

This is when English mathematician and astronomer Isaac Newton made seminal contributions to optics and laid the foundations for classical mechanics; Swedish botanist Carolus Linnaeus introduced binomial nomenclature, the taxonomic system of naming plants and animals by their distinct genus and species; and Scottish geologist James Hutton proved that geological processes such as sedimentation, erosion, and volcanic activity created the Earth's topography, and that the world was inconceivably old, its age being reflected in geologic layers built up over time.

The field of meteorology, the roots of which reach all the way back to Aristotle's treatise *Meteorologica*, written in 340 BCE, also advanced during the Age of Enlightenment. The increasingly widespread use of accurate barometers, thermometers, and rain gauges transformed many people into weather watchers, who often recorded their observations in journals. The most famous American practitioner was Thomas Jefferson, an amateur meteorologist and inveterate weather observer. The rigors of his diplomatic and political life notwithstanding, for forty-two years, from 1776 to 1818, and possibly longer, he kept an extensive daily diary of the weather at his mountaintop home of Monticello, as well as at other locations where he lived during his illustrious career, including the White House. Jefferson's hope was that by measuring a wide variety of what he called "the indexes of climate"—precipitation, temperature, the times at which birds migrated and plants flowered—he could contribute to a theory of the climate and how it changes over time. Although such a theory wasn't developed during his lifetime, Jefferson's meteorological efforts added to the general understanding of daily weather and broader climatic trends. His work was amplified by thousands of other weather diarists in America and Europe who also kept and shared their assiduously maintained records.

Another amateur meteorologist is credited with the "invention of clouds." In 1802, thirty-year-old British pharmacist Luke Howard gave a public lecture titled "On the Modification of Clouds," which he followed soon thereafter with an essay by the same name. Howard took something everyone experienced—ever-shifting clouds overhead—and made sense of them by giving them names. His classification of clouds, based on their characteristics, was simple and elegant. The three basic cloud types were cirrus, cumulus, and stratus—most simplistically defined as, respectively, wispy or feathery clouds, massively towering clouds extending upward from a horizontal base, and clouds that spread horizontally over a great area, creating a covering sheet. Then Howard went one step further by combining the three basic types to create variations on a theme, such as cirrostratus and cumulocirrostratus. Howard's genius was to create a "language of the skies," which enabled a richer and deeper conversation about clouds and their effect on the weather.

While progress in meteorology during the Age of Enlightenment was not insignificant, it was not earth-shattering either. As Jefferson wrote in 1822, "Of all the departments of science no one seems to have been less advanced for the last hundred years than that of meteorology." But at least when it came to the daily and seasonal weather, and the climate and clouds, there was some forward movement. Unfortunately, the same could not be said for the understanding of hurricanes. This deficiency was not for a lack of examples to observe and study. Since Franklin's epiphany during the Eclipse Hurricane, plenty of hurricanes had afflicted America and the Caribbean, and two of the most consequential hit during the American Revolution.

THE FIRST STRUCK AT the beginning of October 1780 and laid waste to Jamaica by flattening buildings, sinking ships, and killing more than a thousand people. Jamaican governor John Dalling described the scene in Savanna-la-Mar, at the southwestern tip of the island, when the hurricane roared ashore: "The sea broke suddenly in upon the town, and in its retreat swept everything away with it, so as not to leave the smallest vestige of man, beast, or house behind." A former plantation owner on Jamaica remarked that the hurricane "will be ever acknowledged as a visitation that descends but once in a century, and that serves as a scourge to correct the vanity, to humble the pride, and to chastise the imprudence and arrogance of men." As the storm transited the island and then swept over

Cuba, it smashed into a number of British naval ships, sinking four and killing most of their crews. The terrifying ordeal of one of these ships, the *Phoenix*, was captured in a letter that its first lieutenant, Benjamin Archer, wrote to his mother.

Engraving, circa 1784, of HMS Hector *and HMS* Bristol *being dismasted on October 6, 1780, during the Savanna-la-Mar Hurricane.*

The *Phoenix* encountered the storm while sailing between Jamaica and Cuba. As the winds rose to hurricane strength, the sailors secured the sails, tied down the guns, and made the ship as snug as possible. In the midst of these preparations, Archer noticed birds literally dropping out of the sky and diving toward the deck, where many of them were knocked unconscious. Upon reviving, they would not leave their haven in the storm, but rather huddled in corners, trying to shield themselves from the wind. The elements brought so much pressure to bear on the hull that all the ship's seams began to leak. Archer had been through rough weather before, but nothing like this. "My God! To think that the wind could have such force!"

Pumping furiously to keep the lower decks from swamping, the sailors worked nonstop through the night, but the hurricane was gaining. Archer lashed himself to a post on the deck, barking out orders as best he could above the deafening din. "If I was to write forever, I could not give you an idea of" the storm, his letter said—"a total darkness all above, the sea on fire, running as it were the Alps, or pikes of Tenerife; mountains are too common an idea; the wind rising louder than thunder . . . the poor ship

*Engraving showing First Lieutenant Benjamin Archer
cutting away the lanyards on the* Phoenix *during the
Savanna-la-Mar Hurricane of 1780, published in
Archibald Duncan's* Mariner's Chronicle, vol. 2 (1804).

very much pressed, yet doing what she could, shaking her sides and groan-
ing at every stroke."

Ultimately, the *Phoenix* plowed into the shore, stern first, about 10
miles east of Cuba's Cape Cruz. The waves forced her so high onto the
rocks that she hardly moved from that spot. When the fury of the hurricane had passed, the ship was a total loss, yet it was still in one piece.
Only five men had been killed, when they were washed overboard by a
breaking wave. Taking in the scene, with many injured men lying about,
Archer "was surprised to find [that] the most swaggering, swearing bullies
in fine weather, were now the most pitiful wretches on earth, when death
appeared before them."

As the storm slowly subsided, the officers and crew of the *Phoenix*
clambered higher up on the shore, away from the pounding surf. In the
coming days, Archer and four other men sailed the ship's cutter to Mon-
tego Bay, where they enlisted three serviceable vessels to ferry the *Phoenix's* remaining crew back to Jamaica. Meanwhile, after leaving Cuba
behind, the hurricane continued its northward march. Tracking hundreds
of miles from the shores of the American colonies, it greatly damaged two
separate British naval fleets, forcing many of the ships into port for repairs.

Less than a month later the Caribbean would be hit by a storm of such magnitude that it came to be known as the Great Hurricane of 1780. Its trajectory took it past the Leeward Islands and between Puerto Rico and Hispaniola. It then curved sharply to the east, dying out over the mid-Atlantic after delivering Bermuda a serious blow. But it had its most devastating impact on Barbados, Martinique, and St. Eustatius, with estimates of the deaths on these islands alone totaling roughly 17,000.

British admiral Lord George Brydges Rodney, commander in chief of the Leeward Islands Station, was on a ship off the coast of New York at the time the hurricane hit, but when he returned to Barbados a few weeks later, he wrote a letter in which he expressed his shock and dismay at the vista that unfolded before him. "It is impossible to describe the dreadful scene [the hurricane] has occasioned at Barbados, and the condition of the miserable inhabitants. . . . The whole face of the country appears one entire ruin; and the most beautiful island in the world has the appearance of a country laid waste by fire and sword, and appears to the imagination more dreadful than it is possible for me to find words to express."

The hurricane also gravely damaged the British and French navies, both of which used Caribbean ports as staging areas for their forces fighting in the American Revolution. The British lost eight ships to the storm, and almost all of their crews, while the French lost more than forty transport vessels, along with the thousands of soldiers on board. The overall death toll of the hurricane is estimated to have reached 22,000, with some sources placing it higher still. In either case, this staggering loss of life earned this storm the title of the deadliest hurricane ever in the Atlantic.

The two hurricanes that slammed the Caribbean in October 1780 raise the question of whether these singular weather events affected the course of the Revolutionary War.* According to historian Nathaniel Philbrick, the hurricanes had a decisive impact because they caused France, America's ally in the war, to reevaluate its stance vis-à-vis sending ships north to fight the British. "The lesson [of the hurricanes] was impossible to ignore," Philbrick argues. The French concluded that remaining in

---

* There was yet a third massive hurricane that hit the Caribbean in October 1780, called Solano's Hurricane, which struck a few days after the Great Hurricane of 1780. Although it gravely damaged the Spanish fleet under the command of Admiral Don José Solano y Bote Carrasco y Díaz, it did not impact the English or French fleets, and therefore did not have a direct impact on the American Revolution.

*Major General Charles O'Hara, surrounded by French and American
soldiers, handing his sword in surrender to General Benjamin Lincoln
at Yorktown on October 19, 1781.*

the Caribbean during hurricane season was too dangerous. "Up until this
point, France had viewed a naval expedition to the north on the behalf of
the United States a possibility but hardly a priority. After that horrendous
October, a different attitude prevailed."

Given their newfound appreciation for the destructive power of hurricanes, the French spent the winter of 1781 in the Caribbean repairing
their ships and strengthening their hold on the French colonies there, then
sent most of their forces north to the American colonies, both to avoid tan-
gling with any more hurricanes and also to aid the Americans. Thus, by
following this course of action the French played a key role in the crucial
Battle of the Chesapeake and the ultimate American victory over the British in the Battle of Yorktown, which ended when Lord Charles Cornwallis
surrendered to George Washington at Yorktown on October 19, 1781—
an event so profound that when the British prime minister, the imperious
Lord North, learned of the surrender he wailed, "Oh God, it is all over!"
He was correct. The surrender effectively ended the war and soon led to
peace negotiations, resulting in the Treaty of Paris on September 3, 1783.

THE WAR AGAINST THE British was over, the Constitution ratified, and the business of running a new nation well on its way. And yet, the forces of nature continued to plague the infant republic. Twin hurricanes hit North Carolina in 1795. The Great Louisiana Hurricane of 1812 destroyed nearly all of the low-lying soil and sand levees that bordered the Mississippi River, as well as most of the houses in New Orleans and surrounding areas. Then, three years later, the Great September Gale of 1815, which was just a hurricane by another name, zipped over the tip of Long Island and delivered a deadly blow to New England.

Barreling north at an estimated speed of nearly 50 mph, this hurricane not only battered coastal areas but also spread its path of destruction far inland before petering out. Famed lexicographer Noah Webster, writing in his diary from his farm in Amherst, Massachusetts, called the storm "a proper hurricane, like those experienced in the West Indies." The sea spray carried aloft by the storm could be tasted in the rain and left a salty glaze on windows and leaves throughout the region. Along with the spray came flocks of seagulls, some of which were blown all the way to Worcester, about 45 miles from the ocean.

Some of the greatest damage occurred in Providence, Rhode Island, where terrific winds coming from the south propelled a gathering bore of water up Narragansett Bay and into the narrower confines of the Providence River, where it violently washed over the city. Wharves collapsed under the onslaught, and forty vessels ripped from their moorings careened into bridges and shot like missiles through the streets, demolishing anything in their way. Roofs flew into the air, chimneys toppled, fences were flattened, and the roiling waters, 15 feet above the highest of high tides, scraped buildings from their foundations. "Destruction and desolation were everywhere," wrote one eyewitness. Amazingly, only two lives were lost, one of which was an elderly woman who, it was claimed by her neighbors, had been baking bread in her house and refused to leave until it was done. Before the bread rose, the house was swept away by the flood.

The hurricane seared itself into the memory of Oliver Wendell Holmes Sr., who was only seven years old at the time and would become one of America's most celebrated essayists and poets. Recalling the storm many years later, he noted, "The wind caught up the waters of the bay and of the river Charles, as mad shrews tear the hair from each other's heads." Holmes's 1836 poem titled "The September Gale" humorously recounted the passing of the hurricane over his Cambridge home, in one of its stanzas telling of the storm's dramatic effect on his wardrobe:

> *It chanced to be our washing-day,*
> *And all our things were drying;*
> *The storm came roaring through the lines,*
> *And set them all a flying;*
> *I saw the shirts and petticoats*
> *Go riding off like witches;*
> *I lost, ah! bitterly I wept,—*
> *I lost my Sunday breeches!*

Despite all of these hurricanes, and many more that pounded the Caribbean and the coast of America during the late 1700s and early 1800s, after Franklin's contribution the well of knowledge about the meteorology of hurricanes remained largely unfilled until William C. Redfield arrived on the scene.

William C. Redfield.

BORN TO A POOR family in Middletown, Connecticut, in 1789, Redfield overcame his modest upbringing and rudimentary education to become a voracious autodidact and successful businessman. When he was thirteen his father died at sea, and the following year his mother sent him off to be a harness maker's apprentice in Middletown Upper-Houses (now Cromwell), the adjoining village, which hugged the western shore of New England's longest river, the gently flowing Connecticut. Four years later, Redfield's mother remarried and moved to Ohio with all of his siblings, leaving him behind to fend for himself. Despite a grueling apprenticeship, his thirst for knowledge gave Redfield the drive and energy to form a local debating society and seek other opportunities for intellectual growth. Fortuitously, a nearby physician, Dr. Tully, took an interest in Redfield, and opened up his considerable library to the young man. Thus began Redfield's lifelong habit of insatiably consuming books, especially scientific ones. After finishing his apprenticeship, Redfield settled down in Cromwell, and by 1821 he had become a respected merchant, running a general store and a saddler's shop.

In early October of that year, Redfield left his home in a horse-drawn wagon. His mission was a depressing one. He was traveling to Stockbridge, Massachusetts, to tell his in-laws that their daughter had died just a few weeks after giving birth to a son, who followed her in death a couple of days later. But in the midst of his anguish, Redfield remained the keen and insightful observer he had always been. It was the trees that caught his attention.

A month earlier, a powerful hurricane had come in off the Atlantic and torn across the Connecticut Valley up through Massachusetts and beyond. It had left behind a ravaged landscape with great stands of trees blown down. During his journey to Stockbridge, Redfield looked at the way those trees had fallen and noticed something peculiar. In and around Cromwell, all of the downed trees were lying with their crowns facing toward the northwest, but in the vicinity of Stockbridge, some 70 miles away and slightly to the west, the downed trees were facing in the opposite direction, to the southeast.

The strange manner in which the trees had fallen greatly puzzled Redfield. The mystery deepened when he began inquiring of people along the route, only to learn that at around 9:00 p.m. on the night of the hurricane, the winds in Cromwell had been from the southeast, while those in Stockbridge were blowing out of the northwest. As Redfield's son John later recalled, "These facts at first seemed" to his father "irreconcilable." He couldn't believe it was "possible that two winds of such violence should be blowing directly against each other at a distance of only seventy miles." Having dismissed this possibility, Redfield landed on the only other logical explanation he could devise—namely, that the hurricane was a great whirlwind, its winds revolving around a central axis. Cromwell had been on one side of the hurricane, and Stockbridge on the other.

At the time, this was just a working hypothesis, and Redfield made no effort to publicize it. Instead, he kept his epiphany to himself for a full decade, during which time he did what he had always done when a topic excited him: he studied it. For him, this meant gathering further information on the hurricane of 1821, as well as reading anything and everything about meteorology and hurricanes that he could lay his hands on—all in the hope of turning his hypothesis into an established fact. While pursuing self-directed meteorological studies in his free time, Redfield proceeded to become a wealthy man, establishing a successful business building steamboats that transported growing numbers of people up and down America's vast network of rivers, as well as along the coast.

Finally, in early 1831, a serendipitous encounter brought Redfield's hurricane insights into the open. While traveling on one of his steamboats from New York to New Haven, he met Denison Olmsted, the Yale professor of mathematics and natural philosophy, who happened to be on board that day. Thirty-nine years old, Olmstead was already famous for his teaching and research in meteorology and astronomy, and Redfield was familiar with some of his work. In particular, Redfield had read Olmsted's provocative theory on the creation of hailstones, and he had a question about it, which he posed to the professor.

In the course of their discussion, Olmsted quickly realized that he was in the company of someone who knew a great deal about meteorology. When Redfield began to share his ideas on hurricane formation and structure, Olmsted was transfixed. He had never heard such musings and thought they were both novel and important—so much so that Olmsted strongly encouraged Redfield to publish his findings in the *American Journal of Science and Arts.** Redfield, both modest and fearful that his lack of formal scientific training might cause people to discount his work, demurred. Olmsted kept pressing until Redfield agreed, but on one condition. Redfield said he would write the paper as long as Olmsted promised to revise the piece as needed and oversee its submittal to the journal. The deal struck, the paper was published in the journal's July 1831 issue.

Titled "Remarks on the Prevailing Storms of the Atlantic Coast, of the North American States," the somewhat dense article detailed much of what was known about hurricanes, including Franklin's observation, and then offered up Redfield's own conclusions. His central finding, now bolstered by extensive data, was his original surmise—namely, that hurricanes took the "form of a great whirlwind."

But Redfield was not the first person to make this suggestion. When famed English explorer and perceptive observer of natural history William Dampier sailed through typhoons in the China Sea during his around-the-world voyage in 1697, he noted that they were "a sort of violent whirlwind." During one typhoon, in which his vessel entered and exited the eye, Dampier noticed that at first the winds came from the northeast, followed by a period of calm, and then a shift in the wind, which now came from the southwest. Similarly, in the early 1800s, both Colonel James Clapper, of the East India Company, and German professor Heinrich Dove identified the whirlwind nature of hurricanes. While these earlier observers had merely hinted at the rotary nature of hurricanes, Redfield marshaled a mountain of data, thus fully demonstrating his clear right to the credit for proving that hurricanes were indeed "violent whirlwinds." Redfield's discovery is all the more impressive because he knew nothing of the limited findings on this topic that preceded his observations.

In subsequent years, Redfield published other articles that, through additional analysis, further refined his conclusions. All together, they painted a much fuller picture of the structure and progression of hurricanes. Besides characterizing hurricanes as whirlwinds, Redfield noted that the winds blow in circles around an axis, and that the direction of revolution is counterclockwise north of the equator, and clockwise to the

---

* This publication later became the *American Journal of Science* and is the oldest continuously running scientific journal in the United States, having been launched in 1818.

south. He also determined that the velocity of the winds increases dramatically as one moves from the outer edge of the hurricane toward its center, and that the entire hurricane moves forward at a variable rate, but always much more slowly than it rotates.

The difference in internal velocity compared to forward velocity means that the part of the hurricane directly to the right of the eye will have the strongest winds, because the speed of the rotating hurricane is added to the speed at which the hurricane is advancing (thus, if the hurricane's sustained winds are 80 mph and the entire hurricane is moving at 30 mph, the actual speed of the wind on the right side is the sum, or 110 mph). By the same token, the winds on the left side of the eye will be the weakest because the advancing speed of the hurricane must be subtracted from the speed of the hurricane's winds (in our example, the calculation is 80 mph minus 30 mph, so the wind speed in the left half of the hurricane is only 50 mph).

Despite Redfield's earlier concerns that his findings would not be taken seriously, on account of his lack of scientific pedigree, they were, and many scientists, as well as more casual observers, applauded Redfield for his seminal contribution to meteorology. There was one well-known scientist, however, who wasn't receptive to Redfield's ideas. In fact, he set out to discredit Redfield and tear his research down. His name was James P. Espy.

ESPY WAS BORN IN rural Pennsylvania on May 9, 1785. While he was still a young boy, his family moved west to Ohio. After graduating with a law degree from Transylvania University in Lexington, Kentucky, Espy returned to Pennsylvania, married, and ultimately settled down in Philadelphia, where he rose to become the head of the classics department at the Franklin Institute. Although trained in law, he had always had a love of and aptitude for science, and by the early 1830s he was actively engaged in meteorological research, with a focus on violent storms.

Using his deep understanding of how gases operate in dynamic systems, Espy postulated that hurricanes are essentially large heat engines, in which warm, moist air rises from the surface of the ocean in the tropics, cooling in the process and forming the droplets of water or ice crystals that make up clouds. This transition from moist air or water vapor to drop-

James P. Espy.

lets or crystals releases latent heat, which causes the air to rise further, and also provides the energy that propels the hurricane's ferocious winds. As the air rises, it creates an area of extreme low pressure—hence the low barometric pressure associated with hurricanes—and given that nature abhors a vacuum, air at the surface rushes into the area of low pressure in an attempt to balance the system. But since the air rushing in is continually heated by the warm water, and also becomes saturated with vapor, it, too, rises upward, thereby continuing the cycle and drawing more air into the area of low pressure.

This was a brilliant insight and, in fact, has been proved to be the driving force that generates and sustains hurricanes. Indeed, the crucial contribution of heat is the reason why hurricanes rapidly weaken after encountering colder waters or land, since they are thereby stripped of their main energy source. Espy also argued that the air rushing in would come in straight lines (envision the wind being represented by the spokes of a bicycle wheel, all converging on a central point). This model was at odds with Redfield's observation that a hurricane was a whirlwind, with wind circulating in a counterclockwise direction in the Northern Hemisphere, around a center axis.

The disagreement between Espy and Redfield spawned what would later become known as the "American Storm Controversy," which played out primarily between Espy and Redfield, and each of their respective supporters, in the rapidly expanding scientific and popular press of the day. Espy, who soon earned the moniker "Storm King" by virtue of his meteorological studies, as well as his very public efforts to promote his theory, viciously attacked Redfield's conclusions. Espy claimed that the evidence from numerous storms, even those from which Redfield had gathered data to support his own arguments, clearly showed that, in fact, Espy was correct. Affronted that anyone—much less a rank amateur like Redfield—would question him, Espy sought to steamroll Redfield with a tsunami of insults and overly academic scientific arguments. Espy even took his show on the road, giving lectures at lyceums throughout the country to drive his arguments home.

But Redfield would not be cowed, and he gave as good as he got, taking on his antagonist in a series of articles that defended his findings and refuted Espy point by point. Observing the raucous debate, the renowned American physicist Joseph Henry insightfully commented, "Meteorology has ever been an apple of contention, as if the violent commotions of the atmosphere induced a sympathetic effect in the minds of those who have attempted to study them." Redfield, however, didn't have to wage his battle alone. By the end of the 1830s, he had gained the support of some powerful allies, the most important of which was William Reid.

COLONEL WILLIAM REID, of the Royal Engineers, had been sent by the British government to help with reconstruction efforts after a powerful hurricane devastated Barbados in 1831, resulting in the death of nearly 1,500 people. One who lived through it compared the roar of the hurricane to "the agonizing shrieks of millions of human beings in the last agony of despair." Reid wanted not only to rebuild the colony but also to better understand hurricanes, specifically "their causes and mode of action," in the hope that such understanding might help people on land and mariners at sea better cope with hurricanes and their impacts.

At first, Reid was stymied in his search for information about the nature of hurricanes—until, that is, he happened upon Redfield's 1831 article in the *American Journal of Science and Arts*. Thinking that Redfield's arguments made sense, Reid set out to see whether the data supported them. He studied, in minute detail, the logs of British naval ships that had survived their encounters with hurricanes, along with any other eyewitness information he could glean from the historical record. He searched for data pertaining not only to the 1831 hurricane in Barbados but also to the Great Hurricane of 1780, as well as a host of other Atlantic hurricanes and Pacific typhoons.

Buttressed by a mountain of data, Reid overwhelmingly confirmed Redfield's conclusions about the whirlwind nature of hurricanes, and by 1838 the two men had struck up a warm relationship, corresponding regularly and sharing ideas. That same year, Reid attended the annual meeting of the British Association for the Advancement of Science held in Newcastle upon Tyne in northern England, where he presented his findings to the thunderous applause of an audience that was thoroughly swayed by the merit of Redfield's arguments and the persuasive power of Reid's data.

Soon after the meeting, Reid published a book titled *An Attempt to Develop the Law of Storms by Means of Facts*, which further elaborated on his findings. Reid's book also built upon an idea first broached by Redfield—namely, that by knowing their location with respect to a hurricane's eye and its revolving winds, mariners could take evasive action and steer clear of danger, either finding the quickest and safest route out of the hurricane or avoiding the hurricane altogether. This concept—that, in effect, mariners could alter their fate by better understanding the nature of hurricanes and reacting appropriately—was groundbreaking.

After reviewing the work of Redfield and Reid, the editors of the *Edinburgh Review* proclaimed "that a real step has been made in the statistics and philosophy of storms." They went on to "predict that no sailor will study these records of atmospherical convulsions, without feeling himself better armed for a professional struggle with the elements." And they warned that the mariner who would sail either to the West or the East Indies "without Colonel Reid's book, will discover, when it is too late, that he has left behind him his best chronometer and his surest compass. In his attempts to escape the Scylla of its incipient gales, he may recklessly plunge himself into the Charybdis of the hurricane."

Englishman Henry Piddington took Redfield's and Reid's idea even further. After spending more than a decade captaining merchant ships in the East India and China trade, Piddington retired from the sea around

1830, when he was in his early thirties, so that he could pursue his broad interests in science. He settled in Calcutta, where he was appointed curator of the Museum of Economic Geology, and he began publishing articles on a wide array of topics, including the discovery of a new fossil dinosaur, fish biology, and the suitability of various soils for cultivating cash crops. Piddington's intellectual meanderings came to an end in 1839, when he decided to focus his considerable energies on the study of storms.

Piddington spent the better part of the next decade studying and writing about hurricanes, but he didn't call them that. Instead, he coined the word *cyclone*, which is derived from the Greek word signifying the coil of a snake, to refer specifically to hurricanes that occurred in the South Pacific and the Indian Ocean. As a former mariner, Piddington strived in all of his work on cyclones to give sailors the tools they needed to safely navigate tempestuous seas. To that end, in 1848 he applied Redfield's and Reid's findings in creating a handy guide with the hefty title *The Sailor's Horn-Book for the Law of Storms: Being a Practical Exposition of the Theory of the Law of Storms, and Its Uses to Mariners of All Classes, in All Parts of the World, Shewn by Transparent Storm Cards and Useful Lessons.*

The triumphant introduction to the book boldly stated that its purpose was "to explain to the seaman, in such language that every man who can work a day's-work can understand it, the theory and the practical use of the Law of Storms for all parts of the world; for this science has now become so essential a part of nautical knowledge that every seaman who conscientiously desires to fulfill his duties . . . must wish to know at all events what this new science is: of which he hears it said, that it teaches how to *avoid* Storms—teaches how best to *manage in Storms* when they cannot be avoided—and teaches how to *profit by Storms!*" Tucked into each copy of the book were two transparent storm cards that, if held up to a map or chart and properly oriented over a ship's location, could be used not only to instruct captains in which direction to sail to most quickly escape a storm's clutches, but also in how to use a hurricane's winds to their advantage in hastening their voyage.

Mariners who had the greatest need for accurate information came down universally on the side of Redfield and Reid in the great storm controversy. Commodore Matthew C. Perry, after returning from his 1854 groundbreaking expedition to Japan, which led to a peace treaty that opened the secretive kingdom to the West, sang their praises. To

Redfield and Reid, Perry intoned, "are navigators mainly indebted for the discovery of a law which has already contributed, and will continue to contribute, greatly to the safety of vessels traversing the ocean." While he admitted that others had added to the understanding of hurricanes, Perry argued that these two should get the credit for "the original discovery of this undeniable law of nature, and its application to useful purposes."

At about the same time, a captain in the British navy who penned a tome quite similar to Piddington's, called *The Storm Compass or, Seaman's Hurricane Companion*, proclaimed that Redfield and Reid "should be remembered by seamen of all nations with feelings of gratitude; for by the simple light of truth . . . they have literally disarmed the storm of its greatest terrors. How many lives would have been saved, had the truth been known in years gone by! How much suffering have been avoided! How many ships, laden with valuable property, [would] have been saved to their owners!"

ESPY WATCHED THESE ASSAULTS on his theory—that the winds in a hurricane rush straight in toward the center as a result of the rising warm air that creates an area of extreme low pressure—with increasing alarm and anger, and he sought to fight Redfield at every turn. Realizing that the epicenter of science was Europe, Espy launched his own tour of the continent. His appearance in Glasgow before the British Association for the Advancement of Science in 1840, however, didn't go as he hoped. Since that august body had already declared in favor of Redfield, they gave Espy a polite but lukewarm hearing. Soon thereafter, Reid wrote to Redfield, "I hear from England that people's minds were satisfied with the revolving theory of storms; so that few cared to listen at Glasgow, and elsewhere, to Mr. Espy's explanations of his particular theory." France's Academy of Sciences gave Espy a much more enthusiastic and supportive reception. According to one account, famed French astronomer and mathematician François Arago, convinced of the value of Espy's work, declared, "France has its Cuvier, England its Newton, America its Espy." In an effort to further his cause, in 1841 Espy published a tremendously long and tedious tome titled *The Philosophy of Storms*, which laid out his theories for the entire world to see.

Espy was so focused on the purported merits of his theory that he would not dispassionately consider any other. Even when presented with evidence that contradicted his view, he would not budge. Alexander Dallas Bache, one of his colleagues at the Franklin Institute, and also a friend, commented on Espy's pig-headed approach, which seemingly made him immune to intellectual conversion. "The earnest and deep convictions of the truth of his theory in all its parts," Bache wrote, "and his glowing enthusiasm in regard to it; perhaps, also, the age which he had reached, prevented Mr. Espy from passing beyond a certain point in the development of his theory. . . . He was not prone to examine and re-examine premises and conclusions, but considered what had once been passed upon by his judgment as finally settled." Former president and current congressman John Quincy Adams was a little less charitable in his estimation of Espy, observing that he was "methodically monomaniac[al], and the dimensions of his organ of self-esteem have been swollen to the size of a goiter."

Redfield died in 1857, and Espy in 1860. Each went to his grave thinking he was correct regarding the nature of hurricanes. As it turned out, they were both *partially* correct. In a hurricane, winds do rush toward the center area of extreme low pressure, as Espy had predicted, but they don't do so in straight lines. And although the winds do rotate around a central point, they do not do so in circles as Redfield thought. Instead, a hurricane's winds spiral in toward the center because they are influenced by the so-called Coriolis effect, which was first hypothesized in 1831 by French mathematician Gustave-Gaspard Coriolis but wasn't applied to meteorology, and more specifically to hurricane behavior, until William Ferrel did so a couple of decades later.

LIKE REDFIELD, Ferrel was largely self-trained, and he possessed a keen mind. Growing up in rural Pennsylvania and Virginia, he had only a rudimentary education and spent much of his time working on his father's farm and others nearby. Using some of his earnings to purchase mathematical books, Ferrel became entranced with the sky, especially solar and lunar eclipses, and before long he was proficient enough in astronomical calculations to predict the arrival of eclipses with considerable accuracy. Ferrel added more mathematical books to his growing library and gained enough skill and promise to enroll in two colleges, where he studied mathematics,

Latin, and Greek, ultimately graduating from Bethany College in West Virginia at the age of twenty-seven, and soon thereafter embarking on a career as a schoolteacher.

While teaching in Missouri, Ferrel continued his self-directed studies, purchasing a copy of Newton's most important work, *Philosophiae Naturalis Principia Mathematica*, or *Principia*, as it is usually called. This treatise on mathematics, physics, and the celestial and terrestrial mechanics of motion opened up a whole new world of inquiry for Ferrel, who continued to acquire the classics of science as he pursued teaching jobs in Kentucky and Tennessee. With his mind fully engaged in the mysteries of the universe, Ferrel focused his efforts on meteorology, zeroing in on the motions of the winds and the ocean.

He published three papers between 1856 and 1860, the key conclusion of which was captured neatly in a single sentence from his second paper ("The Influence of the Earth's Rotation upon the Relative Motion of Bodies Near Its Surface"), which appeared in the *Astronomical Journal* in 1858. "If a body is moving in any direction," Ferrel asserted, "there is a force [the Coriolis force], arising from the earth's rotation, which always deflects it to the right in the northern hemisphere, and to the left in the southern." In other words, Ferrel showed how, in a hurricane, the air rushing in toward a region of low pressure will be diverted or deflected on its course, thus resulting in the hurricane's mesmerizing, spiraling motion.

Apparently, Redfield wasn't aware of Ferrel's work before he died, but Espy read Ferrel's first paper after Joseph Henry forwarded him a copy. While Espy was encouraged by Ferrel's support of his theory on the source of the energy that drove hurricanes—the latent heat coming from the condensation of ascending water vapor—he vigorously disagreed with Ferrel's findings regarding the impact of the Earth's rotation on a hurricane's progress, characteristically preferring to stick to his own rigid views. Nevertheless, Ferrel's contribution was accepted in time, providing a more accurate conception of hurricane behavior. It gave us the final link that created the basic and accepted image of a hurricane as a mass of swirling or spiraling, moisture-laden winds, the velocity of which greatly increases as one approaches the central axis of the storm until one enters the calm, clear, and surprisingly beautiful eye.

By the mid-1800s, hurricanes were no longer an inscrutable force, but rather an explainable, albeit far from completely understood, phenomenon. Still, broadly understanding a phenomenon and protecting oneself from it are two different things. Even though Redfield's, Reid's, and Piddington's work offered guidance on how to avoid or outflank hurricanes at sea, people both at sea and on land still had little warning that a hurricane was heading their way. There might be some signs, such as a red sky or swelling seas that appeared in advance, but by the time those signs were recognized, the hurricane would be on the verge of arrival. To properly deal with hurricanes, what was required was not only an understanding of hurricane dynamics but also a way to predict when and where they would hit, so that people could prepare and take evasive action. As the young nation flourished and populations living in coastal regions swelled, with trade growing apace, what America desperately needed was a means of forecasting the weather and issuing storm warnings.

Seeing into the Future

*Photograph taken by Mathew B. Brady, circa 1850,
of Samuel F. B. Morse, inventor of the telegraph.*

JOHN RUSKIN WAS A PRECOCIOUS EIGHTEEN-YEAR-OLD
undergraduate at the University of Oxford in 1837 when he wrote a letter
to the Meteorological Society of London commenting on the "present state
of the science of meteorology." Showing the deep intellect and literary flair

that would make him one of the most celebrated and influential art and social critics of the Victorian era, Ruskin argued that meteorology—a field of study that had enthralled him for years—had the potential to greatly benefit humankind. One of the most important functions of meteorologists, he believed, was "to trace the path of the tempest round the globe,—to point out the place whence it arose, to foretell the time of its decline."

But, he lamented, meteorologists were hobbled in their attempts to provide such useful information because they operated in isolation. "The meteorologist is impotent if alone; his observations are useless; for they are made upon a point, while the speculations to be derived from them must be on space. It is of no avail that he changes his position, ignorant of what is passing behind him and before; he desires to estimate the movements of space, and can only observe the dancing of atoms; he would calculate the currents of the atmosphere of the world, while he only knows the direction of a breeze." In other words, for meteorology to achieve its potential, meteorologists would need the ability to share their observations in real time, so that they could track the weather and make predictions about the future. Just seven years later, Samuel Finley Breese Morse provided an instrument that could help them to do just that.

BORN IN CHARLESTOWN, MASSACHUSETTS, in 1791, Morse grew up in a household that greatly valued education. His father, the clergyman and geographer Jedediah Morse, was celebrated for authoring the first textbook on American geography ever published—*Geography Made Easy*—which appeared in 1784, for which he earned the sobriquet "The Father of American Geography." Samuel, or Finley as his parents called him, attended Phillips Academy and then Yale, graduating in 1810 having established himself as a solid, though not outstanding, student.

While his formal studies focused on philosophy, mathematics, and science, Morse's first love was painting. Much to the dismay of his parents, who urged him to find a more steady and traditional form of employ, Morse stuck by his desire to become an artist, and with their grudging financial and emotional support he spent a few years in England working on his craft at the Royal Academy of Arts. After returning to the United States in 1815, he hoped to interest Americans in the types of paintings he had studied in England and loved to emulate—large canvases of sweeping historical themes. But Americans much preferred portraits of themselves and famous personages of the day, and in order to feed his growing family, Morse gave them what they wanted while continuing to paint grander works on commission when he could, always hoping for, but never getting, his big break.

In 1826, not long after the tragic death of his first wife, Lucretia, Morse helped found the National Academy of Design in New York, its mission "to promote the fine arts in America through instruction and exhibition." Three years later, still yearning to jump-start his career as a major artist, Morse left for Europe to continue his education, painting his way through the continent with stops in France, Italy, and Switzerland. Upon returning to America in 1832, he was appointed a professor of painting and sculpture at New York University, and he immediately threw himself back into the currents of the art world, trying desperately to elevate his stature. But the commissions were few and far between, and the biggest prize he sought— to paint one of the murals to adorn the Capitol rotunda in Washington, DC—was handed to four of his contemporaries. This snub left him weary and disconsolate, wondering why all his hopes and dreams had yet to be realized. Morse would nonetheless become very famous one day, but his success would have nothing to do with art.

HEADING BACK FROM EUROPE in 1832 on the sailing packet *Sully*, Morse struck up conversations with fellow passengers about the possibility of creating a machine that could transmit information electrically through wires over great distances—in other words, an electric telegraph.* Morse had long been fascinated by electricity, as far back as his days at Yale, where he attended demonstrations of circuits and took chemistry classes with professors who performed experiments involving galvanic electricity and batteries. Some of the *Sully*'s passengers, including a Dr. Charles Jackson of Boston, knew a considerable amount about electricity, and they shared their thoughts liberally with Morse. By the end of the voyage, Morse believed that he could build an electric telegraph and, further,

---

* The word *telegraph* derives from the Greek *tele* ("far off") and *graph* ("writer"). It was first used to describe a visual (nonelectric) signaling system created by Frenchman Claude Chappe in 1791.

Samuel F. B. Morse's Gallery of the Louvre, *oil on canvas, circa 1831–33. One of Morse's goals for this large painting was to expose American audiences to the wonders of European art.*

that the idea was original to him, apparently unaware that others before him had pondered the same possibility and were working to put their own inventions into effect.

Over the next five years, Morse labored, mostly in secret, to perfect his telegraph. Then, in 1837, he got a rude surprise: some Europeans claimed to have developed a machine that sounded similar to Morse's, and they were trumpeting their discoveries in the press. Morse was thunderstruck, but he quickly regained his composure and began a multiyear effort to prove that he was the true inventor of the electric telegraph, and that his machine was the best. Morse's actions during this time involved everything from fighting off claims by, among others, Dr. Jackson, who insisted that Morse had stolen the idea, to publishing articles on his work, consulting other scientists to improve his apparatus, and codeveloping the ingenious system of dots and dashes to transmit words, which would later become known as Morse code. Finally, in 1844, after years of experiments, small-scale demonstrations, and badgering Congress for an appropriation to prove the viability of his telegraph over long distances, Morse got the chance he wanted.

On May 24 everything was set. The 36-mile-long wire running between the chamber of the US Supreme Court in Washington, DC, and a train depot just outside of Baltimore was in place. Morse, who was at the court, tapped the biblical phrase "What hath God wrought!" into the device—which was especially appropriate, given the momentous nature of the event about to unfold. Morse's associate, Alfred Vail, received the message at the depot and immediately confirmed that fact by transmitting the same words back over the wires to the court. Although this event is now a famous marker in the history of technological advancement, it caused hardly a ripple in the popular press of the day, which viewed the telegraph as nothing more than an enigmatic and not very useful toy.

All that changed three days later, when Morse and Vail teamed up again, this time to transmit the proceedings of the Democratic presidential nominating convention taking place in Baltimore. As Morse and Vail spoke to each other, using the telegraph as their intermediary, an ever-increasing crowd of onlookers assembled at both ends of the wire, including many of the most powerful politicians of the day. When the momentous news that the Democrats had nominated James K. Polk as their standard-bearer reached Morse, he immediately informed Vail that those gathered around him had let out "3 cheers" for Polk, and "3 for the Telegraph."

Witnesses to the spectacle suddenly and viscerally understood the historic importance of the revolution in communication that was taking place before their eyes. For most of the history of humankind, messages could travel no faster than one could walk or ride. In the late 1700s, semaphores (visual messaging using flags or specially shaped wooden arms to communicate letters and words from ridgeline to ridgeline) sped things up in the limited places where they were employed. Then, with the advent of steam-powered railroads in the 1820s, messages could travel as fast as the locomotives could take them. But the electric telegraph held out the possibility that information could be sent over hundreds, if not thousands, of miles in an instant.

Morse had handily and decisively beat the competition, and proved the practicability of his electric telegraph system, which one journalist labeled the "Highway of Thought." Morse had "annihilated space and time," another writer proclaimed. The telegraph communicates information "with *lightning speed*," crowed the *Pittsfield Sun*. "Locomotives go at a snail's pace compared with it." And *lightning* was the operative word.

As a result of his towering achievement, Morse became affectionately known as the "Lightning Man." Almost overnight, he was transformed into a national celebrity, lifted to the pantheon of America's greatest inventors, sharing the rarefied air with the nation's founding inventor, Benjamin Franklin.

The question still remained, though: Who would own the telegraph? Morse wanted to sell his patents to the government, thinking the government would be in the best position to capitalize on the new technology and spread it nationwide. But when Polk swept into office, his firm opposition to funding internal improvements killed any possibility of the telegraph becoming a government monopoly. Ultimately, private companies purchased the rights to use the technology, setting the stage for the explosive growth of the telegraph system. By the beginning of the Civil War, it stretched all the way across the country, not only from north to south, but also from east to west, thereby putting the suddenly antiquated pony express out of business.

NONE OTHER THAN WILLIAM REDFIELD first seized upon the potential for the telegraph to revolutionize meteorology and achieve Ruskin's dream of connecting meteorologists so that they could "trace the path of the tempest round the globe." In the November 1846 issue of the *American Journal of Science and Arts*, Redfield wrote, "In the Atlantic ports of the United States, the approach of a gale, when the storm is yet on the Gulf of Mexico, or in the southern or western states, may be made known by means of the electric telegraph. . . . This will enable the merchant to avoid exposing his vessel to a furious gale soon after leaving her port." While Redfield knew that timely warnings would not "disarm the tempest of its power," or eliminate all threats to navigation, he firmly believed that much of the tremendous loss due to shipwrecks "might be prevented by the exercise of timely and intelligent precaution."

Joseph Henry, the first secretary of the Smithsonian Institution, echoed Redfield's optimism in 1847 when he said, "The citizens of the United States are now scattered over every part of the southern and western portion of North America, and the extended lines of telegraph will furnish a ready means of warning the more northern and eastern observers to be on the watch for the first appearance of an advancing storm." Unlike Redfield, however, Henry was in a position to make this system of telegraphic meteorology a reality. He soon reached out to the presidents of the various telegraph companies sprouting around the country and persuaded them to provide the Smithsonian with meteorological information at no cost, in a most ingenious and unobtrusive manner. Normally, telegraph operators began their regular morning transmission with the word *O.K.* to signify that the line was working. Henry got the presidents to tell their operators to begin each morning's transmission with terms describing the weather, such as *cloudy*, *fair*, or *rainy*. To better ensure that the operators' observations were correct, Henry had the Smithsonian provide them with meteorological instruments, and instructions on how to use them.

Joseph Henry, first secretary of the Smithsonian Institution,
who saw in the telegraph much promise for
weather forecasting and meteorological science.

With this rudimentary system in place, Henry was able to present a near-real-time snapshot of the weather. In 1856, in the great hall of the Smithsonian's main building, he erected a weather map displaying conditions as reported by the telegraph operators. There were about thirty operators at the time, covering only the eastern part of the country as far west as Cincinnati, so the map wasn't extremely detailed. But it did give a general picture of the daily weather over that broad area. An iron wire was thrust into the map at the location of each station, and a disk of colored paper, about an inch in diameter, was hung from the peg, denoting the weather conditions, with different colors for snow, rain, sun, and so on. There were eight holes around the edge of each disk, and an arrow painted at its center. Each disk could thus be hung from a particular hole to show the direction of the wind at that locale. The map was a big hit in Washington, with tourists and congressmen alike, who often dropped by to see what was happening, meteorologically, in their states and districts.

The next logical step—forecasting the weather—came just a year later. That is when the *Washington Evening Star* took information and analysis provided by the Smithsonian's telegraph network and printed the nation's first weather forecast. "Yesterday, there was a severe storm south of Macon, GA; but from the fact that it is still clear this morning at that place and at Wheeling, it is *probable* that the storm was of local character." It wasn't much, but it was a start down the road that would ultimately lead to the massive national forecasting apparatus in place today.

Henry's interest was not only forecasting the weather, but also understanding it. To that end, he mustered and nurtured a vast network of volunteer observers throughout the country. Fitted out with Smithsonian-supplied instruments, these citizen reporters recorded their local weather and submitted monthly reports to Washington. There, Henry's team of meteorologists analyzed the data with the aim of unlocking the secrets of the weather and, in effect, perfecting the theory of storms.

Henry's ultimate goal—to marry science and forecasting—received a mortal blow on April 12, 1861, when the Confederate batteries in Charleston, South Carolina, began shelling Fort Sumter, forcing the Union forces defending the fort to raise the white flag of surrender. With that, the Civil War, the bloodiest in American history, commenced. In short order, telegraph lines to the South were cut, and those throughout the North were dedicated to transmitting information about troops, transports, and military strategy, leaving weather reports as one of the war's many casualties. By the same token, Henry's observer network basically fell apart, as virtually all reports from the South stopped and most northern correspondents were swept up by the necessities of the conflict.

After the war ended on April 9, 1865, with General Robert E. Lee's

Mid-nineteenth-century lithograph depicting the wreck of
the steamship Central America, *nicknamed the "Ship of Gold."*
It was traveling from Aspinwall (now Colón), Panama, to New York
with nearly 600 passengers on board, and many tons of gold and silver
from California, when, on September 12, 1857, a Category 2 hurricane
sank it roughly 160 miles off the coast of Cape Hatteras, North Carolina.
More than 400 lives were lost. The ship and the treasure remained hidden
on the bottom of the ocean until the late 1980s, when a team of salvagers
found both and started recovering some of the treasure.

surrender to General Ulysses S. Grant at Appomattox Court House in
Virginia, Henry tried to resuscitate his network of telegraphed weather
reports, as well as his network of voluntary weather observers, but he had
limited success. The Smithsonian was still reeling from a fire on January
24, 1865, that had gutted much of its main building, including Henry's
office, and the nation's telegraph companies balked at providing weather
reports voluntarily, forcing Henry to pay a small amount for this service.
It was increasingly clear to Henry that the federal government needed to
step in and fund an agency to take over the massive task of not only weather
reporting but also forecasting.

That finally happened on February 9, 1870, when President Grant
signed into law a bill that gave the US Army Signal Corps the responsibility

of gathering telegraphic weather reports from military stations throughout the country and using them to issue weather forecasts for the Great Lakes and the East Coast. The army, instead of the Smithsonian or some other agency, was entrusted with this new role because it was believed that the task of weather forecasting would benefit from the precision and discipline provided by the military, and that military men would be more reliable than civilians. Two years later, in 1872, the corps's charge was expanded to issuing forecasts for the entire country.

An early US Army Signal Corps weather map for September 1, 1872.

The corps issued its first storm warning on November 8, 1870, alerting the Great Lakes region to the high likelihood of powerful winds the following day. For the next twenty years, the corps continued to issue forecasts from Washington on a daily basis—although until 1876 they were called *probabilities*, at which point they changed to *indications*, only to finally morph into *forecasts* in 1889. To help make sense of all the telegraphic reports flooding into the Washington office, the army's meteorologists prepared synoptic weather maps of the United States that showed prevailing winds, air pressure, temperature, and the types of weather recorded at reporting locations, with isobars, or lines, connecting points on the map that had the same pressure. By analyzing a series of such maps, one could see and, hopefully, explain and predict the progression of weather over time.

Despite the high hopes for the army's ability to manage the nation's first weather service, it was heavily criticized for its shoddy management, its lack of professionalism, and the inevitable incorrect forecasts that occurred about 20 percent of the time. The army's most embarrassing forecast came on Sunday, March 11, 1888: "Fresh to brisk easterly winds, with rain, will prevail tonight, followed on Monday by colder brisk westerly winds and fair weather throughout the Atlantic states." Instead of fair weather, on Monday one of the worst blizzards in American history hit the vicinity of New York City and then screamed up the coast into the heart of New England, blanketing the region in as much as 4 feet of snow, causing tens of millions of dollars in damage, and killing more than 400 people.

Beyond these highly publicized mistakes, the corps was also mired in controversy, much of it resulting from the appalling behavior of many of its employees. One case involved a weather observer in the Midwest who was an inveterate gambler. To support his addiction, he pawned all of the weather station's expensive equipment and was forced to conduct his daily observations at the pawnbroker's store. Another observer, stationed in the Rocky Mountains, preferred fly-fishing to his job, and to maximize his time on the river he would write multiple telegrams, each one containing weather observations for a different day. He would hand those to the local telegraph operator with instructions to send them out sequentially while he was away from the office. Both of these men, along with scores of other less-than-stellar performers, were relieved of their jobs.

But the most serious and well-publicized controversy was that of Henry W. Howgate, the disbursing agent for the signal corps, who embezzled about $250,000 from the organization. The accumulated baggage finally became too much for Congress, and in 1891 it took weather-forecasting responsibilities away from the corps and transferred them to the civilian Weather Bureau, housed in the Department of Agriculture.

Throughout this period, from Joseph Henry's launch of the telegraphic network to the creation of the Weather Bureau, forecasting hurricanes was not a major focus of government meteorologists. The bureau threw most of its energy and effort into agricultural forecasts and tracking weather moving over the continent, from west to east and south to north, using the expanding but still patchy network of telegraphed weather reports and its growing but incomplete understanding of atmospheric dynamics. Although limited and sporadic weather reports came into the bureau from

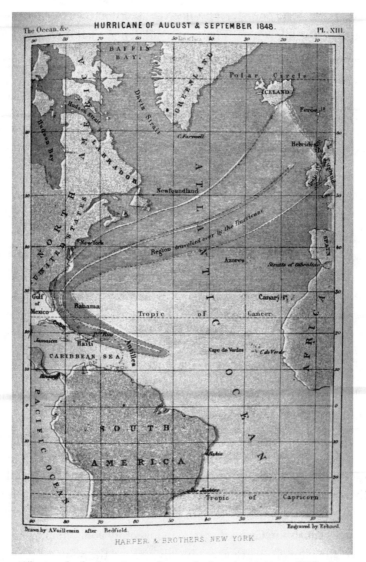

The track of a hurricane that took place in 1848, published in
Élisée Reclus's The Ocean, Atmosphere, and Life *(1873). It is one of*
the earliest hurricane storm tracks ever depicted in an illustration.

six Caribbean stations and the occasional ship heading into port, for the
most part American meteorologists were flying blind until the hurricanes
hit the coast, and even then they had only limited ability to predict the
movements of these storms or alert populations in their paths.

Nevertheless, the corps did issue hurricane warnings on occasion, its
first coming in 1873, when it told of a hurricane approaching anywhere

between Cape May, New Jersey, and New London, Connecticut, which are roughly 200 miles apart. That storm didn't make landfall in the United States, instead coming ashore in Newfoundland and leaving at least 223 people there dead. While the Americans were making little progress in the area of hurricane forecasting, the Cubans were leading the way, almost entirely because of the work of one intrepid man, Father Benito Viñes.

VIÑES WAS BORN IN 1837 in the village of Poboleda in the northwest corner of Spain. Details of his education are conflicting, but sometime during the 1850s he attended a Jesuit seminary where he received training in religious studies as well as science, the latter of which he built upon through his own reading in astronomy and meteorology. In the 1860s he was ordained a priest, and in 1870 he arrived in Havana as the director of the observatory at the Jesuit College of Belén. Viñes's main motivation in his new position was humble and utilitarian. "I do not desire any other reward," he wrote, "besides the one I expect from God, than being useful to my brethren and to contribute in some fashion to the advancement of science and the welfare of humanity." To that end, he chose to focus on unlocking the mysteries of hurricanes, which had caused the Cubans so much suffering over many years.

As a man of the cloth, Viñes didn't discount the power of prayer in forestalling hurricanes. That is why he encouraged his brethren to pray on a very specific schedule—focusing on the locales and the months during which hurricanes were most likely to strike, asking God to keep them away. However, Viñes knew better than to rely solely on divine intervention for protection. He also believed that human ingenuity could help Cuba better cope with any hurricanes that stubbornly resisted the power of prayer and instead barreled into the island. Thus, he set out to learn as much as he could about hurricane behavior, studying the seminal works of Redfield, Espy, Reid, Piddington, and Ferrel, and gathering raw data from the field.

When Viñes took over as director of the observatory in 1870, it was in disarray. Over the next few years, he organized the decades' worth of detailed weather records collected by his predecessors, repaired old equipment, and obtained new state-of-the-art instruments. He also launched a strict regimen of observations ten times a day, gathering readings of temperature, pressure, relative humidity, wind speed and direction, and the location and appearance of the clouds. This information was supplemented by data from observatory instruments, reports from the Cuban navy and from ships docking in Havana, and intelligence provided by a Caribbean-wide network of observers.

A slight man with a gift for detailed observation and extensive data analysis, Viñes soon developed his own empirically based understanding of hurricanes—almost a shorthand of the sky. He wasn't content, however, to simply describe hurricane behavior; he also wanted to use his knowledge to forecast when and where hurricanes would race ashore.

Just as the Taíno Indians had told Columbus that certain signs indicated a hurricane's approach, Viñes, too, relied on signs. In addition to the brick-red sky that often foretold the coming of a tempest, and the long, rolling swells, Viñes paid attention to the rising and then rapidly falling barometer, the presence of cool and dry anticyclonic winds, and the beautiful, clear skies. Most of all, Viñes studied the clouds. The first premonition of a hurricane's approach, he argued, was wispy cirrostratus clouds, which he called "cat's tails," "cock's plumes," or "wind feathers," all names playing off their delicate wraithlike appearance, composed as they are of thin mists of ice crystals. The cirrostratus clouds were followed, he said, by the dense cloud bank of cumulostratus and increasingly dark cumulonimbus clouds, and the ever-more-intense squall lines that broke away from them. But beyond the observable was the ineffable. Like a maestro who creates transcendent music from an entire symphony of musicians, Viñes was able to take all the measurements, signs, and historical data he had gathered and, using his unique synthesizing skills, transform them into a unified whole, a prediction of the weather to come.

Viñes's first foray into hurricane forecasting came on September 11, 1875, when the Havana-based newspaper *La Voz de Cuba* ("The Voice of Cuba") printed his warning that a hurricane, which had passed the Windward Islands days earlier, would come close to the north and east of Cuba but not make landfall. Viñes said that ships' captains should be alerted, and anyone thinking of sailing to the north and east should stay in port for the next few days. The conscientious priest ended his first forecast with a caveat: "These are only my rough estimates based only on the general laws of gyrating storms and a few short years of my direct observations."

When Viñes's predictions actually transpired, local newspapers heartily commended him, and their praise became only more effusive as his record of accurate hurricane forecasts grew. Over time, his network of informants expanded, and he received an increasing number of telegraphed weather reports from Cuban stations, as well as others throughout the Caribbean.

But Viñes's forecasts didn't always pan out. In September 1888, for example, he predicted that a hurricane that had passed north of Puerto Rico and Hispaniola would follow a northeasterly track toward Florida, with the brunt of the storm missing Cuba. But north of Cuba, the hurricane, blocked by a dome of high pressure over Florida, swerved left, coming ashore about a hundred miles east of Havana. One estimate places the number of dead at 600, with more than 10,000 people left homeless.

This and other failures notwithstanding, Viñes was right far more often than he was wrong. According to Dr. Bob Sheets (former director of the National Hurricane Center) and Jack Williams (founding editor of the *USA Today* weather page), Viñes's "successful forecasts were almost certainly more luck than skill, but they weren't *all* luck." Where the line should be drawn can be debated, but there is no doubt that Viñes was able to use the limited information available to him to craft unusually accurate hurricane forecasts.

During the 1880s and early 1890s, the reputation of Viñes and his observatory soared, not only within Cuba but also throughout the Caribbean, Europe, and the United States. Viñes visited the latter in the 1870s as part of an effort to foster closer meteorological collaboration. In 1885, the US Hydrographic Office, impressed by Viñes's track record, printed a translation of his *Practical Hints in Regard to West Indian Hurricanes*, which introduced mariners to the signs that Viñes used to detect a coming hurricane. Two years later, Adolphus Greely, chief of the signal corps, confirmed Viñes's respected position in a letter in which he expressed his thanks for Viñes's valuable telegrams informing the corps of approaching hurricanes.

Early in 1893, Viñes received a singular honor when he was invited to participate in the International Meteorological Conference to be held in Chicago in late August. He was asked by the American organizers to present a paper on the hurricanes of the Antilles. A frail man, for many years Viñes had battled a variety of maladies, and when the invitation arrived he was not well. Nevertheless, he worked assiduously on his paper, even though his vision was failing and his body was "a mere skeleton covered by nerves and skin." He finished the paper but would not have the chance to deliver it. On July 23, at the age of fifty-five, Viñes died of a cerebral hemorrhage. He had lived a full and meaningful life, and he certainly achieved his ultimate goal to "contribute in some fashion to the advancement of science and the welfare of humanity."

SOON AFTER VIÑES'S PASSING, the United States experienced one of its worst hurricane seasons on record, which only proved that America's forecasting capabilities left much to be desired. During the third week of August 1893, four hurricanes were simultaneously churning up the ocean, and all of them were heading toward the United States. In the coming days, two of the four would strike, and neither of them would be forecast with anything resembling precision. They would leave in their wake a horrific trail of devastation.

The first hurricane struck the New York City area around midnight on Wednesday, August 23, earning it the sobriquet "The Midnight Storm." For several days prior, the Weather Bureau had noted that a hurricane was moving northward, but it was thought to be far offshore. Thus, although the bureau urged coasting vessels to beware of rough seas, the official forecast for the New York area that evening was rather tame, calling only for "northwesterly winds" and "light rain on the coast." What came ashore a few hours later, however, was a Category 1 hurricane that shook the very foundation of the city.

Reporting on the storm a few days afterward, the venerable and usually calm and measured *New York Times* devoted nearly the entire first two pages to documenting the "almost unexampled fury" of the "West Indian monster." New Yorkers, the paper proclaimed, "realized how the residents of a small Kansas town feel when a genuine tornado bursts upon them and smashes their houses to kindling wood." Hundreds of chimneys were toppled, roofs were blown off, and broken glass littered the ground. A record-breaking deluge of nearly 4 inches of rainfall within twenty-four hours, on top of heavy rains earlier in the week, combined with the storm surge and aided by extremely high tides, flooded cellars and submerged the low-lying edges of the city, making it appear as if the ocean were consuming New York, block by block.

In Central Park, "more than a hundred noble trees were torn up by the roots, and branches were twisted off everywhere." The park's grounds were strewn with thousands of dead sparrows and other avian corpses, which roving gangs of young boys gathered, hoping to sell them to local restaurants. Telegraph poles and wires crashed to the earth, creating a tangled mess that virtually cut off communication with the rest of the world, isolating New York City until jury-rigged connections were established. Trains and trolleys were swept off their tracks, wharves were transformed into kindling, and vessels up and down the coast were ripped from their moorings and "dashed upon the shore." Thirty-four sailors died at sea when their ships went down.

The hurricane nearly obliterated a small barrier island just off the coast of Queens, opposite the Rockaway community of Edgemere. Accessible from the mainland via a five-cent ferry ride, Hog Island—so called because its shape resembled a hog's back—boasted bathhouses, saloons, and restaurants that summer revelers frequented to escape the torrid heat of the city. The massive storm surge and waves unleashed by the hurricane eroded much of the island and destroyed all of the human-made structures, including a posh eatery and entertainment hall owned by Patrick Craig, which was a favorite haunt of Tammany Hall politicians and other city power brokers.

Craig and his wife and daughter were in their flimsy summer cabin on the island when the hurricane roared ashore, and they likely would have perished if not for the heroics of two young men, Stephen Stillwagon and Matt Raynor, who were also on the island at the time. With no vessel in sight, Stillwagon and Raynor, displaying "undaunted courage," according to the *Times*, "plunged into the water and struck out for the mainland." Dodging floating debris and battling the swift current, they finally struggled onto the beach, secured a boat, and shoved off for the island. Despite being swamped twice, they "pushed on until at last they were rewarded by seeing Mrs. Craig, with her little one in her arms, step upon solid earth out of the reach of the hungry sea." Mr. Craig also survived, although in the breathless reporting of the *Times*, the moment of his stepping ashore was apparently not worthy of mention.

In subsequent years, the summer resort was reconstructed on a smaller scale, only to completely disappear in the early 1900s, when the ceaseless beating of the ocean waves and storms finally eliminated its last vestiges. From that point on, the memories of Hog Island slowly faded away, until the mid-1990s, when Queens College professor and self-proclaimed "forensic hurricanologist" Nicholas K. Coch, and some of his students, began digging on a beach in Edgemere. They uncovered a slew of artifacts, including broken dishes, beer mugs, bricks, and the remains of dolls. Coch surmised that these items were washed onto the beach during the hurricane of 1893, thereby providing mute testimony to the destructive power of the storm.

WHILE THE PEOPLE OF New York City were cleaning up after their exceedingly destructive rendezvous with one hurricane, another zeroed in on the US East Coast. On Friday morning, August 25, the Weather Bureau issued a forecast in which it noted a storm center about 500 miles southeast of Florida, moving in a northwesterly direction. The following day, the bureau predicted that the storm, now officially recognized as a hurricane, would make landfall somewhere along the Eastern Seaboard south of New York City. This swath of potential impact was so immense that effectively no preparations were undertaken, other than warning vessels along the coast to stay in port until the danger had passed.

On Sunday morning, the bureau honed its forecast, warning that the hurricane would strike the coast of Georgia, and that evening it singled out Savannah for a direct hit. But by the time this word was telegraphed to officials in the area, it was too late. Although a few brief notices about an approaching hurricane appeared in papers in Savannah and a little farther up the coast, in Charleston, there was almost no time to prepare, since the hurricane was essentially already there. For those living on the numerous so-called Sea Islands dotting the Georgia and South Carolina coast, where neither telegraph lines nor newspapers reached, the hurricane came as a nearly complete and utterly devastating surprise.

Around midnight on Sunday, August 27, the Category 3 hurricane, packing winds of 116 mph, roared ashore in the vicinity of Savannah, delivering a storm surge as high as 15–20 feet above normal and pushing a boiling wall of water up the Savannah River into the city proper. The violent combination of wind and water destroyed numerous buildings, killed many people, flung train tracks far from their beds, and left a tangled mass of wreckage and the stench of death in its wake. Even in Columbia, South Carolina, roughly 150 miles north of Savannah, and more than 100 miles from the coast, the weakened hurricane still packed a powerful wallop.

As the *State* newspaper reported two days after the hurricane made landfall, the storm "seemed to revel in the destruction it was causing, sweeping with full force over the wooded and gently undulating expanses of the capital city, neglecting no opportunity of descending upon the prosperity of its frightened inhabitants."

But Savannah's and Columbia's suffering was nothing compared with what the Sea Islands endured, especially those to the northeast of Savannah. These islands found themselves on the dirty (right-hand) side of the hurricane, where the storm's fury was most intense. There, from Hilton Head to Charleston and beyond, lies a band of low-lying tidal and barrier islands so crisscrossed with rivers, rivulets, and marshes that they are as much a part of the sea as they are of the land. The profile of the islands is so low that a rise of as little as 20 feet on an island plantation earned it the dubious right to be called a "hill" by the locals.

At the time, these islands were home to tens of thousands of black residents and a smattering of whites. The blacks, known locally as "Gullahs," were originally slaves, mostly of West African descent, who had toiled for their white masters on the rice and cotton fields of the Low Country and were freed after the Civil War. In time they developed a unique English-based language that incorporated Creole and African words, and a vibrant culture based on their language, ancestral ties, and colorful artistic, spiritual, and musical traditions. After obtaining their freedom, the Gullahs continued to raise crops such as corn and sweet potatoes, working either for themselves or as sharecroppers. They also provided most of the muscle for South Carolina's burgeoning phosphate mining industry, performing the laborious work of digging and dredging rivers and marshes to expose the phosphate-rich rocks—so-called "stinking stones"—beneath the upper layers of muck. Once dried and pulverized, those rocks provided the basis for valuable fertilizer shipped throughout the country.

The residents of the Sea Islands, isolated culturally and physically from the mainland, had little or no warning of the atmospheric juggernaut heading their way. While some of the older islanders might have surmised that a storm was coming, on account of their joints aching from the drop in pressure, or because of the long, deep swells hitting the coast, most of them were caught off guard when the wind and water plowed onto the shore, leveling almost everything in its path.

According to Miss Laura Towne, a white resident on St. Helena Island,

"When the tide rose on the 27th at full moon, the wind started to blow a terrific gale, [and] drove the sea over the land, and there it remained for eight hours, raging like breakers on a beach. . . . That tide advanced eighteen feet above high-water mark, and was a raging surf, with boats, trees, boards, and animals tossed helplessly in the midst of it."

The number of people who died during the hurricane is not known, although most estimates say 1,500–2,000, with some claiming that deaths rose as high as 4,000 or 5,000. The vast majority of these deaths occurred on the Sea Islands, where many drowned in the rushing floods. To those totals must be added the untold number of people who died of exposure and disease in the following weeks and months as stagnant pools became breeding areas for malaria-bearing mosquitoes, and unburied bodies putrefied in the blazing sun. The survivors had their lives, but little else. Roughly 30,000 people were left homeless, and since virtually all of the local wells had been contaminated with salt water and most of the crops had been destroyed, there was little water to drink, food to eat, or produce to sell.

Cut off as the islands were from the rest of society, it was a few days before news of the full nature of the catastrophe radiated outward to the region and the nation as a whole. Even then, the pernicious influence of racism and bigotry delayed the response, exacerbating the human toll of the disaster. As historian Marian Moser Jones points out, the white-supremacist governor of South Carolina, Ben Tillman, was slow to call for aid to the Sea Islands, and when he finally did toward the end of September, his motivation was less the well-being of the Gullahs and more the fear that if they weren't given help, they would leave the islands and overrun South Carolina's mainland cities and towns, upsetting public order and sexually threatening white women.

In the absence of any national machinery for responding to a calamity, Tillman reached out to Clara Barton and the American Red Cross. Although the Massachusetts-born Barton had no formal training in nursing, she nevertheless had risen to great and deserved fame by providing medical supplies and ministering to injured Union servicemen during the Civil War, becoming known as "The Angel of the Battlefield." Spurred on by this experience and her exposure to the brilliant humanitarian work of the Switzerland-based Red Cross, Barton founded the American Red Cross in 1881—its goal to serve people in need during times of war and when natural or human-made catastrophes strike. Barton and her small

Red Cross team had responded splendidly to a number of disasters before the Sea Islands Hurricane, including the Johnstown Flood in 1889. In early October 1893, she and her staff of three, along with about a dozen volunteers, descended upon the South Carolina coast to help alleviate the widespread suffering.

Clara Barton, circa 1860s.

"It is a great undertaking," Barton wrote in her diary on September 29, "to feed, clothe, work, doctor & nurse 30,000 human beings . . . , and to do it all upon charity gathered as one goes along." But she and her team worked tirelessly over the next nine months to administer $30,000 worth of aid to the stricken. Although the weekly rations of a pound of pork and a peck (8 dry quarts) of hominy grits per family of six were extremely limited, and families had to supplement this fare with what they could gather or catch, the food provided by the Red Cross was critical to fending off mass starvation.

Since able-bodied men and women were required to work—building houses, planting crops, or sewing clothes—to receive aid, the afflicted assisted in their own resurrection and hastened the recovery process. As

Barton described it, "I had desired to do more than merely make a gift for distribution. I wished to plant a tree. I could have given them their peach, which they would eat, enjoy, and throw the pit away. But I wished them to plant the pit, let it raise other fruit for them." Thus, the Red Cross's intervention threw a lifeline to the Sea Islanders when they were at their lowest ebb and gave them a firm foundation of hope and action upon which they could build, thereby starting the long and laborious process of piecing back together their lives and their communities—a process that continued for many years afterward.

AMID ALL THE MISERY and despair brought on by the hurricane were stories of heroism, none more impressive than that of Dunbar Davis, the keeper of the lifesaving station on Oak Island, North Carolina. Established at key spots along the coast by the federal government, lifesaving stations were manned by men whose sole job was to render assistance to shipwrecked mariners. Although Oak Island was more than 200 miles from the hurricane's landfall in Savannah, the massive seas generated by the storm extended far and wide, and many vessels along that stretch of the North Carolina coast were in grave danger. Fortunately, for some of them at least, Davis was on duty.

Davis was the only man at the station at the time, since the rest of his crew were enjoying their annual work hiatus, which ran from the end of April until September 1. Things had been quiet that summer for Davis, but on the afternoon of Monday, August 28, all hell broke loose. Scanning the horizon, both he and J. L. Watts, the keeper of the nearby Cape Fear lifesaving station, saw the *Three Sisters* offshore just to the east of Bald Head Island. The three-masted schooner, which had been transporting lumber from Savannah to Philadelphia, was clearly in distress, taking on water and pitching back and forth in the mountainous seas. Early that morning, in the vicinity of Frying Pan Shoals, the hurricane's powerful winds had shredded the 286-ton vessel's sails and toppled its mizzenmast. Making matters far worse, the captain and the mate had been washed overboard and drowned. The cook had taken charge of the remaining five-man crew, and it appeared to Davis and Watts that he was attempting to run the schooner ashore. With the seas so angry, the two lifesavers knew that such a course would mean the certain death of all on board. Somehow, Watts managed to signal to the men aboard the *Three Sisters* that they should anchor in place and allow their rescuers to come to them.

That they did. Davis and Watts recruited nine men from the nearby town of Southport, and before dawn on Tuesday, August 29, they all shoved off in their surfboat, rounded Cape Fear, and ultimately ferried the six men on board the *Three Sisters* back to land. Davis's work, however, was not done. When he returned to his station early that afternoon, he scanned the horizon and spotted the *Kate E. Gifford*, a 420-ton schooner out of New Jersey, in distress.

Once again Davis rounded up volunteers, and over the next twenty-four hours he led another strenuous rescue operation, retrieving seven men from the stricken ship. While those men and the volunteers walked back to the lifesaving station, Davis and the mate of the *Gifford* remained behind, hoping to regain their strength by taking turns napping by the bonfire they had built on the beach. But just as Davis was about to doze off, another boat appeared, struggling through the breakers toward the shore. It was a yawl from a schooner that had foundered earlier in the day, and on board were another seven survivors. After he and Davis rescued these seven, the mate of the *Gifford* took the exhausted men to the station in an ox-drawn cart, while Davis stayed by the fire.

When the mate and the cart returned around sunset, the oxen were too exhausted to make another trip. Davis later recalled, "By this time I was getting pretty fagged [worn out]. I had gone without food for two days and without water for twelve hours, and had been wet all the time." So, Davis left the oxen, the cart, and their lifesaving gear behind while he and the mate trudged back to the station.

Dead tired and famished, Davis arrived at the station around 9:00 p.m. on Wednesday, September 30. It was a full house. Many of the ship-wrecked sailors he had helped rescue, including a few who made it there on their own, had taken advantage of the hospitality, food, and nursing services provided by Davis's wife and by the keeper of the Oak Island Lighthouse and his wife, who had come over to help out. Since all of the beds were taken, Davis finally settled on the couch for a well-deserved and long-overdue sleep.

The men saved that day by Davis, Watts, and their volunteers were the lucky ones. Farther down the coast, in the waters off South Carolina and

Georgia, many other vessels were caught in the hurricane's grasp. Eight of them sank to the bottom, killing all fifty-six people on board.

AFTER A PARTICULARLY ACTIVE August, with two destructive landfalls, September 1893 proved to be fairly tame, with only one hurricane hitting the mainland, coming ashore in Louisiana and doing little damage to either humans or their property. But October packed another powerful one-two punch. The first blow was a sneak attack.

The Weather Bureau's forecast for Louisiana and Mississippi on Sunday, October 1, was "fair, preceded by light showers tonight on the coast, southwesterly winds." Nevertheless, by that afternoon the residents of the Barataria region knew something was brewing offshore. On the islands and bayous to the south and west of New Orleans, local fishermen and their neighbors who had grown up in the area saw the signs. The long, deep swells gently crashing on the shore, the drop in pressure, the growing darkness of the clouds on the horizon, and the sudden quietness of the birds all foretold the arrival of a storm.

Andre Gilbeaux was more than just worried; he was resigned to his fate. He lived on Chénière Caminada, an island of sand just 4 feet above sea level at its highest point. It was less than a mile wide and about two and a half miles long, located about 60 miles by boat from New Orleans at the southernmost tip of Jefferson Parish. Gilbeaux was one of the island's many fishermen who supplied the Big Easy's fancy restaurants and markets with fresh terrapin turtles, crabs, oysters, and shrimp. He lived in what most people would refer to as a shack, sporting a palmetto-frond roof and raised on stilts to keep it a bit higher than the highest tides. That Sunday, Gilbeaux summoned his relatives and friends to an impromptu dinner at his house. It was not a celebration, but rather a farewell.

At dinner's end, Gilbeaux stood up with a glass raised aloft. His guests cut short their genial conversations, turning their attention to their gracious host. "This will be the last time we will be together," he told them, "for tonight I will drown." Before anyone could raise an objection, or ask why Gilbeaux was so certain that his time on Earth was up, he continued. "There will be companions with me in my death. You may think that I am crazy, but I cannot help that, for I am firmly convinced that a watery death will be mine. I will now toast to all, and hope peace and rest will be mine. May God bless all that remain behind, and peace to my companions' ashes that will die with me." According to an eyewitness, Gilbeaux's wife and some of the other guests, thinking that he meant to take his own life, urged him not to commit suicide. Gilbeaux calmly responded that he had no such inclination, but instead would die in the hurricane that he thought was bearing down on them at that very moment.

Unnerved by Gilbeaux's premonition about his own demise, his dinner guests dispersed, returning to their homes to prepare for the worst, which came ashore just a few hours later. As the sun set that Sunday evening, the wind and the waves rose, and soon Louisiana's Barataria region was being buffeted by a Category 4 hurricane, with winds in excess of 130 mph. The following day, the tempest ratcheted down to a Category 2 and then a Category 1 hurricane as it scoured the coast of Mississippi and Alabama before becoming a tropical storm heading inland to the northeast.

The Weather Bureau later claimed that the "hurricane advanced suddenly and unexpectedly," and that was certainly true from the bureau's perspective, but that's only because it was entirely unaware of the storm's history. As later analysis showed, the hurricane had been forming for at least five days before making landfall, originating in the western Caribbean, crossing the Yucatán Peninsula on its way to smashing into the Gulf Coast. The bureau simply had no inkling that the storm was on its way, and that's why it was surprised when it roared ashore.

Louisiana suffered the worst, especially Chénière Caminada. A storm surge of as much as 10–15 feet, with crashing waves that went higher still, rolled over the peninsula, destroying nearly everything in its path. Ferdinand Grimeau, the priest of the local Roman Catholic Church, Our Lady of Lourdes, later recounted the horrors that he and his fellow islanders faced that night. As the flimsy fishing shacks and other homes all around began to succumb to the fury of the wind and waves, Grimeau climbed to the upper story of the presbytery where he lived, "holding onto the sill of an open window, powerless to do anything and exposed to the terrific blasts and hearing the cries and agony of my poor dying parishioners."

When the eye of the hurricane passed overhead, "brave and sturdy men" used the temporary lull to go out in skiffs to gather people from the water and bring them to houses that were more solidly built and, therefore, more likely to survive the punishing storm. In this manner many were saved, but in the end even more lives were lost. Of the 300-plus homes

Remains of a house on Chénière Caminada
after the hurricane of 1893.

on Chénière Caminada, only four remained largely intact, providing critical refuge from the storm. Father Grimeau's postmortem of the hurricane offered a grisly tabulation. Out of a population of 1,471, "696 only are now living; 779 are dead. Historic Chénière Caminada is no more."

As he had ominously predicted, Andre Gilbeaux drowned that night, when his boat overturned in the Gulf's churning waters, taking his life along with that of his wife and children. With so many dead, and the living in such distressful circumstances, proper burial was not an option. The corpses littering the island were interred where they were found in hastily dug trenches. But for the scores, if not hundreds, of bodies that had been swept into the Gulf or Caminada Bay, their final resting place was the sea.

The arc of devastation extended well beyond Chénière Caminada. The storm ranged north to New Orleans, and farther to the northeast, ripping through the numerous bayous and communities dotting the coast all the way to Mobile, Alabama. Death stalked people not only on land but on the water as well, where more than 200 luggers* sank. All told, roughly 2,000 people lost their lives as a result of the hurricane. In stark contrast to what had happened in the aftermath of the Sea Islands Hurricane, when many

---

* A *lugger* is a traditional fishing vessel with two or more masts, each of which supports a four-cornered lug sail that, when raised and suspended from a spar, partially overlap the mast.

weeks passed before aid started flowing into the most heavily impacted areas, relief from civic organizations and businesses in storm-battered New Orleans, as well as from farther afield, quickly flowed to where it was urgently needed. Still, a fuller recovery would take years, and some communities, such as on Chénière Caminada, would never rebound from the calamity.

THE FINAL HURRICANE OF the 1893 season came less than two weeks later, making landfall north of Charleston, South Carolina, on October 13 as a Category 3 hurricane, with sustained winds of 120 mph. The Weather Bureau tracked the hurricane as it skirted Florida and then headed north up the coast, issuing ample warnings of its arrival somewhere along the Carolinas. Although it was as powerful as the Sea Islands Hurricane, it did much less damage, and only twenty-eight people died. At that point the 1893 hurricane season mercifully came to an end. Leaving a tally of roughly 4,000 deaths, it was the deadliest hurricane season to date for the United States.

One might assume that with such a terrible death toll, and a mediocre forecasting record, the US government would have given the Weather Bureau more resources. It was obvious that the bureau needed to improve its hurricane tracking and prognostication through more research, increased cooperation with weather organizations in the Caribbean, and the establishment of additional weather outposts along the southeastern and Gulf coasts. Although more reporting stations, especially in Florida, were set up, the shock to the system that the 1893 season provided generated little real change at the bureau or in the halls of government. It would take a war to move the needle.

"REMEMBER THE USS *MAINE*!" became the battle cry that spurred the United States to declare war on Spain on April 25, 1898. The explosion and subsequent sinking of this American battleship in Havana Harbor, however, were just the spark that launched the Spanish-American War. The driving forces behind the conflict were a potent mixture of imperialism, commercial avarice, media hype, and a desire to support Cuba's fight for independence from Spain. At the outset of the war, President William

McKinley had many pressing concerns on his mind, one of which was hurricanes.

In the months leading up to the conflict, Willis Luther Moore, the chief of the Weather Bureau, approached his boss, James Wilson, the secretary of agriculture, with a grave worry. "I knew," Moore wrote, "that many armadas in olden days had been defeated, not by the enemy, but by the weather, and that probably as many ships had been sent to the bottom of the sea by storms as had been destroyed by the fire of enemy fleets." Thus, Moore told Wilson that if war broke out, the US Navy would have to contend not only with the Spanish but with Mother Nature, and she might be the more dangerous foe. Hurricanes, he warned, had the potential to wipe out the American fleet. The best way to avoid such a calamity, Moore argued, was to expand the bureau's weather-monitoring and -reporting network in the Caribbean.

Alarmed, Wilson arranged a meeting with McKinley and took his bureau chief along. According to his own later account, Moore spread out some maps of the Caribbean and gave the president a quick tutorial on the power of hurricanes and their typical paths through the Caribbean. McKinley, "with one leg carelessly thrown across his desk, chin in hand and elbow on knee," intently studied the maps, and then "suddenly he turned to the secretary and said, 'Wilson, I am more afraid of a West Indian Hurricane than I am of the entire Spanish Navy.'" As a result, the president ordered Moore to take whatever action was necessary to improve the Weather Bureau's forecasting abilities in the West Indies.

Before Moore could do much to carry out his charge, the war ended. Not surprisingly, given the vast disparity in power, the hostilities were over in a little less than three months, with the unconditional surrender of Spanish forces in Cuba on July 16; the official end of the war came on December 10, 1898, when a peace treaty was signed in Paris.* At war's end, however, Moore took quick advantage of Cuba's new status as a protectorate of the United States by establishing the headquarters for Caribbean weather forecasting in Havana and installing William B. Stockman as its chief. In addition, other observation stations were set up on Dom-

---

* Under the terms of the peace treaty, Cuba became a protectorate of the United States (this status ended in 1902, when Cuba gained its formal independence), Guam and Puerto Rico were ceded to the United States, and the United States purchased the Philippines for $20 million.

inica, Barbados, St. Kitts, Panama, and Puerto Rico, the latter of which had also come into the American orbit as a result of the war.

This foothold in Cuba had the potential to be a forecasting bonanza. For years, Cubans had taken the lead in the science and art of hurricane prediction as a result of Viñes's efforts, and his acolytes continued the Viñes tradition of weather forecasting after he was gone. But instead of drawing on Cuban expertise, the Americans not only ignored it but actively disparaged it. The price of such conceit became abundantly clear in September 1900.

CHAPTER 4

Obliterated

*Memorial to the Galveston Hurricane of 1900, on the seawall
in Galveston, Texas. Sculpted by David W. Moore, it was commissioned
by the Galveston Commission for the Arts and installed in 2000.*

JUST AFTER SUNRISE ON SATURDAY, SEPTEMBER 8, 1900, a real-estate agent and insurance broker named Buford T. Morris awoke in his weekend home in Galveston, Texas, looked out the window, and was greeted by a wondrous sight. "The sky seemed to be made of mother of pearl," he later recalled. "Gloriously pink, yet containing a fish-scale effect which reflected all the colors of the rainbow." This surreal and serene morning scene didn't last long. The brilliant colors soon faded, the sky darkened, and rain began to fall.

Nobody in Galveston was particularly worried about the weather that morning. Although a strong tropical storm had dumped more than 2 feet of rain in Cuba during the previous week, skimmed by the tip of Florida, and then planted itself in the Gulf of Mexico, the US Weather Bureau's forecasters didn't think the storm would become a hurricane, nor did they think Galveston would be hit too hard. Minor flooding and strong winds, perhaps, but nothing the city hadn't handled before.

The Weather Bureau, however, was drastically mistaken. The storm that would hit the Galveston area was a Category 4 hurricane, and it would level thousands of buildings and claim at least 6,000 lives. It was a tragedy of epic proportions, and one of its central characters was an American meteorologist named Isaac Monroe Cline, who simply didn't think anything like this could ever happen.

ALMOST A DECADE EARLIER, in early July 1891, a Category 1 hurricane made landfall near Matagorda, Texas, about 110 miles southwest of Galveston. The outer bands of the storm had drenched Galveston, causing significant flooding. In the wake of the hurricane, the editor of the *Galveston Daily News* posed a question to the twenty-nine-year-old Cline, who was at the time the chief at the Weather Bureau's Galveston station, and the overseer of the bureau's Texas operations. The editor wondered how vulnerable Galveston was to a hurricane at some point in the future. In other words, should Galvestonians worry about one day being battered by hurricane-force winds and massive waves? Given his position, the precocious young bureau official was certainly the right person to ask.

Cline was born in Monroe County, Tennessee, on his family's prosperous fruit farm, where he learned the value and rewards of hard work and also developed a keen interest in the natural world, especially the workings of the weather. He excelled in school, attending Hiwassee College in Madisonville, Tennessee. Soon after he graduated in 1882, a strong rec-

Isaac Monroe Cline.

ommendation from the college's president landed Cline a job at the US Army Signal Corps's weather service.

Initially posted at the weather office in Little Rock, Arkansas, Cline was next sent to Abilene, Texas, and then on to Galveston in 1889, where he took over the reins of the station from an incompetent and lazy army private who had allowed the station to fall into disrepair and had earned the enmity of area merchants because they had lost all faith in his ability to provide useful forecasts. Cline quickly established a sterling reputation for the station and himself, becoming a respected member of the local community and a voice of authority in all things weather related. Given Cline's reputation, it is no wonder the editor of the *Galveston Daily News* posed such a question to the young meteorologist, for Galveston had a lot to lose.

TWENTY-EIGHT MILES LONG, and only 1–3 miles wide, Galveston was a barrier island composed entirely of sand, marshes, grass, and a smattering of bushes and trees, with the Gulf on one side and Galveston Bay on the other. Situated about 2 miles from the mainland, Galveston had a very low profile, its highest point barely 9 feet above sea level,

Bird's-eye view of Galveston; lithograph, 1871.

with an average elevation of only 4½ feet. Upon this rather unimpressive geologic foundation a major city had risen—one with a meteorologically tempestuous past.

After ousting the Spanish from Galveston in 1817, Jean Lafitte, the notorious pirate, smuggler, and war hero who helped Andrew Jackson's forces successfully defend New Orleans in the final act of the War of 1812, settled on the island. Jean and his older brother, Pierre, established a pirate kingdom on Galveston called Campeche. It boasted as many as 2,000 inhabitants and more than 100 buildings, including saloons, whore-houses, and Lafitte's imposing headquarters, the two-story Maison Rouge, which was surrounded by ramparts and cannons trained on the harbor. Between plundering ships in the Gulf of Mexico and the Caribbean Sea, and enriching themselves, the pirates faced a number of difficulties, one of which was a powerful hurricane that struck Galveston in September 1818. The storm inundated most of the island, destroyed nearly all of its build-ings, and sank many of the pirates' ships anchored in the harbor.

Lafitte and his men quickly regrouped and rebuilt, but their tenure on the island would not last much longer. A few years later, when some of Lafitte's men unwisely attacked an American naval cutter, the United States retaliated, hanging some of the offenders and ordering the pirates to vacate Galveston. Not wanting to tangle with the American navy, the pirates left, but in a final flourish they set their settlement ablaze.

Texas gained its independence from Mexico in 1836, establishing itself as a republic, and by the early 1840s Galveston had grown from a devastated pirate settlement into a small but increasingly important port with a few thousand people and about 300 buildings. In 1842, Galveston was hit by another hurricane that flooded nearly the entire island and destroyed half of the city's buildings. When a British travel writer and novelist by the name of Mrs. Houstoun visited Galveston the following year, the city was already on the mend, rebuilding lost structures and adding new ones. Upon being told of the hurricane's destructive power, she offered a prescient comment about the fragility of Galveston's very existence: "The tremendous hurricane that occurred last September, as it was described to us, is calculated to give one the impression that on some future day the flourishing city of Galveston may be swept away by the overwhelming incursions of the sea."

In 1845 the Republic of Texas became the state of Texas, bringing to twenty-eight the number of stars on the Union's flag. Over the next five decades, Galveston continued to grow at an impressive rate, with the exception of the Civil War years, when the city's commerce was hobbled and much of its population fled to the mainland to escape the shelling of the city. By 1891, when the *Galveston Daily News* editor posed his question to Cline, Galveston was by far the leading port in Texas, even though the shallowness of its harbor forced larger ships to transport their cargo to the wharves on smaller, shallow-draft vessels known as lighters. Galveston's cosmopolitan and multiethnic population stood at nearly 30,000, closely packed at the east end of the island, on a geometrically precise, grid-like array of streets and avenues, many of which were lined with stately homes owned by the city's wealthier class. The city's future was looking even brighter, since the massive dredging project under way would soon transform Galveston Harbor into a deepwater port, making it still more of a magnet for trade.

WHEN READERS OF THE *Galveston Daily News* perused Cline's response—an article on July 16, 1891—they must have smiled and let out a sigh of relief. In essence, he told them they had nothing to be concerned about. The lengthy piece, replete with impressive maps showing the course of hurricanes in the Gulf of Mexico, painted a picture of Texan exceptionalism. Cline asserted that in the previous two decades, twenty hurricanes had come off the Atlantic, passing over the West Indies and "the southern coast of the United States," but, he said, "only two [of them] have reached Texas." The reason, he argued, was that hurricanes barreling across the Atlantic "nearly always turn to the north and northwest" between the Bahamas and the western tip of Cuba, and then generally curl toward the northeast, either making landfall in Florida or along the East Coast, or spiraling off into the Atlantic Ocean.

So certain was Cline of this trajectory that he made a bold claim: "The coast of Texas is according to the general laws of the motions of the atmosphere exempt from West-India hurricanes and the two which have reached it followed an abnormal path which can only be attributed to causes known in meteorology as accidental." He also noted that during that same twenty-year period, seven hurricanes had originated in the Gulf of Mexico, and therefore did not fall in the category of West Indian hurricanes. Like their West Indian counterparts, these Gulf hurricanes tended to avoid Texas, with only two of them hitting the state's coast. Galvestonians, therefore, should rest easy.

Despite his characteristic certainty and confidence—traits that some felt veered into arrogance—Cline was simply wrong on many counts. There were no such "general laws" that preordained the course of West Indian hurricanes, thereby keeping them away from Texas, and there was no basis for claiming that such hurricanes that hit the Texas coast did so because of a meteorological accident. Nothing in the current, and still fairly limited, understanding of hurricanes supported Cline's assertions. Furthermore, when it came to West Indian hurricanes, Cline's numbers were off. Between 1871 and 1891, the years he considered, seven—not just two—such hurricanes had hit parts of the Texas coast. And while his tally of two hurricanes originating in the Gulf *and* hitting the Texas coast during this period was accurate, his implication that two out of seven hurricanes is an insignificant number, and therefore not worthy of concern, seems wrongheaded.

Then there is the broader issue of his time frame—twenty years. Why stop there? Had Cline looked further back in the records, he would have discovered that during a longer period, the Texas coast had been raked by many hurricanes, a few of which did considerable damage to Galveston.

In addition to the hurricanes of 1818 and 1842, there was the Category 2 hurricane that just missed making landfall near the mouth of the Rio Grande on October 3, 1867, and devastated a number of towns, including Brazos Santiago, Port Isabel, and Brownsville. It then skirted the Texas coast, heading east. When it passed close to Galveston, it submerged much of the city and severely damaged or destroyed numerous buildings, in many cases blowing off their roofs and bulldozing them off their foundations. So great was the damage to and impact on the city that historians and meteorologists often refer to this storm as the "Galveston Hurricane of 1867." Writing a few days after the hurricane, the editor of the *Ranchero*, a newspaper in battered Brownsville, Texas, proved as insightful as Mrs. Houstoun. "What would happen," he asked, "if a similar storm struck Galveston directly as it had the lower coast?"

By looking deeper into the past, and broadening his view a bit, Cline would have found another reason to question his position. A hurricane that destroyed Isle Dernière, a popular resort off the Louisiana coast, in 1856 tracked only about 200 miles to the east of Galveston. That sounds like a significant distance, but given the huge size of some hurricanes, a slight deviation in the hurricane's trajectory to the west could have spared Isle Dernière and savaged Galveston. Such a margin of error should have given any meteorologist pause.

As for the two West Indian hurricanes that Cline asserted had hit Texas "accidentally" within the prior twenty years, he further discounted them by claiming that neither had caused significant property damage. "In each of these two cases," he wrote, "the loss of property aggregated less than that which often results from a single tornado in the central states." Even if this were true, which is not at all clear, Cline failed to take into account the human toll of the hurricanes. Those fatalities were, in fact, the more serious losses, and the ones that would have concerned the newspaper's readers the most.

Both of these so-called accidental hurricanes bore down on the town of Indianola, Texas, located a mere 125 miles southwest of Galveston. Hugging the edge of Matagorda Bay, about 14 miles from the Gulf, and behind a row of barrier islands, Indianola was a prosperous city of 5,000 when the first hurricane visited, on September 16, 1875. Winds in excess of 115 mph, accompanied by surging seas, overwhelmed the city, creating a trail of absolute devastation. Indianola's district attorney, D. W. Cram, sent out a heartrending letter to local newspaper editors a few days after the hurricane had passed. "We are destitute," he wrote. "The Town is gone. One quarter of the people are gone. Dead bodies are strewn for twenty miles along the bay. Nine-tenths of the houses are destroyed. Send us help, for God's sake." The official death toll was 176, but since so many visitors and tourists were in town at the time, the ultimate number of people who died will never be known.

View of Indianola *(Texas); lithograph by Helmuth Holtz, 1860.*

Indianola partially rose from the wreckage, and by 1886 it was touting itself as a tourist destination with some of the most beautiful beaches on the Gulf Coast. But in a repeat performance, on August 20 of that year another, even more powerful, Category 4 hurricane delivered a knockout blow. Many died, although the final tally is unknown, and virtually all of the city's buildings were reduced to rubble and heaps of splintered wood. There would be no coming back this time. Indianola simply ceased to exist.

Neither of these hurricanes spared Galveston, where lives were lost, much of the city was flooded, and damage was widespread. After the 1886 hurricane, the editor of the *Austin Weekly Statesman* took stock of the situation and offered a warning to Galvestonians, echoing earlier comments by Mrs. Houstoun and the editor of the *Ranchero*: "Take it all in all, it was a disaster almost as appalling as that of 1875, and when the results of the cyclone are studied, the conclusion is reasonable that, some time or other, a tidal wave, driven by some howling tempest as swift and terrible as that which swept over Indianola may yet engulf Galveston Island. It may have been submerged by these tremendous sea storms before the recollection of civilized man. It may be again, and the proud city which sits on the sands of the gulf share the same fate as her more southerly sister, Indianola."

Galvestonians seemed to have come to the same conclusion. Six weeks after the 1886 hurricane, a collection of the city's most prominent merchants issued a call for action. They urged the citizenry to back the building of a massive seawall that would protect them and their property from any inundation that a future hurricane might bring. The editors of the local *Evening Tribune* ballyhooed the project, and assured its fruition. "When men such as these say that work on seawall protection should be commenced at once and pushed to completion, the public can depend upon it that something tangible will be done—and that without unnecessary delay."

The editors were wrong. The clarion call for change did spur the city to prepare a plan for the wall, and a state bond was passed to pay for it, but in the end the fire for change was extinguished by that most potent of project killers, the out-of-sight, out-of-mind mentality. According to E. M. Hatrick, Galveston's engineer, by the time the bond was passed, many months after the hurricane, "the attitude was, oh, we'll never get another one—and they didn't build."

As historian Erik Larson points out in his seminal book on the 1900 Galveston Hurricane, *Isaac's Storm*, "If Galveston had any lingering anxiety about its failure to erect a wall, Isaac's 1891 article would have eased them." Galvestonians would have taken particular comfort in Cline's ringing conclusion: "The opinion held by some, who are unacquainted with the actual conditions of things, that Galveston will at some time be seriously damaged by [a hurricane] . . . is simply an absurd delusion and can only have its origin in the imagination and not from reasoning; as there is too large a territory to the north which is lower than the island, over which the water may spread, it would be impossible for any cyclone to create a storm wave which could materially injure the city."

Confident in their future, and having been reassured by their local and well-respected meteorologist, Galvestonians moved toward the twentieth century unconcerned that a hurricane might upset the city's grand ambitions. And, indeed, as the city approached the new millennium, Galveston experienced an explosion in population and development. The number of residents jumped to more than 38,000, and the flood of immigration gave Galveston a truly international flair, its streets filled with a babel of tongues. Now the fourth largest city in Texas, and a center for trade and tourism, Galveston was connected to the mainland by three train trestles and one wagon-and-pedestrian bridge. The dredging project completed, Galveston's port—the third busiest in the nation—welcomed a steady stream of deep-draft vessels that delivered cargoes ranging from coffee and wine to cement and twine. In turn, heavily laden ships left the port each year with an astonishing array of goods, including nearly 2 million bales of cotton and large quantities of grain, sugar, cattle, corn, zinc, and lumber, with a cumulative value approaching $100 million.

Stately brick and stone edifices with ornate architectural features reflecting Galveston's commercial ascendance dotted the downtown, among them the four-story Cotton Exchange, the nation's first. The major streets were paved with blocks hewn from the heart of cypress trees, while avenues were covered inches deep in crushed shells gathered from the sea. In the wealthier parts of the city, electric trolleys and clomping horses pulling stylish surreys passed by magnificent mansions, fancy restaurants, thriving businesses, and massive churches, all surrounded by fragrant oleander, towering live oaks, swaying palms, and well-manicured gardens that seemed to be perpetually in bloom. Tourists flocked to Galveston's many hotels, most notably the opulent 250-room Tremont, which was a favorite of the rich and famous, and boasted the luxury of electricity. Those in search of entertainment could attend the opera, listen to a concert, walk through one of the city's six public parks, fish for mighty tarpon, or lounge on a gorgeous beach that was lined with bathhouses and a midway where food and souvenirs were always for sale.

Galveston was riding high by the summer of 1900. It boasted more millionaires than tony Newport, Rhode Island, and its main commercial thoroughfare, the Strand, was dubbed the "Wall Street of the Southwest," which seemed only appropriate, since the entire city had been labeled the "New York of the Gulf." Amid all this flourishing and explosive growth, a storm began to take shape.

THE FIRST NOTICE OF the disturbance that was to morph into the Galveston Hurricane of 1900 took place on August 27, when a ship's captain in the mid-Atlantic encountered a "moderate breeze" that he attributed to a squall in the distance. Over the next few days, other ships recorded encounters with an increasingly strong storm as it approached the Lesser Antilles, and observers on the outer islands tracked it entering the Caribbean Sea. On Monday, September 3, the southwestern part of Cuba was drenched by torrential downpours, and two days later the storm was in the Straits of Florida, north of Cuba.

By this point, the Weather Bureau was focusing more intently on the storm, anticipating that it would almost certainly impact the American mainland. Forecasting kicked into high gear, with the Washington, DC, headquarters in control. According to bureau policy, headquarters was solely responsible for issuing regional forecasts and storm warnings. After weather stations throughout the country delivered their observations and meteorological data to headquarters, it was Washington that made the final call on what weather was expected in different parts of the country.

The bureau claimed that the storm in the Florida Straits was only of moderate intensity, and that it would curve toward the northeast and cross into Florida. It would then travel up the Eastern Seaboard, perhaps affecting areas as far north as southern New England, before dissipating harmlessly over the North Atlantic. Not until the morning of Friday, September 7, did the bureau become convinced that the storm, which it now called a tropical storm, had not gone north over Florida but instead had entered the Gulf and was heading northwest. Still, the bureau felt there was no cause for serious concern. The storm was not major and was predicted to bring only rain and high winds. It certainly wasn't a hurricane. The Cubans, also tracking the storm, didn't agree, but the bureau didn't care, because it didn't respect their opinions.

IN HIS 1899 REPORT to Congress on the expansion of the "West Indian Service," bureau director Willis Moore told a lie. "At first," he wrote, "it was difficult to interest the people [of the West Indies] in the [hurricane] warning service, since they are by nature very conservative and slow to adopt any change in their accustomed methods and modes of living. The issue of warnings of hurricanes was the most radical change, the inhabitants being accustomed to hear of these phenomena only upon their near approach."

This was simply not true, especially for the Cubans, who were, in fact, ahead of the Americans in understanding and forecasting hurricanes. Moore, like so many others in the United States, had a deeply condescending view of the people of the Caribbean, and it colored his estimation of their skills and potential. He thought Cubans were governed too much by their passions, instead of cold, hard reason, and that they were too quick to label any serious storm a hurricane. Added to this bias was Moore's propensity for self-aggrandizement and his desire to consolidate control of all things weather. He was very ambitious and wanted his bureau to be *the* voice when it came to forecasting hurricanes or any other weather-related phenomenon. To admit that the Cubans, or anyone else, had something of value to offer was, in Moore's eyes, an admission of weakness, and unfortunately this hubristic position was shared by William B. Stockman, Moore's man in Havana.

Despite the increasing tensions between the American and Cuban meteorologists in Havana, when the 1899 report was written, Cuban meteorologists were still allowed to use the telegraph lines to gather information, submit forecasts, and communicate with their American counterparts. But by August 1900, Moore had had enough. Even though there was no evidence, he believed that the Cubans were stealing American data and weather maps to improve their own forecasts so that they could compete with the Weather Bureau. To put an end to Cuba's purported conniving, Moore asked the War Department, which controlled the telegraph lines on the island, to ban the Cuban meteorologists from using them for any purpose. The only weather reports coming from Cuba should, Moore argued, be those filed by the Americans stationed there. The military consented, and the Cubans were cut off.

Cuban meteorologists protested this punitive decision, with one of them arguing that it showed "an extraordinary contempt for the public," which relied on Cuban weather expertise to warn them of approaching danger. The injunction couldn't have come at a worse time, this being the height of the hurricane season.

Had the Americans listened to the Cubans, they would have heard a far different story from the one they were telling themselves. Way back on August 31, Cuban meteorologists thought the storm had the makings of a hurricane. On Wednesday, September 5, when it was in the Florida Straits and bureau staff predicted it would move to the northeast over Florida, their Cuban counterparts began calling the storm a hurricane. The following day, Father Lorenzo Gangoite, Benito Viñes's successor at the Havana observatory, issued a warning published in the newspaper *La Lucha* ("The Fight") stating that the hurricane was heading into the Gulf. By Saturday morning, Gangoite thought the hurricane had already plowed into Texas. He was right about Texas, but wrong about the hurricane's location. It was only just approaching the coast.

ON FRIDAY MORNING AT 9:35, Weather Bureau headquarters in Washington, DC, telegraphed Galveston, instructing Isaac Cline to hoist the storm-warning flag—a small, black square emblazoned on a larger, red square background—up the pole atop the station's building. A communication from the bureau later that day noted that the storm was to the south of Louisiana, moving to the northwest, and would bring high winds and heavy rain. Still, no cause for alarm, it was thought. Isaac, along with his brother Joseph and John D. Blagden, both of whom also worked at the station, continued monitoring the situation. Heavy swells were breaking on the beach, and the temperature was holding steady at an oppressive 90 degrees, while the barometer's mercury, which had been inching down for days, rose slightly in the evening. At midnight on September 7, the reading was 29.72, which was a little low, but nothing particularly noteworthy. At this point, Joseph left the station to return to his room in Isaac's home, just a few blocks from the beach. Isaac was already asleep, and Joseph dozed off shortly thereafter.

At about 4:00 in the morning, Joseph woke up with a start. "In some obscure way," he later recalled, "I sensed that the waters of the gulf were already over our backyard." Upon looking outside and seeing that that was indeed the case, he rushed to wake up his brother to tell him that "the worst had begun." While Joseph went back to the office to prepare information for the 7:00 a.m. report to be sent to headquarters, Isaac harnessed his horse to his two-wheeled hunting cart and headed for the beach to investigate. This is what he saw: "Unusually heavy swells from the southeast, intervals one to five minutes, overflowing low places south portion of the city three to four blocks from the beach. Such high water with oppos-

ing winds never observed previously." Isaac would later write that some of
the "usual signs which herald the approach of hurricanes were not present
in this case." There was no brick-red sky, nor were there the high, wispy
cirrus clouds that often indicated a coming tempest.

According to Isaac's own account of what happened next, penned
decades later, the unusually high tide and large swells tipped him off, "as
though it was a written message that great danger was approaching." He
rushed to the station to dash off a telegram to headquarters, alerting them
about the swells and the winds, and then raced back to the beach. Riding
from one end of the beach to the other, he told everyone in sight "a great
danger threatened them, and advised some 6,000 persons from the inte-
rior of the state who were summering along the beach, to go home immediately." He also said he warned those who lived within a few blocks of
the beach to move to higher ground because soon their houses would be
inundated "by the ebb and flow of the increasing storm tide and would be
washed away."

Isaac knew it was official policy that only headquarters could issue
storm and hurricane warnings, but he asserted that he couldn't wait to ask
approval from Washington. Instead, he continued, "I assumed authority
in the emergency and warned the people of Galveston of their danger and
advised them what action was necessary to protect their lives and property." Isaac would later claim that his actions saved "some 6,000 lives."

In Larson's convincing history of the Galveston Hurricane, a totally different story emerges. Larson reviewed the voluminous personal accounts
of people who survived the hurricane, and none mention the Paul Revere–
like ride of Isaac, heralding the coming hurricane and warning people to
flee the city or head to higher ground. The inevitable conclusion is that
Isaac's heroic and self-serving account is simply not true. Larson notes that
even if Isaac had issued such warnings, the hurricane was so close that
there wouldn't have been the time or enough train cars to accommodate a
horde of fleeing citizens.

The scene at the beach early that morning was one characterized by
wonder, not alarm. Crowds came down to watch the rising waters and
impressive swells, viewing it as a dramatic spectacle of nature, not an ominous portent. And why would they think otherwise? Although the weather
station had raised the storm-warning flag, Galveston had weathered many
storms before, and the proud Galvestonians assumed they would do so

again. Few of them had any inkling that a historically powerful hurricane was on the way.

As the winds picked up and the waters rose higher, first engulfing and then smashing the bathhouses and the midway, the mood at the beach changed rapidly. No longer intrigued and excited, people now became increasingly alarmed, and they started rushing for higher ground, which was fast disappearing. By early afternoon, even the most sanguine of observers, who might have assumed that the storm would flood much of Galveston but no more, knew something was terribly wrong. The winds were rapidly increasing, and water was rushing in and appeared to be overwhelming the city.

Isaac, too, was becoming alarmed. Back at the station, he updated headquarters every two hours on the worsening conditions, fielded phone calls from distressed citizens, and answered the questions of the many people who came to the station in search of counsel about what to do. Around 3:00 in the afternoon, Isaac wrote an urgent dispatch for Moore at headquarters, "advising him of the terrible situation, and stat[ing] that the city was fast going under water, and great loss of life must result, and stress[ing] the need for relief."

Wading through fast-surging water, Joseph took Isaac's message to the telegraph office, only to find that the telegraph lines were down. He then went to the telephone building and managed to relay the message on the one working line to Houston, minutes before the line went dead. All communication with the outside world had been cut off, leaving Galveston utterly alone.

Believing that there was nothing else he could do at his desk, and extremely worried about the fate of his pregnant wife, Cora, and their three young daughters, Isaac struggled 2 miles through waist-deep water to get to his home. Between dodging pieces of wood and roof tiles whizzing through the air, and fighting through the remains of destroyed buildings swirling in the seething waters, he did not arrive until about 5:00 p.m. Along the way, Isaac saw an almost surreal tableau. As he later recalled, water "already covered the island from the Gulf to the Bay. In reality there was no island, just the ocean with houses standing out of the waves which rolled between them."

While Isaac went home, Blagden remained behind at the station, periodically checking the instruments. At 5:00 p.m. the barometer stood at 29.05 inches and the wind had reached 100 mph, at which point the anemometer blew away. Galveston was facing a growing meteorological disaster. And the water was still rising fast—a fact that must have astonished Isaac.

IN HIS 1891 ARTICLE, Isaac had argued that it was an "absurd delusion" to think that Galveston could be "seriously damaged" by a "storm wave" generated by a hurricane. His confidence, however, was based on an incomplete understanding of hurricane dynamics and how those might impact the city. He and his fellow meteorologists at the bureau believed that each inch of reduction in atmospheric pressure would result in roughly a 1-foot increase in the height of the sea. Thus, even during a major hurricane, where the pressure could drop 2 inches or more, one could expect a sea-level rise of, at most, about 2 feet. Isaac and his peers also knew that wind-generated waves could cause a rise in sea level and be incredibly destructive to anything in their path. But Isaac didn't think that such waves would have a major impact on Galveston, because of what was offshore.

Since the waters near Galveston, for many miles out to sea, are relatively shallow, Isaac believed that the waves would break far from the beach, and the massive amounts of water they brought with them would tend to spread out over the broad, shallow shelf, resulting in only a small sea-level rise. While the "storm wave" resulting from reduced atmospheric pressure and wind-generated waves was not trivial, it wasn't particularly impressive either, and it was thought that much of the city would be spared. To the degree that the waters rose during a hurricane because of a drop in pressure and the action of waves, Isaac thought that instead of inundating Galveston, most of that high water would flow over the lower lands to the north, across the bay.

Isaac was correct about the influence of atmospheric pressure and the behavior of waves encountering the shallows, and to some extent he was correct about the ability of the low-lying mainland behind Galveston to absorb some of the stormwaters. But he wasn't taking into account some other extremely important factors that affect storm surge, because neither he, nor any of his fellow meteorologists at the Weather Bureau, appreciated them at the time. Among these were the impact of wind in piling up water, and the related influence of offshore topography. As a hurricane moves, the most powerful winds on the right side of the eye cause the water to mound up ahead of the storm, and that mounding generally takes place on the right side as well. The height of that mound, or storm surge, is further increased by the water-level rise caused by a reduction of atmospheric pressure. On top of the mound ride the wind-generated waves.

How this mound behaves as it approaches land depends on the coastal topography. In deeper water, gravity forces the mound down, and it flows away as underwater currents. But when the mound encounters the shallows, it has no place to go, and instead of being carried away by such currents, it gets pushed up, reaching even greater heights. This is what was happening in Galveston. The eye was located southwest of the city, so the city was on the right side of the hurricane. Making matters worse was the hurricane's angle of approach: it crashed into the Texas coast head-on, almost perpendicular to the shore, such that its powerful storm surge flowed straight into the city.

Certain other factors unknown to Isaac affected the intensity of the storm. As a hurricane travels over deeper parts of the ocean, it churns up the waters, mixing the warm top layer with the colder waters beneath. This mixing cools off the water closest to the surface, and since cooler water has less of the energy needed to fuel the hurricane, the storm weakens. Such mixing is less of a factor in the waters near Galveston for two reasons: First, the Gulf is very warm to a considerable depth, thereby reducing the potential influence of mixing.* Second, the waters very near Galveston are so shallow that there is no deeper, colder layer to be churned up—the entire water column is very warm all the way to the shore. Thus, the hurricane got added boosts of energy as it was traveling over the Gulf and zeroing in on the city.

Because of all these factors, Galveston was confronting a storm surge of biblical proportions. And beyond the surge was the roaring wind. Already, some residents of the city had died, and many more would be added to their ranks. In sharing his observations of the disaster a few days

---

* The relatively deep warm layer of water in the Gulf is due to the eddies that break off from the Loop Current, which is part of the main Atlantic Current that flows out of the Caribbean through the Yucatán Channel, curves back (or loops) on itself in the Gulf before exiting the Gulf between Florida and Cuba, and then flows between Florida and the Bahamas, becoming the Gulf Stream.

later, local reporter Richard Spillane said, "The people of Galveston were like rats in traps. . . . To leave a house [or any building] was to drown. To remain was to court death in the wreckage."

WHEN ISAAC GOT HOME, the water was waist deep outside, and he found about fifty people sheltering under his roof. They had gathered there because his was one of the sturdiest houses in Galveston, having been built, per Isaac's specifications, to withstand hurricane-force winds. In fact, the home's builders and their families, confident in its construction, were among those Isaac saw huddled on the first floor.

At 6:30, when Joseph arrived, the water was higher still, and he told Isaac that the barometer had fallen below 29 inches right before he left the station an hour earlier—a clear indication that the hurricane was continuing to strengthen. The two men had no way of knowing it, but the mercury would continue its precipitous fall until 8:30 p.m., when it bottomed out at 28.48 inches, the lowest barometer reading the Weather Bureau had ever recorded up until that point. (Later analysis by the National Oceanic and Atmospheric Administration, or NOAA, determined that the hurricane was even more intense, its lowest barometric reading being 27.64, but that was in the eye, which didn't pass directly over Galveston.)

Yelling so that his voice could be heard above the din, Joseph pleaded with his brother to leave for higher ground in the city's center. All the other houses in the neighborhood were being smashed by the water and wind, and Joseph feared that Isaac's house would soon follow. Isaac wouldn't budge, arguing that it would be "suicidal to attempt to journey through the flying timbers." Furthermore, Cora was pregnant and ill, and Isaac was concerned about moving her in that condition. So they stayed.

At 7:30, Isaac was standing at his front door, peering out into the maelstrom. Suddenly, within the span of four seconds, the water rose 4 feet, causing everyone inside to flee to the second floor. In the next hour, the water rose nearly 5 feet more, bringing it to 20 feet above sea level. This tremendous surge had been amplified by a dramatic shift in the atmosphere. The winds, which were blowing offshore in the morning, had swung around and were now rushing onshore. And they were much stronger than they had been earlier in the day. At its peak that evening, the hurricane is estimated to have had sustained winds of more than 138 mph, with gusts approaching 180 mph or more.

The tremendous current running east to west across the island, combined with the lashing winds, was propelling all manner of wreckage against the outer walls of Isaac's house, but it stood fast, anchored to its foundation. Then, out of the darkness came a new threat. A streetcar trestle, about a quarter of a mile long and located not far from Isaac's house, had held fast for a while against the surging waters, acting as a dam behind which a massive amount of debris had accumulated. When the trestle finally gave way under the increasing pressure, carrying with it a veritable mountain of wreckage, it became an almost unstoppable battering ram, mowing down any structures that stood in its way. Those included Isaac's house, which shuddered for perhaps ten or fifteen seconds after the trestle hit, and then violently crashed into the water, its walls, floors, and ceilings buckling under the terrific strain.

Just before the trestle struck at around 8:30, Joseph had been standing next to a large window with Isaac's two older daughters, Allie May and Rosemary. As the house toppled over, Joseph smashed the window, grabbed the girls' hands, and jumped through the frame, landing on the outside wall as it collapsed. Meanwhile Isaac, Cora, and their six-year-old daughter, Esther Bellew, who had been in the center of the room, were flung against the chimney, and then all three went down with the house.

Pinned between timbers beneath the water, Isaac assumed this was the end. His last thought before he lost consciousness was that he was going to die, and that it was "useless to fight for life." But he soon came to, sputtering and gulping for air. Timbers had floated to the top of the water, taking him along for the ride.

Isaac could barely see anything in the inky darkness. Suddenly, a bolt of lightning illuminated the terrible scene, and he saw Esther nearby, floating on some wreckage. Struggling to free himself from the wood's embrace, Isaac swam to Esther and grabbed her tight. Another flash of lightning revealed Joseph, along with Isaac's two older daughters, a short distance away, clinging to their own raft of debris. Isaac, with Esther under one arm, swam to them. Reunited atop a tangled mat of wreckage, Isaac and Joseph used their bodies to shield the children from the wind and projectiles flying through the air. To protect themselves from the airborne debris, and distribute the force of impact should they be struck, the two brothers grabbed planks from the water and held them to their backs.

For three hours they drifted, having no idea where they were or if the end was near. A few times, one or both of the brothers were knocked off the raft, only to fight their way back and resume their protective positions. Two more people joined them on their terrible journey: a four-year-old girl who they plucked from some wreckage, and a woman who climbed aboard. "While being carried forward by the winds and surging waters," Isaac would later recall, "through the darkness and terrific downpour of rain we could hear houses crashing under the impact of the wreckage hurled forward by the winds and storm tide, but this did not blot out the screams of the injured and dying."

Around 11:30, as the waters were fast subsiding and flowing back into the Gulf and bay, the raft came to rest on solid ground only 300 yards from where their hellish voyage had begun. Isaac and Joseph led the children to a nearby house, where they remained for the rest of the night. They were the lucky ones. Of the fifty or so people who had sought shelter in Isaac's house, only eighteen survived. Isaac's wife, Cora, and their

Lithograph, circa 1900, titled Galveston's Awful Calamity—
Gulf Tidal Wave, September 8th 1900.

unborn baby were among the dead. It would be days, though, before her body was found, not far from where the rest of her family had landed. "Even in death," Isaac would say, "she had traveled with us and near us during the storm."

THERE WERE OTHER TRAGIC stories as well. The crowd at Ritter's Café and Saloon in downtown Galveston on Saturday, composed primarily of businessmen and city power brokers, wasn't going to let a mere storm interrupt lunchtime plans. As the winds rattled the restaurant's windows and the waters rose just beyond the door, the men eating inside shared intelligence, struck deals, and expressed little concern about the nasty weather; in fact, they were laughing about it. When one of them noted that there were thirteen men in the room, another diner shouted back, "You can't frighten me, I'm not superstitious." But their jocular banter hid a rising fear of what might be in store, should the storm get any worse.

In the next instant, a mighty gust ripped the roof off the two-story building, weakening the structure so much that the ceiling gave way and the heavy printing presses on the second floor crashed onto the men below, killing five and seriously injuring five more. Ritter sent one of his black waiters to fetch a doctor, but soon after leaving the establishment, the waiter was engulfed by turbulent waters and drowned.

ST. MARY'S ORPHANAGE was almost an island unto itself, located about 3 miles from downtown Galveston, with only a few ramshackle homes nearby. Its two wings—the girls' and boys' dormitories—each with two floors, housed ninety-three children ranging from newborns to early teens, who were cared for by ten nuns. Situated mere yards away from the beach, the orphanage was separated from the surf by only some low dunes and a white picket fence.

As the waters rose, surrounding the orphanage and cutting off any escape route, mother superior Sister M. Camillus Tracy herded everyone into the chapel. The sisters then took a clothesline from outside, cut it into short sections, and tied groups of six or eight of the younger children together by their wrists. They connected each of those groups, in turn, to a nun or to the two workmen by tying the end of the sections around their waists. The older kids were left to fend for themselves.

To try to maintain calm, Sister Camillus led the children in singing hymns. With water rising in the chapel, everyone climbed to the second floor of the girls' dormitory. The howling wind grew even louder, and soon there was a tremendous crash as the boys' dormitory collapsed in a heap, swallowed by the angry waters.

Finally, the elements won, and the building crumbled, killing everyone within except for three of the older boys whose wrists had not been tied to a section of clothesline. They managed to climb through a transom and clamber onto an uprooted tree that was floating by. Before it could be swept out into the deeper waters of the Gulf, the tree became entangled in the mast of the schooner *John S. Ames*, which had sunk offshore not far from where the orphanage had stood. The boys remained in that spot throughout the night, buffeted by waves, winds, and surging waters. In the morning, the tree broke free and floated onto the beach, and the boys hiked into town.

After the hurricane had passed, a man walking along the beach, searching for the living and the dead, came upon a child whose body was partly buried in the sand. When he tried to lift the body, he discovered it was connected by a clothesline to another body, and then to six more, including a nun. The rope that had been meant to keep the children safe and together had only served to drag them all down with the wreckage to their death.

SUNDAY, SEPTEMBER 9, DAWNED with a clear sky, brilliant sunshine, gentle breezes, and placid seas. It was, Isaac said, "a most beautiful day," but one that "revealed one of the most horrible sights that ever a civilized people looked upon." More than 3,500 homes had been utterly obliterated. Wharves were smashed; scores, if not hundreds, of vessels had been sunk or driven ashore; bridges were washed away; and an untold number of businesses, along with many houses of worship, hotels, and hospitals, were either severely damaged or destroyed. So much timber was scattered about and mounded up in great piles that it looked as if a vengeful giant had raided an enormous lumberyard and thrown everything wildly up in the air. The remains of buildings listing at odd angles or shorn of one or

A body in the wreckage on the wharf
after the Galveston Hurricane of 1900.

more of their walls peeked out from the rubble, ghostly vestiges of the once proud city. The cost of the damage was pegged at $20–$30 million. But property loss was ultimately not the real tragedy.

Dead and mangled bodies were found under, over, within, and next to the wreckage. Bloated corpses, covered in silt and sand, with arms and legs contorted into unnatural positions, littered the macabre landscape—a silent testament to the hurricane's power. Most contemporary accounts place the number killed at 6,000, but there is little doubt that it was higher still. The unusually hot weather had brought numerous visitors to Galveston to enjoy the surf and sand, but just how many of them died is unknown. An untold number of people were also swept out to sea or into the bay, and never seen again. Thus, the death toll might have been 8,000, 10,000, or even more.

Martial law was declared, as policemen, the local militia, and many regular citizens banded together to maintain order, apprehend looters,

Collecting dead bodies after the Galveston Hurricane.

and impress men to help with the cleanup when necessary. They also ensured that relief supplies were fairly distributed among the 8,000 people rendered homeless, as well as those who still had roofs over their heads yet were in dire need of assistance. To discourage unruly behavior, the mayor ordered all saloons to be closed on Sunday afternoon, and to reopen only after martial law ended.

Under the beating sun, and with temperatures still sweltering, the dead quickly putrefied, creating gaseous emissions that assaulted the senses and cast a nauseating pall over the city. The sheer number of deceased and their decaying condition created a public health emergency that forced local officials to face the difficult task of disposing of the bodies quickly. Traditional burial alone was not an option for such a large quantity of cadavers, so the living of Galveston decided to sink or burn the dead.

Black men were forced at gunpoint by soldiers to load corpses onto boats that took them miles offshore, where the bodies were weighed down and pitched over the side into their watery graves. Despite such precautions, many of these bodies floated to the surface, where the wind, currents, and waves deposited them on the beach, forming a grisly wrack line. Some of the bodies that washed ashore were interred in place in trenches or shallow graves, but many more, along with other bodies found scattered throughout the island, were heaped into piles and burned. For days, Galveston was shrouded in a miasma of burning flesh and decay that transformed the city into a living hell.

Nellie Carey, a stenographer who lived through the hurricane, wrote to her parents on September 12, giving voice to the horrors she had witnessed: "Thousands of dead in the streets, the gulf and bay strewn with dead bodies. The whole island demolished. Not a drop of water—food scarce. If help does not reach us soon there will be great starvation for everybody. . . . It is so pitiable to see husbands, with a look of despair in

Searching for valuables among the ruins of the Galveston Hurricane.

their eyes, searching for their wives and children; wives for their loved ones; and, most pitiable of all, the comparatively few children—although they are enough, God knows, to be left orphans and homeless—looking into every one's face with frightened, appealing eyes. It is heartrending."

As word of the disaster spread, the nation's and the world's papers shared the shocking story with their readers. Along with blow-by-blow descriptions of the hurricane's fury, there were vivid and disturbing depictions of the aftermath and the human cost of the calamity. One of the dominant themes of the newspaper articles, as well as many of the quickly produced book-length treatments of the hurricane, was looting. Lurid accounts of men, repeatedly referred to as "ghouls," roaming alone or in gangs and stripping corpses of their valuables, became a staple of the extensive media fare.

It wasn't just any men who were accused of such abominable behavior, but mainly black men who were singled out for excoriation. Representative of this type of coverage was a dispatch sent out by a reporter in Texas two days after the hurricane, which was picked up by multiple news outlets nationwide. It told of "ghouls [who] were holding an orgy over the dead. The majority of these men were negroes, but there were also whites who took part in the desecration. . . . Not only did they rob the dead, but they mutilated bodies in order to secure their ghoulish booty. A party of ten negroes were returning from a looting expedition. They had stripped corpses of all valuables and the pockets of some of the looters were fairly bulging out with fingers of the dead, which had been cut off because they were so swollen the rings could not be removed. . . . not only were fingers cut off, but ears were stripped from the head in order to secure jewels of value." This behavior, the reporter said, "incensed" the unidentified onlookers, who shot the looters. Such retribution was widespread. All over the city, the reporter continued, people charged with maintaining order, as well as private citizens, had "endeavored to prevent the robbing of the dead and on several occasions killed the offenders. It is said that at one time eight were killed and at another time four. Singly and in twos and threes the offenders were thus shot down until the total of those thus executed exceeds fully fifty."

While there is no doubt that there were both black and white looters, a few of whom were shot, the sensational coverage of hordes of out-of-control men—primarily black men—rampaging through the streets of Galveston was simply not true. These reports were more a function of yellow journalism that reflected the racial prejudices and stereotypes of the day. As the circumspect managing editor of the *Galveston Tribune*, Clarence Ousley, said at the time, reports of as many as seventy-five "ghouls" being shot were quite overblown. "Diligent inquiry fails to discover conclusive proof of one-tenth the number."

In the wake of the hurricane and its extensive coverage, a flood of financial and material aid went to the city, administered by all sorts of groups and individuals. Red Cross president Clara Barton was overwhelmed with shock and sadness after her arrival on the scene. "The tale is too dreadful to recall—the funeral pyre of at least five thousand human beings," she wrote later. Even Germany's Kaiser Wilhelm II, moved by the disaster, cabled President William McKinley with a message of sympathy, saying that he "sincerely hope[d] that Galveston will rise again to new prosperity."

Galveston did rise again, but the prehurricane trajectory that had positioned it to become the undisputed economic and commercial center of Texas had been derailed. That mantle would go to nearby Houston, whose bayous were dredged to make it a major inland port, and whose prosperity was fueled by the gusher of black gold that started spewing from Texas's oil fields around the turn of the century. Instead, Galveston became more of a tourist destination and vacation spot, yet it still remained an important port with a vital business community.

Galvestonians, waylaid by the hurricane, knew they had to do something to protect the city from another such blow. So they latched on to the previously ignored idea of building a seawall. Realizing that a wall alone would not do the trick, they approved a two-pronged plan. First, they would build a massive seawall to a height of 17 feet above mean low tide; then they would raise the entire city anywhere from 1 to 11 feet, depending on a location's initial elevation above sea level.

It took ten years, but they did it, accomplishing one of the most amazing engineering feats of the era. The 17,593-foot-long cement seawall was completed first, in 1904.* With its curved surface facing the sea, the wall was 16 feet wide at the base, tapering to just 5 feet at the top. It weighed a whopping 40,000 pounds per foot and was flanked

---

* Since then, the seawall has been extended seven times. It is currently more than 10 miles long.

Man standing on the Galveston seawall before its completion.

on one side by a 100-foot-long embankment. Six years later, the last of 2,000 buildings, along with all the associated water pipes, not to mention streetcar tracks, had been jacked up and underlain with more than 16 million cubic yards of sand and mud dug from the ocean bottom just beyond the harbor's mouth.

The first major test of Galveston's two-pronged engineering solution came in August 1915, when another Category 4 hurricane slammed into the city. Although part of the wall was damaged and much of the city flooded, the wall and the higher elevation of the buildings proved their value, as only eleven people died in Galveston, and the financial toll was much less than had been the case in 1900.

ISAAC CLINE WOULD NOT be in Galveston to watch the city being transformed. Moore had transferred him to the newly created forecasting office in New Orleans with responsibility for multiple states bordering the Gulf and beyond, where he worked until his retirement in 1935. Cline never remarried, and he continued to mourn the loss of Cora and his unborn child, feeling that he was to blame for their death by not doing what his brother had urged and abandoning his house for higher ground.

During his time in New Orleans, Cline produced some well-regarded works on hurricanes, with a special focus on the dynamics of the storm surge, which he now correctly viewed as a hurricane's most deadly feature. In his autobiography—*Storms, Floods and Sunshine*—he defended his actions in September 1900. To bolster his case, he included a comment by an Associated Press reporter who, Cline said, had told him a few days after the hurricane that "nothing more could have been done than was done." Cline did, however, admit that he had misjudged the fury that a hurricane could unleash. "This being my first experience in a tropical cyclone," Cline wrote, "I did not foresee the magnitude of the damage which it would do."

WHAT ABOUT THE WEATHER BUREAU? How did its reputation fare in the wake of the hurricane? According to the editors of the *Houston Daily Post*, it was in tatters. On September 14, 1900, they wrote, "The practical utility of the National Weather Bureau, for certain sections of the country, at least, was never so conspicuously shown as on Friday and Saturday last when south Texas was left without any warning of the coming storm, or at least its severity. . . . With the weather bureau saying that Saturday would be 'fair; fresh, possibly brisk, northerly winds on the coast,' of East Texas, who would have looked for the most destructive hurricane of modern times on that coast on that date?" Although the editors were wrong about the bureau calling for fair skies—it actually called for rain—the rest of the forecast was correctly stated.

When Moore read this editorial, he exploded in rage, and then took up his pen. His letter to the editors—a full-throated defense of the bureau—was published in the paper two weeks later. He lied and said that warnings about "the coming hurricane" had been "thoroughly distributed" throughout the Gulf region days before the storm hit, and then he claimed that the storm warnings posted in Galveston on Saturday morning "were changed to hurricane signals" a few hours later. Moore called Isaac Cline "one of the heroic spirits of that awful hour," who had not only warned thousands on the beach, and in houses nearby, to flee to higher ground, but also had continued to do his duty as a weatherman, keeping headquarters apprised of the worsening situation, until he could be of service no more; and only then did he leave his station to be with his wife and family.

Moore's arguments were not new. In fact, he had been trumpeting the purported effectiveness of the bureau's actions ever since the hurricane struck. In the end, Moore's version of events is the one that was most widely accepted by newspapers throughout the country. For example, the *Boston Herald* argued that "the excellent service rendered by the Weather Bureau . . . is deserving recognition," while the *New York Sun* opined, "The value of the Weather Bureau's forecasts of what was destined to happen at Galveston cannot be overstated."

THE GALVESTON HURRICANE OF 1900 has not relinquished its unique and tragic place in the pantheon of hurricanes. It remains even to this day the deadliest natural disaster in American history. It is the storm against which all others are measured, and every year it becomes part of the national conversation swirling around the relentless march of hurricane season, as news outlets trot out the Galveston Hurricane's gruesome particulars for comparison's sake. No matter what the future brings, its story will continue to enthrall us and serve as a cautionary tale about the dangers of human arrogance in the face of the awesome power of nature.

CHAPTER 5

Death and Destruction in
the Sunshine State

Flooding in Miami Beach during the Great Miami Hurricane of 1926.

HE FIRST THREE AND A HALF DECADES OF THE TWENTIETH century were a period of relative stasis for hurricane forecasting in the United States, as a result of bureaucratic, budgetary, scientific, and data limitations. Having congratulated itself for a job well done after the Galveston Hurricane of 1900, the Weather Bureau continued with business as usual. Rather than giving more responsibility for issuing warnings to the local meteorologists who were best positioned to monitor evolving situations, headquarters tightened its grip. Not only did the issuance of hurricane warnings remain solely the prerogative of officials in DC, but once the occupation of Cuba came to an end in 1902, the bureau recalled most of its hurricane forecasting personnel from the West Indies, leaving behind a small office in Puerto Rico with responsibility for issuing warnings just for the island and its immediate surroundings.

Another bureaucratic limitation was time. Although hurricanes strike around the clock, the bureau and its stations operated just twelve to fifteen hours per day. Making matters worse, the bureau issued its national weather maps and storm warnings only twice daily, meaning there was a significant lag in reporting developing events. And the bureau's ability to issue any type of hurricane communication was further curtailed by President Calvin Coolidge's (1923–29) budget cutting, which reduced by six weeks the time that bureau employees spent monitoring for hurricanes during the traditional hurricane season.

The science of hurricanes, too, saw minimal progress. In fact, Isaac Cline's work on tropical cyclones—in particular, the nature and impact of storm surges—was one of the only scientific works produced during this period. Finally, with respect to data or information about the movement of hurricanes, there were promising developments in wireless communication, but even that was of mixed value.

Samuel Morse's invention of wire telegraphy in the 1840s ushered in a new era in weather forecasting, enabling meteorologists to communicate in real time and, therefore, not only to "trace the path of the tempest round the globe," but also to combine their understanding of meteorology with far-flung observations to predict the coming weather. One of the major limitations of wire telegraphy, however, was the wire itself. If a wire didn't reach a location, immediate information from that spot could not be obtained. Thus, the usefulness of Morse's invention ended at the edge of land, or, in the case of an island, at the edge of the island, as long as it was connected to the mainland by an underwater cable. The invention of wireless telegraphy changed all that.

Wireless telegraphy burst onto the international scene in the early 1900s after years of trial and error by an array of inventors, including Guglielmo Marconi and Nikola Tesla. It was Marconi who took the lead in promoting wireless technology and became its public face. On December 12, 1901, he sent the first "message"—simply the Morse code for the letter *s*—2,100 miles across the Atlantic, from Cornwall, England, to St. Johns, Newfoundland. A little more than a year later, on January 19, 1903, Marconi and his team sent the first transmission across the ocean that was actually worthy of being called a message. Emanating from Wellfleet, Massachusetts, and reaching to Poldhu in South Cornwall, the transmitted letter from President Theodore Roosevelt to King Edward VII read, "In taking advantage of the wonderful triumph of scientific research and ingenuity which has been achieved in perfecting a system of wireless telegraphy, I extend on behalf of the American people most cordial greetings and good wishes to you and all the people of the British Empire." The king replied, in part, "I thank you most sincerely for the kind message which I have just received from you, through Marconi's transatlantic wireless telegraphy."

The potential application of wireless telegraphy—or *radio*, as it was later called—to weather forecasting was quickly recognized. Now there was a way to communicate with ships at sea and, more important, to obtain information from them about the development and movement of storms they encountered offshore. Using such shipboard observations, a meteorologist on land could track storms and issue warnings of their approach well in advance, giving people time to prepare.

The first transmission of this type came from the steamship *Cartago*, which crossed paths with a hurricane in the Yucatán Channel on August 25, 1909. The *Cartago* was able to send messages to the weather station in New Orleans, 600 miles away, reporting the storm's character and course. Using that information, Weather Bureau headquarters issued hurricane warnings for the Texas coast near the Mexican border. Once the storm had passed, bathers who had been on South Padre Island credited the bureau with saving their lives by giving them enough time to head to shelter. "Had it not been for the warnings," they said, "every one of them might have been drowned."

Ship-to-shore radio communications were a boon to mariners as well, since they could quickly learn of serious storms at sea and chart their course so as to avoid them, or not leave port until the tempest had passed; indeed, many ships were spared run-ins with hurricanes in this manner. That very reasonable urge to scatter or stay in port, however, limited the usefulness of radio in tracking hurricanes as they approached land. As Ivan Ray Tannehill, a weather historian who had served as a high-ranking official in the Weather Bureau's forecast division from the 1920s to the 1950s, put it, "Vessel masters soon learned that it was dangerous to be caught in the predicted path of a hurricane, and when a warning was received by radio, they steamed out of the line of peril as quickly as possible. Thus, as the storm advanced, fewer and fewer ships were in a position to make useful reports and in a day or two the hurricane was said to be 'lost,' that is, there were too few reports to spot the center accurately, or in some cases there were no reports at all. The storm hunters could only place it vaguely somewhere in a large ocean area. When it is impossible to track the center of a hurricane accurately, it is also impossible to issue accurate warnings." As a result, despite the advent of ship-to-shore radio, people on land would often not become aware of a hurricane until it came ashore.

While the art and practice of forecasting hurricanes stagnated in the first three and a half decades of the twentieth century, the United States was pummeled by more than sixty hurricanes. Three of the worst hit Florida and are especially noteworthy for the death and destruction they left in their wake. The first, in 1926, battered Miami.

HENRY MORRISON FLAGLER PUT Miami on the map, literally and figuratively. Born in 1830 in Hopewell, New York, he had some limited success in his early career in the salt-mining and grain business before striking it rich with "black gold." In 1870, Flagler, along with John D. Rockefeller Sr. and a few other lesser partners, founded Standard Oil, which fast became the nation's preeminent petroleum-producing, -refining, and -transporting company, and one of the world's most powerful and wealthy corporations. Its phenomenal success, however, would become its undoing. In 1911 the Supreme Court ruled that Standard Oil was a monopoly in violation of the Sherman Antitrust Act and must, therefore, be broken up into smaller independent entities. Among the companies that were the ultimate offspring of that decision are ExxonMobil, ConocoPhillips, and Chevron.

Standard Oil made Flagler one of the richest men in the country, and he invested much of that wealth in Florida. He fell in love with the Sunshine State after visiting it with his first two wives and decided that it offered irresistible business opportunities both for tourism and for broader economic development. Flagler's first foray was to build the luxurious, 540-room Ponce de Leon Hotel, which opened in 1888 in the city of St. Augustine.

Henry Morrison Flagler.

Realizing that the key to a flourishing hotel was to ensure that paying customers could easily get there, Flagler invested in railroad service into the city. People came, and the money flowed.

Buoyed by his success in St. Augustine, Flagler decided on an ambitious goal. He would extend railroad service down the east coast of Florida. At promising locations along the route, he would construct extravagant destination hotels to act not only as a lure for the rich and famous, but also as an anchor around which both he and other developers would build. When those areas became thriving cities, Flagler would earn more money by transporting people and freight on his railroad.

In the ensuing decades, Flagler's Florida East Coast Railway snaked its way down the shoreline, finally arriving in Key West in January 1912. The eighty-two-year-old business titan, who would die the following year, had achieved his goal. Along the way he had built or bought and refurbished iconic deluxe hotels in Ormond Beach, Palm Beach, and Miami.

When Flagler set his sights on Miami in the mid-1890s, there was no Miami. The area was called Fort Dallas after an abandoned military outpost and had only a few hundred residents. Among them was Julia Tuttle, a wealthy widow from Cleveland, Ohio, and her family. Tuttle dreamed of making Fort Dallas into a thriving city, and to that end she spearheaded the effort to convince Flagler to extend his railroad to the area, build a hotel, and take the lead in local development. As an enticement, she promised him a substantial amount of land.

In 1895, Flagler accepted her offer, and his railroad arrived the next year. Soon thereafter, the thrilled and confident residents of Fort Dallas decided to incorporate as a city. They wanted to name it Flagler, in honor of their benefactor, but Flagler demurred. Instead they called the city Miami, after the nearby Miami River, whose name, in turn, was derived from the word "Mayaimi," the name of a local Indian tribe. In 1897, Flagler held up his end of the bargain, opening up the 350-room Royal Palm Hotel on the edge of Biscayne Bay, yet another one of his grand hotels, which perfectly reflected the celebration of wealth that epitomized the Gilded Age in America.

TUTTLE'S PLAN SUCCEEDED far beyond her wildest dreams. Up through the mid-1920s, Miami was one of the fastest-growing cities in the country. Between 1900 and 1910, the population rose over 200 percent, from 1,681 to 5,471. In the next ten years, despite the disruption on the home front caused by World War I, Miami's population grew 440 percent, to 29,517, and by 1925 it stood at an astonishing 84,258. Accompanying this explosive growth was an equally explosive construction boom. With so much demand for houses, hotels, and office buildings, land was quickly gobbled up and the real-estate market zoomed upward. In 1925 alone, $60 million's worth of new construction sprang up in the city, and 2,000 real-estate offices bustled with 25,000 very busy agents cutting deals. Speculation ran rampant, fueled by extravagant assumptions and outlandish expectations. Properties changed hands at lightning speed, and at ever-increasing prices.

Miami's prosperity bubbled over into the neighboring city of Miami Beach, which incorporated in 1915. Located on the other side of Biscayne Bay from Miami, Miami Beach was originally a relatively narrow, low-lying barrier island comprising sand and mangrove swamp. After various failed attempts to raise crops on the island, a group of investors transformed it into a tourist mecca. Mangroves were cut down, causeways to the mainland were constructed, and enormous quantities of soil were trucked in to build up the island and make it ready for its new, glamorous life. Just ten years after incorporation, Miami Beach had become, in the words of historian Ted Steinberg, "a real estate theme park" with a sprawling array of lavish hotels, numerous apartment complexes, and nearly 1,000 private residences.

Few places in the United States were more emblematic of the Roaring Twenties than Miami and Miami Beach at mid-decade. There was an unmistakable energy and vitality in the air, fueled by the massive amounts of money surging through the local economy. Partying, fun in the sun, and newfound sexual freedom were the orders of the day. Even Prohibition could not dampen the exuberant mood. The liquor flowed in speakeasies, and flappers bobbed their hair, sported short dresses, and gyrated to sensual jazz compositions, not caring a lick what proper society thought of their purported transgressions. No wonder Miami was referred to by contemporaries as "the world's playground," "Wonder City," and "Magic City."

Above all, conspicuous consumption was the goal. Not only real estate, but everything and anything one could buy. One sign of the region's amazing prosperity, hedonism, and dynamism could be seen in the July 26, 1925, Sunday edition of the *Miami Daily News*. It weighed a hefty 7½ pounds and ran to 504 pages, making it the largest newspaper ever published up to that point in history, and also the one with the most advertising. Almost no one stopped to consider the craziness of the boom, the ridiculousness of the prices, and the shallowness and greed that were reflected in so many people's behavior. As John Kenneth Galbraith wrote in his book *The Great Crash 1929*, "The Florida boom was the first indication of the mood of the twenties and the conviction that God intended the American middle class to be rich."

Although the real-estate market in Miami and Miami Beach had begun to cool a bit by 1926, no one had any real concerns that the good times were coming to an end, and the thought that a hurricane might put a dent in the area's prosperity was hardly entertained. The last hurricane to impact the city had been way back in October 1906, but that one had done most of its damage when it came ashore in the Florida Keys, killing 124 laborers who were working on Flagler's railroad extension to Key West. By the time it rolled over Miami, much of the storm's energy had been spent. Quite a few houses were seriously damaged, and many of the streets were impassable because of flooding, but nobody was killed.

Since 1906, other hurricanes had struck the Keys, the west coast of Florida, and the panhandle, but the Miami area had remained out of the crosshairs. Therefore, few, if any, of the people in Miami or Miami Beach had lived through a hurricane, and most of the residents seemed to believe they had little cause to fear that another one would visit the area. When prospective homebuyers broached the topic of hurricanes hitting Miami or Miami Beach, local realtors simply dismissed their apprehensions, assuring them that would never happen. Even when a hurricane came ashore at the end of July in 1926, a mere 70 miles north of Miami, causing significant damage in Palm Beach and farther up the coast, Miamians remained blissfully unconcerned. After all, the storm had only brushed Miami, resulting in minor wind damage and hardly any flooding. A few days after the hurricane, Richard W. Gray, the meteorologist at the Weather Bureau's Miami office, gave a talk before the members of the Miami Kiwanis Club in which he said they "need not fear serious damage from a hurricane." If he wasn't worried, why should they be? As both Gray and his fellow Miamians would soon find out, their confidence was horribly misplaced.

ON TUESDAY, SEPTEMBER 14, 1926, Weather Bureau headquarters informed Gray that a tropical storm was heading toward the Bahamas. At noon three days later, when the storm was thought to be nearing Nassau, the bureau instructed Gray to raise the storm warning. There was still no talk of a hurricane, and the *Miami Herald* informed its readers that only a "tropical storm" would hit the city that night.

Back at his office, Gray continued to monitor the situation. Throughout the day and into the early evening, he saw nothing alarming. Winds were light, the barometer had fallen only slightly, and the rain that typically preceded a tropical storm was not present. Then, after 10:00 p.m., the winds picked up and the barometer began dropping fast. Gray's sudden fear that something more than a tropical storm was in the offing was confirmed at 11:16, when he received a message from headquarters to display the hurricane warning—two square flags, one on top of the other, both with a red background and a small black square in the center.

Gray rushed to raise the flags—one on the weather station's roof and another at the storm-warning tower at the city docks a half mile away. He also telephoned the warning to the offices of the railroad and Coast Guard, as well as to the long-distance operator, who relayed the urgent message to area exchanges in Miami and nearby cities and towns. But it was too late. Most people were asleep, and by 3:00 in the morning the gales had become so strong that the telephone lines in Miami and Miami Beach were severed. The hurricane had arrived in full force.

Winds measured 115 mph at 4:30 a.m., minutes before the instrument shelter atop the Weather Bureau building flew off the structure and plummeted to the ground. Shortly after 6:00 that morning, the eye of the hurricane passed directly over Miami. Most Miamians, who had never lived through a hurricane, or didn't imagine that one would ever hit their fair city, had no idea that hurricanes had eyes, much less what they were. So, when the winds subsided, many people came out of their buildings, thinking the worst was over, to view the wreckage and celebrate their survival.

Front page of the Miami Daily News, *September 18, 1926.*

Gray, of course, knew better, and he ran into the street yelling, "The storm is not over! We're in the lull! Get back to safety! The worst is yet to come!" He might as well have just shouted to the heavens. A handful of people in the vicinity heeded his call, but most were well beyond the reach of his entreaty and were left with their ignorance. When the eye passed by about thirty-five minutes later and the winds rapidly ramped up to hurricane force, numerous people were taken by surprise, and many of them died when they were struck by flying debris or swept into the churning waters.

During this "second storm," wind speeds of 128 mph were recorded atop the Allison Hospital in Miami Beach. Not long after, the anemometer blew away. The wind speed was estimated to reach 145 mph, making it a Category 4 hurricane.

The winds, combined with a 9-foot storm surge, greatly damaged or destroyed much of Miami and Miami Beach. The latter was completely covered with water at the height of the hurricane, and when the waters receded, all of the streets closest to the ocean were blanketed in mountains of sand. The entire bayfront section of Miami was similarly coated, and hundreds of boats, including magnificent yachts and large commercial ships, were strewn about like children's toys. The tidal bore that surged up the Miami River sank many vessels and deposited others high along the riverbank. In these two communities alone, thousands of houses, many hastily and poorly constructed to fulfill the demands of the building boom, were simply blown or washed away, and virtually all of the rest were seriously scarred. According to the *New York Times*, "The Floridana Club, the once brilliant dream of a fashionable Anglo-American society winter resort, has been transformed into a swamp, above which the long rows of street lamps, all bent double, appear to bow mockingly."

"The intensity of the storm and the wreckage that it left cannot be adequately described," Gray would later write. "The continuous roar of the wind; the crash of the falling buildings, flying debris, and plate glass; the shriek of the fire apparatus and ambulances that rendered assistance until the streets became impassable; the terrifically driven rain that came in sheets as dense as fog; the electric flashes from live wires have left the memory of a fearful night in the minds of the many thousands that were left in the storm area."

Building destroyed by the Great Miami Hurricane of 1926.

As author Marjory Stoneman Douglas observed, "The city built on wild promises and hopes, paper and unchecked speculation, like acres of flimsy buildings and billboards, was gone." Although Miami and Miami Beach bore the brunt of the hurricane, they were not the only areas impacted. All the cities and towns surrounding Miami were also devastated. Leo Francis Reardon's account of what his family endured in Coral Gables, 6 miles west of Miami, offers another glimpse of the terrors that the hurricane delivered.

REARDON LEFT HIS OFFICE at the Coral Gables Construction Building at about 4:00 p.m. on Saturday to play a round of golf. He and his friends were unfazed by the weather forecast. They had handled tropical storms in the past and would do so now. After the game they repaired to Leo's home to eat dinner, and his friends left at 11:00 p.m., just as the weather was beginning to get nasty.

Leo locked the windows and barred the double doors connecting the sun parlor with the living room. A few minutes later, a gust ripped an awning off the side of the house and sent a projectile crashing through the window in his bedroom. Rattled, Leo woke his eight-year-old son and grabbed his six-year-old daughter, and he sent both of them to stay with his wife, Deanie, in her room on the second floor, while he continued to monitor the house.

As the wind rose, another terrific gust tore the awnings off the other side of the house. Then the lights went out. Now somewhat panicked, Leo and Deanie scrambled to dress their children while windows shattered and the walls heaved in and out in rhythm with the blasting wind outside. To see whether they could make a run for it to a sturdier building, Leo ventured out the front door into the maelstrom. The wind flung him along the side of the house for several yards before he was able to arrest his motion by grabbing on to one of the awning bars bolted into the wall. Using those supports, he struggled back to the door and reentered the house.

Leo knew he had to get his family to a safer location, so he went back upstairs, where he found Deanie and his kids barricaded in her room. He led them, crawling along the hallway and down the stairs, to the attached garage. He thought that if the house blew away, the safest place was in their car, a heavy open-air roadster. In they piled, and for extra protection Leo placed an old mattress on top of the car in case the ceiling caved in. Then he laid his body over his wife and children to further shield them from any blow.

For nearly five hours they remained hunkered down in the car, with the wind howling outside and trees crashing all about, "expecting every moment," as Leo later recalled, "to be buried under tons of stucco and Cuban tile or swept away entirely." Around dawn, the wind suddenly died down, and the Reardon family, like so many others, thought the hurricane was over. They breathed a sigh of relief and went back inside the house to survey the damage.

Worried that there would be a run on food, Leo drove twenty blocks around downed trees and wreckage until he found an open grocery store. He hoped to get bottled water, since the tap at his home was dry, but the store was already out. He bought some food, and by the time he placed it in the trunk, the winds were whipping again. "Filled with fear and dread," he raced back home.

Leo and Deanie wrapped their arms around each other and their children near the front door, thinking that they could crawl to the car parked in the driveway if necessary. "Never abating for an instant, the wind rose still higher until it sounded like hundreds of steamer whistles blowing at once." After the wooden double doors in the living room blew open, Leo placed Deanie and the children behind a heavy trunk in the foyer and crawled along the wall to the doors, attempting to push them shut. Having closed one and wedged his foot behind it, he grabbed the second one and had it nearly closed when, as Leo said, a "titanic gust of slashing wind picked me up bodily and hurled me against the dining room buffet forty feet distant."

Fearing that the house would collapse at any instant, Leo led his family to the laundry room, where he and Deanie put the kids in two large, slate washtubs and covered them with pillows. Looking out of "the yawning window frames east and west, we could see the tall Australian pines twisting, writhing and tumbling before the rushing wall of wind. The air was streaked with garbage cans, automobile tops, doghouses, furniture, and parts of buildings."

A little after noon on Sunday, as the winds lessened, the Reardon family left the relative safety of the laundry room and walked through the remnants of their house. It presented, Leo said, "a scene of sickening desolation." They gathered some clothes and began the long walk to the Everglades Hotel in Miami, where they took a room. Along the way, Leo recorded the sights and sounds. "Few people were to be seen. . . . those we did see were either laughing hysterically or weeping. . . . [in Miami] whole sides of apartment blocks had been torn away, disclosing semi-naked men and women moving dazedly about the ruins of their homes. . . . Ambulances rushed in every direction, their wailing sirens reminiscent of the storm. There's a boy covered with blood running blindly across the street. Where are his parents?"

EVEN COASTAL COMMUNITIES 25–30 miles north of Miami suffered mightily, having been hammered by the very powerful right side of the hurricane. Many people there had poignant stories to share. In Hollywood, a young man who had worked for months preparing his bungalow for his new bride proudly welcomed her to their finished home on Friday, September 17, the night the hurricane hit. Unfortunately, the house was not strong enough to withstand the storm, and when it came tumbling down, it crushed her to death. Rescuers found the husband the next morning. He had three broken ribs, a fractured arm, and a broken heart.

A few miles to the north, in Fort Lauderdale, another home collapsed on a married couple. The husband was pinned under the rubble, and the wife marshaled all of her strength to try to wrench him free, but couldn't do it. She knelt next to him as the water continued to rise, and held his head up to keep him from drowning. He begged her to leave him behind to save herself as the water crept higher, nearing his chin and partially submerging her. Finally, she tearfully relented and gave him a kiss goodbye, then fled to safety.

THE MARCH OF DEVASTATION did not end with Miami and its environs along the coast. The hurricane tracked northwest across the Florida peninsula, delivering an especially savage blow to the town of Moore Haven, on the southwest edge of Lake Okeechobee. Okeechobee means "big water" in the Seminole Indian language, and the lake lives up to the name. The third-largest natural freshwater lake contained entirely within the United States—the first being Lake Michigan, and the second, Lake

Detail of an 1846 map of Florida, by Joseph Goldsborough Bruff.
Below Lake Okeechobee it says "Pah-Hay-O-Kee or Grass Water Known
as the Everglades."

Iliamna in Alaska—Okeechobee covers 730 square miles, making it a little more than half the size of Rhode Island. Despite its large surface area, the lake is relatively shallow, averaging only 9 feet.

Like the other farming communities that skirted the lake, Moore Haven was built on land that used to be part of the Everglades. Labeled the "river of grass" by Marjory Stoneman Douglas, the Everglades had originally extended from the lake all the way to the tip of Florida. As water from the lake sluggishly flowed over vast expanses of saw grass down to the ocean, it deposited a layer of rich, organic sediment on the land. This *black muck*, as it was called, formed the basis for a complex ecosystem that provided valuable habitat for a great diversity of animals and plants. But developers and farmers in the early twentieth century viewed the Everglades as a fetid swamp, a vast wasteland, and a blighted landscape. To them, the black muck was agricultural gold, and they wanted the fertile land around the lake, so they took it. They cut down, burned, and plowed under the grass, and dredged canals to drain off the water. They called it *reclamation*, just another word for forcing nature to serve humankind's needs.

By 1926, Moore Haven was the largest town along the edge of Lake Okeechobee, with a population of 1,200, most of whom were farmers growing vegetables, citrus, and sugarcane. The lake would periodically overflow, and the people of Moore Haven took those events in stride, especially since the waters brought with them rich sediment that settled on the fields. But in 1922 the lake rose too much for the locals' liking. During the spring and summer, it rained nearly 100 days, lifting Okeechobee's waters 4½ feet, flooding Moore Haven and surrounding communities, and drowning their crops. To keep this from happening again, the state built a dike that ran for nearly 50 miles. It was made of mounded dirt and was 5–9 feet tall, and 20–40 feet wide at the base. The farmers replanted their fields in the following years right up to the edge and on top of the dike. At the same time, the Everglades, already gravely wounded by the spread of farms and drainage projects, took another blow, as the vital water from the lake on which it had long depended to thrive was cut off.

Neither the state nor the locals felt that this makeshift dike was sufficient. What was needed, they argued, was a more permanent, larger, and specially engineered dike that would offer true protection for decades from any wet conditions that might arise. The cost of such a scheme, however, proved prohibitive, at least to those county and state officials who would have to authorize the funding. So the plan died. In the meantime, the weather remained dry, and the dirt dike performed beautifully.

In the summer of 1926, however, the heavy rains returned, raising the lake higher, until the water was just a foot below the top of the dike. Although some people urged that the lake should be lowered by the release of water through locks that discharged into area rivers, water managers resisted, wanting to stockpile this valuable resource for drier times ahead. When the water continued to rise, however, the managers relented and opened the locks. But it was too late. The hurricane was about to hit the Florida coast.

Fred A. Flanders, the state engineer in charge of water control in and around Moore Haven, had been informed by telegram late Friday evening, September 17, that a hurricane was approaching Miami. He and his fellow townspeople were only mildly concerned, believing it wouldn't significantly impact them, since they were 90 miles from the city. But conditions worsened. While Miami was just beginning to be buffeted by hurricane-force winds, heavy rain was already falling on Lake Okeechobee. The open locks notwithstanding, the lake level started rising again, coming dangerously close to the top of the dike. Alarmed, Flanders turned on the fire siren. All of the men who came running were sent to pile sandbags on top of the dike. They worked through the night, but it was all for naught.

When the right side of the hurricane plowed into Okeechobee in the early-morning hours on Sunday, the normally docile lake was transformed into a destroyer. Hurricane-force winds generated large waves and piled up enormous quantities of water in the southwest corner of the lake, right at Moore Haven's doorstep. Overwhelmed by the great pressure, the dike breached in multiple places, and a great wall of water as high as 17 feet surged into the town.

Most of Moore Haven's houses crumpled in the face of the flood and the ferocious winds, and many residents perished in the wreckage, while others who ran outside were swept up by the torrent and drowned. Still, the majority of the town's population survived, either by clinging to floating debris or by climbing to the second floor or onto the roof of those buildings that remained standing.

After laying waste to Moore Haven, the hurricane continued across the state, exiting into the Gulf of Mexico, where it picked up energy from the warm Gulf waters and came ashore again in Pensacola, Florida, which sustained major damage from both flooding and wind. The hurricane continued inland over Alabama, Mississippi, and Louisiana, slowly disintegrating along the way.

ALTHOUGH CONTEMPORARY ACCOUNTS OFFERED different estimates for the death toll from what came to be known as the Great Miami Hurricane of 1926, a recent in-depth analysis concludes that the most reliable number is 372. That estimate includes 132 who perished in Miami and Miami Beach (about half of whom died on boats in Biscayne Bay), and 150 in and around Moore Haven. The real number of dead is probably higher than 372, given that some people were missing and not added to the total, and there were undoubtedly unidentified migrant workers in and around Moore Haven who weren't captured in any reporting. In addition to the dead, many thousands more were injured. Estimates for the cost of the hurricane also vary, but the Weather Bureau set the number at $105 million.* In the end, the storm left more than 40,000 people homeless.

For the once-thriving areas of Miami and Miami Beach, the hurricane was devastating. As historian Arva Moore Parks put it, "A lot of people who'd come down to speculate left because of the hurricane. It squished the boom and started our depression three years early." Potential buyers evaporated and real-estate values plummeted.

Miamians, however, were resilient and determined. An editorial in the *Miami Tribune* written just a day after the hurricane was a rallying cry. "Chicago had her fire, and a new Chicago was born," the piece said. "San Francisco had her earthquake and prospered thereafter. Galveston's premier position in the shipping world today is traceable to a mighty tidal

---

* A study in 2018 normalized hurricane damage from historic hurricanes using multiple methodologies. As the authors state, "A normalization estimates direct economic losses from a historical extreme event if that same event was to occur under contemporary societal conditions" (in other words, if the Great Miami Hurricane had taken place in the second decade of the twenty-first century instead of in 1926). The main methodology employed "adjusts historical loss data for inflation, per-capita wealth and the population of affected counties." This analysis establishes the Great Miami Hurricane as the most damaging hurricane between 1900 and 2017, resulting in "$236 billion [of normalized damage] in 2017." Jessica Weinkle, Chris Landsea, Douglas Collins, Rade Musulin, Ryan P. Crompton, Philip J. Klotzbach, and Roger A. Pielke Jr., "Normalized Hurricane Damage in the United States: 1900–2017," *Nature Sustainability* (December 2018), 808–13.

wave that almost annihilated that island city. Adversity struck those cities with such intensity that it seemed their difficulties were insurmountable." And just as those cities would bounce back, so, too, would theirs. The editorialist urged his fellow Miamians to "look bravely to the future. That is the spirit of Miami, out of which a new city will arise to face whatever storms the future shall bring."

The city did rebound eventually. In the near term, the University of Miami, which welcomed its first-ever class of students in the fall of 1926, decided to name its football team the Hurricanes in honor of the storm that had just blown through. Continuing the theme, the university chose the white ibis as its official mascot, a nod to the ibis's reputation of being the first bird to take shelter from an oncoming hurricane, and the first to return after it has passed.

The people of Moore Haven, with the help of the military, also began to recover. It was a gruesome task. It took weeks for the water to finally recede, while unsanitary conditions and fears of spreading disease caused the National Guard to order all residents to leave the area until they could complete the initial cleanup. Bodies were everywhere—in the fields, floating in the lake, and scattered throughout the saw-grass swamps. Many of the corpses were virtually unrecognizable, on account of decay and visits by animals that feasted on the dead.

When the beleaguered residents of Moore Haven returned, they built new houses and repaired the few that were left standing. They threw a party on Christmas Day to relieve stress and to usher in a return to normalcy. In subsequent years, they replanted their crops and looked to the repaired dike as their protection from the lake, hoping it would never be so tested again. Unfortunately, another hurricane hit, this time even closer to home.

THE FIRST SIGN OF what would later morph into the Lake Okeechobee Hurricane of 1928 came on Sunday, September 9, when the SS *Commack* recorded a lowering barometer and gale-force winds (39–54 mph) about 600 miles east of Barbados. From that point on, this "tropical disturbance of considerable intensity," as the Associated Press soon dubbed it, continued to strengthen and march in a northwesterly direction. On September 12, having progressed from powerful tropical storm to full-fledged hurricane, it battered Guadeloupe, leaving the French outpost in ruins, with a death toll perhaps as high as 1,000. Next in line was the island of Montserrat, where more than forty people died. After that, St. Croix in the US Virgin Islands was struck. While only a handful of people there died, virtually all of the buildings were damaged or destroyed.

On September 13 the hurricane deluged Puerto Rico with up to 25 inches of rain. A storm surge and 160-mph winds decimated almost every building on the island, and much of its infrastructure. At least 300 people died, with some estimates going much higher, and roughly 700,000 people were left homeless. The cost of the damage was estimated to exceed $80 million. In Puerto Rico this storm is known as the San Felipe Segundo Hurricane, and as such it is the first known Category 5 hurricane to have made landfall in the United States, and one of only five such massive hurricanes known to have hit the country since record keeping began in 1851.*

After the hurricane left Puerto Rico, the Weather Bureau forecast that it would travel toward the Bahamas but almost certainly curve or arc, missing Florida, and instead head in a northeasterly direction, either up the coast or into the North Atlantic. It did, in fact, smash into the Turks and Caicos islands, and it also devastated much of the island Eleuthera in the Bahamas. But in the evening of Saturday, September 15, the Weather Bureau started hedging its bets. Meteorologists were now saying it was likely that after the storm passed slightly to the north of Nassau early on Sunday, the outer edges of the hurricane would graze the southeast coast of Florida with gale-force winds. On Sunday, however, the situation drastically changed.

New analysis indicated that the hurricane would not curve, but instead barrel straight into Florida early that evening, coming ashore near Jupiter, just north of Palm Beach. The bureau telegraphed an urgent message to the Miami and Palm Beach stations, ordering that hurricane warnings be hoisted at 10:30 a.m. from Miami to Daytona, and that word of the impending strike be shared far and wide. At 1:00 p.m. the bureau sent out an updated alert, predicting that landfall would come not in the evening, but that afternoon.

---

* The other four are the Labor Day Hurricane of 1935, which struck the Florida Keys; Camille, which plowed into Louisiana in 1969; Andrew, which hit southeastern Florida in 1992; and Michael, which came ashore on the Florida Panhandle in 2018.

Station managers did their best to alert area newspapers and radio stations of the threat, with limited effect. Newspapers had already come out with their morning editions, which shared the now old information that the Florida coast would likely receive only a glancing blow. Although some radio stations broadcast the news, personal radios were still a relatively new and expensive prospect, so very few Floridians had one. Nevertheless, quite a few people along the coast did receive warning that a hurricane was coming, either directly from the radio, or via informal phone trees and word of mouth. But by the time the message spread, there was not much locals could do, since the edge of the hurricane had already arrived.

Not long after the 1:00 p.m. update, strong winds began buffeting Palm Beach. By 7:00 p.m., when the eye was overhead, the barometer had sunk to 27.43. That was 0.18 inch lower than the bottom reached during the Great Miami Hurricane of 1926, and the lowest pressure ever recorded up to that point for a hurricane in the United States. The storm continued inland in a westerly direction, traveling at about 15 mph.

The storm was many hundreds of miles wide, generating powerful winds felt from Key West to Jacksonville. Damage along the coast was extensive from Pompano to Jupiter, with the wealthy enclave of Palm Beach and the more working-class West Palm Beach taking the worst beating. Maximum sustained wind speeds were officially measured at 145 mph, making it a strong Category 4 hurricane. Although damage along the coast was widespread and at least twenty-six people died, the true tragedy of this hurricane came later, when it slammed into Lake Okeechobee.

THE DEVASTATION IN MOORE HAVEN as a result of the Great Miami Hurricane of 1926 had spurred renewed calls to improve the dike system surrounding the lake. Representatives from area towns appealed to the state legislature to fund the project, but the bills proposed were repeatedly voted down. The hurricane of 1926 was part of the reason for this inaction because the storm's impact on Florida's economy helped tip the state into a deep recession. Money was scarce, and fixing the lake's dikes was low on the list of priorities. And as memories of the 1926 hurricane faded, the urgency of the project receded as well. But Lake Okeechobee remained a ticking time bomb, and on the evening of September 16, 1928, it exploded.

After leaving the coast, the hurricane made a beeline for the lake, some 40 miles inland. It had been an exceptionally wet summer, raising water levels similar to those reached just before the hurricane of 1926. This time, however, the winds that descended on the lake were far more powerful than those that had struck it two years earlier. This was no glancing blow, but rather a head-on assault.

Traveling over flat, sparsely settled, and wet, marshy ground, the hurricane weakened only slowly as it approached. Although anemometers at two federal research stations along the lake's edge blew away early on, when the wind was a mere 75 mph, it was later estimated that winds ultimately surpassed 120 mph.

Fortunately, some people around the lake were able to prepare for the onslaught because they had heard the warnings earlier in the day on the radio, or had received telephone calls from the coast. For most area residents, though, the hurricane came as a complete surprise. This was especially true for the thousands of black migrant workers who had come from other southern states and the Caribbean to plant and pick the crops, and who lived in ramshackle houses isolated from the outside world.

Just as with the 1926 hurricane, the wind piled up the lake's water, but this time the major flash points were in the southern and southeastern parts of the lake, not the southwest where Moore Haven was located. Roughly 22 miles of the dike in this area was either completely or partly breached, sending a flood of water more than 20 feet high at many places into the neighboring towns of Lake Harbor, Belle Glade, South Bay, Chosen, and Pahokee.

In her classic 1937 novel *Their Eyes Were Watching God*, Zora Neale Hurston described this elemental force of nature in especially memorable terms: "The monstropolous beast had left his bed. The two hundred miles an hour wind had loosed his chains. He seized hold of his dikes and ran forward until he met the quarters; uprooted them like grass and rushed on after his supposed-to-be conquerors, rolling the dikes, rolling the houses, rolling the people in the houses along with other timbers. The sea was walking the earth with a heavy heel."

Even before the dike gave way, the wild waters of the lake were claiming victims. Late Sunday afternoon, the residents of Torry, a small island near the southern shore of Okeechobee, were warned of the coming hurricane and were preparing to return to the mainland via the causeway, but they missed their window for escape. The lake's surging waters had already blocked their exit. Twenty-three of those who had attempted to flee then rushed to a local packinghouse, where they scampered on top of tractors and crates to keep dry. As the water rose, they climbed all the way to the rafters, where they placed boards on top of the roof ties to create platforms to sit on. According to one witness, the wind-driven rain pelted the iron roof with such fury that it made noise like "a hundred fire-hose streams."

Toppled trees slammed into the packinghouse, forming a dam that the wind and waves rammed against the building's side, which ultimately gave way under the strain. All twenty-three people within tumbled into the water, as the building crashed down on their heads. In the end, only thirteen survived. One of the most heartrending deaths was that of the youngest of Ralph Cherry's five boys. Able to extricate himself from the building's wreckage, Ralph held on to the boy with one arm, while grabbing the branch of a cypress tree with the other. As he desperately tried to gain better purchase on the limb, a piece of floating wood hit him, causing him to lose his grip on both the branch and his son. Ralph swam to a nearby house, where he remained until the storm passed, but his son was swept away.

A few hours later, the dikes began to crumble, and in the towns ringing the southern and southeastern shores of the lake, similarly dreadful scenes played out. As the wind screamed and the waters rose, people took refuge in any and all types of buildings, many of which succumbed to the elements. Roofs were lifted into the air, walls collapsed, and entire houses were wrenched from their foundations.

Near Pahokee, for example, all but one of farmer Charles Moran's nearly sixty workers drowned when their living quarters were washed away. Robert Calhoun, the lone survivor, later recalled the horror he had witnessed when four entire families—a total of twenty-one people—perished. "I could hear the women and children scream as the water started rising. Some of the older children were holding these youngsters. Their cries grew terrible as the houses started to fall and the water rose. I heard the older children call to their parents that they could not hold the babies longer. Gradually the cries stopped one by one and there was no screaming. They must have drowned."

———

*At Belle Glade, loading the bodies of those who had perished
in the Lake Okeechobee Hurricane of 1928.*

WHILE THE ULTIMATE COST of what later became known as the Lake
Okeechobee Hurricane was about $75 million, the death toll is subject
to debate. The Red Cross's number was 1,836. Contemporary articles
in Florida newspapers claimed the number of deaths to be in the neighborhood of 2,200–2,300. More recent and persuasive estimates place the
number at 2,500–3,000. Whatever the overall number, one thing not in
dispute is that the vast majority of the victims were in the vicinity of Lake
Okeechobee. As one of the survivors in Belle Glade said the day after the
hurricane, "Ugly death was simply everywhere."

As one would expect in America at this time, and especially in the
South, rescue efforts before and after the hurricane were plagued by racism. For example, when South Bay businessman Frank Schuster heard
that the hurricane was heading toward Okeechobee, he jumped into his
car and made multiple trips in and around his town "for the purpose of
collecting *white residents* and moving them to a large barge," whereby 211
people were saved.

After the hurricane passed, the task of disposing of the dead was overwhelming and nauseating, similar to the 1900 Galveston Hurricane's aftermath. A number of black men were forced, often at gunpoint as had been
the case in Galveston, to aid in gathering and burying bodies. One of them,
Coot Simpson, was shot and killed by a National Guardsman under sus-

picious circumstances. There are multiple stories about exactly what happened. A version told by some of Simpson's relatives claimed that he was one of those rounded up in West Palm Beach to help collect the dead, and after working for a few days he said he wanted to go back home. The guardsman said he couldn't leave, and when Simpson went to find the foreman of the work detail to let him know his intentions, the guardsman shot him. In another version, Simpson refused to go with the guardsman and then attacked him with a bottle, but was shot down. Whatever really happened, the local newspapers reported that Simpson had attacked the guardsman, who claimed he acted in self-defense. During the brief inquest that followed, the jury determined it was, in fact, a case of self-defense, and the court freed the guardsman on the grounds that his action was a justifiable homicide.

Most of the dead were either burned in place or buried in mass graves around the lake, the largest being at Port Macaya, where, according to one estimate, as many as 1,600 bodies were interred, although some have argued that that number is much too high. In addition, many hundreds of bodies, stacked like cordwood, were loaded onto trucks and buried in West Palm Beach, where the racial divide was especially stark. The 69 white victims, most of them in coffins, were interred in a mass grave at the whites-only Woodlawn Cemetery. For twelve to twenty-four hours before burial, people were given a chance to inspect the bodies in order to identify their loved ones, and the grave site was identified with a communal tombstone. The 674 black victims, in contrast, were given no coffins and were placed in a large trench dug beside the city's incinerator, at Tamarind Avenue and Twenty-Fifth Street, a location long used as a pauper's burial ground. People had no grace period to search for their kin. Although a few of the black victims were identified with toe tags, most were not, and all of them were pitched into the trench and sprinkled with lime. When the trench was covered over, no headstone or marker was erected to memorialize the dead—maintaining, in death, the segregation and injustice that these men and women had suffered in life.

On September 30, 1928, West Palm Beach's mayor, Vincent Oaksmith, ordered all workers at the two mass grave sites to cease their activities for an hour to allow for ceremonial services. Five thousand white mourners showed up at Woodlawn, while 3,000 black mourners went to the Tamarind Avenue site. At the latter, Mary McLeod Bethune, a black educator and activist best known for founding Bethune-Cookman University at

Daytona Beach, participated in the service that was organized by the area's black churches. Reflecting on that experience, she later wrote, "Our hearts were torn at the sight of the one large mound containing the hundreds of bodies of men, women and children. Those who had been spared stood with tear-stained cheeks, wringing their hands, because many of them had lost entire families, or many, many members of their families had been taken. The sadness of this scene fell upon us like a pall."

Funeral service at Woodlawn Cemetery in West Palm Beach
in the aftermath of the Lake Okeechobee Hurricane of 1928.

It would take another seventy-three years for the city to attempt any reparation for the injustice done to the black victims. In 2001, after years of lobbying by local activists, the city of West Palm Beach and the Florida Department of State finally placed a historic marker at the site of the mass burial site. The following year, the site was listed on the National Register of Historic Places.

THE BREACHING OF THE Lake Okeechobee dike during the hurricane and the tragedy that ensued were enough to convince the federal and state governments to fund a massive construction project. The new earthen dike completed by the US Army Corps of Engineers in 1938 was 85 miles long, 34–38 feet high, 125–150 feet wide at the base, 10–30 feet wide at the top, and punctuated by numerous drainage canals, hurricane gates, and locks. Since that time, the dike, christened the Herbert Hoover Dike in the 1960s, has been heightened and lengthened to 143 miles, so that it now encompasses nearly the entire lake. Thus far, the dike has withstood many storms, but none of the magnitude of the 1928 hurricane. What would happen if such a hurricane slammed into Lake Okeechobee today is unknown, although the hope is that the dike would prevent another catastrophe.

LIKE A HURRICANE, the Great Depression came roaring ashore in the United States with the stock market crash on October 29, 1929, forever immortalized as Black Tuesday. Tens of billions in value simply vanished, wiping out the investments of millions of people. Although some believed that this precipitous sell-off would soon be followed by a rapid rebound, the latter failed to materialize. The US economy went into freefall, and by 1933, 15 million Americans, or roughly 15 percent of the workforce, were unemployed; nearly half the banks had failed; and not only economic but also mental depression had a firm grip on the nation. Bankruptcies were commonplace, suicides spiked, and long bread lines popped up in cities and towns large and small. The hit tune on the radio was E. Y. "Yip" Harburg and Jay Gorney's "Brother, Can You Spare a Dime?" which perfectly captured the national mood and became the Depression's mournful anthem.

Despite the Depression, the government did not grind to a halt. It ramped up as never before, as the buoyant and confident President Franklin Delano Roosevelt used old and new federal agencies to nudge the economy back on track. His administration also searched for ways to make the government more efficient and effective, and the Weather Bureau's hurricane operations benefited from this approach.

In 1933, Roosevelt tasked the newly created Science Advisory Board, under the National Research Council, with reporting on ways in which government science activities could be improved to better serve the public. The board's analysis found the Weather Bureau's hurricane forecasting program to be severely wanting—a perspective that was wholeheartedly

President Franklin Delano Roosevelt, December 1933.

endorsed by the bureau's chief, Willis R. Gregg, who labeled the program "sadly sketchy." Among the board's most urgent suggestions were to increase the number of daily hurricane advisories from two to four, and to focus more on long-range forecasting.

The impetus for change received a major boost while the board was developing its recommendations, because 1933 was a banner year for tropical storms and hurricanes in the Atlantic. Twenty-one were officially recognized, including five hurricanes that hit the American mainland. Many of the Weather Bureau's forecasts for these storms were inaccurate, and as a result, the public began clamoring for change.

The following year, another event occurred that further underscored the need for a new approach. Early on a Sunday in late August, the forecaster at bureau headquarters in Washington, DC, issued a hurricane warning for the Galveston area. He then left the office, planning to return in the evening when the next forecast was due. In the meantime, people in Galveston were becoming agitated, especially since, according to the morning advisory, the hurricane should have already arrived, yet the skies were a brilliant blue and there were no clouds on the horizon. Still wary of the approaching storm, a local chamber of commerce wired headquarters for an update. The response was a note from the map plotter, who replied perhaps a bit too truthfully, "Forecaster on golf course—unable to contact." As one observer noted, "In Galveston, the weather remained quiet, but temperatures in the Chamber of Commerce rose rapidly." Ultimately, this relatively minor hurricane only grazed the coast of Texas, to the southwest of Galveston.

By the time the Science Advisory Board sent its recommendations to Roosevelt in October 1934, the Weather Bureau had added a few of its own, and when Congress took up the issue of reform in 1935, it appropriated $80,000 to implement a wide range of improvements to the hurricane program. Under the reorganization to take effect on July 1, 1935, more money was invested in the science of forecasting, while headquarters was stripped of the responsibility for issuing hurricane warnings, except when a storm moved north of latitude 35° north, approximately the location of Cape Hatteras. To cover the rest of the coast, three new hurricane forecasting centers were established, each responsible for a different area: San Juan would issue forecasts for the Caribbean Sea and islands east and south of Cuba; New Orleans would cover the Gulf Coast west of Apalachicola, Florida; and Jacksonville* would be responsible for the remaining parts of the Atlantic, Caribbean Sea, and Gulf of Mexico.† The rationale behind this move was that regional meteorologists were closer to the action and had valuable local knowledge, so they were in the best position to monitor tropical disturbances and issue hurricane forecasts and warnings.

Furthermore, hurricane forecasts and warnings were to be issued four times a day, so as to give the public more real-time information about impending threats. And when a hurricane was about to make landfall, warnings would be issued every hour. Finally, at New Orleans and Jacksonville, forecasters would be on duty around the clock to better monitor evolving situations, and a greater effort would be made to gather additional observations from foreign stations located throughout the West Indies.

These changes, and the newfound sense of purpose resulting from the reorganization, caused the Weather Bureau to become overly confident. Right after the reorganization went into effect, the bureau launched an advertising blitz to convince coastal residents that their government

---

* In 1943, the hurricane forecasting center at Jacksonville was moved to Miami.

† In 1940, a fourth hurricane forecasting center was established in Boston, taking over from headquarters the responsibility of forecasting hurricanes and issuing warnings for storms traveling north of latitude 35° north.

weather watchdogs had solved the problem of hurricanes making a surprise landfall and catching people off guard. In newspapers around the nation, the bureau's pitch told readers, "Uncle Sam has perfected his hurricane service for this area, perfected it to the extent of putting a decided crimp in their stealthy approach."

To put it bluntly, that was hyperbole and wishful thinking. Although the organizational changes were most welcome and certainly an improvement over the past, they were not earth-shattering, nor did they suddenly transform the Weather Bureau into an unerring hurricane forecasting machine capable of accurately tracking storms and telling the public whether and exactly where they would land (even today, such feats of precision are beyond the reach of meteorologists). In the mid- to late 1930s, determining what hurricanes were doing at sea before they came ashore remained pretty much a mystery, severely limiting forecasting capability, as two exceptionally powerful tempests would soon prove.

THE FIRST BEGAN AS a minor atmospheric disturbance north and east of the Turks and Caicos islands, noticed initially on Friday, August 30, 1935. The next day, the bureau grew more concerned. Off Long Island in the Bahamas, the disturbance had become more organized and was now a tropical depression. Although the storm was small in stature, the wind was approaching gale force near its center. Warnings were raised in Florida from Fort Pierce to Miami, and vessels traveling in the area were warned to beware of rough seas. The storm was heading, the bureau said, toward the general vicinity of southern Florida and the Florida Keys.

The Keys are a roughly 200-mile-long coral archipelago that includes 1,700 islands curving in a graceful arc from Virginia Key off Miami through Key West to the Dry Tortugas. The remnants of ancient coral reefs and sandbars, the keys are bordered on one side by the Atlantic Ocean, and on the other by Biscayne Bay and Florida Bay, a shallow estuary connected to the Gulf of Mexico. Barely peeking out from the water, virtually all of the land on the Keys rises less than 5 feet above sea level, making it particularly vulnerable to the angry moods of the ocean, especially hurricanes.

Key West, the southernmost city in the contiguous United States, is located at the bottom of the archipelago on the edge of the Straits of Florida, which separates the Keys from Cuba, a mere 90 miles away. The tropical disturbance approaching at the end of August 1935 got the attention of Key West's most illustrious resident, Ernest Hemingway. He first visited Key West in the summer of 1928 at the recommendation of his friend, American novelist John Dos Passos, who said that the town was "like no other place in Florida," and "something seen in a dream."

Already a famous author by this time, having published *The Sun Also Rises* in 1926, Hemingway spent much of his first summer on the island completing his next major work, *A Farewell to Arms*. In subsequent summers he returned and fell in love with Key West. The fishing, the balmy weather, and the relaxed lifestyle all appealed to him. "It's the best place I've ever been any time anywhere," he wrote to a friend, "flowers, tamarind trees, guava trees, coconut palms. . . . Got tight last night on absinthe and did knife tricks." In 1931, Hemingway and his second wife, Pauline Pfeiffer, purchased a stately French Colonial home in the oldest part of town, right across from the Key West Lighthouse. He lived there until 1939, adding to his literary pedigree such works as the short story "The Snows of Kilimanjaro" and the novel *To Have and Have Not*. Ultimately, these and other later works, such as *The Old Man and the Sea*, earned Hemingway the Nobel Prize in Literature in 1954.

Ernest Hemingway in 1939.

After writing until the early evening on Saturday, August 31, 1935, Hemingway retired to his porch to drink and peruse the local paper. When he read the Weather Bureau's warning that there was a storm heading in his direction, his mood soured. "Work is off until it is past," he would later write, "and you are angry and upset because you were going well." He took out the September storm chart for the Keys, which had the tracks of all the hurricanes that had afflicted the region since 1900, and made his own calculations of where this new storm might travel in the coming days, based on the information he could glean from the bureau's advisory. Concluding that if the storm hit Key West, it would likely not do so until Monday, Hemingway spent Sunday and early Monday preparing his house and his beloved 38-foot fishing boat, *Pilar*, for the potential blow. Meanwhile, about 70 miles away, slightly to the north and east, hundreds of World War I veterans were also thinking about the storm.

THE VETERANS WERE AT three government work camps in the Florida Keys' village of Islamorada. Camps 3 and 5 were on Lower Matecumbe Key, and camp 1 on Windley Key.* The reason the men were there traced back to a promise the nation had made to veterans of World War I, known as the Great War. In 1924, Congress had rewarded the veterans for their valiant service with certificates or bonuses—$1 for each day of service on the home front, and $1.25 for each day overseas—that were redeemable in 1945 for up to $1,000. Then, the Great Depression intervened, knocking many of those veterans, who were already having a difficult time reintegrating into society, back on their heels. Hoping for compassion and a helping hand, a group of roughly 15,000–20,000 veterans and many of their families—the so-called Bonus Army—marched to Washington, DC, in the summer of 1932, demanding that the federal government immediately give them their money.

Although President Herbert Hoover obstinately refused to meet with the marchers, congressional leaders took up a bill to pay the debt. While that bill was being debated, the veterans lived along the banks of the Anacostia River in abandoned government buildings and a hastily erected shantytown of tents and shacks. The bill passed the House but was voted

---

* Camps 2 and 4 were in St. Petersburg and Clearwater, Florida, respectively.

Bonus Army camping out near the Capitol
on July 13, 1932.

down in the Senate. Disconsolate at this loss, many of the veterans returned home, while thousands remained behind to continue their vigil near the Capitol Building, with some of them vowing to stay until 1945 to get paid.

Hoover viewed the Bonus Army as a potential threat to the capital, even though the veterans had been remarkably peaceful in pursuing their demands. The only real flare-up came on July 28, when local police evicted veterans from the old National Guard Armory. In the brief melee that ensued, veterans threw bricks and punches, and the police, in turn, roughed up many of them, shooting and killing two in the process. Fearing an escalation of tensions, and possibly more bloodshed, Hoover quickly ordered Douglas MacArthur, the chief of staff of the army, to use military force to drive the veterans from DC.

Hoover wanted the troops to "use all humanity consistent with the due execution of the order," but the imperious MacArthur had other ideas. Despite virtually no hard evidence to support his deluded and paranoid perspective, MacArthur believed that a significant number of communists, criminals, and other agitators intent on leading a revolution against the government had infiltrated the Bonus Army and were about to carry out their dastardly plan. To guarantee that this wouldn't happen, MacArthur intended to react with overwhelming force. What followed was not a battle but a rout. In the early evening of July 28, hundreds of mounted cavalrymen with sabers drawn, and soldiers whose guns were fixed with bayonets, backed up by tanks and machine gunners, descended on the veterans, lobbing tear gas and grenades to clear the way. By midnight, the last remnants of the Bonus Army had been run out of the capital, and their shantytown set ablaze.

That scene, of America's military attacking fellow Americans—in the nation's capital, no less—which was recounted in newspapers and in newsreels at movie theaters throughout the country, enraged the public and helped secure Hoover's blowout loss to Roosevelt in the fall election. According to Supreme Court justice Felix Frankfurter, when Roosevelt heard on the radio about the attack, he turned to his friend and said, "Well, Felix, this will elect me."

Roosevelt, however, soon had his own Bonus Army to contend with. A few months after his inauguration, 3,000 veterans returned to the capital to resume their protest, and in subsequent years more veterans arrived. Instead of giving them their bonus, Roosevelt gave them jobs. The philosophical motivation behind the president's action was neatly summed up by his close adviser, and the administrator of the Federal Emergency Relief Administration (FERA), Harry Hopkins, who said, "Give a man a dole and you save his body and destroy his spirit. Give him a job and pay him an assured wage, and you save both the body and the spirit." Roosevelt placed most of the veterans in the newly created Civilian Conservation Corps, where they were sent nationwide to work on a great variety of conservation projects. The remaining veterans were shipped off to FERA work camps with state oversight, in South Carolina and Florida. About 700 of them ended up in the camps in the Florida Keys, where their job was to help save Key West by building a highway to replace Mr. Flagler's railroad.

———

WHEN HENRY FLAGLER STEPPED off the train in Key West on the morning of January 22, 1912, he was exceedingly happy. His triumphal visit celebrated the completion of the "railroad across the ocean." Critics had long derided his ambitious scheme to connect Miami and Key West by rail, calling it "Flagler's Folly." But the industrialist's tens of millions of dollars, and the skill of the thousands of men he employed, had accomplished this gargantuan feat, creating what many called "The Eighth Wonder of the World." Flagler believed that the railroad would succeed brilliantly by becoming the major conduit for goods and produce from Central and South America to enter the commercial bloodstream of the United States.

But Flagler's gamble didn't pay off, although he wasn't around to see the railroad's demise, having died on May 20, 1913, well before things started to fall apart. The expected flood of cargo never materialized, and the middling passenger traffic did little to offset that loss. The Great Depression made things worse. Key West became a depreciating asset, going from a population of about 20,000 in 1910 to fewer than 13,000 in 1930. The increasingly decrepit and insolvent railroad had gone into receivership in 1931, and in 1934 the city of Key West declared bankruptcy. Just as Key West was figuratively sinking under the waves, the federal government threw it a lifeline. Hoping to kick-start the city's faltering economy, FERA decided to build a highway from Miami to Key West.

Much of the highway was already in place, in the form of local roads and bridges traversing the Upper and Lower Keys. But right in the middle was a large gap. People driving to Key West reached the end of the road in Lower Matecumbe Key, where they could catch a car ferry to transport them the next 35 miles to No Name Key, at which point the road picked up again, taking them to their destination. Slow, unreliable, and small, the ferry was a huge bottleneck to traffic heading down to the Lower Keys. FERA planned to eliminate the bottleneck by building a road to close the gap. Once the road was complete, FERA believed that tourists would flock to Key West and help propel it out of bankruptcy. Laborers were needed to build the road, and that's where the veterans came in.

The 700 or so veterans at the camps on Lower Matecumbe and Windley Keys, who earned about $1 a day, were a motley group to be sure. Having fought in the most brutal and deadly war the world had ever known, many of them suffered from what at the time was called *shell shock*—what we refer to today as post-traumatic stress disorder. Beaten down by their own demons and the pitiless economic realities of the Depression, many of the veterans turned to drink to dull their pain and often spent their salary on liquor at the camps' canteens, where drunken brawls were common. While "some were hard, useless characters," as Marjory Stoneman Douglas said, others were just doing their best to get by. One of the camp administrators who worked closely with the veterans said, "Sure, there were a few who were problems. But most of them were good men."

The camps themselves were shoddy affairs, especially the living quarters. The veterans' bunks were tents or hastily built, simple wood-frame shacks, 20 feet on a side, with wooden roofs covered with tar paper or canvas. Most were only slightly elevated off the ground, on cinder blocks or wooden pilings, while some were bolted to coral outcroppings or held in place by sand mounded around their edges. Other buildings, such as the canteens, mess halls, and the makeshift hospital, were not much sturdier, and all of them were located very close to the shoreline, which is hardly surprising, given that the Keys they were on are extremely narrow—for the most part far less than a half mile wide, with many stretches just a few hundred feet across.

Not far from the veterans' camps lived the locals, or Conchs (pronounced "konks"), as people born in the Keys were often called on account of the ubiquity of the queen conch (*Strombus gigas*) shell in coastal waters, as well as its importance as an icon and a source of food. The number of Conchs in the area was fairly small. Between Key West and mainland Florida, there were fewer than 1,500. They were a tough, proud, and resilient people who had an often uneasy coexistence with the veterans, but for the most part the two groups got along. The Conchs were amazed at the flimsiness of the veterans' bunks, remarking that they would never survive a severe storm, much less a hurricane. As it turned out, even the locals' significantly more solid homes were in danger as well.

THE CAMPS WERE QUIETER than normal that weekend in late August and early September 1935, since Monday was Labor Day and a few hundred of the veterans had gone to Miami to watch a baseball game. Ray Sheldon, the camps' director, kept an eye on the approaching storm, following the Weather Bureau's reports and checking barometers for movement. On Saturday, August 31, there were some worrying signs. Many of the Conchs started boarding up their houses, and some local fishermen saw fleets of tarpon swimming between the Keys, heading from the Atlantic into the bay—a retreat often seen when bad weather was on the way. Colonel Ed Sheeran, the head of road construction, told Sheldon the Conchs were worried that the approaching storm was a hurricane. Sheeran urged Sheldon to order a relief train from Miami to evacuate the camps, but Sheldon, noting that the barometer registered a normal reading, about 30 inches, said such action was not warranted. Anyway, the storm was far off, so Sheldon felt he still had plenty of time to change his mind.

On Sunday morning, the sun shone and winds were light. As the day wore on and night fell, however, conditions deteriorated. Winds picked up, rain fell intermittently, barometers began inching down, and the telltale deep swells heralding the approach of a hurricane began hitting the coast. Weather Bureau reports from Jacksonville reiterated the warnings and said that the very compact storm was south of the Bahamas' Andros Island, but it had grown in strength, possibly with hurricane-force winds near its center, and was heading toward the Straits of Florida. The bureau ordered storm-warning flags to be raised from Miami to Fort Pierce, and urged vessels around the Keys to head either to port or away from the area.

The bad weather was the talk of the camps. Most of the veterans had never witnessed a major tropical storm, and they were excited about the possibility that it would turn into a hurricane. "Naturally we were all interested in seeing a hurricane or experiencing one," said one veteran from New York, "and we all hoped it would blow the mosquitoes away and cool things off." Sheldon didn't share this perspective. He knew that a hurricane could greatly damage the camps and place veterans' lives, not to mention his own, at risk. It was up to him, in conjunction with Fred Ghent, the Jacksonville-based director of Florida's veterans' work camps, to decide whether the veterans should be evacuated by train to Miami. As of Sunday evening, their answer was still "Not yet," so they went to sleep.

Overnight, the tropical storm sucked energy from the open ocean waters west of the Bahamas, which were an unusually warm 86 degrees. This infusion of raw power and a favorable atmospheric pattern caused the formerly unremarkable storm to turn into a tightly wound yet incredibly strong hurricane. Since there were no ships or weather stations in the area, this violent transformation went unnoticed, and the Weather Bureau remained oblivious to the oncoming threat.

On Monday morning, Labor Day, the bureau came out with two more warnings that were similar to the one issued the night before and gave no indication of the rapid intensification that had taken place. According to the bureau, the storm was now 200 miles east of Havana, likely with hurricane-force winds near its center, and it was still heading toward the Florida Straits, where it would possibly pass through in the next twenty-four to thirty-six hours. The bureau's new warning did, however, add another wrinkle, saying that high tides and gale-force winds should be expected throughout the Keys.

Sheldon could see that the barometer was continuing to drop, and that squalls were rolling in, but as of late morning he still didn't think the camps were in any immediate danger, *despite* the fact that the latest advisories said the entire Keys would likely experience high tides and gale-force winds. Sheldon finally spoke to Ghent at about 1:30 p.m., and while they were in the midst of deciding what to do, the radio crackled with a new Weather Bureau alert. It labeled the storm a hurricane for the first time and ordered the district of Key West to hoist the hurricane warnings. By that afternoon or evening, the alert continued, the strait should be experiencing hurricane-force winds, while the islands to the north of Key West and south of Key Largo—precisely where the camps were—would be hit by gale-force winds. This ominous news, and the hurricane warning, finally convinced Sheldon and Ghent to act. They immediately called the dispatcher at the Florida East Coast Railway and asked him to send the relief train from Miami. The dispatcher said the train should arrive at the camps around 5:00 or 5:30 p.m.

But the situation was far more serious than the alert had indicated, for the Weather Bureau's forecast was dead wrong. Although the bureau's meteorologists did not know it at the time, the hurricane was no longer heading through the strait and past the Keys. Instead, it had taken a sharp turn to the right and was at that moment on a collision course with the Lower Matecumbe and Windley Keys.

AS WORD THAT THE train was on the way spread throughout the camps, the veterans gathered critical items for the trip. While they packed and waited, the weather rapidly worsened, causing many of the veterans who had been looking forward to experiencing a hurricane to change their minds.

The barometer continued to fall, waves grew higher, squalls strengthened, and the wind rose to gale force.

In the midafternoon, the Weather Bureau received information from Havana that prompted it to radically change its forecast. Cuban meteorologists had been tracking the hurricane and were both concerned and puzzled by the Americans' predictions that the storm would continue westward through the Straits of Florida, very close to, if not hitting, Cuba. Barometers in Havana had been rising since Saturday, indicating that the hurricane was moving away from, not toward, the island. To get more data to pinpoint the storm, and to determine whether Cuba was in real danger, Cuban weather authorities asked the country's air force to send one of its planes on a reconnaissance mission. The man chosen for the task was Captain Leonard James Povey, an American test pilot and barnstormer who had been hired to reorganize and train the air force and also to serve as the personal pilot for Cuban military leader and strongman, Fulgencio Batista y Zaldívar.

Povey hopped into his 25-foot-long Curtiss Hawk II biplane, with an open cockpit, and took off in search of the hurricane, which he soon spotted. As he later told a reporter, "I was unable to fly close to the disturbance, visible to me for miles. It appeared to be a cone-shaped body of clouds, inverted, rising to an altitude of 12,000 feet. The waves in the sea below broke against each other like [they were] striking a sea wall."

Although he didn't get too near the hurricane, he was close enough to determine that it was farther north than the Americans thought. Instead of heading through the Straits of Florida, it was veering away from Cuba and approaching the Keys. Upon landing, Povey shared this information with Cuban meteorologists, who quickly relayed it to their American counterparts. As a result, the Weather Bureau issued a bulletin at 4:30 p.m. stating that the hurricane had, in fact, turned to the right and would be hitting the Keys head-on. The bureau thought that Key West was the likely target, but the veterans knew better. A half hour later, the outer bands of the hurricane arrived, with winds whipping up to 125 mph. Unfortunately, the relief train was running late.

SHELDON AND GHENT THOUGHT that their arrangement with the Florida East Coast Railway required the latter to have a train ready to go at a moment's notice during hurricane season. The railway, however, thought it had agreed to get a train ready only after receiving advance warning. So, when the dispatcher got the go-ahead from Sheldon and Ghent, he wasn't in a position to send the train right away. First he had to gather a crew, and this being a holiday weekend, that took time. It was another hour for the locomotive's boiler to build up the head of steam necessary to move the train. That was not the last of the delays. No sooner had the train pulled out of the Miami station than it had to stop at a drawbridge for about ten minutes while boats passed by. At 5:15 p.m., the train reached Homestead, the last station before the Keys. At this point, the engineer decided to reposition the engine to the rear, enabling him to back the train down to the Keys and then pull the train north again through the heavy weather that was expected. This switch took another half hour. As a result of all of these delays, it was almost 7:00 p.m. before the train finally reached Windley Key.

The engineer, J. J. Haycraft, had planned to continue to the lower camps, load veterans there, and pick up more veterans on the way back. But suddenly the train ground to a halt. An inch-thick cable from a derrick had fallen across the track between two train cars and held tight. It took about forty minutes to disentangle the train, which then chugged on. While the men had been working to remove the cable, the Weather Bureau came out with yet another advisory. Finally, it got the track correct. The hurricane, the advisory said, was approaching Upper Matecumbe Key. But the bureau's timing was off. The hurricane wasn't *approaching* the key; it was already there.

The train pulled into the station on Upper Matecumbe Key at about 8:00 p.m. When Sheldon and others began running toward it, their feet were already covered in water, but by the time they began boarding, the water was up to their waists and rising fast. Entering the locomotive's cab at about 8:20 p.m., Sheldon tried to inject some levity into the grim situation, saluting Haycraft with a jocular "You're the man we've been looking for."

Sheldon then asked Haycraft whether he thought the train could continue down the Keys to camps 3 and 5, where hundreds more veterans were waiting. Haycraft wasn't sure but said he would try. Just a few moments later, however, the train again ground to a halt. The conductor sent to investigate the matter returned with horrible news. The wind had pushed one of the train's 75-ton boxcars off the track, initiating the automatic brakes. Before they could even consider decoupling and free-

Relief train sent to pick up the veterans, shown knocked off the rails in Upper Matecumbe Key by the tremendous winds and storm surge.

ing the boxcar, the water in the engine's cab rose up to chest height, extinguishing the fire heating the boiler. Without steam, the train was not going anywhere.

A few moments after that, the train was broadsided. As one of the passengers described it, "A wall of water from 15 to 20 feet high [the storm surge] picked up our coaches and swirled them about like straws. We felt them going and I imagine everyone thought it was the end. I know I did." Only the 160-ton locomotive stayed on the tracks. Amazingly, all of the people on the train survived. Tragically, the same could not be said for the other people in and around the camps.

———

J. E. DUANE WAS a cooperative observer for the Weather Bureau and caretaker of a fishing camp on Long Key, which was only a couple of miles to the south of the veterans' camps 3 and 5 on Lower Matecumbe Key. Given this proximity, his detailed diary provides an excellent blow-by-blow account of the weather that the people in the area were experiencing during the hurricane.

At 6:45 p.m., Duane's barometer read 27.90. The wind was turning debris into missiles, including a 6×8-inch beam that flew 300 yards and clear through the walls of Duane's house, barely missing three people inside. About two hours later, the barometer stood at 27.22 as the eye arrived. During the hour-long calm, Duane and about twenty others retreated to the sturdiest cottage on the key. While the eye was overhead, Duane said, the sky was clear and the "stars [were] shining brightly, [but the] water was a terrible sight to see on the ocean side. Never will I forget the water raising—no, not a wave but looked just like a vacuum drew it right up, then let go."

The surge lifted the cottage off its foundation, and then set it down quite some distance away. A little after 10:00 p.m., just before the cottage was blasted apart by the wind and waves, Duane took one last look at the barometer, which registered 26.98 inches. As the cottage disintegrated, Duane was pitched into the water, where he grabbed onto the fronds of a coconut tree with a viselike grip. Airborne debris then knocked him unconscious, and when he awoke nearly five hours later, he was lodged in the crown of the tree some 20 feet off the ground. By 5:00 a.m. on Tuesday, the hurricane had finally passed, but gale-force winds and rain continued throughout the day.

The barometric reading of 26.98 that Duane had captured was amazing enough, but the absolute low was even more astonishing. At the diminutive Craig Key, about a mile from the veterans' camp 3, Ivar Olsen rode out the hurricane on his boat, which was tied up next to one of the railroad embankments. He watched his aneroid barometer as it sank lower and lower, finally reaching the lowest value engraved on the dial. The level indicated by the needle continued to plunge, so Olsen scratched marks in the barometer's brass case to track the fall. Olsen later gave that barometer to the Weather Bureau, and after determining that it had been properly calibrated, the bureau concluded that the pressure had dropped to 26.35 inches—still an all-time record for the lowest reading ever measured by a hurricane upon landfall on the US mainland.

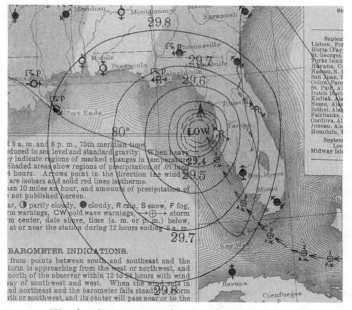

*Weather Bureau map showing the progression of
the Labor Day Hurricane of 1935 through the Florida Keys
and up the west coast of the state.*

Maximum sustained winds were 185 mph, with gusts as high as 200 mph or more, launching the storm into the hurricane hall of fame. Add to that the tremendous storm surge and massive waves, and the epic proportions of this beast reveal themselves. It was also an incredibly compact hurricane, its eye only about 6 miles in diameter, and the entire storm on the order of 50–75 miles wide.

SURVIVORS OF WHAT CAME to be known as the Labor Day Hurricane of 1935 were met with a scene on Tuesday that beggared description. Virtually every structure on Windley and on Upper and Lower Matecumbe Keys was obliterated, and hundreds of people were killed. Their contorted bodies were strewn about, many of them stripped of clothes, and some with their skin literally sandblasted away. In subsequent days, as relief and rescue crews arrived, the full scope of the tragedy came into view, and horrific stories were spread in newspapers and on the radio to the broader world.

When word of the disaster reached Hemingway, he was heartbroken, since many of the veterans were his friends. He had drunk with them plenty of times when they visited Key West on payday benders and frequented his favorite hangout, Sloppy Joe's Bar. He particularly relished swapping war stories and recalling his service driving an ambulance for the Red Cross in Italy. Since the hurricane had only grazed Key West and Hemingway's boat, *Pilar*, and his majestic house had made it through largely unscathed, he immediately volunteered to bring emergency food and medical supplies to the veterans' camps and assist in collecting the dead. He hitched a ride on one of his friend's boats, which pulled into the ferry slip on Lower Matecumbe Key early Wednesday morning.

"The brush was all brown," Hemingway observed, "as though autumn had come to these islands where there is no autumn . . . but that was because the leaves had all been blown away." The surging ocean had deposited a thick layer of sand on the island's ridge, and the enormous bridge-building equipment was all knocked on its side. "The biggest bunch of dead were in the tangled, always green but now brown, mangroves. . . . You found them everywhere and in the sun all of them were beginning to be too big for their blue jeans and jackets that they could never fill when they were on the bum and hungry."

In a letter to his editor, Maxwell Perkins, Hemingway wrote, "We were the first into Camp Five of the veterans who were working on the Highway construction. Out of 187, only 8 survived. Saw more dead then I'd seen in one place since the Lower Piave [River, in Italy] in June of 1918. . . . We made five trips with provisions for survivors to different places, but nothing but dead men to eat the grub. Max, you can't imagine it, two women, naked, tossed up into trees by the water, swollen and stinking, their breasts as big as balloons, flies between their legs. . . . [I] recognize them as the two very nice girls who ran a sandwich place and filling-station three miles from the ferry."

Other stories were equally horrific. Also on Wednesday, Dr. G. C. Franklin, who had come from Coconut Grove to help tend to the injured, took a boat to Lower Matecumbe Key. At camp 5 he came upon veteran Elmer Kressberg, who was impaled by a two-by-four that went clean through his chest, entering just under the ribs and exiting over the kidneys. Kressberg was still alive and amazingly calm, given the circumstances. Franklin told him he wanted to pull out the piece of wood and offered him a shot of morphine to dull the pain. Kressberg refused, telling the doctor it didn't matter, since he was going to die as soon as the wood was removed. What he really wanted was a last drink, and he asked for two beers, which were quickly provided. After finishing them, Kressberg said, "Now pull." The doctor did, and Kressberg died.

Survivors, too, had dreadful tales to tell. Clifton and John Russell, both part of a clan of Conchs on Upper Matecumbe Key with roots in the area reaching back to the mid-nineteenth century, had taken their families to the highest point of the island, about 12 feet above sea level. There, Clifton, his wife, and five of their children, along with John, his wife, and four of their children, piled into a hurricane shelter that the brothers had built. It proved no match for the storm, and when the surge destroyed the shelter, only the two brothers and one of Clifton's children survived. Unfortunately for the Russell clan, that was but a fraction of the horrors the day would bring. Of the more than seventy Russell family members living on Upper Matecumbe Key, only eleven made it through the hurricane alive.

Jack Clifford, a veteran from Virginia, said, "When the buildings began to crack, men ran out like scurrying rabbits, only to be picked up and blown in the air in every direction." Another veteran, from Connecticut, stated, "I would rather face machine-gun fire than go through an experience like that again."

About 1,200 people helped recover bodies. It was physically demanding, grisly, and haunting work. One of those thus engaged was Edney Parker, the constable on Upper Matecumbe Key. He had handled corpses before with stoic professionalism but, as a father of twelve, he was overcome with emotion while dealing with very young victims. "I could take out the bodies of dead men, alright," Parker said. "At Camp 5 we found 39 dead stacked by the water in a heap like you stack cordwood. But I came upon a pool where five children drowned. There was a little fellow floating face down, and I took him out. 'Why, your mama just dressed you,' I said, and I broke and cried."

Because many bodies were not recovered, and there is no way of knowing exactly how many people were in the area when the hurricane hit, estimates of the number who perished vary. The most comprehensive accounting sets the number at 485, of which 257 were veterans, while the rest were civilians who perished not only on Windley Key, and on Upper and Lower Matecumbe Keys, but also on some neighboring islands.

Although President Roosevelt originally wanted the veterans transported to Washington for burial at Arlington National Cemetery, the logistics of transporting so many putrefying bodies more than a thousand miles quashed that plan. Instead, most were cremated in the Keys, while the rest were either buried at Woodlawn Cemetery in Miami or shipped to relatives for burial. Most of the civilians were also cremated; the rest were buried in various cemeteries or turned over to relatives to lay to rest.

Almost all of the surviving veterans either were sent to Civilian Conservation Corps camps or, after being compensated for their losses, simply reentered the lives they had left behind. Their condition improved a bit in 1936, when Congress overrode a presidential veto and awarded the veter-

Inscription: "Dedicated to the memory of
the civilians and war veterans whose lives were lost
in the Hurricane of September second, 1935." Located in
Islamorada, this memorial was dedicated
on November 14, 1937.

ans of World War I their bonus nine years early. As for the Conchs who had survived, most regrouped, rebuilt, and reclaimed their lives on the Keys with which they were so intimately connected.

The hurricane put the final dagger in the railroad to Key West. Its right-of-way was sold to the state of Florida, and the road project received a new infusion of money and manpower. The completed highway down to Key West was opened to the public on March 29, 1938, and tourists followed, spurring development all along the archipelago.

After leaving the Keys, the hurricane continued into the Gulf of Mexico, paralleling the Florida coast and slowly weakening to a Category 1. It then traveled over the Florida Panhandle and into Georgia, and marched far inland as a tropical storm, finally exiting into the Atlantic near the mouth of the Chesapeake Bay. Along the way, it left a trail of floods and significant wind damage. Once back over the ocean, it strengthened into a Category 1 before fading away in the North Atlantic.

SOON AFTER THE HURRICANE left the Keys, the recriminations began. Leading the charge was Hemingway, who wrote an article with the provocative title "Who Murdered the Vets?" that appeared in the September 17, 1935, issue of *New Masses*, a Marxist magazine associated with the American Communist Party. Who, he asked, sent the war veterans "to live in frame shacks on the Florida Keys in hurricane months? Why were the men not evacuated on Sunday or, at the latest, Monday morning, when it was known there was a possibility of a hurricane striking the Keys *and evacuation was their only possible protection*? Who advised against sending the train from Miami to evacuate the veterans until four-thirty o'clock on Monday so that it was blown off the tracks before it ever reached the lower camps?" Although the article didn't accuse any specific person or organization, in a letter to Perkins, Hemingway made it perfectly clear who he thought should be blamed. "The veterans in those camps were practically murdered," he wrote. "The people in charge of the veterans [Sheldon, Ghent, and their state and federal government associates] and the Weather Bureau [for supposedly downplaying the severity of the storm] can split the responsibility between them."

There were multiple investigations to determine who was to blame for not evacuating the veterans in time—conducted by Congress, FERA, the Veterans Administration, the American Legion, and the state of Florida. They all concluded that nobody was at fault, and that the response had been as good as could be expected, given the circumstances. As the joint FERA and Veterans Administration report said, "To our mind, the catastrophe must be characterized 'as an act of God' and was by its very nature beyond the power of man or instruments at his disposal to foresee sufficiently far enough in advance to permit the taking of adequate precautions capable of preventing the death and desolation which occurred."

A second investigation launched by the Veterans Administration, however, concluded that there had been negligence, and it laid most of the blame on Sheldon and Ghent, who, it was felt, had received plenty of warning that the approaching storm would be severe, regardless of which track it took, despite the shortcomings of the Weather Bureau's advisories. The report posited that Sheldon and Ghent should have requested the relief train much earlier than they did, for that would have been the prudent thing to do. Had they done so, many lives would have been saved. Despite this rather convincing conclusion, however, nobody was formally blamed for the catastrophe or held to account.

Almost no one, other than Hemingway and a few newspapers, faulted the Weather Bureau for its forecasts and advisories, instead assuming that the bureau had done the best it could, given its limitations. Not unsurprisingly, the bureau agreed wholeheartedly with this conclusion. In its analysis of the hurricane published in December 1935, the bureau admitted that it had had a very hard time tracking the storm. "During the developing stage of the hurricane, as it was moving over remote islands and shoals of the southern Bahamas, where there were no ships or island stations to report the passage of the small vortex, the problems of accurately locating the center and its line of advance and forecasting its probable movement were extremely difficult. Nevertheless, timely and generally accurate advices were issued by the forecast center at Jacksonville." Adding to the difficulty of forecasting this hurricane was its rapid and explosive intensification—a feature of some hurricanes that even modern meteorologists are still working hard to understand and predict.

In a letter written soon after the hurricane, the chief of the Jacksonville Weather Bureau office, Walter James Bennett, offered an additional defense of the bureau's performance: "We maintain that if the storm warnings were not considered sufficient for actual evacuation, they certainly should have been sufficient for preparations to be made to evacuate, by having the train ready. Storm warnings were ordered 36 hours in advance of storm winds, and hurricane warnings at least 8 hours ahead of the arrival of the storm center." To put the bureau's forecasts in context, Bennett added, "It should be remembered that Meteorology is not an exact science and probably never will be. It is impossible to tell very far in advance just exactly where the storm center will reach land, and just exactly how severe it will be." Three years after the Great Labor Day Hurricane of 1935, another hurricane would slam into the United States and drive home the wisdom of Bennett's words.

CHAPTER 6

The Great Hurricane
of 1938

*Waves striking a seawall during the Great Hurricane
of 1938 give the appearance of geysers erupting.*

IT HAD BEEN EXCEPTIONALLY RAINY DURING THE SUMMER OF
1938 in the Northeast, but Wednesday, September 21, was shaping up to

be a nice reprieve, starting out warm and mostly sunny, promising to be a beautiful day. Despite the pleasing weather, however, the news was full of storm clouds on the horizon. A little more than a week earlier, announcers at CBS Radio had set the stage for the German chancellor's address to a Nazi rally in Nuremburg by telling their listeners, "The entire civilized world is anxiously awaiting the speech of Adolf Hitler, whose single word may plunge all of Europe into another World War."

In the ensuing days, the United States and the rest of the world got healthy doses of Hitler's vitriol and his ruthless determination to take back the Sudetenland, a part of Czechoslovakia with 3 million ethnic Germans that had been stripped from Austria by the Treaty of Saint-Germain at the end of World War I. Readers of the *New York Times* on September 21 were given page after page of unnerving reports and commentary about Hitler's aggressive stance and his ultimatum that Czechoslovakia turn over the region, or else he would take it by force. Czechoslovakia's purported allies, France and England, were actively debating whether to abandon their pledge to defend Czechoslovakia against foreign aggression—in this case from Germany—and later that day they did just that, siding with Hitler. This move paved the way for the Munich Agreement on September 30, in which England and France essentially gave the Sudetenland to Germany. Lauding the agreement, English prime minister Neville Chamberlain proclaimed that it had achieved "peace for our time," a naïve boast that proved to be grossly untrue.

After wading through twenty-six pages of international and domestic news in the September 21 issue of the *New York Times*, readers in New York and New England would have seen, nearly hidden in the bottom left-hand corner of page 27, a short article on an approaching hurricane, which had been born a few weeks earlier in Africa. On September 4, a French weather observer at the Bilma oasis in northeastern Niger noted a slight disturbance in the atmosphere, perhaps as mundane as shifting winds or a thunderstorm. Although no one realized it at the time, that disturbance became an easterly wave that morphed into a Cape Verde–type hurricane, which marched across the Atlantic, arousing the attention of meteorologist Grady Norton.

NORTON HAD JOINED THE US Weather Bureau in 1915. His early assignments focused on general forecasting, but he switched to hurricanes after an affecting encounter in late September 1928. On the way to visiting relatives in Florida, he stopped to watch as men shoveled dirt into a trench filled with the decomposing bodies of people killed by the Lake Okeechobee Hurricane. He overheard a woman behind him say, "There's something wrong with them forecasters or Joe would have got away in time." Norton later recalled, "I took what that poor woman said to heart, and I knew then and there that what I wanted to do most in life was to prevent such senseless destruction."

Norton got his big chance when he became chief hurricane forecaster at the bureau's Jacksonville office just a few months before the Labor Day Hurricane of 1935. The tragic outcome of that devastating storm, especially the great loss of life, only increased his determination to improve forecasts. So when he heard via radio on September 16, 1938, that a Brazilian steamer, the SS *Alegrete*, had reported a very low barometric reading and hurricane-force winds about 1,000 miles northeast of the Leeward Islands, Norton sprang into action, focusing all his attention on the approaching storm.

In subsequent days, additional reports from ships and land-based stations showed the hurricane to be advancing at 20 mph, heading toward the Bahamas and Florida. On the morning of September 19, Norton ordered storm warnings along the Florida coast, from Jacksonville to Key West, and he urged Floridians to make initial preparations for a possible strike. By late that afternoon, however, new data gave cause for optimism. Barometric readings on the Bahamas were hardly dropping at all, indicating to Norton that the hurricane was curving toward the northeast. The following day, Norton's suspicions were confirmed. The hurricane would miss Florida, but the danger wasn't over yet; reports and barometric readings indicated that the hurricane was heading toward Cape Hatteras. Norton ordered storm warnings as far north as Atlantic City, New Jersey, and he advised caution for all vessels in the storm's path, recommending, in particular, that small craft from Charleston to the Virginia Capes remain in port. The fact that many vessels heeded the warning was a mixed blessing, since then there were virtually no ships at sea to provide the bureau with updates on the storm's path and behavior.

As the hurricane moved up the coast, tracking responsibility shifted from the Jacksonville office to Washington, DC, where a thirty-year veteran of the bureau named Charles Mitchell was the chief forecaster. Look-

Weather Bureau forecasting office in Washington, DC, in 1926.

ing at the sparse data, Mitchell concluded that the storm would do what Cape Verdean hurricanes almost always did—namely, continue curving around the high-pressure dome in the North Atlantic called the Bermuda High, which is typically located in the western North Atlantic near Bermuda. Since the Bermuda High rotates in a clockwise direction, it tends to steer hurricanes north, parallel to the coast, and then east as they skirt the edge of the high, meaning that they ultimately veer away from the mainland into the open ocean. Mitchell also assumed that as the hurricane traveled farther north, it would rapidly weaken over the colder ocean waters, transitioning from a hurricane to a gale before dying out in the frigid North Atlantic.

Every meteorologist in the office but one agreed with the chief. Charles H. Pierce, a talented twenty-eight-year-old junior forecaster who had been with the bureau for less than a year, looked at the same data and came to a radically different conclusion. He determined that since the Bermuda High was much farther north than usual, it would pull the hurricane in a more northerly direction, meaning that the storm would likely come ashore in the vicinity of New York and southern New England. He assumed that the strong winds from the south measured in the DC area were indicative of similar winds throughout the region, which would give the hurricane an added boost of speed as it traveled north. Pierce also noted that there was a strong cold front, or trough of low pressure, farther inland in the upper atmosphere, which, he argued, created a pathway between it and the Bermuda High that was ideal for rapid movement of the storm up the coast, especially since that pathway was already flooded with moist, warm, tropical air.

Since Mitchell was the chief forecaster, he had the final say on advisories. As a result, the bureau's official forecast late on Tuesday, September 20, told the public that the storm would be heading away from land. The *New York Times* article on September 21 echoed Mitchell's confidence in the hurricane's track, reporting that the storm would weaken as it sailed off into the North Atlantic. It might cause gale-force winds and high surf later in the afternoon or evening along portions of the coast, but those effects were not of great concern.

Readers of the *Times* article were certainly not surprised by the forecasted trajectory. It was conventional wisdom among northeasterners that hurricanes menaced the southeastern and Gulf coasts of the country, not their part of the world. While hurricanes had, of course, struck Long Island and New England before, the last one that had even come close had been thirty-five years earlier, in 1903, and that storm had been relatively minor. Before that, one had to go back to the mid-nineteenth century before finding a major hurricane that had hit so far north. Few people in the Northeast had lived through or remembered the 1903 hurricane, and fewer still knew anything about the region's earlier history with such storms.

ON THE MORNING OF September 21, Pierce grew more concerned about the hurricane. One of the only ships to report on the storm after Norton issued his warning on September 19 was a British luxury liner, the RMS *Carinthia*. In the early-morning hours of September 21, the *Carinthia* was a few hundred miles northeast of Florida, caught in the thick of the hurricane and furiously rolling in the mountainous seas. Its upscale passengers were hanging on for dear life, barely able to stand, surrounded by rivers of their own vomit. While desperately trying to keep the ship from capsizing, the captain radioed in an extremely low barometric reading of 27.85. Just an hour or so later, the ship exited the hurricane, still intact but seriously damaged. The captain's report convinced Pierce that the hurricane was still extremely powerful and would remain so for quite a while.

This new data from the *Carinthia*, combined with other reports filtering in from coastal stations, caused Mitchell to alter the official forecast slightly. In its 2:00 p.m. advisory on September 21, the bureau said that the storm would come ashore late in the afternoon or early that evening in the vicinity of Long Island and Connecticut, but still as only a gale, not a hurricane. That forecast, unfortunately, was terribly wrong.

As Pierce alone had predicted, the still powerful hurricane zoomed north, making a beeline for the coast. It came ashore in Suffolk County, Long Island, and then blasted into southern New England as a Category 3 hurricane, packing sustained winds of up to 120 mph.* Even Pierce must have been shocked at how fast the hurricane approached. It raced over the open ocean at the blistering speed of 50–60 mph, rather than the 20–30 mph that is more typical of Cape Verdean hurricanes in the North Atlantic. The Great Hurricane of 1938 moved so fast that journalists dubbed it "The Long Island Express."

The disagreement between Mitchell and Pierce is often presented as high drama, painting Mitchell as a villain. It pits the older, arrogant forecaster, mired in the ways of the past, against a brash, younger meteorologist who was schooled in newer methods of forecasting, and who tried in vain to persuade his superior to see the error of his ways. As the portrayal usually goes, Mitchell imperiously dismissed Pierce's concerns, essentially telling him to stay in his lane and leave the forecasting to the men with decades of experience. But, as Lourdes B. Avilés, a meteorology professor at Plymouth State University, points out, no contemporary accounts depict such a dramatic showdown. Instead, that narrative arose decades later, when historians attempted to re-create the encounter.

The truth is there is no way of knowing exactly what transpired between the two men, since neither of them, nor any of their colleagues, ever elaborated on the events of that day. Because Mitchell was a highly respected forecaster with decades of experience, "most of the time," Avilés contends, he "would have been the one who was right and the inexpe-

---

* Gusts of up to 186 mph were recorded at the Blue Hills Observatory outside of Boston, but that measurement was taken at roughly 650 feet aboveground, and by that time the storm was no longer officially a hurricane, but rather an extratropical storm.

rienced junior forecaster or analyst would be the one learning from his experience; but this one time at least, when it mattered most, Mitchell was wrong or seemingly unaware of what was going on in the atmosphere."

Mitchell also was seemingly not sufficiently impressed by history. While he was correct that the vast majority of Cape Verde–type hurricanes weaken considerably as they go north and then slingshot around the Bermuda High into oblivion, that had not always been the case. The devastating New England hurricanes of 1635, 1815, and 1821—not to mention other hurricanes that hit the region in 1869, 1878, 1893, and 1903—should have at least caused him to question his forecast, or to take more precautions by expanding the zone of concern. Tragically, Mitchell's apparent lack of historical perspective and his decision not to give more credence to Pierce's analysis meant that when the hurricane struck the coast, the people in its path were caught totally by surprise.

THE HURRICANE MADE LANDFALL on Long Island at around 3:00 in the afternoon. Observers on the South Shore looking out to sea were at first puzzled by what appeared on the horizon, and then alarmed. We thought it was "a thick and high bank of fog rolling in fast from the ocean," one of them said. "When it came closer, we saw that it wasn't fog. It was water." The hurricane could not have come at a worse time. It was during an unusually high tide, which, when combined with the driving wind, low pressure, and storm surge, generated monumental storm tides along the coast, up to 25 feet above average low water. Waves thunderously crashing on the shore were reported to be 30–50 feet high. The storm destroyed so much of the local communication systems, including phone and telegraph lines, that many of the places hit first had no way of alerting those who were next in line, so those places were similarly unprepared for the maelstrom that suddenly enveloped them.

The rapidity of the onslaught is reflected in the story of a man on the eastern end of Long Island who had been waiting for a package delivery with great anticipation. Ever since he was a boy, he had been fascinated by the weather and wanted a top-of-the-line barometer to track the vagaries of the atmosphere. On the morning of September 21, the package arrived. He eagerly opened the box from Abercrombie & Fitch, which at the time sold all manner of outdoor equipment, and out came a gleaming barometer. But his delight quickly turned to disgust. The barometer's needle was pointing to a "stormy" reading so low that it could only mean a hurricane was approaching or was already there, yet outside the sun was shining through wispy cirrus clouds, and neither the sea nor the wind betrayed anything ominous on the horizon. He shook the barometer in the hope of setting it right, but there was still no change. Greatly annoyed, and believing the barometer to be broken, he wrote the manufacturer an angry note and went to the local post office to mail it. He shouldn't have been so rash. By the time he returned from town, the Great Hurricane of 1938 had blown both his house and his precious barometer away.

THE ACTRESS KATHARINE HEPBURN was caught equally off guard. Already famous for starring in *Little Women* and *Morning Glory*, for which she received her first Oscar, Hepburn was at her family's rambling Victorian summer home in the Fenwick area of Old Saybrook, Connecticut, on the day of the hurricane. Taking advantage of the prime beachfront location, the thirty-one-year-old Hepburn went for a swim at 8:00 a.m., with the sun beaming down, a light breeze playing over the sound, and mere ripples on its surface. After breakfast she played nine holes of golf with her friend Jack Hammond and, despite the quickening winds, launched a perfect drive on the par 3 ninth, scoring a hole-in-one and contributing to her personal best on the course.

Back home after the triumphant outing, Hepburn and Hammond went swimming at the beach again, but this dip was quite different from the one she had taken earlier in the day. The wind was whipping now, and the surf rapidly increasing. They had fun jumping the waves, and when they got out it was impossible to stand without leaning into the wind. The sand flying through the air stung their exposed skin.

Running back to the house, they joined Hepburn's mother, Katharine; her brother, Dick; Fanny the cook; and a repairman who was there to fix the screens on the porch. As it turned out, the repairs would not be necessary. While he was working on the screens, the repairman's car, which had been parked in the driveway, was lifted off the ground by a gust of wind and hurled into a nearby lagoon. Immediately thereafter, the laundry wing was ripped from the house. At that point, all work ceased, and the only goal was survival.

Fearing that the entire house would soon crash to the ground, Dick led everyone out of the dining room into the storm. In fast-flowing water up to their knees, and while clinging to the same rope, the group trudged for about fifteen minutes across a field to higher ground. "Looking back," Hepburn would later recall, "we saw the house slowly turn around, sail off to the northeast and start down the brook which fed the swamp-lagoon. It just sailed away—easy as pie."

With the storm seething around them, the six people now took shelter at the closed-for-the-season Riversea Inn by forcing their way in. The next morning they went to investigate, and where Hepburn's family house had once stood, all that was left was "a bathtub at a cockeyed angle and a toilet." Upon reaching the Saybrook Telephone Company offices, Hepburn finally got through to her father in Hartford. She assured her father of the family's safety, and when she told him that the house was gone, he responded, "I suppose you didn't have brains enough to throw in a match before it disappeared. I'm insured for fire."

Katharine Hepburn, digging where her family's summer home once stood, looking for valuables and family items after the Great Hurricane of 1938.

AT THE SAME TIME that Hepburn and company were fighting for their lives, just 25 miles farther up the coast the hurricane was crashing into Napatree Point, a long, narrow spit of sand jutting out from the village of Watch Hill, which, in turn, is part of Westerly, Rhode Island. On one side of the point is the Atlantic, and on the other, Little Narragansett Bay. The point was named in 1614 by Dutch explorer and trader Adriaen Block. Seeing that it was heavily wooded, Block called it "Nape (Neck) of Trees," which, over time, morphed into "Napatree." That name, however, lost its relevance two centuries later, when the Great September Gale of 1815 denuded Napatree of all its eponymous trees, as well as a few buildings, leaving it bare and exposed.

Napatree didn't remain barren, and by the early twentieth century it was a vibrant summer community for the well-heeled, with thirty-nine cottages, a yacht club, a beach club, and a bathing pavilion. One of the cottages was owned by Geoffrey Moore, a successful businessman whose Westerly-based company made elastics that went into products ranging from golf balls to ladies' underwear. On September 21, 1938, there were ten people at the three-story cottage: Geoffrey; his wife, Catherine; their four children, ranging in age from four to twelve; a family friend; and three employees who helped run the house and take care of the children.

Right after lunch, Geoffrey, or Jeff, as he was called, felt a severe pain in his chest and slumped over in his chair. His family and staff got him to the sofa in the living room, and Catherine immediately called the doctor. He came right over, said that Jeff had had a mild heart attack, and prescribed three days of bed rest. Soon after the doctor left, Catherine helped Jeff up to their bedroom. Minutes later, the hurricane crashed into Napatree Point.

"Tons of water were being hurled against the house," Catherine recalled, and through the window she saw a cottage next to theirs blown over by the wind and waves. A few minutes later there was a loud knock at the front door. When Catherine opened it, eighteen-year-old Jim Nestor was standing there, out of breath and clad only in his underwear. It was his family's cottage that Catherine had seen swallowed by the hurricane, and when she asked Jim where the rest of his family was, he replied, "Gone."

Somehow Jeff rallied, got out of bed, and took charge of the situation, ushering everyone to the center of the house to stand under a thick door casing separating two rooms. A religious family, all of the Moores began praying. On a more practical note, Catherine told everyone to take off their shoes in case they had to swim.

When the house started breaking apart, Jeff screamed for everyone to rush upstairs to the third floor, so that if the house collapsed, they wouldn't be buried under a pile of rubble. As soon as they made it to the third-floor landing, the second floor pancaked into the first. Fearing that the roof would soon give way, Jeff smashed the bathroom window and was about to lead everyone out into the storm. At that moment the roof section

Before and after images of the Watch Hill Beach Club on Napatree Point, showing the utter destructive force of the Great Hurricane of 1938.

over the maid's room flew off, and, as Catherine said, "They made for it, [as] it was the best raft in sight, with two iron pipes sticking up through the floor to hold onto."

And hold on they did, as the floor was wrenched from the rest of the house by a crashing wave. They literally sailed off, with the wall at one end of the floor catching the wind and sending them scudding across Little Narragansett Bay. Despite being pummeled by waves and floating debris, all eleven people hung on to the raft, which finally came to rest on Barn Island in Connecticut, a little more than a mile from where their hair-raising voyage had begun.

The power of the Great Hurricane of 1938 can be seen in this picture,
which shows the US Lighthouse Service tender Tulip, *thrown up*
on the tracks of the New Haven Railroad in New London, Connecticut.

Appropriately enough, they found the remains of a barn, and that is where they spent the night, wet and shivering in the hollows of a haystack, which helped shield them from the still ferocious wind. During the night they saw a brilliant orange glow off in the distance, reflected in the sky, and thought it must be the nearby town of Stonington, ablaze. They were off by about 10 miles. That glow was coming from New London, whose storied waterfront was on fire. The next morning Jeff found a mirror in the wreckage, and with the sun shining brightly, he used the mirror to send distress signals in different directions. A short while later, a local fisherman, seeing the glinting light, rescued them.

Reflecting later on their ordeal, Catherine said, "I sometimes feel that we have had a preview of the end of the world. . . . For some it was the end of their earthly existence; it might easily have been for us. . . . We shall never forget the feeling of helplessness, in the face of the elements let loose. We who have been through this hurricane, I am sure,

Atlantic Avenue in Westerly, Rhode Island, before and after the Great Hurricane of 1938.

have gained a deeper, richer, more complete outlook on life than we ever could have otherwise." Of the forty-two people that were on Napatree Point that day, only twenty-seven survived, each one of them, no doubt, having the same life-altering experience that Catherine recounted. As for the cottages, the yacht club, the beach club, and the bathing pavilion, all were gone. Today, the point is a conservation area where the only inhabitants are the wildlife of the shore.

ANOTHER 30 MILES UP the coast, the hurricane took the lives of a group of children, in what is one of the storm's most haunting stories. It was around 3:00 p.m. when bus driver Norman Caswell picked up eight kids at the Thomas H. Clark Elementary School in Jamestown, Rhode Island, at the mouth of Narragansett Bay. He was responsible for getting them home, come hell or high water, and on this day both had arrived with the hurricane. Caswell's route required him to drive across a narrow causeway connecting the two main parts of Jamestown. On the southern side of the causeway was Mackerel Cove, typically a relatively placid body of water where area kids learned how to swim. At that moment, however, it was a frenzied sea with crisscrossing waves crashing into one another, spume flying from their crests. The water in the cove had risen so high that it was covering the causeway to a depth of a few feet, and Caswell could see abandoned cars in the distance. He had a decision to make. Should he turn around or continue?

Dairy farmer Joseph Matoes Sr. had watched Caswell drive down the hill toward the causeway, and he waved wildly for him to stop. Four of Matoes's five children were on the bus, and he knew that if Caswell continued, he would be courting disaster. Just a short while before, Matoes had attempted to cross the causeway himself, but at a low spot his truck was swept into the water. He had saved himself by swimming to shore and huddling next to a rock wall at the edge of a cemetery.

Caswell either didn't see Matoes or ignored the warning. Either way, he wasn't turning back. He put his foot on the gas, hoping that the height of the bus would allow him to power through. Partway across, the bus stalled, and then two huge waves hit it broadside. Caswell remembered thinking, "We'd better get out, or we'd drown like rats." He opened the back door, helped the kids down, and screamed that they should hold hands and he would lead them to shore. Just then, another wave struck and they were all pitched into the churning waters.

Relatively safe on land, Matoes could only watch this horrific drama play out. Conditions were so bad that an attempted rescue was out of the question, even for a father watching his children being swept away. Out of the corner of his eye, Matoes spied a dark shape moving through the water, which came to rest on the shore. Upon investigation, he found that it was Caswell, lying motionless, face down on the grass. Matoes kicked him to see whether he was alive. Caswell grunted and, according to Matoes, said, "Please let me die. I lost a whole bunch of kids I had in the school bus. Everything's gone. Please don't move me. Let me die."

Caswell didn't get his wish. He would die a few years later, a broken man. As a fellow Jamestown resident said, "He died from the shock of this thing." The only other person to survive the bus incident was Clayton Chellis, the twelve-year-old son of the lighthouse keeper at Beavertail Light, at the tip of Jamestown. A very strong swimmer, Clayton successfully battled the current and the waves to make it to shore.

Clayton's seven-year-old sister, Marion, had also been on the bus. According to a contemporary account, her last words to her brother before they exited the bus were, "Clayton, don't let the water get in your eyes." Tragically and ironically, Clayton, the boy whose excellent swimming skills enabled him to survive the hurricane, died in 1946 when he drowned off a beach in distant Saipan, where he and his navy brothers had gone to celebrate their imminent return to the states.

SITUATED ON THE BANKS of the Providence River not far from the head of Narragansett Bay, Providence was, in a manner of speaking, a sitting duck on September 21, 1938. The city's problem began at the coast. Located just to the east of the protective shield of Long Island, Rhode Island had no barrier to the ocean's onslaught, and it was fully exposed to the seas that had been building to mountainous heights as the hurricane flew toward New England. According to one observer, a "series of waves, each higher than the previous one, were lashed into a seething, foaming fury to the height of thirty feet" as they thundered onto Rhode Island's beaches. These waves accompanied the storm surge, which swept up the broad bay and funneled into the increasingly narrow river, causing the water to rise to astonishing heights, and transforming the city's downtown into a roiling lake.

The apogee of this aqueous assault reached 13 feet, 8½ inches above mean high water, beating the old record set by the Great September Gale of 1815, during which the water peaked at 11 feet, 9¼ inches. People who live through hurricanes are often at a loss for words to adequately describe the nightmarish experience. Not so David Cornel De Jong, acclaimed novelist, poet, and short-story writer who documented what happened to him and his fair city of Providence when the 1938 hurricane crashed into it.

Enjoying a cup of coffee that afternoon in the cafeteria at the offices of the *Providence Journal*, De Jong had an inkling that bad weather was on the way when the reporters he was chatting with were called away to cover the coming storm. Through the spitting rain and gusting winds, De Jong trudged over to a market to buy some food. While he was busy shopping, conditions deteriorated outside. His purchase made, he paced the aisles for a half hour, hoping the storm would subside, but it only grew worse. Finally, he left the store to brave the elements.

A few steps later a gust of wind pinned him to a wall, and "buckets of water" drenched him. He struggled to the steps of the stately Arcade, which was built in 1828 and is the nation's oldest indoor shopping mall. There, about 500 feet from the river, he joined fifty other sojourners in the storm, who "scurried from one entrance of the Arcade to the other, victims of the wind's weird caprices." Upon finding a spot near the Arcade's massive Doric columns, where the wind was a little less fierce, De Jong "decided to make" his stand "if only for the safety of my bacon and eggs. . . . It was fairly dangerous where we stood, because streetlights kept shattering and the enormous clock above us keeled and teetered madly. On the street, people were flattened against buildings or fell prone on the sidewalk."

When a sheet of tin roofing flew through the air, knocking a man down, De Jong lost confidence in his improvised redoubt and, during a lull, began running toward home. The wind, however, quickly returned, and at that moment a huge storefront window shattered, showering him and those nearby with shards of glass. "Just ahead of us an old woman had her neck sliced by a pane of glass; she tumbled, straightened herself, bent her head, and brunting the storm went on, leaving a trail of blood behind her." When De Jong and the others went to assist her, another blast of wind flung them against a wall, "spattering the woman's blood over our faces."

The wind pushed them along the side of the building into the embrace of its revolving doors. As the doors turned, they deposited their human flotsam, two and three at a time, into the lobby, "where a crowd laughed foolishly at us, until they saw the injured woman." While a waitress tended to the woman's wound, someone shouted, "Look at the water," which was "suddenly swirling and billowing down the street. . . . turbulent with whitecaps," with people and cars struggling against the flow. When water began filling the lobby, people rushed for the stairs. On the way up, De Jong ran into a lawyer friend, who ushered him to his third-floor office, where others joined them.

In the deepening darkness, De Jong and his fellow refugees watched as the hurricane swallowed the city, occasionally cracking jokes in a feeble attempt to lessen the horror of what they were witnessing. "Beneath us the city lay helpless in a sea, in gray waves in which people perished." Strange sights rolled by. "A yellow-haired store dummy, bobbing up between black beams, holding her head high, her visage vacant, never sinking, pirouetted on the flood like a well-mannered debutante. . . . Whole shoals of vermillion tennis balls issued out of a broken store window like puffed exotic fish." A human chain, sixteen individuals long, in water up to their chins, snaked its way to the safety of a building. Submerged cars, their lights still on and their short-circuited horns blaring, made for a surreal traffic jam.

And then there were the looters, the vermin who far too often are the handmaidens of tragedy. "They came, neck deep, or swimming, holding flashlights dry above them, rising out of the water and disappearing through the demolished store windows. At first there were few, then there were hordes, assisting each other. Some climbed into the stores, others received the stolen goods and piled them into rowboats or stuffed them into burlap sacks. They seemed organized, almost regimented, as if they'd daily drilled and prepared for this event, the like of which hadn't happened in a hundred and twenty years. They were brazen and insatiable; they swarmed like rats; they took everything. When a few policemen came past in a rowboat, they didn't stop their looting. They knew they outnumbered the police; beside[s,] the latter were intent on rescue work."

De Jong and the others waited in the building, wary of the dangers that might lurk in the still-flooded lobby, until firemen and their trucks arrived to help evacuate its trapped occupants. "The sudden hard lights" that the firemen used "threw in gross relief only devastation, and gloomy

Plaques registering the maximum heights of the
Great September Gale of 1815 and the Great Hurricane of 1938,
located on the southwest corner of the Old Market House
on North Main Street, Providence, Rhode Island.

water mirroring devastation." De Jong climbed aboard one of the trucks, still clutching his package of food, holding it up to keep it out of the water. The truck took him and many others to higher ground on the other side of the river, where "a mildly cheering crowd greeted us." De Jong pushed on through the mass of people but was stopped by a policeman who demanded to see what he had in his bag, thinking he must be a looter. When De Jong showed him what was within, the policeman "shook his head in misgiving, but let me go." Making his way home at last, and exhausted, De Jong went to bed, and when he awoke the next morning the sun's rays cast a harsh light on his broken city.

AMID ALL THE TRAGIC and sad stories, there were a few humorous ones as well, both real and imagined. A woman in one of the villages on the South Fork of Long Island, who had been in her car when the hurricane struck, pulled up at a public garage, hoping to find shelter. The attendant opened the garage doors to let her in, but in an instant the garage's rear wall blew off into the storm, and all the windows caved in. "I think I've done enough damage," the woman was heard to say. "I'll try to get on home." And off she drove.

Vincent McHugh, a writer for *The New Yorker*, took a different tack in reporting the news of the day and, with tongue firmly in cheek, told some whoppers about the hurricane and its aftermath. One story featured a wealthy forty-nine-year-old man, his twenty-one-year-old wife, and their Finnish cook, young Venetian gardener, and French maid, all of whom lived in a large house on the edge of Narragansett Bay. The wife was taking a bath when she began yelling to her husband that the kitchen door was making a racket. Upon investigation, he found that the wind had blown it open, and it wouldn't stay shut, so he walked to his neighbor's to get a hammer and some nails. When he returned, his house, along with his wife, the cook, and the gardener, had disappeared.

The husband, McHugh noted, "was not greatly disturbed" by this turn of events. "His wife had left him twice before and each time returned within a day or two." Then he saw his house in the distance, floating toward Providence. The husband "remained all night on the beach in a distraught condition, with the French housemaid attempting to comfort him." Meantime, the Finnish cook washed ashore some distance up the coast near a fancy restaurant, which hired her on the spot. As for the wife, the next morning the husband spied her in the distance, "in the bathtub with the young Venetian gardener perched on its rim whistling 'Santa Lucia' and paddling like a gondolier with what the husband saw at once was an ironing board that had belonged to his grandmother." Not surprisingly, McHugh reported, "the couple have since been divorced."

AS THE HURRICANE MOVED inland, it slowly weakened and lost hurricane status, but it still had plenty of power as it raced through New England at a blistering pace of nearly 50 mph before dying the next morning in the farther reaches of Canada. The fact that it remained so strong, even far from the coast, was unusual. Typically, upon encountering land, hurricanes rapidly fall apart, both because of increased friction with the ground and because their main source of heat energy, the ocean, is gone. But when the storm smacked into the low-pressure system to the west, the temperature differential gave the storm a big boost of energy and spread it out, expanding its area of impact. Yet another important factor was speed. The Long Island Express was moving so fast when it came ashore, and continued to move extremely fast over land, that it did not have much time to weaken.

The band shell in Bushnell Park, Hartford, Connecticut, functioning as a reflecting pool in the aftermath of the Great Hurricane of 1938.

By the time it was over, the hurricane had killed 680 people—more than half of whom were in Rhode Island—and seriously injured nearly 2,000. Had it struck just a month or so earlier, when summer season was at its peak and the beaches were packed, the death toll would have undoubtedly been much higher, perhaps reaching Galveston levels. The hurricane damaged or completely demolished roughly 20,000 homes and farm buildings, 26,000 cars, and more than 3,000 boats (another

2,500 were lost at sea), and 95 percent of those losses were uninsured. Nearly 63,000 people requested emergency aid. Vast areas were temporarily jettisoned back to the previous century, as the conveniences and, some would say, necessities of modern life were ripped away. Twenty thousand miles of electrical and telephone wires were brought down, leaving half a million people in the dark and unable to make a call. Railroad service along the eastern corridor from Boston to New York was severed for one to two weeks (creating a temporary surge in airline passengers along that route).

Rivers, already at flood stage because of the exceptionally wet summer, were transformed into rampaging beasts by the deluge from the sky, which dropped more than 7 inches of water in some places. They ripped through the landscape like liquid bulldozers, washing away hundreds of roads and bridges, and turning cities and towns into lakes. A 200-mile-wide swath of slicing winds marched through the eastern end of Long Island and the heart of New England, snapping or toppling a few billion trees. Many of them were relative pushovers, since their roots couldn't gain a solid purchase in the waterlogged ground—a dynamic that one fourth-grader from Connecticut captured beautifully in a two-line poem that read, "The wind was oh so very bold / The earth the trees just could not hold."

Nearly 15,000 of New Haven's stately elm trees, many of them already weakened by Dutch elm disease, succumbed, leaving the city and the campus of Yale University looking like an arboreal war zone. In many places, so many downed trees were draped across roads and highways that driving was impossible for days or weeks, and even walking made people feel as if they had been placed in a massive obstacle course that forced them to snake, duck, and jump just to move about. Trees that remained standing were stripped of most of their leaves, and the leaves that were still attached had turned brown and crinkled by the salt spray saturating the air, which coated the landscape up to 50 miles from the coast. Even when the greatly weakened storm reached as far north and inland as storied Mount Washington in New Hampshire, wind gusts of up to 163 mph were registered, and large sections of the Cog Railway's trestle leading to the top of the mountain were blown down. All told, the damage from the Great Hurricane of 1938 was estimated to be as high as $300–$400 million. It still ranks as the most destructive natural disaster to strike New England, and one of the worst disasters of any kind in American history.

*Whether at sea or on land, the eye of a hurricane often acts as an
aviary of colossal proportions. Birds caught in a hurricane frequently fly into the calm eye and attempt to travel along within it
to avoid being cast back into the maelstrom. That is why ships in a
hurricane sometimes become landing pads for the weary birds. By the
same token, when the eye passes over land, entrapped birds literally
drop from the sky to find shelter on the ground. Thus, it is common
for birders who follow in the wake of a hurricane to identify species
that are a long way from home. A white-tailed tropicbird (shown here
in multiple poses)—the national bird of Bermuda—was caught up in
the eye of the Great Hurricane of 1938 and was carried all the way to
Woodstock, Vermont, where it was found dead, undoubtedly having
succumbed to exhaustion or blunt-force trauma. It was the first time
such a bird had ever been seen in the state. More typically, it is found
from Bermuda to the Caribbean, and in Hawaii.*

The 1938 hurricane was so sudden, jarring, widespread, and devastating that it left an indelible impression on anyone who lived through it.
Capitalizing on people's strong desire to share their experience, an entre-
preneurial man reportedly walked around Boston Common with a sandwich board hung from his shoulders that read, "For twenty-five cents, I'll

listen to your story of the hurricane." To this day, old timers and their children are quite fond of regaling anyone who will listen with tales of what happened when the hurricane struck.

ONCE THE SKIES CLEARED and the nation had some space for reflection, the failure to forecast the hurricane brought an avalanche of criticism down on the Weather Bureau. John Q. Stewart, a professor of astronomical physics at Princeton University, spoke for many when he claimed, "In the long and laudable annals of the government's forecasters, that day's record makes what must be the sorriest page." Because there "had been no warning worth the mentioning," he asserted, "a sophisticated population died by the hundreds, with little or no knowledge of what raw shape of death this was which struck from the sky and the tide."

Dr. Charles Clark, acting chief of the Weather Bureau at the time, did his best to deflect the barbs. The *Boston Evening Transcript* reported Clark as stating, "On the basis of the data on hand [the forecasters] could hardly have given any greater advance warning, for the tropical storm—the worst in the history of the Northeast—was a freak; it did not follow the usual pattern. . . . Up to the time it reached Hatteras, there was no indication that it would be particularly dangerous, and it seemed quite likely that it would go out to sea well off the Atlantic seaboard." Another time, he added, "Had the storm not moved with such unprecedented rapidity, there can be no doubt but that Weather Bureau warnings by radio and through the press would have reached nearly everyone in the affected area."

Clark's defense of the forecasting was only partially persuasive. Yes, the hurricane was a freak, at least with regard to its speed and its trajectory, in that it didn't follow the usual pathway. And if the hurricane had proceeded at a more typical speed of 20–30 mph, there is good reason to believe that many, if not most, people in the danger zone would not have been caught completely off guard and would have had a little more time to react. Other parts of Clark's defense were weaker. After all, Pierce, using the same data as everyone else, had correctly forecast the course of the hurricane. Had his arguments held sway, the Northeast would have received more advance warning, giving people more time to prepare. The extremely low barometric reading reported by the captain of the *Carinthia*, which Pierce picked up on, was clear proof that the hurricane was still quite dangerous as it was closing in on Cape Hatteras. And, as noted earlier, any serious student of New York's and New England's meteorological history would have known that, although this was an unusual and even a freakish event by historical standards, other very dangerous hurricanes had plowed into the region with disastrous results.

Still, the Weather Bureau should not be blamed too harshly. Although Pierce had made what turned out to be an accurate forecast, the available data was indeed quite limited. Pierce was correct, but he just as well might have missed some of the signs, or failed to put them together, and been wrong. There was virtually no data about the hurricane for the seven hours before it came ashore, while it was zooming up the coast from Cape Hatteras to Long Island. Exactly what it was doing during that time was anyone's guess.

The lack of data, of course, was not a new problem. Ever since the Weather Bureau had begun forecasting hurricanes, its efforts had been severely hampered by the paucity of real-time data about what was happening over the ocean. Sure, there were times when ships not already scattered because of earlier warnings provided valuable information. And if the hurricane passed near or over an island that had a weather station, another data point was generated. But what the bureau desperately needed to avoid forecasting debacles like the calamity of the Great Hurricane of 1938—not to mention those relating to the Great Miami Hurricane of 1926, the Lake Okeechobee Hurricane of 1928, and the Labor Day Hurricane of 1935—was more data about hurricanes at sea, as well as better science to understand and predict their behavior.

Fortunately, all of this and much more was coming. Throughout the remainder of the twentieth century, and up until the present, our understanding of hurricanes and our ability to monitor them and forecast their movement and behavior improved tremendously. Airplanes, satellites, radar, high-tech measuring devices, and computers all played critical roles. But those aren't the only changes that took place during this dynamic era. The manner in which we name and report on hurricanes also evolved in new and intriguing ways.

CHAPTER 7

Into, Over, and Under
the Maelstrom

Artist's impression of NOAA's Hurricane Hunter Kermit,
a WP-3D Orion (registration number N42RF),
inside the eye of a hurricane.

SINCE THE LATE 1800S, METEOROLOGISTS INVOLVED WITH tracking and forecasting hurricanes have looked to the sky for answers. Their ability to get them, however, was severely limited because information came mainly from observations on the ground or from a small number of ships that just happened to be unlucky enough to be in the storm's path. By the 1930s, weather balloons carrying instruments aloft were increasingly employed by the Weather Bureau, but they were no match for a hurricane's vicious winds, which often destroyed the balloons and the instruments before valuable data could be gathered. If only there were a way to get closer to hurricanes to obtain data as they traveled over the ocean, far from land; then, meteorologists mused, tracking and forecasting them would be much easier. World War II made such monitoring possible.

Since time immemorial, wars have spurred innovation and ingenuity while also sowing death and destruction. Nothing focuses the mind like a threat to one's existence, and World War II certainly had that impact on America, where the imperative to win fueled advances in numerous fields. Meteorology, and hurricane science in particular, became one of the beneficiaries.

Weather doesn't comply with the needs of war; therefore, US military commanders knew that pilots had to be capable of flying in good conditions and bad if they were to take full advantage of every strategic and tactical opportunity. That meant the pilots had to rely on their instruments, and not just visible landmarks, to guide their way (flying by visible landmarks is called contact flying). To teach its pilots how to master *instrument flight*—the art and science of being able to fly even when weather conditions hide the ground and the horizon as a reference—the air force asked pilot Joseph B. Duckworth to lead the way.

BORN IN SAVANNAH, GEORGIA, in 1902, Duckworth earned his air force wings in 1927 and went into the private sector, ultimately becoming a pilot for Eastern Airlines in 1930. As a commercial pilot intent on keeping to a schedule and flying in all types of weather, he taught himself the art of instrument flying, which had only been developed in 1929. When he returned to active duty in 1940, Duckworth began training air force pilots to gain the same proficiency.

By 1943, Duckworth, now a lieutenant colonel, was the commanding officer of the air force flying school in Bryan, Texas. He taught his students instrument flying on the AT-6 "Texan" trainer, a single-engine, two-seater workhorse that was nearly 30 feet long, with a 42-foot wingspan. On July 27, the Weather Bureau alerted the military that a hurricane in the Gulf of Mexico would soon be coming ashore in Galveston. This warning

AT-6C Texans, circa 1943.

prompted the air force to consider flying the AT-6's to another base farther inland to protect them from harm. That's when the ribbing started.

Among Duckworth's students were a bunch of grizzled British flying aces who had earned their stripes battling the German Luftwaffe over the skies of Europe. They had no experience with hurricanes, however, and viewed them as nothing more than bad thunderstorms. When such storms threatened in Britain, planes remained on the tarmac. So, when the Brits heard over breakfast on the twenty-seventh that the military brass were thinking of sending the planes inland in advance of the hurricane, they started making fun of the supposed fragility of the AT-6.

The lanky Georgian sat up straight in his chair, cast his British trainees a wry smile, and offered them a wager. After disabusing them of the idea that hurricanes were merely bad thunderstorms, Duckworth bet them that he could fly an AT-6 into the hurricane and then return to the base. Such a flight would vindicate the strength of the plane, as well as the reliability of instrument flying. The loser, Duckworth said, would buy the winner a drink of his choice.

Duckworth needed a navigator, so he asked the only one at the base that day, Ralph O'Hair, to join him. O'Hair was hesitant. His main concern was what would happen if the heavy rain within the hurricane flooded the plane's single engine and it stopped working. The most likely answer—that they would crash and die—was hardly reassuring. The thought of ejecting from the crippled plane and parachuting to safety didn't seem like a practical or safe alternative either. Nevertheless, O'Hair agreed to go along, as he later recalled, because of "the respect he had for Duckworth's skill as a pilot."

Since this "experimental instrument flight" into a hurricane's path would be a first and was potentially very risky, Duckworth didn't think he could get clearance from his superiors at headquarters. So he didn't ask. Early that afternoon, the two men flew in the direction of the Category 1 hurricane as it swept in over the coast. On the way, they radioed Houston's air traffic control tower. When they informed the startled operator that they were heading to Galveston, he thought he must have heard wrong, and he asked them whether they knew there was a hurricane at Galveston. "Yes, we do," O'Hair responded. "We intend to fly into the thing." Since the operator couldn't stop them, he asked that they report in every now and then to keep him updated. "Evidently," according to historian Ivan Ray Tannehill, "he wanted to be able to say what became of the plane if they went down in the storm."

Though Duckworth and O'Hair were outwardly cool, their pulses certainly quickened as they approached the unknown. When they entered the hurricane at an altitude of between 4,000 and 9,000 feet, a gray darkness descended, torrents of rain poured down, and visibility went to near zero as the plane was buffeted by violent updrafts and downdrafts. O'Hair said it felt like they were "being tossed about like a stick in a dog's mouth."

Originally, the plan was to fly into the outer edge of the hurricane and then come back. But before Duckworth could execute a turn, the plane broke through the eyewall. While circling inside, surrounded by what O'Hair called "a shower curtain of darker clouds," the men could see the Texas countryside below. Duckworth exited the eye and returned to the airfield about two hours after their trip began.

Word of their unauthorized flight had filtered through the ranks, and when they landed, the base's weather officer, Lieutenant William Jones-Burdick, was there to greet them. Disappointed that he had not been asked to go on the first excursion, but still eager to take advantage of so momentous of an opportunity, he convinced Duckworth to make a second flight so that he, too, could see the hurricane up close. Jones-Burdick took O'Hair's place, and off they went. Unlike the first flight, during which neither men took notes, this time both Duckworth and Burdick-Jones recorded as much data as they could, including descriptions of the hurricane's structure and temperature variations.

That evening there was a joyous celebration at the officers' club, where all of Duckworth's students, most especially the British, toasted their fearless teacher. Although he had broken the rules by taking off that day without permission and venturing into the hurricane, Duckworth was later awarded the Air Medal for his singular act of meritorious achievement.

NEWS OF THE HISTORIC flights excited Francis W. Reichelderfer, who had become chief of the Weather Bureau a few months after the Great Hurricane of 1938. Ever since Captain Povey had flown reconnaissance on the Labor Day Hurricane of 1935, the bureau had wanted to explore the possibility of flying near hurricanes to gather information. Despite lobbying for such flights, the bureau had failed to gain any traction for its bold idea. Duckworth's success, however, changed the calculus by proving that planes could fly not only in the vicinity of hurricanes but also directly into them.

The flight also attracted the military's attention. Despite being only a Category 1 storm, the July 1943 hurricane caused considerable damage to Texas's oil industry and temporarily shut down the refinery that provided most of the nation's aviation fuel. This painful disruption jolted the Joint Chiefs of Staff into action. Now that Duckworth had proved that airplanes could monitor a hurricane's progress, the Joint Chiefs authorized additional flights in the hope that they would provide earlier warnings of a hurricane's approach. That way the military could better prepare, should a hurricane threaten a base or suppliers of critical war matériel.

Reichelderfer was overjoyed by this turn of events because the military was not going it alone. While the air force and the army would be flying the planes, the flights would be supervised jointly by the military and the Weather Bureau out of the latter's facility in Miami, which replaced Jacksonville in 1943 as the nation's primary hurricane forecasting office.*

---

* In 1940, the Weather Bureau was transferred from the Department of Agriculture to the Department of Commerce.

Admiral William F. "Bull" Halsey's disastrous experience with typhoons in the Pacific gave the military even more encouragement to support Hurricane Hunter flights. In December 1944, and again in June 1945, the US Third Fleet, commanded by Halsey, was clobbered by a typhoon. These two storms, dubbed "Halsey's Typhoons," delivered a traumatic blow, sinking three destroyers, damaging scores of ships, demolishing 222 planes, and killing more than 800 men. Although military courts of inquiry placed most of the blame on Halsey for poor decision-making, another major cause of these two debacles was faulty or nonexistent forecasts provided by both Halsey's own meteorologist and the navy's Fleet Weather Center in Pearl Harbor, which caused Halsey to steam into, instead of away from, the typhoons. One of the main recommendations to come out of these inquiries was that the navy should conduct more weather reconnaissance flights so that its fleets could outflank typhoons and other bad weather.

Bureau meteorologists would be on the planes to gather valuable data. The man who would decide when those flights would launch and where they would go was Grady Norton, the bureau's chief hurricane forecaster.

The value of so-called Hurricane Hunter flights became apparent the following year. Responding to news of a strong tropical disturbance in the

Atlantic about 250 miles north of Puerto Rico, Norton dispatched a navy plane to investigate on September 10, 1944. It found a fully developed hurricane with tremendous winds roughly estimated to be 140 mph. At several points during that flight, the pilot feared that the plane might burst apart or crash into the ocean, and when it returned to base, an inspection showed that 150 rivets had been sheared off one of its wings. So powerful was this storm that the bureau dubbed it the Great Atlantic Hurricane of 1944.

Over the next four days, as the hurricane continued north, paralleling the coast, Norton sent out six more reconnaissance flights. When the hurricane finally made landfall, plowing into eastern Long Island and southern New England on September 14, it had winds in excess of 100 mph, with gusts much higher. It then tracked over Rhode Island and Massachusetts before heading into Massachusetts Bay and the broader Atlantic.

While this hurricane bore some similarity to the Great Hurricane of 1938 in terms of trajectory and landfall, it was far less damaging to people and property. Of the 390 deaths, only 46 occurred on land. The rest came from the sinking of ships at sea, most notably the USS *Warrington*, which lost 247 men when it capsized about 450 miles east of Vero Beach, Florida; 68 crewmen survived and, after forty hours in the water, were saved by other ships. The cost of the hurricane was $100 million. Although the bulk of that damage occurred after landfall, there was considerable destruction from the mid-Atlantic north, as the massive hurricane sideswiped the coast.

The Great Hurricane of 1944 was much less damaging than the one in 1938 in part because it was weaker on landfall, it hit at low tide and at an oblique angle to the coast, and, since so many buildings had been destroyed six years earlier, there were fewer left to damage. But the reconnaissance flights deserve much credit as well. The information they provided helped the bureau issue timely hurricane advisories. As *Time* magazine reported a few weeks later, "Hour after hour, radio stations from Delaware to Maine cried the alarm, like pygmies running ahead of a mad elephant. The people listened to the loudspeakers. Families were evacuated from coastal areas where people had been trapped in 1938." The officers on the *Warrington*, too, had received multiple weather advisories telling them that a hurricane was headed toward them, but for reasons that are not entirely clear, they ignored the warnings. The result of their refusal was a death toll higher than it might otherwise have been.

FROM THESE HUMBLE BEGINNINGS grew today's impressive fleet of hurricane hunting planes, which are now operated by the Air Force Reserve Command's 53rd Weather Reconnaissance Squadron and the National Oceanic and Atmospheric Administration (NOAA). These planes get their marching orders from the National Hurricane Center in Miami, Florida, which is part of NOAA's National Weather Service (the Weather Bureau was absorbed into NOAA in 1970, and renamed the National Weather Service).

When the National Hurricane Center identifies a tropical disturbance of note that is close enough to land to be reached by a round trip on a

Mrs. Estella Hode, Miss Hurricane Hunter 1956. Estella was selected for this honor by the 59th Weather Reconnaissance Squadron at Kindley Air Force Base, Bermuda. The logo to her left shows the typical hurricane swirl with the hurricane warning flags in the middle. The wording on the logo reads "Hurricane Hunters" and "Pro Bono Publico," which translates to "for the good of the public." Each year for many years, apparently, a woman was crowned with this title.

single tank of fuel, it sends Hurricane Hunter planes to investigate. These planes, which include Lockheed WC-130J's and WP-3D Orions, are flying data-collecting marvels full of high-tech instruments and trained meteorologists, not to mention first-rate pilots and navigators, whose job is to gather information that is used by the National Hurricane Center to assess the disturbance and, if need be, issue tropical storm or hurricane watches or warnings.

One of the key instruments on board is radar (which stands for "radio detection and ranging"), a technology developed during World War II. Originally intended to detect enemy aircraft, radar was also found to have meteorological applications. More specifically, it uses the scattering and reflection of microwaves to identify, visualize, and analyze all sorts of weather phenomena, including hurricanes. Among the many things that radar can do is locate and display the outlines of the hurricane, such as the eye and eyewall, as well as measure rainfall intensity. Radar is deployed not only on Hurricane Hunters but also on land, where it provides the same services to meteorologists tracking tropical storms and hurricanes as they come closer to the coast and travel inland.

Another critical instrument is the *dropsonde* (or dropwindsonde), a cylindrical and expendable weather device packed with sensors that measure temperature, humidity, and pressure. It also contains a global positioning system antenna and receiver that make possible the tracking of wind speed and direction. As the name implies, the dropsonde is dropped from a Hurricane Hunter through a launch chute that extends through the plane's fuselage. Deploying a miniparachute, the dropsonde floats down through the hurricane while its radio transmits all the measurements back to the plane every 0.5 second. One other key piece of equipment is the Stepped-Frequency Microwave Radiometer (SFMR), which can measure wind speed just above the ocean's surface, as well as precipitation rates, in real time.

There have been thousands of Hurricane Hunter flights over the years. Despite the violence of hurricanes, such flights are relatively safe. One Hurricane Hunter pilot said that "the most dangerous part of his day is not flying through the eye of a hurricane, it's driving to the runway and climbing a steep ladder to get on board the plane."

The main danger during a Hurricane Hunter flight is not the straight-line winds—after all, commercial jets often fly in the jet stream with or against winds of 150 mph or more—but rather sudden updrafts or down-drafts. Under the best of circumstances these can make for a very bumpy flight, and in the worst cases they can rip the plane apart. While most hurricane hunting flights are relatively routine, if not quite grueling, more than a few have been downright scary. Early Hurricane Hunter crews called such flights "hairy hops."

During one hairy hop in 1945, the navigator provided a colorful description of his experience flying through a hurricane with wind speeds of 125 mph. "One minute this plane, seemingly under control, would suddenly wrench itself free, throw itself into a vertical bank and head straight for the steaming white sea below. An instant later it was on the other wing, this time climbing . . . at an ungodly speed. To ditch would be disastrous. I stood on my hands as much as I did on my feet." A short while later, this man, who had more than 1,500 hours of flight time and had never once been airsick, lost his "cookies."

A September 1989 flight into Hurricane Hugo, a Category 5 that was approaching the Lesser Antilles and would later make landfall in South Carolina as a Category 4, was one of the worst. As the NOAA plane *Kermit*, named after the beloved Muppets character, flew through the eyewall at a very low altitude of 1,500 feet, Dr. Jeff Masters, the flight director, recounted the terror.

> Darkness falls. Powerful gusts of winds tear at the aircraft, slamming us from side to side. Torrential rains hammer the airplane. . . . A fierce updraft wrenches the airplane, slams us into our seats with twice the force of gravity. Seconds later, we dangle weightless as a stomach-wrenching downdraft slams us downward. . . . Thick dark clouds suddenly envelop the aircraft. A titanic fist of wind, three times the force of gravity, smashes us. I am thrown into the computer console, bounce off, and for one terrifying instant find myself looking DOWN at a precipitous angle. . . . A second massive jolt rocks the aircraft. Gear loosened by the previous turbulence flies about the inside [of] the aircraft, bouncing off walls, ceiling, and crewmembers. . . . A third terrific blow, almost six times the force of gravity staggers the airplane. . . . Terrible thundering crashing sounds boom through the cabin; I hear crewmembers crying out. . . . We are going down. . . . The aircraft lurches out

of control into a hard right bank. We plunge towards the ocean, our number three engine in flames. Debris hangs from the number four engine. The turbulence suddenly stops. The clouds part. The darkness lifts. We fall into the eye of Hurricane Hugo.

Gravely injured but still flying, *Kermit* circled within the eye. To lighten the load so that the plane could ascend to a safer altitude before attempting to exit the hurricane, the pilot dumped 15,000 of the 50,000 pounds of fuel. The meteorologists continued to collect what weather information they could, and to help get rid of additional weight they deployed all twenty-two of the expendable bathythermographs on board, which radio back measurements of water temperature and ocean current speed and weigh about 30 pounds each. The main goal at this point shifted from data gathering to sheer survival, and on that score *Kermit* received a huge assist from two other Hurricane Hunters that had been sent out with *Kermit* to explore Hugo—NOAA's *Miss Piggy* and the air force's *Teal 57*.

Upon learning of *Kermit*'s dire situation, *Miss Piggy* and *Teal 57* entered the eye. They circled and penetrated the eyewall at various locations, searching for a "soft spot" where the turbulence was less. Finally, *Teal 57* found it at about 7,000 feet, and *Kermit* followed the air force plane out of the hurricane. The exit was another wild ride, with winds of 170 mph, gusts up to 190 mph, and a few terrific updrafts, but it was not as bad as the entry, and within a couple of minutes it was all over. "Praise God!" yelled the exuberant Masters. "The sun never looked so good. We are alive!" *Kermit* returned to the airfield on Barbados. It sat out the rest of the 1989 hurricane season but, after repairs, was back in action the next year.

As terrifying as *Kermit*'s flight was, there are a few that were far worse. Six Hurricane Hunter planes have crashed, killing all on board. Of those, five were doing reconnaissance on typhoons in the Pacific. The only Hurricane Hunter lost in the Atlantic was in 1955, when a crew of eleven, including two reporters, flying out of Guantánamo Bay, went down over the Caribbean Sea while investigating a Category 4 hurricane named Janet. The last clear radio transmission, which came in at 8:30 a.m. on September 26, ended with "beginning penetration." Almost two hours later, another message arrived, but it was garbled. Despite a massive search operation, not a single piece of debris was ever found.

Hurricane Hunter planes are key to tracking and analyzing storms once they are located, but what of locating them in the first place? Historically, meteorologists relied on reports from ships and island-based weather stations to alert them to approaching storms. In 1960, a radically new and game-changing device—the weather satellite—came on line. The Russians—and the Cold War—deserve part of the credit for this achievement.

ON OCTOBER 4, 1957, the Soviet Union successfully launched Sputnik 1 into orbit, the world's first artificial satellite (*sputnik* originally meant "fellow traveler" in Russian, but now it is a synonym for "satellite"). It was only about the size of a beach ball, weighing a mere 184 pounds, but when it passed over the United States, emitting a chirping sound, American observers on the ground were shocked. The Russians not only had proved that they could successfully launch a satellite but also had spawned fears that the missile that sent the satellite into orbit could also be used to rain nuclear warheads down on Europe and America. "Never before had so small and so harmless an object created such consternation," observed one historian. America's long-held belief that it was the world's leader in science and technology was shaken, and that the blow had come from its sworn Cold War enemy, the Russians, made this new advance all the more difficult to comprehend and accept. Russia struck again just a few weeks later. On November 3 it launched Sputnik 2, which carried a heavier payload and a 14-pound dog named Laika (Russian for "barker").

America's response to the Russian challenge was to initiate its own satellite program and create the National Aeronautics and Space Administration (NASA) in 1958. The United States began sending satellites into orbit, and on April 1, 1960, the TIROS-1 (Television Infrared Observation Satellite), the nation's first successful weather satellite, was launched. An experiment intended to test various operational features, TIROS-1 lasted only seventy-eight days in orbit. But it offered a glimmer of just how important satellites could be in tracking hurricanes, by transmitting to Earth a photograph of a typhoon about 800 miles east of Brisbane, Australia, that local meteorologists didn't even know existed.

Weather satellites have evolved tremendously since then and are extremely sophisticated and critically important tools in the National Weather Service's armamentarium for monitoring and understanding

TIROS-1, the nation's first weather satellite.

hurricanes. Bob Sheets, a former director of the National Hurricane Center, called satellites "the greatest single achievement in observing tools for tropical meteorology."

Jointly with NASA, NOAA operates two types of satellites. Weather satellites of the Polar-orbiting Operational Environmental Satellite (POES) series, located about 520 miles above Earth, orbit in a north–south direction over the poles and collect images within a 1,740-mile-wide swath of the globe on each pass. They observe most locations on Earth twice daily—once at night and once during the day.

Satellites of the Geostationary Operational Environmental Satellite (GOES) system, on the other hand, orbit the Earth at the same rate as the Earth's rotation, and therefore have a fixed location. GOES satellites are located 22,300 miles above the Earth's equator and are able to capture images of large sections of the planet, covering the entire Western Hemisphere. The great value of GOES satellites is that they take continuous footage, beamed down to Earth as frequently as every thirty seconds, show-ing changes in the atmosphere over time—a meteorological movie of sorts.

Satellites are an indispensable supplement to Hurricane Hunter flights. Whereas planes are limited in range by the amount of fuel they carry, satel-lites can monitor the entire Atlantic and Pacific Oceans. Thus, they enable meteorologists to track hurricanes from their inception to their dissolu-tion. No longer can these storms launch a surprise attack. In addition to monitoring the movement of hurricanes over time, satellites, like hurri-cane hunting planes, have plenty of high-tech instruments on board that help meteorologists analyze a variety of parameters, including sea surface temperature and height, cloud and precipitation data, heat energy, and water vapor concentration.

The data gathered by Hurricane Hunters and satellites, as well as through additional means, such as weather balloons and oceanic buoys, helped meteorologists make great strides in understanding hurricane dynamics. Key discoveries since the 1940s include identifying the role of African easterly waves in the genesis of hurricanes and highlighting essen-tial factors in hurricane development, among them water temperatures of at least 80 degrees Fahrenheit to a depth of about 150 feet, and low vertical wind shear. Other breakthroughs include a better understanding of the influence of upper-atmosphere steering currents in determining a hurri-cane's path, and a much richer and fuller picture of the anatomy of hurri-canes from top to bottom.

THE MAIN REASON FOR collecting data and conducting basic research is to improve our ability to forecast the track and intensity of hurricanes to provide enough advance warning for people to prepare and, if neces-sary, leave the area. With lives in jeopardy, and the prospect of spending potentially millions of dollars on evacuations, and losing millions more as a result of lost economic output, it is incredibly important that these forecasts be as accurate as possible. That is a difficult task, since, as MIT professor and meteorologist Kerry Emanuel states, "no natural phenome-non poses a greater challenge to forecasters than the hurricane."

The most valuable hurricane forecasting tool is computer modeling. First developed in the United States, it has come a long way since its incep-tion in the early 1950s, when computers themselves were only just entering the mainstream. Today, by feeding huge amounts of data into mathematically based models of hurricane behavior that are run on powerful supercomputers, meteorologists can generate predictions of what a hurricane is likely to do and become in the coming hours, days, and even weeks.

The National Hurricane Center uses a great range of models that vary tremendously in terms of complexity and design. In brief, there are statistical models that rely heavily on the short-term behavior of the hurricane, as well as on tracks of past hurricanes that have followed a similar path, to predict future movement. This is the simplest type of model and is rarely used for forecasting, and then only as a benchmark against which to check the accuracy of other models. More complex and reliable dynamical models ignore historical data, instead creating output based on the mass of data gathered about the particular hurricane in question, and the weather that surrounds it. Statistical-dynamical models combine elements of both approaches.

Dynamical models divide the globe into three-dimensional grids composed of different shapes, such as squares or hexagons. Each grid point, which can be on the order of 6–60 miles on a side and of varying thickness, contains all of the data—atmospheric pressure, temperature, wind speed, and so on—that meteorologists have gathered from various sources, which characterize what is happening at any given moment. This snapshot description, or meteorological bio of the grid points, is called the *initial conditions*. When the model is run, the initial conditions are input into a computer, and the computer iteratively solves an array of elaborate equations to predict how the hurricane will evolve over time. The complexity of these models is reflected in the fact that they often take hours to run and they require the solution of as many as 10 million equations.

There are numerous hurricane forecast computer models, with different strengths and weaknesses. Among the best known are the European Centre for Medium-Range Weather Forecasts model (run out of the United Kingdom) and two National Weather Service models: the Global Forecast System model and the Hurricane Weather Research and Forecasting model. Meteorologists, however, do not rely on only a single model in making hurricane forecasts. Instead, they take into account the results from a range of models—a so-called multimodel ensemble—weighing and balancing the strengths and weaknesses of each to come to a consensus prediction. According to the National Hurricane Center, the ensemble or consensus approach "significantly increase[s] forecast accuracy over any individual model by canceling out biases found in individual models. Think of a modeling ensemble as you would a musical ensemble: while each individual instrument is vital, it is the unified whole that accomplishes harmony."

And it's not just model outputs that meteorologists consider when forecasting a hurricane or the promise of one. Added to the mix is their personal knowledge of and intuition about hurricane behavior, because forecasting is a combination of science *and* art.

Despite all the data, the sophisticated computer models, and meteorologists' accumulated wisdom, forecasting hurricanes remains a rather tricky endeavor. That is why forecasters employ a *cone of uncertainty*, which brackets the probable track of the center of the hurricane from its last recorded position out into the future. In other words, it offers a graphic illustration of where the hurricane is most likely to make landfall. To create the cone of uncertainty, the National Hurricane Center averages its hurricane forecast errors over the previous five years at intervals of 12, 24, 36, 48, 72, 96, and 120 hours. Then it draws circles around the predicted track of the hurricane's center so that "two-thirds of historical official forecast errors over a 5-year sample fall within the circle."

Since the cone captures only two-thirds of the historical forecast errors, there is a one-third chance that the hurricane center will stray outside of the cone's boundaries. And since forecasting errors become larger the farther out one goes in time, the cone of uncertainty also increases over time. Thus, according to the National Hurricane Center, in 2018 the radius of the two-thirds probability circle twenty-four hours out was 49 miles. In other words, a 2018 forecast that predicted a hurricane's center would be over New York City in the next twenty-four hours would mean there was a two-thirds chance that the hurricane's center would not be over the city, but instead would veer either 24½ miles to the north or south, with a one-third chance that it would be outside that distance. Note that the cone of uncertainty says nothing about the actual size of the storm. It tells only the rough odds of the hurricane's *center* remaining within the cone.

The good news is that over time, the cone of uncertainty for hurricanes has narrowed considerably, mirroring the improvement in forecasting accuracy as a result of better data and more sophisticated models. According to a recent paper in *Science*, "Modern 72-hour predictions of hurricane

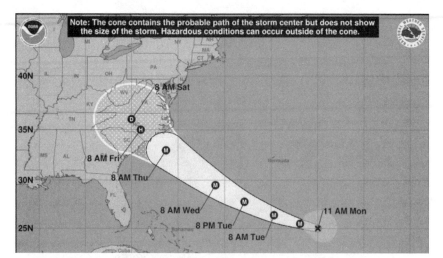

National Hurricane Center graphic showing the expanding cone of uncertainty for Hurricane Florence, which made landfall near Wrightsville Beach, North Carolina, as a Category 1 hurricane on September 14, 2018.

tracks are more accurate than 24-hour forecasts were 40 years ago." The bad, or at least disappointing, news is that the cone of uncertainty will never disappear. Edward N. Lorenz's groundbreaking work proved that.

REFLECTING ON HIS YOUTH, Lorenz said, "As a boy I was always interested in doing things with numbers, and was also fascinated by changes in the weather." He followed those passions by pursuing advanced degrees in mathematics and meteorology and then becoming a professor of meteorology at MIT. In the winter of 1961, while working in his Cambridge, Massachusetts, lab, Lorenz made a discovery that fundamentally changed how we view the world in general, and weather forecasting in particular. Like many great advances, his was triggered by a serendipitous accident.

To better understand the complexities of forecasting, Lorenz devised a relatively simple mathematical model to simulate weather patterns, which was based on twelve variables, such as wind speed and temperature. He ran the model on a Royal-McBee LGP-30 computer that was about the size of a large desk. The printouts showed columns of numbers representing how the simulated weather changed over weeks and months, according to the model's calculations. At one point, Lorenz stopped the computer to

Edward Lorenz.

examine the results more closely. Then he ran the simulation again and, in the meantime, went out to grab a cup of coffee. When he returned about an hour later and looked at the data, he was surprised to see that the two simulation runs had spit out wildly divergent results, when they should have been the same. Those divergences, which started off small at the beginning, became greater the farther out in time he looked. In fact, when he examined what the data for the two runs looked like a couple of months out, they bore absolutely no resemblance to each other.

Thinking there must have been a malfunction with the hardware, Lorenz checked the computer. But he found nothing amiss, so he turned to the results, and the problem came into focus. The computer carried numbers out to six decimal places, but to save space on paper, Lorenz had instructed the computer to round off its calculations to three decimal places when it printed out the results. When Lorenz ran the simulation the second time, he used the rounded-off numbers from the printout as the starting point instead of the actual, slightly larger numbers that the computer had used during the first simulation—for example, .506 in place of .506127. That minor change, an error of one in 5,000, made all the difference.

It was an astonishing discovery. Lorenz had shown that small changes in initial conditions can result in dramatic changes or outcomes over time. In a seminal paper published in 1963, he concluded that "[weather] prediction of the sufficiently distant future is impossible by any method, unless present conditions are known exactly. In view of the inevitable inaccuracy and incompleteness of weather observations, [the possibility of] precise very long-range forecasting would seem to be non-existent."

Although Lorenz's paper had focused on weather prediction, his startling findings had much broader implications and laid the foundation for the field of chaos theory, in which the "sensitive dependence on initial conditions" plays a key role in the behavior of a whole range of phenomena, from irregular heartbeats to the shapes of river deltas to population dynamics. In time, this principle became known in popular culture as the *butterfly effect*, a term that owes its origins to a paper that Lorenz presented in 1972, in which he posed the provocative question, "Does the flap of a butterfly's wings in Brazil set off a tornado in Texas?" Lorenz's answer was, basically, you can never know; it might or it might not, because the outcome is unpredictable. His point was not to draw a line between cause and effect, but rather to drive home his central thesis that a small change in initial conditions (such as a butterfly flapping its wings) can result in a big change or effect in the future (like a tornado in Texas).

"Remember that hurricane a thousand miles away? That was me!"

New Yorker *cartoon by Charlie Hankin, published in May 2016.*

Lorenz's findings unnerved many meteorologists at the time. As historian James Gleick observed, "The fifties and sixties were years of unreal optimism about weather forecasting." The advent of computers, satellites, and complex numerical models of weather behavior led some to believe that the problem of forecasting would one day be solved, resulting in weather predictions that were incredibly, if not unerringly, accurate far into the future. Ultimately, a good deal of that optimism was warranted, and over time forecasting did become much more accurate, but Lorenz showed that there are clear limits to such improvements.

According to Kerry Emanuel, "Experiments with sophisticated weather prediction models, having millions of equations, show the same behavior as Lorenz's simple model: very small differences in the initial state eventually amplify to render the forecasts useless. These same experiments have shown that even with excellent and very extensive measurements of the atmosphere, and very good models, it will be impossible to make detailed weather predictions beyond about two weeks." That conclusion applies to all types of weather, including hurricanes.

Given Lorenz's findings, one relatively recent method that meteorologists use to try to improve their hurricane forecasts is to run individual models many different times with different initial conditions to account for our inability to measure exactly what the atmosphere is doing at any specific moment in time. According to the European Centre for Medium-Range Weather Forecasts, "By generating a range of possible outcomes . . . [this] method can show how likely different scenarios are in the days ahead, and how long into the future the forecasts are useful. The smaller the range of predicted outcomes, the 'sharper' the forecast is said to be."

But no matter how many forecast models there are or how many variations of each model are run, meteorologists can't overcome what is called the *limit of predictability*. As meteorologists Christopher W. Landsea and John P. Cangialosi wrote, "Despite incredible improvements in tropical cyclone track forecast errors and skill, it is well accepted that making perfect forecasts will never happen." And, they conclude, we might be very close to reaching the limit of predictability, if we aren't already there.

FORECASTING HURRICANES IN REAL time is one thing; predicting how many hurricanes are likely to occur in a particular year is a very different challenge. This latter activity, called seasonal hurricane forecasting, looks much more broadly at historical records and various long-range atmospheric influences to give rough estimates of how many named tropical storms and hurricanes might develop in the Atlantic basin during a single hurricane season, and whether that number will be above or below average. Forecasts also list how many are expected to be major hurricanes, and some include a prediction of the probabilities that at least one major hurricane will hit the East Coast, the Gulf Coast, or track into the Caribbean. Seasonal hurricane forecasts are broad-brush. They say absolutely nothing specific about when or where hurricanes might strike.

William M. Gray, a professor of meteorology at Colorado State University, produced the first-ever seasonal hurricane forecast in 1984, and the Tropical Meteorology Project he founded has been issuing them ever since. These forecasts, which Gray oversaw until his death in 2016, take into account the impact of an array of factors on hurricane activity, such as sea-level pressures in the Atlantic and the El Niño–Southern Oscillation, which is the occurrence of above-average sea surface temperatures in the central and eastern tropical Pacific Ocean.

Since Gray blazed the path, roughly two dozen organizations have followed suit, issuing seasonal forecasts based on their own methodologies. These organizations include NOAA's Climate Prediction Center, IBM's Weather Company, and Tropical Storm Risk, based at University College London. The track record for seasonal hurricane forecasts is highly variable. In some years, predictions match quite well with what actually transpires, while in other years they are far off the mark. That variability applies to the efforts of all forecasting organizations. One analysis of twenty-five years' worth of forecasts from the Tropical Meteorology Project concludes that forecasts have become better over time, but they still have plenty of room for improvement.

METEOROLOGISTS ARE INTERESTED NOT only in forecasting hurricanes; for a time at least, they also wanted to control them. This impulse to modify the weather is nothing new. Humans have sought to do so since ancient times, from performing rainmaking dances to offering sacrifices that would encourage the gods to douse parched land. Given the life-nurturing power of water, it is perhaps no surprise that the first proposal for weather modification in the United States also focused on rain. In the mid-1800s, James Espy advanced the idea of making it rain by lighting forests on fire. He believed that the rising heated air would entrap water vapor, and once this moist, warm column of air ascended high enough, it would cool, thereby condensing the vapor into water and creating rain. Fellow scientists thought this a ridiculous and dangerous idea, and it was never tested. A century later, another weather modification idea took flight in America, this time focusing on hurricanes.

On October 13, 1947, a B-17 bomber dropped 180 pounds of dry ice (solid carbon dioxide) into the outer edges of a hurricane 415 miles east of Jacksonville, Florida, with the goal of weakening the storm by altering its structure. This audacious experiment grew out of Project Cirrus, a joint effort of the General Electric Research Laboratory, the US Naval Research Laboratory, and the US Army Signal Corps that was intended to explore whether seeding clouds with dry ice could induce precipitation.

This idea was the brainchild of General Electric's Irving Langmuir, winner of the 1932 Nobel Prize in Chemistry, Vincent J. Schaefer, and Bernard Vonnegut (Kurt Vonnegut's older brother). Together, they pioneered the idea of cloud seeding. They found that if a nucleus such as dry ice or silver iodide was introduced into a cloud filled with supercooled water (colder than 32 degrees Fahrenheit, but not frozen), the water droplets would coalesce around the nucleus, forming snow or ice crystals, which would fall to the ground still frozen, or melt on the way down, thus becoming rain.* Project Cirrus's main focus was to introduce dry-ice nuclei into

---

* From 1947 to 1951, Kurt Vonnegut worked as a publicist at General Electric. While there, he heard about a visit that the science fiction writer H. G. Wells had made to the lab, during which Langmuir suggested an idea for a book revolving around a scientist who invented a new substance that freezes or crystallizes at room temperature. When it is dropped in the ocean it becomes a seed crystal that initiates a chain reaction that turns all the water to ice. Although Wells showed no interest, Vonnegut did. When he finally left General Electric to pursue a writing career, Vonnegut featured a substance with similar characteristics, called "Ice Nine," in his book *Cat's Cradle.* Ice Nine works in much the same way that dry ice and silver iodide do in a cloud, creating a nucleus around which water coalesces, forming Ice Nine ad infinitum. I won't spoil the ending, but let's just say that Ice Nine does not benefit humankind. See Sam Kean, *Caesar's Last Breath: Decoding the Secrets of the Air around Us* (New York: Little, Brown, 2017), 276; and James Rodger Fleming, *Fixing the*

a variety of cloud types to see whether they could produce snow and rain, which would have practical applications in drought situations and during times of war, when the ability to cause rain or snowfall on cue could be a very effective way of slowing down the enemy. The project also sought to manipulate hurricanes, which is what led to that October 1947 flight. In its most basic form, the thinking was that transforming the supercooled water in the hurricane's clouds into ice would release latent heat that would, in turn, decrease the hurricane's stability, thereby reducing its strength.

Seeding a hurricane was a risky proposition, to say the least. The biggest fear was that the storm would change direction and hit land, raising concerns that project sponsors might be held liable for any deaths and destruction that ensued. To minimize that possibility, the researchers waited for the *right* hurricane to arrive. So, when a hurricane that the military had named King swept northeastward over the tip of Florida and into the Atlantic on October 12, the B-17 Flying Fortress took off the next day. After all, King was far offshore, heading away from the coast, and weakening. Even if it changed direction, it was thought, the chance that it would hit land was remote.

While the B-17 dropped the dry ice, two other supporting airplanes watched the clouds to detect changes. What they saw was confusing. One group of clouds appeared to break up, while another grew a bit. The following day, the planes returned to record any additional changes, but the hurricane wasn't where they thought it would be. Instead, further searching revealed that the hurricane had made a sharp turn—135 degrees to the left—and was now heading west toward land. Furthermore, the hurricane had become stronger. On October 15, against all assumptions, King came ashore at Savannah, Georgia, killing one person and causing millions of dollars in damage.

Newspapers were quick to pounce, implying, and sometimes claiming, that seeding had caused the hurricane to swerve and, therefore, Project Cirrus was to blame. "In Savannah last week," *Time* magazine reported, "Southern blood bubbled toward the boiling point. A Miami weatherman had hinted that last month's disastrous hurricane might not have been an Act of God, but just a low Yankee trick." Langmuir only made things worse when he said he was "99% sure" that seeding was the reason the hurricane had changed direction.

Sky: The Checkered History of Weather and Climate Control (New York: Columbia University Press, 2010), 46.

Weather Bureau personnel working on Project Stormfury pose in front of a Douglas DC-6 plane in 1966 in Miami, Florida.

His Nobel Prize notwithstanding, Langmuir was wrong. The Weather Bureau later proved that the hurricane had actually begun turning west before the seeding, and the bureau also shared information about other hurricanes that had exhibited similar behavior. The damage, however, had been done. Project Cirrus was eyed warily from then on, and it steered clear of hurricanes. The project finally shut down in 1952, but the idea of seeding hurricanes would not die with it, resurfacing in 1962 at the inception of Project Stormfury.

THE NATIONAL HURRICANE RESEARCH PROJECT, which would later morph into NOAA's Hurricane Research Division, implemented Stormfury in cooperation with the navy. In essence, it was a much more sophisticated and well-funded version of Project Cirrus and, as science writer Sam Kean pointed out, it had a "kickass" name. This time, however, the sole focus was modifying hurricanes through seeding. Instead of dropping dry ice, Stormfury's nucleus of choice was silver iodide.

The project, which lasted twenty-one years, continuing until 1983, conducted only four flights into hurricanes. Part of the reason so many years elapsed between missions is that researchers were well aware of the skewering that Project Cirrus had received, and they didn't want to be blamed if a hurricane suddenly turned and headed straight for the coast. Therefore, just like those who had run Project Cirrus, they waited until the *right* hurricane showed up, hoping they would have better luck than their predecessors. Not only did the hurricane have to be far from the coast and show no signs of turning toward land, but it also had to be mature, with a well-developed eyewall.

The results of Project Stormfury were mixed. On two of the runs, the hurricane's winds decreased by 10–30 percent. But the other applications failed to do anything, and the lack of effect was blamed, in part, on faulty execution. Reflecting on the limited positive results, the researchers ultimately concluded that the project had "two fatal flaws: it was neither microphysically nor statistically feasible. Observational evidence indicates that seeding in hurricanes would be ineffective because they contain too little supercooled water and too much natural ice. Moreover, the expected results of seeding are often indistinguishable from naturally occurring intensity changes." One of the Stormfury pilots later admitted his frustration with how things turned out. "It was disappointing to concede we couldn't really do it. But the storms were so big, and we were so small." Nevertheless, Stormfury was not a bust. Funding provided by Congress enabled NOAA to purchase two hurricane hunting planes, and the research that Stormfury supported contributed mightily to the general understanding of hurricane behavior.

SINCE THE MID- TO LATE 1900S, many other methods besides cloud seeding have been suggested for controlling and even eliminating hurricanes, all of which are creative, if not outlandish and totally impractical. Some of the most fanciful ideas include flying an enormous fleet of propeller-driven planes around a hurricane, in a clockwise direction, to "unwind" the storm; towing icebergs from the Arctic to the tropics to cool the ocean and sap hurricanes of energy; having supersonic jets circling a hurricane create a sonic boom that would shatter the storm by disrupting the upward flow of warm air; shooting lasers at hurricanes; and locating a phalanx of enormous windmills on the coast to blow an approaching hurricane away from the shore. Then there is one of the most popular suggestions of all: nuke 'em! Just drop a few nuclear bombs into a hurricane and blow it apart. Every year, the National Hurricane Center receives letters advocating this purportedly wonderful solution.

The most fundamental reason why these ideas won't work, other than the fact that some of them can't pass the laugh test or are technically infeasible, is the same one that the Stormfury pilot lamented: hurricanes are simply much too massive and powerful to be subdued by the likes of these relatively puny human efforts. Even nuclear bombs would be swallowed whole by a hurricane, which would just keep chugging along in the wake of the explosion. And let's not forget about the worry of nuclear fallout!

Beyond the technological and scientific hurdles standing between us and our ability to control hurricanes, ethical questions remain. The fact that humans don't have the best track record when it comes to manipulating nature should perhaps give us pause. We don't know what the world would be like without hurricanes, or with fewer or weaker ones, and to succeed at creating such a future might release a Pandora's box of unforeseen consequences.

ALONG WITH THE MANY advances in tracking, analyzing, forecasting, and understanding hurricanes that took place between the 1940s and the present, there was also a dramatic change in the way hurricanes are named. Until the 1940s, hurricanes were christened in a variety of ways. Sometimes they were named after the year they struck or the area most directly affected, and often a combination of the two. Thus we have the "Great Colonial Hurricane of 1635," the "Great September Gale of 1815," the "Great Miami Hurricane of 1926," and the "Great Hurricane of 1938," all of which lend credence to the notion that when it comes to naming hurricanes, our forebears were exceptionally fond of the adjective *great*.

Hurricanes in the Caribbean were often named after the saint whose feast was celebrated on the day the hurricane arrived—for example, the "San Narciso Hurricane," which struck the Danish West Indies and Puerto Rico in 1867. A few hurricanes were unofficially named after living people, as was the case in 1949 when President Harry Truman was in Miami addressing the Veterans of Foreign Wars while the first hurricane of the season was heading toward the Caribbean. This confluence of events prompted the *Miami Herald* to label the storm "Harry's Hurricane." To give equal billing to Truman's wife, when another hurricane struck Florida later that year, some called it "Hurricane Bess." In addition, many hurricanes deemed not worthy of a name have slipped unheralded into the mists of history.

During the late 1940s and early 1950s, sometimes so many hurricanes formed that the public had a difficult time identifying, tracking, and keeping them separate, especially when they occurred close together or hit land at roughly the same time in subsequent years. In 1951, the Weather Bureau decided to remedy this situation by adopting the military's method of identifying hurricanes using the Joint Army/Navy Phonetic Alphabet— Able, Baker, Charlie, Dog, Easy, and so on.*

This system worked fine for a year, but in 1952 the International Air Transport Association adopted a different phonetic alphabet for naming hurricanes, which began Alfa, Bravo, Coca, Delta, Echo. Just as things started to get really confusing—was it hurricane Able or Alfa?—the bureau, in conjunction with the military, decided to scrap the phonetic system and start naming hurricanes after women. This peculiar choice was based on a very interesting history, and it all started with a unique and memorable man named Clement Lindley Wragge.

FROM 1887 TO 1902, Wragge was the chief weather forecaster for the Australian state of Queensland. Fearless, egotistical, well versed in the classics, and blessed with a clever wit, Wragge, who was tall and thin and had a "mop of flaming red hair and explosive temper to match," turned weather forecasting into an art form. Starting off rather tamely in the mid-1890s, he began naming tropical storms and typhoons that threatened the Australia coast by using letters from the Greek alphabet. He soon branched out, applying names of Greek and Roman gods, ancient military heroes, and imaginary native women, whom he invariably referred to as maidens.

Never one to leave his names unadorned, Wragge gave them a little personality. Tropical storm Elina was a "dusky maiden," while for another disturbance, dubbed Mahina, he warned his readers, "We fear that Mahina

---

* Actually, the bureau had been using this system internally since 1947, but only in 1951 decided to make it public.

Clement Wragge, circa 1901.

will not prove so soft and gentle as the Tahitian maiden of that name." Wragge once told his readers that he viewed himself as a "godfather, giving them [tropical disturbances] the soft bubbling names of bewitching maidens of the South Sea Islands."

When his stint as Queensland's official forecaster ended in 1902, because of a lack of funding, Wragge started his own weather bureau that, although private, still depended in part on government support. That's when the trouble began. His reports went from artistic and relatively innocuous to combative and biting. The focus of his wrath was the politicians who either blocked funding for his bureau, or annoyed him in some other way. To get even, and perhaps even prompt a change in course, Wragge named storms after local and regional politicians in the most unflattering way. One of his more pointed digs noted an "Antarctic disturbance named 'Jenkins'—in honor of the Premier of South Australia, who takes such a warm interest in this office that he will not even assist us by a fractional part—is now southwest from Melbourne. Gradients on the eastern side of 'Jenkins' are steep, ugly, and suspicious, and shipping and passengers over the Upper Tasman Sea will remember him for many a long day."

Although Wragge had many followers, his attacks earned him the enmity of the one group—politicians—that could help him dig out of his ever-deepening financial hole. Hemorrhaging money, he was forced to close his weather bureau in July 1903, which put an end to his naming scheme as well. Wragge spent much of his time until his death in 1922 on the lecture circuit in Australia and beyond, struggling to provide for his family.

The notion of naming storms after women gained new life in 1941, when prolific novelist George Rippey Stewart wrote a book titled *Storm*. In doing the research for the book, Stewart read about the irascible Wragge and his penchant for naming storms after women, and decided to do the same. The plot of Stewart's book revolves around a massive storm, not a typhoon or hurricane, that travels across the Pacific and slams into California. One of the book's main characters, a recently hired junior meteorologist at the Weather Bureau, gets creative and begins naming the storms after girls he has known, as well as famous actresses and heroines. After all, he believes that each storm is "an individual," with its own personality and characteristics. The names he chooses, however, are for his amusement alone, and he dare not share them with his colleagues.

At one point, while in his office scanning maps and plotting data that is coming in over the wires, the fictional junior meteorologist notes an "incipient little whorl" southeast of Japan. As he has done with all the other storms he has tracked, he decides "he must name the baby." His choice is "Maria." "As if he had been a minister who had just christened a baby, he found himself smiling and benign, inchoately wishing it joy and prosperity. Good luck, Maria!" Over the next eleven chapters, one for each day of the storm's life, the book follows the course of Maria, and for most of that time the junior meteorologist keeps mum about naming storms. In the chapter covering the ninth day of the storm, however, he shares his secret with the chief meteorologist, who, sheepishly, tells the young man that he has done the very same thing! But instead of women, the chief names storms mostly after famous men and conquerors of history.

Storm became a bestseller and was included as one of the books sent to the GIs fighting overseas. The book's success contributed to, if not being the sole reason for, the military's decision to informally start naming Pacific typhoons after women in 1944.

Maria, Stewart's favorite storm, became even more famous in 1951, when the hit musical *Paint Your Wagon* opened on Broadway. It included a song titled "They Call the Wind Maria," which became a hit on the radio as well. Even though the play is not about a storm, but rather concerns love and loss in a mining town during the California gold rush, the connection between Stewart's book and the song is undeniable. Those who have heard this wonderful ballad know that the name Maria is sung as if it had a silent *h* at the end ("mar-eye-uh"), and in fact, Stewart had written in the 1947 edition of *Storm* that that is just how Maria's name was supposed to be pronounced.

Taking up the practice, in 1953 the Weather Bureau and the military jointly agreed to start naming hurricanes after women on a trial basis. Unsurprisingly, the decision angered many. In subsequent years, the bureau received considerable, and often quite spirited, pushback from the public, complaining that it was inappropriate, if not downright insulting, to name hurricanes in this manner, and asking the bureau to reconsider. One observer argued that associating women with the "tragedy and havoc created by hurricanes [is] a personification of extremely poor judgment." Another was a bit less serious but still not amused, saying, "She would rather have an unnamed hurricane hit her house than a storm named after one of her husband's old girlfriends." The bureau, however, would not be swayed. It stuck fast to its naming system, making it permanent in 1956. Protests died down—that is, until Roxcy Bolton spoke up.

CALLED THE "FOUNDING MOTHER of Florida's modern feminist movement" by the *Miami Herald*, Bolton was a national vice president of the National Organization for Women (NOW), which was a leader in the battle for women's equality. In 1968, Betty Friedan, legendary author of *The Feminist Mystique* and cofounder of NOW, recalled that Bolton wrote to her "all incensed at the practice of using women's names to name hurricanes." Two years later, Bolton gave priority to the cause of compelling the National Weather Service to stop. The obviously gendered and misogynistic way in which hurricanes were discussed in the press, on radio, and on television infuriated her. She was tired of reading and hearing media accounts in which female-named hurricanes were variously described as "witches," "capricious," "furious," "savage," "bad girls," "unladylike," "vicious," "erratic," "eccentric," "treacherous," a "slut," and acting "like a woman in

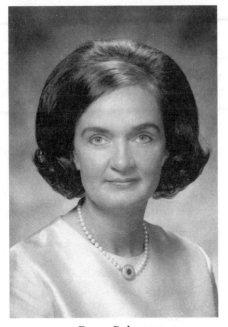

Roxcy Bolton.

labor," to name just a few of the aspersions. Cartoonists, too, had a field day depicting hurricanes as vengeful women terrorizing the coast.

Bolton didn't just complain; she acted, sending a "cease and desist" order to the National Weather Service, demanding that it stop calling hurricanes by female names because it "reflects and creates an extremely derogatory attitude toward women." She added, "Women are human beings and deeply resent being arbitrarily associated with disaster."

Bolton offered some alternatives. Hurricanes could, she said, be named after birds, or perhaps US senators, especially since they "delight in having streets, bridges, [and] buildings" named for them; just add hurricanes to the list. "Can't you just see the headlines, like 'U.S. Sen. Barry Goldwater Annihilates Louisiana' or 'U.S. Sen. Jacob Javits Destroys New York'?" Bolton once said. She even recommended that hurricanes be called "himicanes" instead. To drive her point home, Bolton attended hurricane conferences sponsored by the National Weather Service and appealed directly to those who were in charge of the naming system. Although she certainly raised the profile of this issue, the service refused to budge. Then, US secretary of commerce Dr. Juanita Kreps took up the cause.

Appointed by President Jimmy Carter in January 1977, Kreps was the first woman ever to hold this position—yet another positive sign of changing attitudes toward gender equality. A self-described feminist, Kreps heartily supported Bolton's initiative, and she looked to Australia for inspiration and guidance. In 1975, the "Land Down Under" decided to honor the spirit of the United Nations' International Women's Year by switching from naming hurricanes only after women—which it had been doing since 1963—to naming them after women and men, on an alternating basis. Soon after taking office, Kreps ordered that the United States do the same. There was one slight problem, though. The United States no longer controlled the naming system. Recent changes had passed that responsibility on to a committee of the World Meteorological Organization. Even if that organization agreed with the change, it would take a few years to implement, since the slate of names for a specific hurricane season was selected a couple of years in advance.

In the end the United States proved persuasive, and in 1979 gender equality won out over tired bureaucracy. From that point forward, Atlantic tropical storms and hurricanes would alternate between male and female names. Coming at a time when sexism was being challenged in many areas of society, the new naming system garnered widespread coverage in the press, and almost no opposition. A few voices, however, were raised in favor of eliminating gendered names entirely, and instead identifying hurricanes by another system that was devoid of any social connotation, such as a numbering scheme.

Today, six lists, each containing twenty-one names, are used in rotation. If in any year there are more than twenty-one named storms, subsequent storms are assigned a letter from the Greek alphabet. As was the case even before the male-female naming scheme went into effect, if a particularly deadly and/or costly hurricane occurs, its name is retired because reusing it is viewed as being insensitive to those who suffered. Since 1953, roughly ninety names have been retired. When a name is retired, an international committee of the World Meteorological Organization chooses a replacement.

Perhaps the sweetest story about hurricane names comes from 2017, when Hurricanes Harvey and Irma struck one after the other in late August and early September. This juxtaposition was followed by a spate of articles highlighting Harvey and Irma Schluter of Spokane, Washington,

"If they want us to take these storms seriously, they have to start giving them scarier names."

New Yorker *cartoon by Emily Flake, published in November 2012, in the wake of Hurricane Sandy.*

who were 102 and 92, respectively, at the time and had been married for seventy-five years. What a coincidence! It was the first time that hurricanes bearing those two names had struck in succession, and it would be the last, since both names were retired.

ANOTHER NEW METHOD of identifying hurricanes went into effect just about the time that Bolton was starting her crusade against the inherently sexist naming convention. Since the late 1800s, meteorologists had struggled to alert the public to the severity of approaching hurricanes so that people could take appropriate action. They could use a range of adjectives, such as *powerful* or *major*, but still people had a hard time grasping the potential danger they faced. Relief agencies, too, found it tough to figure out what type of response a hurricane might merit. What was needed was a shorthand method of identifying the risk posed by hurricanes. Herbert S. Saffir and Dr. Robert Homer Simpson provided just that.

Robert Simpson (left), with Cecil Gentry at the National Hurricane Research Project Research Operations Base in West Palm Beach, Florida, 1956. Notice the hurricane project logo on the building, showing the universal symbol for a hurricane—the swirl.

Saffir was an engineer who had done work for the United Nations, evaluating the impact of hurricanes, typhoons, cyclones, and other such storms on low-cost housing throughout the world. To delineate the damage that would ensue from storms of varying intensity, he created a wind scale that ran from 75 to 155 mph, and divided it into five categories based on speed. In 1971, Saffir showed his scale to Simpson, the director of the National Hurricane Center, and a man who had been emotionally scarred by a hurricane in his youth.

Born in Corpus Christi, Texas, in 1912, Simpson spent his early years in a two-story home a little more than a block from Corpus Christi Bay. On Sunday, September 14, 1919, a hurricane demolished much of the city, including Simpson's house. He and his family, thankfully, were not harmed, since they had evacuated to the city's courthouse, which was on higher ground. There, on the sixth floor, Simpson and the other evacuees watched helplessly as the hurricane tore through their beloved city. One scene in particular was seared into Simpson's memory. He saw a man holding on to a baby, precariously perched atop a cistern bobbing down the street. When it reached an intersection, the swirling and crosscutting currents caused the cistern to spin, pitching the man into the water. After what seemed like an eternity to Simpson, the man resurfaced without the baby, and then immediately dove back into the water to find his child. This time, however, he didn't reemerge. "What a dreadful experience to be thrust on a 6½-year-old lad," Simpson would later recall. He also appreciated how lucky he had been. Had the hurricane struck on Friday instead of Sunday, Simpson, along with countless other Corpus Christi children, would have been in the school at the time, which was completely destroyed on that deadly day.

Following this traumatic experience, Simpson would become, decades later, one of the nation's most respected meteorologists, whose research focused squarely on hurricanes. When he saw Saffir's scale, he pounced on the possibilities it opened up. He had long been thinking about how the National Hurricane Center could improve its communication of hurricane risk, and he realized that the scale provided an excellent foundation to build on. A version of the eponymously named Saffir-Simpson Hurricane Wind Scale, which ranks hurricanes from Category 1 through 5, is still in use today.*

So widespread has use of the scale become that it is almost impossible to imagine discussing a hurricane without mentioning its category. As another sign of the scale's resonance, the most devastating category has made its way into the popular culture as a synonym for absolute annihilation. As meteorologist Robert Henson put it, "I once heard the financial meltdown of 2008 described as a Category 5 storm. That tells you something about how deeply the Saffir-Simpson scale has penetrated the consciousness of the American public."

---

* The earliest versions of the Saffir-Simpson scale incorporated central pressure, storm surge, and flooding impact as components of the categories, but those factors were later dropped in favor of focusing solely on wind speed, for a number of reasons—for example, the great variability of storm surge based on local bathymetry, the size of the hurricane, and the angle at which it strikes the coast.

SAFFIR-SIMPSON HURRICANE WIND SCALE

CATEGORY	SUSTAINED WINDS*	TYPES OF DAMAGE
1	74–95 mph 64–82 kt 119–153 km/h	**Very dangerous winds will produce some damage:** Well-constructed frame homes could have damage to roof, shingles, vinyl siding, and gutters. Large branches of trees will snap and shallowly rooted trees may be toppled. Extensive damage to power lines and poles likely will result in power outages that could last a few to several days.
2	96–110 mph 83–95 kt 154–177 km/h	**Extremely dangerous winds will cause extensive damage:** Well-constructed frame homes could sustain major roof and siding damage. Many shallowly rooted trees will be snapped or uprooted and block numerous roads. Near-total power loss is expected with outages that could last from several days to weeks.
3 (major)	111–129 mph 96–112 kt 178–208 km/h	**Devastating damage will occur:** Well-built framed homes may incur major damage or removal of roof decking and gable ends. Many trees will be snapped or uprooted, blocking numerous roads. Electricity and water will be unavailable for several days to weeks after the storm passes.
4 (major)	130–156 mph 113–136 kt 209–251 km/h	**Catastrophic damage will occur:** Well-built framed homes can sustain severe damage with loss of most of the roof structure and/or some exterior walls. Most trees will be snapped or uprooted and power poles downed. Fallen trees and power poles will isolate residential areas. Power outages will last weeks to possibly months. Most of the area will be uninhabitable for weeks or months.
5 (major)	157 mph or higher 137 kt or higher 252 km/h or higher	**Catastrophic damage will occur:** A high percentage of framed homes will be destroyed, with total roof failure and wall collapse. Fallen trees and power poles will isolate residential areas. Power outages will last for weeks to possibly months. Most of the area will be uninhabitable for weeks or months.

*kt = knots.

Source: National Hurricane Center, "Saffir-Simpson Hurricane Wind Scale," accessed September 2018, https://www.nhc.noaa.gov/aboutsshws.php.

AS THE MANNER OF naming and categorizing hurricanes evolved, so, too, did the way in which the media reported on them. In the late nineteenth and early twentieth centuries, newspapers were the main source of information about hurricanes. The advent of radio in the 1920s provided another avenue for such news. But reporting on hurricanes really exploded in the 1950s, during the Golden Age of Television.

One of the first to realize the inherent drama of bringing hurricane coverage visually into people's living rooms was Edward R. Murrow. The most influential and respected journalist of his generation, Murrow had earned his position through his unflinching and heroic radio reporting from Europe for CBS on the rise of Hitler, the subsequent war, and, most memorably, the horrific bombing of London, known as the Blitz. When Murrow returned to the United States, he continued his broadcasting career with CBS. One of his signature shows in the early 1950s was the Emmy-and-Peabody-award-winning television newsmagazine and documentary series *See It Now*, in which Murrow presented to viewers an insightful analysis of the week's top news stories. In mid-September 1954, he chose to highlight a hurricane that was threatening the East Coast.

On September 10, the forty-six-year-old Murrow and his film crew stepped on board one of the Hurricane Hunter planes, a specially modified air force B-29 Superfortress with the 53rd Weather Reconnaissance Squadron. With the cameras rolling, they flew out to meet Hurricane Edna as she raced north about 100 miles west of Bermuda. As they approached, Murrow noted that the public had received at least twenty-four hours' advance warning of the hurricane, "her movements . . . [being] reported as completely as those of the President or of a movie star." He added, "The general opinion up here seems to be that Edna is not going to behave like a lady."

The early parts of the flight were relatively uneventful. "We seem to be flying through milk," Murrow commented as clouds enveloped the plane. When he said that thus far things had been quite smooth, the pilot responded that "flying was sometimes long hours of boredom interspersed with a few minutes of sheer terror." As the camera looked down, Murrow was impressed by the view: "The whole surface of the ocean is undulating like some huge giant was shaking a carpet. Each huge wave seems to be dragging along another behind it."

Then the plane started to shudder as it was buffeted by the wind. After a few "sharp blows," they broke through into the eye. Carried away in the moment, Murrow shouted ecstatically, "There it is, [the eyewall] . . . thousands of feet, as high as Everest. . . . What a beautiful sight! We're in an amphitheater surrounded by clouds. It looks like a lovely alpine lake surrounded by snow." At the eye's center, far below, Murrow marveled that there was a lone ship battling the frothing waves. The plane then turned around and headed back to base.

After riding along into Edna's eye, Murrow's viewers were shown scenes of what happened when the Category 2 hurricane made landfall in New England. Images of flooding, people battling to keep their footing, trees whipping violently back and forth, and hurricane flags being shredded in the wind streamed by. Back in his studio, Murrow looked into the camera for his grand summation: "In the eye of a hurricane you learn things other than of a scientific nature. You feel the puniness of man and his works. If a true definition of humility is ever written, it might well be written in the eye of a hurricane."

AS AN EVER-EXPANDING NUMBER of new television stations popped up during the 1950s, almost all of them included weather forecasts as part of their lineup. Threatening hurricanes were duly reported, but not as dramatically as Murrow had done. How could they have been? Graphics were rudimentary, and simple lines and images drawn on a board could not possibly convey a hurricane's grandeur and power. Weather forecasters added riveting details about the hurricanes when possible but, again, words often left a lot to be desired in this relentlessly visual medium. In 1961, television reporting on hurricanes took another leap forward when Hurricane Carla struck Texas.

On September 5, the Weather Bureau identified tropical storm Carla off Honduras, heading in a northerly direction. The following day, as it rounded the Yucatán Peninsula, the storm became a hurricane. That is when journalist Dan Rather took notice. A thirty-year-old news director and anchorman at Channel 11, KHOU, the CBS affiliate in Houston, Rather had a keen eye for a developing story. He told the program director, Cal Jones, that Carla was worth watching. Although Rather was not a meteorologist, he was a weather buff, and being from Texas, he was very familiar with hurricanes. "I'd been dealing with them all my life," Rather once said. "I knew how dangerous they could be." Hurricane season was, he said, "probably the second most interesting season in the state—after football." If Carla got worse, he wanted to cover it.

By the evening of September 7, as a strengthening Carla entered the Gulf of Mexico, Jones called Rather and told him to "start gearing up." Jones wanted the storm reporting to be done from Houston, but Rather argued for Galveston. He knew that the most dramatic impact was going to be along the coast, and there was an even more important consideration— radar. The Galveston Weather Bureau had recently installed a WSR-57 radar, one of the newer technologies for tracking weather. Rather wanted to be at the bureau office and have access to the meteorologists using the radar so that he could better keep tabs on Carla. This gave Jones an idea. "Do you mean," Jones asked, "if this thing hits, we could actually see it on radar?" Rather said yes, and an enthusiastic Jones suggested they film the radar and put it on television. Rather didn't know whether the bureau would allow that, but it was worth a try.

When Rather and his cameraman arrived at the Galveston bureau on Friday, September 8, Vaughn Rockney, the bureau's chief of observation, greeted them. He was cautious about Rather's idea, since it had never been done before. Rockney's main concern was that showing the radar image would threaten public safety. "You'd be putting an awesome-looking monster on the screen," Rockney told Rather. "Panic is a possibility." To persuade Rockney to take a chance, Rather pointed out that since the bureau often complained about the difficulty of convincing the public to take hurricane warnings seriously, showing the radar might make them pay more attention. Instead of inducing panic, Rather believed that letting the public know early and graphically about Hurricane Carla's approach would save lives. Rockney walked into a private office to consider the proposal. Whether he called headquarters to consult, Rather did not know, but when Rockney reemerged, he told Rather, "Let's do it. It's a damned good idea."

Over the next couple of days, Rather reported around the clock on Carla's every move, often showing the radar, on which you could make out Carla's swirling and growing presence. When, at Jones's recommendation, Rather threw a transparent map of the Texas coast and the Gulf of Mexico on top of the radar screen, it brought everything into perspective. Rather

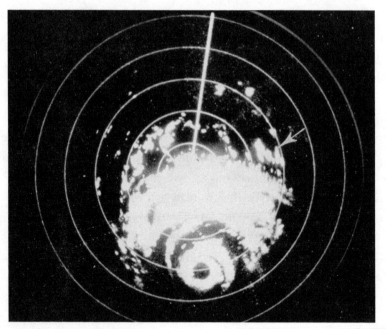

*Hurricane Carla as it appeared on the WSR-57 radar screen
at the Galveston Weather Bureau on September 8, 1961.*

later recalled, "When I said, 'This is actual scale, there's the state of Texas, one inch equals fifty miles,' you could hear people in the studio gasp. . . . The picture took your breath away. The storm actually covered much of the Gulf of Mexico."

On Sunday, September 10, Carla, now labeled as a Category 5 hurricane, was coming very close to the coast, so local government authorities ordered a mass evacuation of Galveston and the surrounding lowlands—a total of 500,000 people. The next morning, Carla came ashore as a Category 4 near Matagorda, about 120 miles southwest of Galveston. Located in the dreaded right side of the hurricane, Galveston was slammed. Nevertheless, Rather and his team continued broadcasting live, subsisting primarily on candy bars. At various points, the cameraman went to one of the Weather Bureau's windows on the fifth floor of the post office building, opened it, and leaned out to film what was happening outside.

To this day, Carla is still the second-most-powerful hurricane to hit Texas since 1851, when reliable record keeping began. Topping the list is the Indianola Hurricane of 1886. The storm surge generated by Carla caused massive flooding and extensive damage along the coast, but only forty-six people died. While any number of dead is too many, given the hurricane's great size and strength the outcome could easily have been far worse.

The Weather Bureau claimed that the media's warnings of the hurricane's arrival and its dissemination of the evacuation orders saved many lives. Although KHOU was just one of many media outlets reporting on Carla, it deserves much of the credit for this result, for there is no doubt that Rather's groundbreaking newscasts convincingly communicated the scope of the danger to the viewers, motivating them to better prepare and leave the area for safety.

One other by-product of Rather's reporting was more personal in nature. CBS News in New York had hooked into Rather's reports and beamed them to CBS stations around the country. The CBS brass liked what they saw, and they offered Rather a job as correspondent, which he accepted. Rather would later say, "With the exception of my wife, Jeannie, the lady who had the most influence on my career was named Carla."

MUCH MORE GROUNDBREAKING THAN showing radar images on television was broadcasting satellite imagery. In the 1960s, as more satellites came online, a few adventurous weather forecasters supplemented their stories with satellite still images. Certainly novel, these shots were often rather grainy and fairly unimpressive. Not until the advent of GOES satellites in the late 1970s and early 1980s did weather forecasters start using dynamic satellite imagery, or *satellite loops*, as they are called, which piece together pictures taken every half hour to create a movie that shows the movement of weather systems over time. In subsequent years, imagery continued to improve with each successive generation of satellites.

The availability of high-quality satellite images ramped up the wow factor of television reporting on hurricanes. Weather forecasts now show brilliant movies of hurricanes marching over the ocean, each step in their evolution captured by the satellite's unblinking eye. By enhancing those images with vibrant reds, yellows, and greens, it is possible to visualize the temperature of the hurricane's clouds. Much as the first astronauts to see the Earth from space were amazed by the beauty of our blue planet seemingly floating in a vast sea of black, we are also stunned by the beauty of hurricanes as they are revealed by satellites coursing through the sky.

NETWORK AND CABLE NEWS STATIONS DO an excellent job of covering the weather, including hurricanes, but that is only part of their mission. The Weather Channel, in contrast, is all weather all the time, and it has raised hurricane reporting to an art form. An army of reporters and experts in the studio and on the scene covers hurricanes from every possible angle. One of the Weather Channel's best-known personalities is Jim Cantore, a trained meteorologist who has been covering the weather for more than thirty years with a unique theatrical and informative style. As one writer said, "In Cantore you have science and show business all wrapped up in one spiffy Gore-Tex package." He is famous for literally throwing himself into a hurricane and reporting while being battered by the wind and rain, and occasionally pelted by flying debris. During Hurricane Isabel in 2003, which made landfall on the Outer Banks of North Carolina, Cantore's cameraman was knocked off his feet by a wave, and although he was fine, the $60,000 camera was a total loss.

Television's major investment in hurricane coverage not only benefits the public, which gets ample warning of threatening storms, but also is excellent for business. One of the main reasons people tune in to network and cable news is to see the weather forecast. Hurricanes only make the weather forecast more compelling, thereby boosting viewership, advertising, and profits. As Cantore observed, "People want to see what's going on. They don't want the map. They want to feel the power of the weather. Technology has brought the weather into our living rooms. Now you're watching it in high-definition, unthinkable images. That's what weather is today: the quintessential reality TV." Hurricanes provide one of the most pulse-pounding, eye-catching, and deadly shows on Earth.

While newspapers, radio stations, and television shows will continue to play a significant role in hurricane reporting, since the new millennium the internet has increasingly taken center stage as the medium for information dissemination. Many websites are simply digital versions of more traditional news outlets, and they report similar stories. But there are other websites people can visit to get the latest on hurricanes. Far and away the best sources for the most up-to-date and accurate hurricane forecasts, tracks, and advisories are the National Weather Service websites, especially the one run by the National Hurricane Center (https://www.nhc.noaa.gov).

In fact, the data provided by those government sites is what virtually all reputable private media outlets use to develop their own custom hurricane reports, which are often packaged in a manner that is especially easy for the general public to understand.

By enabling instant access to real-time, accurate information on hurricanes, websites and the associated weather apps provide an extremely valuable public service that helps to protect human life and property. However, the internet can also be a potent source of incorrect information or even misinformation. Amateur forecasters, which some professional meteorologists call "social mediarologists," have at times posted misleading information online, such as claiming that a worst-case-scenario forecast, or the most severe model, is the final and official prediction of where the hurricane will strike. The incredible ability of Facebook, Twitter, and other social media platforms to rapidly and widely transmit such erroneous information greatly increases the risk that people will make poor decisions that put them in harm's way.

From a broader perspective, the fractured and crowded media landscape threatens the quality of hurricane reporting and our ability to effectively respond to these massive storms. As meteorologist Bryan Norcross observed, "People are bombarded with myriad opinions and an overwhelming amount of data, including continuous fragments of messages and minimessages via social media. There is no one trusted, credible source set up to deliver a cohesive message. This problem is aggravated by economic and social factors—traditional media outlets operate with a much smaller staff of far less experienced people than they did a couple of decades ago. In addition, distrust of government and the media is extremely high. These factors combine to make critical crisis communications much more difficult."

Another problem with hurricane reporting is sensationalism. Famed essayist and *New Yorker* staff writer E. B. White artfully raised this issue way back in 1954. He was home in Brooklin, Maine, when Hurricane Edna came calling. He penned a fascinating piece for the magazine that expressed the considerable power of the radio to alert listeners to an oncoming storm while at the same time sending them into a potentially counterproductive, and even deadly, tizzy. "Hurricanes are the latest discovery of radio stations and they are being taken up in a big way," he wrote. "The idea, of course, is that the radio shall perform a public service by warning people of a storm that might prove fatal; and this the radio certainly does. But another effect of the radio is to work people up to an incredible state of alarm many hours in advance of the blow, while they are still fanned by the mildest zephyrs. One of the victims of Hurricane Edna was a civil-defense worker whose heart failed him long before the wind threatened him in the least."

White noted that the radio announcers had begun their breathless reports of Edna almost two full days before she arrived, and they quickly ran out of new nuggets of information to share with their audience, so they reverted to the mundane and, sometimes, the ridiculous. To make that point, White relayed an exchange he had heard when a reporter was bantering with the announcer about what he had found out in the field.

> "How would you say the roads were?" asked the tense voice [of the announcer].
>
> "They were wet," replied the reporter who seemed to be in a sulk.
>
> "Would you say the spray from the puddles was dashing up around the mudguards?" inquired the desperate radioman.
>
> "Yeah," replied the reporter.

"It was one of those confused moments, emotionally, when the listener could not be quite sure what position radio was taking—*for* hurricanes or *against* them."

White's observations were prescient. Now, many decades later, we are still trying to balance the role of the media in informing us about impending hurricanes, while simultaneously not allowing their reports to become so over the top that we start ignoring them altogether, by virtue of their repetitive and alarmist nature. It is a fine line that separates effective reporting from hype that numbs the senses.

These problems notwithstanding, it is truly amazing to look back and see how far we have come in hurricane coverage. Just a century and a half ago, people had virtually no warning of a hurricane's arrival, other than what they could discern by looking to the sky or the ocean's swells. Today, Americans can watch hurricanes every step of the way as they march across the globe, and report on their progress. Although we often take that capability for granted, it is an astonishing achievement.

National Hurricane Center building on the campus of Florida International University in Miami, Florida. The NHC moved to this new hurricane-resistant facility in 1995.

AN UNTOLD NUMBER OF radio broadcasts, articles, television shows, and, more recently, internet sites have reported on the more than 120 hurricanes that have struck the United States since the end of World War II. All of those hurricanes left scars on the people and landscapes they affected. But some storms loom larger in our collective memory on account of the damage, destruction, and death they caused.

A Rogues' Gallery

*Kentucky Air Guardsman looking down from a helicopter
on a flooded Houston during rescue operations after
Hurricane Harvey hit in August 2017.*

THE HURRICANES OF '54 AND '55

In 1954 and 1955, four hurricanes and one tropical storm altered the landscape of life in the areas where they struck, and also changed the trajectory of hurricane research and forecasting for the better. That first year, a trio of storms—Carol, Edna, and Hazel—made their mark on the East Coast.

Hurricane Carol was first identified by the Weather Bureau in late August of 1954, when it stalled near the Bahamas, gaining strength. Its torpor ended on the thirtieth, when it raced up the East Coast, grazing Cape Hatteras and rushing toward New England at nearly 50 mph. The following day, the Category 3 hurricane swept over the eastern tip of Long Island, raked Block Island with 115-mph winds, drowned one-third of Providence in a 10-foot storm surge, destroyed thousands of homes and boats, and flew through New England on its way to Quebec, leaving sixty people dead and causing nearly $500 million in damage.

In a case of déjà vu, the Weather Bureau failed to warn of Carol's impending blow until the very last minute, much like what had happened with the Great Hurricane of 1938. Carol's unexpected speed caught the bureau off guard, and the timing of her arrival also presented difficulties. As one official told a reporter, by the time the bureau realized that Carol was on a collision course with the Northeast, it was the middle of the night and we "couldn't get that in the papers of the night before or on the radio networks that had already signed off."

Even before the public outcry over the failed forecast could die down, another hurricane roared up the coast. Edna, the hurricane that Murrow famously filmed, followed a path similar to Carol's, but a bit farther to the east, and at a more leisurely pace. It made landfall at the tip of Cape Cod on September 11 as a strong Category 2 hurricane, and then slammed into Maine in the vicinity of Eastport. Twenty people died, and damage was estimated to be $43 million.

THE OCCURRENCE OF TWO hurricanes striking New England back-to-back sent shock waves throughout the region. Normally, New England could expect five to ten hurricanes in a century; two in one year was unheard of. Most of the people affected by Carol and Edna were old enough to remember the Great Hurricane of 1938 and the Great Atlantic

The most iconic casualty of Hurricane Carol was the steeple on the
Old North Church in Boston, which tumbled to the ground. It wasn't
the first time this happened. The original steeple was built in 1740
and made famous on the evening of April 18, 1775, when two lanterns
shone from it for just one minute. That brief signal told Paul Revere
and his rebel associates that the British were leaving Boston by sea, not
land, and set the stage for the Battles of Lexington and Concord the
following day, igniting the American Revolution. During the Great
Gale of Boston in October 1804, the steeple was launched into the air.
On its way down it demolished a house, whose fortunate inhabitants
were out of town. A new steeple was erected in 1806, but when Carol
ripped through, it, too, succumbed to the wind. This time, at least,
its fall was amazingly clean, and only one building across from the
church was slightly damaged. In 1955, yet another steeple was raised
aloft, but the church took no chances. This third and, hopefully,
final steeple is reinforced with steel so that it should be able to handle
anything that Mother Nature can dish out. This image is a montage,
showing the toppling steeple and the aftermath.

Hurricane of 1944, both of which had also ravaged New England, as well as Long Island. What was happening? It was as if the world had turned upside down. Florida and the Gulf Coast, and even the Carolinas, were used to being pummeled by hurricanes every few years. It was part of their history. But the Northeast? Newspaper articles raised the possibility that something might have shifted meteorologically. Could it be that Carol and Edna were harbingers of a new reality? Even though Weather Bureau officials tried to allay the public's concern, pointing out that the two hurricanes within twelve days of each other was just "one of those coincidences in nature that no one can explain," people were worried.

Enter Hazel, the most devastating hurricane of the 1954 season. Spotted east of Grenada on October 5, it soon entered the Caribbean Sea and turned north as a Category 4 hurricane. Bringing heavy winds and torrential rains to Haiti, Hazel killed an estimated 400–1,000 people, many of them buried in landslides. Haiti's 8,000-foot peaks weakened Hazel, but once back out over the warm ocean waters, the storm rejuvenated. On the morning of October 15, with winds approaching 135 mph, Hazel made landfall near the border of North and South Carolina. At speeds of up to 50 mph, it zoomed through North Carolina, Virginia, Washington, DC, Pennsylvania, and New York, and finally into Canada. Hazel caused $281 million in damage and killed ninety-four people in the United States. In Canada, the respective toll was $100 million, and eighty-one dead.

One other notable death occurred well before Hazel struck the Carolinas. Sixty-year-old Grady Norton, the Weather Bureau's senior hurricane forecaster, had long suffered from high blood pressure and migraines, and his doctor had repeatedly begged him to retire or risk dying from the stress. But retiring was not in Norton's nature. So, when Hazel appeared near Grenada, Norton was on the job. As the storm marched through the Caribbean, Norton logged twelve-hour days to track its progress and issue warnings. His body couldn't take the punishment. On the morning of October 9, he suffered a stroke at his home, and he died later that day.

FAR TOO OFTEN, politicians fail to act until forced to do so by a crisis. Rhode Island senator Theodore F. Green thought such a crisis was at hand. Carol and Edna had unnerved him and his fellow New England politicians, and then Hazel had extended the worries down the coast. Now,

*Grady Norton (seated), often referred to by coastal residents
as "Mr. Hurricane" on account of his calm and reassuring
hurricane forecasts, shown at the Miami hurricane warning center,
surrounded by center staff.*

a powerful block of senators and congressmen, representing a huge swath
of the American population and some of the wealthiest states with the
most to lose, wanted to know what the Weather Bureau could do to better
understand hurricanes and improve its forecasts and warnings. Robert H.
Simpson, the man who would later introduce the Saffir-Simpson Hurricane Wind Scale, had the answer.

Simpson had been with the bureau since 1940 and had gained experience working as a hurricane forecaster in New Orleans and Miami. In the
early 1950s, he was stationed in Washington, DC, where he was an assistant to director Francis Reichelderfer, who asked him to develop a plan to
beef up the bureau's hurricane program. With the advent of radar, Hurricane Hunters, and computers, Simpson knew there were phenomenal
tools that meteorologists could use to conduct valuable hurricane science
and improve forecasting. He soon had a plan ready to go; what was lacking, however, was money. Reichelderfer had repeatedly added funding for

Simpson's plan to the bureau's budget proposal, but each time, President Dwight D. Eisenhower's budget masters eliminated it.

Not long after Hurricane Hazel, Senator Green held hearings on Capitol Hill to consider what should be done to improve the nation's hurricane warning system. Reichelderfer appeared, along with Harry Wexler, the bureau's director of research, as well as Simpson, who was there as a technical expert. Since Simpson's plan had been axed from the budget and Reichelderfer didn't want to undermine the administration's position, Reichelderfer said nothing about it. But when one of the committee members asked Simpson directly what he thought Congress should support, he saw his opportunity and took it. While his bosses looked on nervously, Simpson presented his plan. The seed was planted, but what was needed was one last nudge, which Hurricane Connie soon provided.

On August 12, 1955, after deluging Puerto Rico and the US Virgin Islands with rain and heading in a northwesterly direction, Connie made landfall near Morehead, North Carolina, as a weak Category 2 hurricane. What Connie lacked in wind power, it made up for with water. Traveling north close to the coast and then inland toward the Great Lakes, Connie's rains sparked flooding over a wide region, as far north as New England. Damage rose to $85 million, and seventy-four people died.

Consideration of Simpson's plan had been wending its way through Congress when Connie hit, and the storm provided just the right incentive for the plan to be fully funded. If Congress needed any reassurance that it had made a wise investment, the confirmation came a few days later when Diane arrived. Smashing into Cape Fear, North Carolina, on August 17 as a strong tropical storm, Diane curved up through the mid-Atlantic states, exited back out to sea near the tip of Long Island, and then hugged the coast until it reached Cape Cod, at which point it sailed off into deeper water. Coming on the heels of Connie, and just as full of moisture, Diane swamped the region, especially New England, where many rivers crested at all-time highs. Nearly 200 people died, most from drowning, and damage approached $1 billion.

Simpson's plan came into being as the National Hurricane Research Project, the goals of which were to better understand the formation, structure, and dynamics of hurricanes, explore the potential for hurricane modification, and improve forecasting. Although it was slated for only a three-year run, the project was continued for many years, ultimately mor-

*Flooding damage on Main Street in Winsted, Connecticut,
due to tropical storm Diane.*

phing into today's Hurricane Research Division of the National Oceanic
and Atmospheric Administration.

As for Hurricanes Carol, Edna, Hazel, and Connie, they received a
posthumous honor of a sort. In recognition of their tremendously destructive natures, their names were retired, making them the first of many hurricanes to achieve this terrible distinction.

CAMILLE, 1969

The Woodstock music festival began on Friday, August 15, 1969, on Max
Yasgur's farm in upstate New York. Billed as an "Aquarian Exposition of
Peace, Love, and Music," Woodstock became a symbol of youth countercul-
ture and arguably the most iconic event in the history of rock and roll. For
four days, roughly 500,000 predominantly young people danced, drank,
sang, smoked, took drugs, and made love as they were serenaded by many

of the greatest performers of the era, including Jimi Hendrix, the Grateful Dead, Janice Joplin, Jefferson Airplane, Joan Baez, and Santana. It was not all fun and games, however. The audience also contended with a lack of food and water, horrific sanitary conditions, massive traffic jams, and torrential downpours that turned green pastures into a vast expanse of mud.

While Woodstock seared itself into the cultural landscape, becoming a touchstone for a generation, another dramatic event was unfolding more than 1,000 miles to the southwest, along the coast of Louisiana. It, too, would leave an indelible mark, and in this case a tragic one, on American history.

On the same day that Woodstock began, Hurricane Camille, a relatively small storm with winds up to 100 mph, was making its way north through the Caribbean, approaching the western end of Cuba. Simpson told reporters that it might curve and hit the Florida Keys, but it was still too early to tell. Over the next twenty-four hours, it did curve, but only slightly as it clipped Cuba. Then it curved again and headed to the northwest, sucking energy and moisture from the warm Gulf waters as it steadily grew into a Category 3 hurricane. Simpson was alarmed by Camille's rapid intensification, and the satellite images only compounded his concern. Camille had, he later recalled, "the most wicked eyewall I have ever seen."

Simpson needed a closer look, and he got it Saturday afternoon when a Hurricane Hunter plane entered Camille's eye and reported a barometric pressure of 26.81 inches. Simpson could hardly believe it; that was the lowest reading ever measured by a Hurricane Hunter in the Atlantic, and it would make Camille one of the most intense hurricanes on record. As for where Camille was headed, Simpson and his colleagues still believed that it would curve to the east, coming ashore along the Florida Panhandle.

But Camille didn't curve. Over the next day, subsequent weather advisories had it tracking farther to the west. Hurricane warnings went into effect from New Orleans to Apalachicola, Florida. Camille was now an extremely powerful, though relatively compact, Category 5 hurricane with winds estimated to be as high as 190 mph. It was expected to generate a truly astounding storm surge of up to 20 feet. The Weather Bureau urged people along the coast from the mouth of the Mississippi River to Mobile, Alabama, to listen to area politicians and civil defense coordinators and immediately evacuate to higher ground.

Fishing vessel driven ashore by Hurricane Camille.

Camille came ashore at 11:00 p.m. on Sunday, August 17, 1969, in the vicinity of Bay St. Louis, Mississippi, with maximum winds of 175 mph, making it a very strong Category 5. Just to the east of Bay St. Louis, in Pass Christian, where the notorious forward right-hand quadrant of the hurricane hit, the storm surge reached 24.6 feet, higher than any previous surge on record. Calls to evacuate prompted 81,000 of the 150,000 people in the evacuation zone to flee. Among those who decided to ride out the storm was a group of people at the Richelieu Manor Apartments in Pass Christian.

POLICE OFFICERS STOPPED BY the apartments a couple of times on Sunday, pleading with residents to evacuate, but most of them shared the perspective of the Richelieu's manager, Merwin Jones. He had heard about the approaching hurricane but believed that the building would be safe. After all, the U-shaped apartment complex just a few hundred yards from the beach had withstood other hurricanes. When Betsy hit the coast in 1965, for instance, there had been serious flooding on the first floor, but other than that not much damage. It was, Jones thought, a solid building, and it was an officially designated civil defense shelter. If things got bad and the first floor flooded, the residents could climb to safety on the second or third floor. So, while a few residents listened to the police and evacuated, most remained and spent much of the day buying supplies, moving cars to higher ground, and helping Jones nail boards over the windows and haul furniture from the ground level to upper floors.

By early evening, most of the remaining residents had retreated to the third floor, gathering in a few apartments, where they ate, watched television to get the latest on the storm, and peered nervously out the windows at the increasingly angry Gulf. Thirty-three-year-old Mary Ann Gerlach and her sixth husband, thirty-year-old Frederick, or Fritz as he was called, a navy Seabee, were one floor below trying to get some rest. She had returned home early that morning after working all night as a cocktail waitress at a local nightclub. He had also worked very late the previous night, at the nearby officers' club.

At 10:00 p.m. the electricity went out. A few minutes later, the surging Gulf rose to the second floor, and the building shuddered violently under the assault. As the windowpanes exploded around them, the Gerlachs ran to their bedroom and shut the door. Mary Ann retrieved a pool mattress from the closet, blew it up, and handed it to Fritz, who, amazingly, given his navy job, could not swim. The rapidly rising water was now up to their chests and climbing higher still. Grabbing a floating pillow cushion, Mary Ann swam out through the broken window, urging Fritz to follow. No sooner had she exited the building than she became entangled in a mass of wires. It took a couple of minutes for her to break free, and in that time she saw Fritz follow her out, screaming, "Help me! Save me!" before he disappeared under the water.

Mary Ann struggled throughout the night, swimming and bobbing in the water amid and sometimes atop great mats of floating debris. At dawn, the pile of splintered wood, furniture, and trees she was clinging to came to rest near some train tracks. Shivering and barely clothed, she was found a short while later by a local doctor, who helped her reach shelter.

Not long after Mary Ann's escape from her flooded apartment, the water reached the third floor of the Richelieu, and the entire building started coming apart. Suddenly, in addition to the roar of the wind and the rat-a-tat-tat of the pelting rain, the residents heard the shrieking of nails being pulled from wood, and the bullet-like reports of plasterboard, cement, and two-by-fours breaking. When the ceiling ripped open, twenty-three-year-old resident Ben Duckworth thought that their best chance for survival might be to shelter on the roof, in the hope that the building would remain standing until the worst of the storm had passed. But first he needed to see whether his plan was even possible.

With a boost from other residents, Duckworth poked his head above the roofline and found that he was very close to the air-conditioning condensing unit, which partially blocked the full force of the whipping winds and rain. Perhaps, he thought, it could protect them all. So he climbed onto the roof, braced himself as best he could, and reached back down to help the others follow his lead. Unfortunately, the condensing unit did not offer enough protection from the hurricane's extreme violence, and as each resident was hauled onto the roof, the vicious winds swept them into the surging waters. In the end, it didn't matter. Even if the condensing unit had been able to shield them, it would have provided only a short reprieve because Camille's waters soon swallowed the building whole.

Like Mary Ann Gerlach, Duckworth struggled throughout the night to stay alive, alternately swimming and grabbing on to debris. Finally, just when his strength was waning and he was giving up hope, he knocked into a mighty oak whose crown was peeking above the water. He grabbed a branch, crawled along it to the trunk, and held on tight. The next morning, a search party found him high off the ground in the tree, shivering and bloody, his clothes in tatters. They helped him down and brought him to the high school, where relief workers took care of him.

In the days after the storm, Mary Ann Gerlach told any reporter willing to listen her version of what had happened in the Richelieu on the night of the hurricane. When she had heard that Camille was on the way, she said, "The first thing that popped into my mind was party time!" Other residents agreed, and they all convened on the third floor for a "hurricane party," replete with hors d'oeuvres, sandwiches, and plenty to drink. Neither Mary Ann nor Fritz attended, on account of being too tired. She also told reporters that she was the only person from the Richelieu who had survived.

Mary Ann's story made national news. When the "most trusted man in America," CBS News anchor Walter Cronkite, visited the Louisiana coast in the aftermath of the hurricane, he reported from Pass Christian. "This is the former site of the Richelieu Apartments," Cronkite somberly told his audience, "where twenty-three people laughed in the face of death, and where twenty-three people died."

Richelieu Manor Apartments in Pass Christian, Mississippi,
before and after Hurricane Camille.

There were, however, serious problems with Mary Ann's story. For one thing, she wasn't the only survivor. Of those who stayed through the storm, at least eight others are known to have survived. As for the party, neither Duckworth nor any of the other survivors ever said there was such a party, and in fact, Duckworth has repeatedly and vigorously denied that it ever happened. Many have pointed out that there are other reasons to doubt the veracity of Mary Ann's story and her reliability as a witness. In the twelve years after the hurricane, Mary Ann married seven more times, and in 1981 she was arrested for murdering her thirteenth husband— whom she had recently divorced—by shooting him with a .357 magnum. At the trial, she said she couldn't recall the event, in large part because she claimed that her ordeal during Camille had caused her to become legally insane. Nobody witnessed the shooting, but the jury still found her guilty on circumstantial evidence, and she was sentenced to life in prison. In 1992, however, she was released for good behavior. Perhaps, not surprisingly, while in jail she had married twice more.

Despite the compelling evidence that there was no party at the Richelieu, it has remained a persistent urban legend and still gets hauled out occasionally in stories about Camille. That is not to say that nobody partied as Camille came ashore. Many undoubtedly did. In virtually any hurricane in modern times, there are those who laugh and drink in the face of danger, however foolish that might be. Indeed, a day before Camille struck, a recent transplant to New Orleans who had never experienced a hurricane asked the owner of a local hardware store what he should do to get ready for the storm. "Get yourself a bottle of good whiskey and sit back and relax," was the reply.

OF THE MANY PEOPLE who suffered along the coast during Camille, none had a greater burden to bear than forty-nine-year-old Paul Williams Sr. Longtime caretaker at the Trinity Episcopal Church in Pass Christian, Paul and his wife, Myrtle, had fifteen children and lived in a small house on church property. The night that Camille came ashore, twelve of their children were with them, along with a few of those children's spouses and assorted grandchildren. Paul and Myrtle chose not to evacuate, but rather to stay in the auditorium attached to the church. It seemed a prudent choice. Trinity was erected in 1849. More than a dozen hurricanes

Trinity Episcopal Church in Pass Christian, Mississippi,
before and after Hurricane Camille.

had rolled through over the years, and the church, a mere block from the beach, had withstood them all. Although the auditorium was not part of the original building, it, too, was sturdily built.

Soon after the Williams family ate dinner and most of them had lain down to sleep on makeshift beds, water started rushing under the auditorium's door. Paul hurried everyone up the ladder into the attic. As the water continued to rise, Paul prayed and prepared to move the kids even higher, into the rafters. Before he could do so, the building violently shook and collapsed, pitching everyone into the maelstrom. Paul didn't know how to swim, so he thrashed about, grasping for something to hold on to and finally grabbing a board that was floating by. When the board crashed into a live oak, he jumped into the crook of the tree and stayed there through the night.

The next morning, Paul climbed down from the tree and realized he was in the church's cemetery. The church, the rectory, the auditorium—everything was gone. Massive piles of rubbish, some as tall as 15 feet, littered the landscape.

Paul heard voices begging for help. It was Malcolm, his sixteen-year-old son, and his son-in-law Nick. Reunited, together they began searching through the rubble, and they were soon aided by others in their gruesome task. One after another, the dead were located, and Paul's grief deepened. In the end, eleven of his children had perished, along with one grandchild and his beloved Myrtle. Years later, Paul would share his unrelenting sorrow with an interviewer: "I look at their pictures and just wish they were here with me. . . . Oh Lordy mercy, nobody knows. Nobody knows how I miss them. This is a painful thing, what I lost. It's real painful and I just have to go around and hold tight and do the best I can. But God knows I miss them so much. I wish they were here."

THE NUMBER OF PEOPLE killed in Louisiana and Mississippi by Camille is subject to debate, but it was in the vicinity of 200, and as many as a quarter of the deceased were never found, their bodies most likely claimed by the Gulf. According to the Red Cross, 5,652 homes in those two states were destroyed, and 13,865 sustained major damage. In Buras, Louisiana, a town of 6,000 on the lower reaches of the Mississippi, only six structures survived the hurricane. Nearly 100 boats were sunk or grounded on the river, and many offshore oil rigs and onshore pipelines were smashed, resulting in extensive oil slicks lapping the shore. Five thousand cattle drowned, and tens of thousands of acres of pecan and orange trees were leveled. An air force pilot who flew reconnaissance in the days after the hurricane commented, "The Gulf Coast looks like a war zone. Destruction fits one of two categories—demolished or gone." After his tour of the coast, Simpson said the scene reminded him "of the meat chopper action of a Midwest tornado. It looked more like two or three dozen Midwestern tornadoes had followed each other between central Pass Christian and East Long Beach, Mississippi." Damage along the coast added up to $1.4 billion. But Camille's reign of destruction was not over. It had a vicious second act.

AS CAMILLE TRAVELED NORTH through Louisiana and Mississippi and on into Tennessee and Kentucky, it rapidly lost strength, first dropping to tropical storm status, then becoming just another one of the many anonymous and amorphous storms that travel across the land. For the most part, Camille and her shadow were welcomed along the way, bringing much-needed rain and finally ending the severe drought that had plagued much of the area. The Weather Bureau called for continued precipitation as the storm petered out—nothing out of the ordinary, nothing to be concerned about.

But on Tuesday, August 19, when the still very wet remnants of Camille exited Kentucky and ran into the Blue Ridge Mountains in Virginia, something totally unexpected and menacing happened. Instead of quickly rising over the mountains and continuing on their way toward the coast, the remnants came up against a cold front, and the two systems entangled in a violent meteorological embrace, essentially stalling in place. All of this energy and moisture generated billowing clouds that rose to monstrous heights, growing blacker and blacker by the minute. In the early evening, an observer viewing this development from Nelson County, Virginia, said that the clouds looked like "a hornet's nest."

Nestled along the eastern flank of the Blue Ridge Mountains, rural Nelson County had about 12,000 residents, most of whom made a living farming or working in area factories. The county comprised many small, tight-knit communities where life moved at a less hurried pace and everyone seemed to know everyone else. The summer of 1969 had been a wet one, and when the threatening black clouds appeared on the horizon, the ground was already well saturated. The three relatively small and shallow rivers that run through the county—the Tye, Piney, and Rockfish—were higher than normal. It had rained on and off that day, and the air was thick with humidity. The forecast called for showers overnight. As the evening progressed, though, the rain picked up and became constant and heavier.

In the coming hours, the billowing black clouds unleashed torrential downpours. As a result, many residents of Nelson County would not see the light of day. The Raines family would suffer an especially cruel blow.

The Raineses lived in the village of Massies Mill in a house just a few hundred feet from the edge of the Tye. Carl and his wife, Shirley, had six children, ranging in age from seven to nineteen, but only five were home at the time. The oldest, Ava, was living on her own in Lynchburg. At 2:00 in the morning on Wednesday, August 20, the phone rang. Startled, Carl answered, and the woman at the other end of the line, who lived nearby, told him that her house was flooded and that her car had just floated away. Carl thought she must be mistaken and tried to calm her down, but to no avail. After he got off the phone, he walked to the window to look outside. Suddenly, the reason for the woman's call became crystal clear. The Raineses' house was surrounded by water, although Carl wasn't sure whether it was just puddles or the Tye breaching its banks. Worried, but trying to remain calm in front his family, Carl told them to get dressed and be ready to leave. The phone rang again. This time it was Page Wood, their neighbor from across the street. Page asked if he could send over his four kids. His wife was wheelchair bound, and he couldn't leave her, but if the Raineses decided to evacuate, Page hoped they could take his kids as well. Sure, send them over, Carl said, and in a few minutes the four of them arrived, wet, cold, and shaking.

With the water rising by the minute, Carl asked sixteen-year-old Carl Jr. to pull the station wagon around front. In the meantime, Carl and Shirley lugged a few prize pieces of furniture to the second floor. With the car ready to go, the Raineses and the Wood kids piled in, but when Carl put the car into gear, it stalled and wouldn't restart. By then, the water was knee-deep and flowing fast. Carl ordered everyone out of the car. They would have to walk to higher ground, which was only a few hundred yards away.

Arm in arm to support one another, they trudged forward. In an instant, the water rose several feet and the mighty current accompanying it ripped the human chain apart and sent all of them careening downstream. Warren Raines, fourteen, grabbed on to a bush near the edge of the road. When a fusillade of lightning strikes illuminated the scene, he saw his mother, two of his sisters, and one of the Wood kids hanging on to the branches of a tree just a short way off. Shirley saw Warren as well, and she screamed to him, "Let go, we'll catch you." Warren took a deep gulp of air and released his grip. But by the time he reached the spot where his mother had been, she and the others had all been swept away by the rushing water that now had Warren in its clutches.

Flailing about, Warren crashed into an old willow tree. He threw his arms around the trunk, hanging on for twenty minutes while being pelted from behind by all manner of debris. Then the mighty willow slowly fell over, but its extensive roots held fast, so the tree lay partially submerged in the surging waters. Warren crawled farther up the trunk and grabbed hold of one of the tree's long and flowing branches. Each bolt of lightning revealed a new round of horrors, the storm's terrible harvest. Trees, cars, boats, houses, and even cows desperately fighting for air flew past Warren, sometimes with only inches to spare.

Then Warren heard a voice in the distance yelling his name. It was his brother, Carl Jr., perched higher on another tree about 60 feet away. There was no way for them to get any closer to each other, so both held tight where they were through the night, mostly in silence, shivering and raw. The next morning, men in a rescue boat found the boys and ferried them to shelter. Over the next day or two the boys searched in vain for the rest of their family. All of them, along with two of the four Wood kids, had perished. Most, but not all, of their bodies would be found in the ensuing days and weeks.

It turned out that staying put would have been the wiser choice for the Raineses, but there was no way of knowing that at the time. During their search, Warren and Carl Jr. went back to their home and found it still standing, although the windows on the first floor were smashed and the entire first floor was slathered in mud and debris. They heard a noise coming from the second floor and found that their dog, Bo, had survived. The reunion with their beloved pet was the one bright spot in an otherwise hellish few days. The two boys were taken to Lynchburg and delivered into the hands of their only remaining sibling, Ava, and their grandparents, who shared their unbearable grief.

Stories like that of the Raineses and the Wood kids occurred throughout the area with different and sometimes more tragic particulars. The hardest-hit family was the Huffmans of Davis Creek, West Virginia, who lost twenty-two of their clan. In the end, roughly 120 people perished in Nelson County, and a few dozen more elsewhere in Virginia. Flooding damage in the state totaled nearly $150 million. Since there were no official measurements of the rainfall, the exact total will never be known, but estimates range from 27 to 46 inches, with the actual number probably falling somewhere in between. Some meteorologists said that it was a one-in-1,000-year or, perhaps, even a one-in-5,000-year or one-in-10,000-year event. This deluge turned rivulets and streams coursing down the sides of the Blue Ridge Mountains and through Nelson County into violent rivers, destroying everything in their path. In many areas the rushing waters scoured the soil down to bedrock, leaving a deep gash on the land.

ANDREW, 1992

Bryan Norcross wasn't even supposed to be in Miami. His contract as the chief meteorologist at the local television station WTVJ was set to expire in December 1992, and much earlier in the year his bosses had told him they weren't going to renew it. This advance notice gave him plenty of time to find a new weather-reporting job, and come mid-August he had landed one in New York City. By Wednesday, August 19, he was packed and ready to leave but was having second thoughts. He had been tracking a tropical storm named Andrew, which was about 1,500 miles southeast of Miami. Although most meteorologists, including Norcross, thought the storm would likely curve to the north and miss Florida, the path wasn't a sure thing. Since his replacement had not yet arrived, Norcross, who had deep roots in Miami and a strong connection with his audience, canceled his trip so that he could stay one more day to see whether Andrew would make the anticipated turn.

Andrew wasn't all that impressive. In fact, by the next day, the storm had lost its circulation, and the National Hurricane Center considered stripping it of its name but decided to wait a bit, so as not to create confusion if the storm strengthened again. The computer models didn't agree; some showed Andrew heading north, while others had it heading in a more westerly direction, toward northern Florida. Norcross, who by this time had decided to postpone his move to New York City indefinitely, continued to keep a close eye on Andrew, and WTVJ was happy to have him stay on to see them through the storm.

On Friday, August 21, the wisdom of keeping the name became clear, as Andrew strengthened and started developing an eyewall. Although the models tended to indicate that Andrew would turn enough to miss southeastern Florida, Norcross grew more concerned because the actual track of the storm kept veering more to the west than the models predicted. Much worse, the models had tropical storm Andrew morphing into a hurricane by Sunday. On Friday afternoon, Norcross told his viewers that a hurricane might be on the way in the next couple of days, and he urged them to stay tuned for further developments.

Most Miamians were not too concerned, at least not yet. For more than two decades, not a single hurricane had struck anywhere nearby, and they had been lulled into complacency. The last hit had come from Hurricane Betsy, all the way back in September 1965. Betsy made landfall to the south of Miami, near Key Largo, at Category 3 strength. It was a large hurricane, and its strong winds, with gusts well over 100 mph, caused major power outages in Miami and damage at the coast. Since Betsy, the population of Miami-Dade County* had roughly doubled, from about 1 million to 2 million, meaning that a huge percentage of the people in the county had never experienced a hurricane roaring through. So why worry now? Norcross, however, had an entirely different perspective. Steeped in Florida's hurricane history, he knew that devastating hurricanes had struck Miami before, and one day would do so again.

On Saturday, as Andrew's pressure fell, tension in Miami grew. During the day Andrew strengthened from a Category 1 to a Category 2 hurricane, and instead of turning to the north, it continued to drift westward toward the Bahamas—a trajectory that set it on a collision course with southeastern Florida. Norcross and his colleagues stayed on the air from noon until 2:00 p.m., answering questions from area residents about the hurricane and how to prepare for its possible arrival. At 5:00 p.m., the National Hurricane Center issued a hurricane watch for the coast from Titusville to the Florida Keys, meaning there was a risk of hurricane conditions along that stretch within the next thirty-six hours. This alert ratcheted up the level of concern, and the six o'clock news at WTVJ also ran for two hours, with much of that time taken up by more hurricane coverage. Other Florida television stations, as well as radio outlets and newspapers,

---

* Before 1997, Miami-Dade County was called Dade County. To minimize confusion, it will be referred to as Miami-Dade throughout this book.

were also devoting an ever-expanding amount of reporting time to Andrew and its approach.

Miami Herald reporters brilliantly captured the spreading sense of impending calamity: "Throughout south Florida, the thought materialized in the morning like a darkening blip on the horizon: This could be it. And by Saturday night, this thought billowed into something that was not quite fear, but close enough. Call it advanced apprehension: This really could be it. We'd better get ready." That is the message that local civil defense coordinators were sending out. Don't panic, stay alert, listen to media coverage, and be ready to evacuate if necessary.

Syndicated humorist Dave Barry, who lives in Miami, wrote a column about a week after the hurricane in which he poked fun at the instructions that local television and radio personalities had shared with their audience. "Everywhere we went," Barry wrote, "we could hear announcers telling us things we need to do IMMEDIATELY." Among the items were the following: " 'CAULK UP YOUR BATHTUB!' 'REMOVE YOUR PUMP MOTOR!' 'SEPARATE YOUR KITCHEN UTENSILS ACCORDING TO ZINC CONTENT!' 'I SAID DON'T PANIC, DAMMIT!!' 'REMOVE ALL HELIUM MOLECULES FROM THE GARAGE!' 'YOU'RE STARTING TO PANIC, AREN'T YOU??' "

Come evening, South Floridians were seriously gearing up for the storm. Patio tables and chairs were tied down or brought inside, storm shutters were lowered into place, and in areas close to the water, where a storm surge would likely roll through, furniture and valuables were moved to higher floors. Gas stations were mobbed, and store shelves were emptied of food, water, flashlights, batteries, radios, generators, and plywood, as people rushed to prepare their homes and businesses, and themselves, for Andrew's arrival. Sales at one Costco surged by 40 percent, its manager stating, "Today was like a Christmas day for us. It's flying out." Boat owners moved their vessels to protected coves and upriver, or secured them more solidly to their moorings or docks.

The center's new advisory was issued at 11:00 p.m., forecasting Andrew to come ashore farther south, in the vicinity of Miami, as a Category 3 hurricane. This alert prompted Norcross to deliver another two-hour slug of coverage. He signed off the air at 1:00 a.m., telling his viewers, "I'm going to go home now, and get some sleep and I suggest you do, too. Tomorrow is going to be a very big day for our city, and I'm not sure we're going to get sleep tomorrow night."

Sunday morning, August 23, Miamians were greeted by a bold headline on the front page of the *Miami Herald*: "**Bigger, Stronger, Closer.**" When the paper was put to bed the night before, Andrew was closing in on becoming a Category 3 hurricane. By the time people read the article, Andrew had reached Category 3, and the 8:00 a.m. advisory declared a hurricane warning for the coast from Vero Beach down to the tip of the Florida Keys, meaning that hurricane conditions were likely within the next twenty-four hours.

Evacuation orders had already been issued for Broward and Miami-Dade Counties and the Keys. Norcross, sitting at the anchor desk, went on the air at 9:00 a.m., and he and his colleagues would continue reporting nonstop for the next twenty-three hours. They gave updates on the hurricane when available but spent most of their time answering questions, presenting on-scene reporting, telling people which shelters were open, and providing advice and emotional support for their viewers. That advice and support proved critical, since the news about Andrew got worse by the hour.

The 11:00 a.m. National Hurricane Center advisory warned, "DANGEROUS CATEGORY FOUR HURRICANE HEADING FOR SOUTH FLORIDA. ALL PRECAUTIONS TO PROTECT LIFE AND PROPERTY, INCLUDING EVACUATIONS, SHOULD BE RUSHED TO COMPLETION." Hurricane Hunters flying into Andrew revealed that Andrew was not only incredibly powerful, but also very compact, with hurricane-force winds extending only 30 miles from the center. After getting things in order as best they could, roughly 700,000 South Floridians got into their cars, trucks, or mobile homes and evacuated, while tens of thousands more went to area shelters.

At 5:00 p.m., Andrew made landfall on the northern edge of the Bahamian island of Eleuthera as a Category 5 hurricane. Its estimated 170-mph winds caused $250 million in damage on the island and killed four people. Contact with land took a bit of the edge off Andrew, and the storm sustained another, bigger hit when *eyewall replacement* occurred, a process in which the original eyewall disintegrates and is replaced by another eyewall a little farther out—a transition that typically weakens a hurricane. The storm did weaken during eyewall replacement, with winds dropping to about 150 mph. But once Andrew moved over the warmer waters of the Gulf Stream in the early morning hours of Monday, August 24, it quickly reintensified and was now only about 60 miles east of Miami—and closing in fast.

AT THE NATIONAL HURRICANE CENTER, director Bob Sheets, supported by his capable staff, was doing yeoman's work tracking the hurricane and updating media outlets, as well as government officials, every half hour. Located in the Miami suburb of Coral Gables, the center was on the sixth floor of a twelve-story building. On the roof stood an array of weather instruments, including a 1-ton radar dish that was enclosed in what looked like a giant golf ball but was, in fact, a protective fiberglass dome. By 4:00 a.m., the building was being buffeted by 107-mph winds, at which point a nearby transformer exploded, cutting outside electricity and causing the building's generator to kick in. Every few minutes, one of the meteorologists called out the speed registering on the roof's wind gauge. It was going in only one direction: higher.

Between 4:28 and 4:33, the wind rose from 134 to 147 mph. The building started swaying wildly, causing one center staffer to say he felt seasick. Then there was a sudden crashing noise that "almost sounded like a brick wall" hitting the building. Since the radar stopped working at that moment, the center staff surmised that the radar dish and its protective dome had blown over, and that is exactly what happened. After the hurricane passed, the dish was found lying prone on the roof, with fragments of the dome widely scattered on the ground well away from the building. Though the radar was damaged, the wind gauge continued to work, registering 164 mph at 5:52 a.m. This, however, would be the last reading that day, as the wind gauge, too, was knocked out of commission. Moments later, Andrew, whose eye was a mere 9–12 miles wide, made landfall at Fender Point, Florida, about 15 miles south of the Hurricane Center. It was as bad as everyone had feared—a Category 5 hurricane with 165-mph winds.

IN THE HOURS BEFORE landfall, the team at WTVJ was facing its own difficulties. At 2:45 a.m., Norcross began to fear for the stability of the building's roof and the studio's ceiling. He thought it would be wise to have a safer spot to broadcast from, in the event that wood and plaster started flying. To that end, the studio manager and the production manager readied a nearby storage area under sturdy concrete steps to serve as the backup location. They called it "the bunker." In addition to protecting the broadcast team if things got rough, Norcross thought that the bunker could serve another purpose: "If we move off this desk to a place of safety, people will see that we are taking this seriously."

At 3:20 a.m., a power failure knocked WTVJ off the air, but Florida Power & Light quickly restored the connection. However, just because the station was broadcasting didn't mean that viewers could watch. In fact, large portions of southern Florida were already without power, and by the time the hurricane was over, nearly 1.5 million people would be in the dark.

Norcross knew that this problem would arise if a major hurricane ever hit the Miami area, and he also knew it meant that the only way to reach his audience would be to have the broadcast go out over the radio. That way, people with battery-operated radios could hear him, even if they couldn't see him on TV. Therefore, in the spring of 1992 Norcross had urged WTVJ to establish a telephone link with the Fort Lauderdale radio station WHYI-FM (Y100). In a case of fortuitous timing, just one week before Andrew formed, WTVJ had finalized the connection, and now it had come time to use it. Right after WTVJ's power was restored, Y100 started broadcasting the television feed live, and Norcross told his viewers to tune in to the radio station in the event of another power outage.

Bryan Norcross (left), with reporters Kelly Craig and Tony Segreto in the "bunker" during Hurricane Andrew.

A few minutes after the power was restored, the entire building started to shake. Fearing it might no longer be safe to remain at the anchor desk in the main studio, Norcross and his team moved into the bunker and started broadcasting from there.

Norcross continued giving updates on the hurricane and offering helpful advice on how to survive it. In his estimation, one of the most important things he told his audience as Andrew approached came from reading Leo Francis Reardon's book on the Great Miami Hurricane of 1926. To protect his family during the storm, Reardon had covered them with a mattress and pillows to cushion the blow, should anything come crashing down. Norcross shared that lesson on the air just a short while before Andrew made landfall. "Friends," Norcross recalled saying, "here's what I want you to do. Get a mattress off the bed and have it ready. When you go to your safe spot, get your family in there, get the mattress over them, and wait this thing out." In subsequent days, the great value of that advice would become apparent, as many people told Norcross they had survived the hurricane by doing just that.

ANDREW RACED ACROSS SOUTHEASTERN Florida at 18–20 mph, reemerging over the Gulf of Mexico just four hours after it had crashed into Florida's east coast. Still a major hurricane, Andrew sucked energy from the warm Gulf waters, and on Wednesday morning at around 8:00 it came ashore as a Category 3 hurricane in a relatively unpopulated stretch of the Louisiana coast about 100 miles southwest of New Orleans. It pushed ahead of it a storm surge of 8 feet and spawned no less than fourteen tornadoes. Damage in Louisiana totaled roughly $1 billion. Eight people died as a direct result of the hurricane, and another nine were indirect fatalities.* While that was a traumatic and tragic blow, it paled in comparison to what happened during Andrew's rampage in Florida.

Andrew tore a 30-mile-wide swath of misery through Miami-Dade County that covered an area equal to twelve Manhattan Islands. How fast the winds blew during Andrew's transit can never be definitively deter-

---

* To understand what is meant by *indirect fatalities*, and how they compare to *direct fatalities*, please see Author's Notes at the beginning of this book.

*A piece of plywood driven through the trunk of a royal palm
by the powerful winds of Hurricane Andrew.*

mined, since the National Hurricane Center's equipment was crippled at
right about the time of landfall. But there is evidence that gusts approached
200 mph. The storm surge crested at 16.9 feet, a record for southeastern
Florida, leveling or flooding many structures along the coast.

Most of the damage occurred to the south of Miami. A staggering
126,000 homes were damaged or destroyed, while another 9,000 mobile
homes were shredded beyond recognition. More than 160,000 people were
made homeless overnight—the equivalent of nearly one out of every ten
people in Miami-Dade County. Fifteen thousand boats were thrown onto
land, sunk, or stacked up at marinas and cul-de-sacs along the coast, many
of them never to sail or motor again. Businesses were severely battered,
resulting in nearly 100,000 lost jobs, which, not coincidentally, is roughly
the number of people who permanently moved out of Miami-Dade County
after the hurricane. At Kendall-Tamiami airport (now Miami Executive
Airport), about 13 miles southwest of downtown Miami, 275 corporate jets
and personal, as well as historic, planes were tossed around like feathers
in the wind and damaged beyond repair. The working-class city of Homestead, population 26,000, was nearly wiped clean off the face of the Earth.

Andrew's whipping winds knocked over a huge number of trees and
bushes, and those that remained standing were stripped of all their leaves,

Vehicles in the National Hurricane Center parking lot thrown about by Hurricane Andrew. One of them belonged to a CNN reporter, the other to a center employee. The latter found out about the damage to his car while watching CNN's coverage of the hurricane!

transforming them into naked sentinels attesting to the storm's great fury. Witnessing the defoliation on the islands of Biscayne Bay National Park, Rick Gore, *National Geographic*'s senior assistant editor, commented that they "look as if they have been drenched with Agent Orange." Many of the flexible and resilient royal palms, which evolution designed to withstand powerful winds that would level most trees, were also humbled by Andrew and knocked to the ground.

Miami MetroZoo (now Zoo Miami) was especially hard-hit. "The devastation is unbelievable," assistant curator Ron Magill said. "I have no words for it. It will be months just to clear the debris." About 300 rare birds were lost when the zoo's aviary was smashed. Scores, perhaps hundreds, of monkeys and baboons escaped from research and breeding facilities, panicking many residents, who feared, incorrectly, that the animals were infected with the AIDS virus or rabies. Many of them were shot by locals, and although most were eventually rounded up, some remained on the lam. Parrots, capybaras, and a huge number of lizards were also released into the wild. Some of the animals survived, contributing to Florida's well-earned reputation as the state with the most invasive species.

Andrew's great power could be seen just offshore, where it damaged a number of the artificial reefs that are so important to recreational anglers. The most dramatic example concerns the nearly 200-foot-long, 330-ton *Belzona Barge*. Before the storm, it was lying on the bottom, 60 feet down, its deck covered by 600 tons of concrete, the remnants of a bridge. The waves generated by Andrew not only blasted about 90 percent of the concrete off the deck, along with all of the attached wildlife, but also moved the barge two football fields away from its original position and sheared off many of the hull's steel plates.

Total damage in Florida due to Andrew approached $27 billion, making it the most expensive hurricane ever to have hit the United States up to that point. Despite the enormous financial toll and violence of the storm, in Florida Andrew caused only fifteen deaths directly, and another twenty-nine indirectly—incredibly low numbers, attributable in part to the success of emergency preparations and evacuations.

BRYAN NORCROSS CONTINUED broadcasting until 8:00 on Monday morning, August 24, at which point the worst was over, even though there were still occasional gusts of wind as high as 80 mph. He and his colleagues left the bunker, and Norcross, voice hoarse after twenty-three hours on the air, curled up on the floor of an office in the station's building to finally get some rest. With clear answers and steady assurance, he had helped calm his audience's fears. Widely hailed for his performance, Norcross was lauded by the *Miami Herald* as "the man who talked south Florida through" the hurricane. The *Herald* also said that he had "distinguished himself as local television's most valuable player during the coverage of Andrew." On a more personal and professional note, Norcross's stellar performance caused his bosses at WTVJ to reconsider their decision to let him go. Instead, they offered to renew his contract and give him a nice raise, convincing him to stay in South Florida and abandon his plans for New York.

ON TUESDAY, AUGUST 25, in the brilliant light of day, the extent of the devastation became painfully apparent. More than 3 million cubic yards of debris was strewn throughout Miami-Dade County. Homes were blasted into kindling, cars were overturned and smashed, wires were downed, streetlights had toppled, the sides of apartment buildings were ripped off, appliances littered the streets, and people's most cherished items were scattered everywhere, or had vanished forever.

Stunned by the enormity of the event, people began to pick up the pieces of their fractured lives. Judi Whiteman, whose home in Country Walk, even with its $8,200 hurricane shutters, was obliterated by Andrew, reflected on the quicksilver nature of life and the strange calculus of disaster. "Richard and I have been married 29 years," she said. "We've saved and done everything right. Sometimes everything you do isn't enough. It's all gone in an instant. I'm still crying at times. I'll never be the same. But my husband and I are alive. We have faith in the Lord. I know during the storm we were praying constantly, not just for ourselves, but [for] our friends and relatives, that everyone would get through it. And they did. But I didn't pray for this storm to go elsewhere. I couldn't wish this ill wind on anyone."

As is so often the case in the aftermath of hurricanes, there was widespread looting. Many, desperate for food and supplies, stole to survive, making their actions, if not praiseworthy, at least understandable, given the circumstances. Others, however, were nothing more than opportunistic thieves, taking what they could while law enforcement officials were overwhelmed. In the void, some people took matters into their own hands. At the Keg South burger and beer joint in Naranja, owner Bud Nemeth stood vigil during Andrew and for days afterward, with a double-barrel shotgun at the ready, fending off scores of would-be thieves.

ON THE AFTERNOON OF August 24, the day the storm hit Miami-Dade, President George H. W. Bush declared a state of emergency in Florida, activating the Federal Emergency Management Agency (FEMA), which would now be responsible for coordinating the federal financial and physical assistance to hurricane victims. Created in 1979 by President Jimmy Carter, FEMA was intended to consolidate disparate federal emergency and relief programs under a single agency, one reliable source for states to receive federal aid/assistance during times of natural or human-made disasters, in cases when state and local authorities are overwhelmed and cannot handle the response to the disaster on their own. By the time Andrew came in 1992, FEMA had a checkered history. It was often starved of funding and viewed as a patronage dumping ground, where good friends or supporters of the president got plum jobs even if they had no experience or skills that would recommend them to the posts. After Hurricane Hugo in 1989, FEMA was ridiculed for its inadequate response to the ensuing crisis in the Southeast. South Carolina's junior senator at the time, Democrat Ernest F. Hollings, angry over FEMA's poor performance, labeled agency personnel "the sorriest bunch of bureaucratic jackasses I've ever worked with."

The same day that Bush declared a state of emergency, he flew to Miami-Dade County, arriving at Opa-locka Airport at 6:00 p.m. With his Secret Service protection and reporters in tow, Bush was driven to the Cutler Ridge Mall for a press conference in front of a store that had been looted, during which he promised that the federal government would provide relief and help the area recover. After the conference, his motorcade raced to the airport, and within two hours of setting foot in Florida the president was on his way back to Washington.

Although Bush didn't see the true extent of the devastation that Andrew had wrought, the worst of which was farther to the south, Florida officials were hopeful that federal aid would be arriving in force any minute, yet were a bit puzzled that it wasn't already there. Florida National Guard troops had started deploying on Monday, but other than that there was little evidence of any federal response.

As the days dragged on without external aid, the situation in Miami-Dade County became dire. Food and water for the 2 million residents who lived there grew scarcer, and tempers flared. Finally, on August 27, three days after Andrew, Kate Hale, Miami-Dade's emergency director, vented on live TV. At a press conference in front of a gaggle of reporters, she stood her ground and shared the frustration and anger felt by all of Andrew's victims. "Enough is enough," she said. "Quit playing like a bunch of kids. . . . Where in the hell is the cavalry? For God's sakes, where are they? We're going to have more casualties because we're going to have more people dehydrated. People without water. People without food. Babies without formula. We need food, we need water, we need people down here. We're all about ready to drop and the reinforcements are not going in fast enough. . . . President Bush was down here. I'd like him to follow up on the commitments he made."

Hale's emotional plea got the Bush administration's attention, and the federal response finally kicked into high gear. The following morning, the cavalry did indeed arrive. Thousands of army troops and marines, bearing planeloads of tents, cots, blankets, field kitchens, food, water, and generators, fanned out, providing succor to those in need and establishing law and order.

There would be considerable finger-pointing in the ensuing days, with much of the blame for the slow, and initially wholly inadequate, response being laid at the feet of the federal government. Even though Bush had declared a state of emergency right away, and troops at Fort Bragg, North Carolina, had food and supplies ready to send to Florida immediately after Andrew struck, neither Bush nor FEMA gave the order for the military to deploy until after Hale made her urgent plea. The administration argued that it was waiting for Florida governor Lawton Chiles to submit a formal request for aid before initiating a response. Although it was true that Chiles had not sent such a written request, he shot back that he had verbally requested aid early on but had been rebuffed by federal officials, who argued that the state needed to take the lead, after which the Feds would follow. Part of the administration's slow response can be attributed to the fact that it didn't initially comprehend just how serious the situation was, since on his lightning-quick Monday trip to the area, Bush had seen only the edge of the devastation, and not the worst of it.

Bush defended his administration, stating that the federal government had "responded properly." He also said that he wasn't "going to participate in the blame game." Others, of course, had no compunction, and criticism of the administration's response was widespread. One meteorologist observed, "FEMA was prepared to do essentially nothing, and that's what it did for days." Chiles, too, was blamed for not making a formal request sooner. To his credit, Bush returned to Miami-Dade on September 1 and toured more of the area, offered compassion for those suffering, committed the federal government to continued recovery efforts, and urged Americans to "pitch in, in any way you can." Still, some have argued that Bush's botched response in the early days after Andrew contributed to his election loss to Bill Clinton in November 1992.

JUST TWO DAYS AFTER Andrew, the *Miami Herald* issued a sober assessment of the situation and a clarion call: "Thousands of South Floridians have the numb feeling of mourners, seeing little reminders of normal life that offer sharp contrast to the depth of despair." After noting that some had lost comforts like electricity, while others had lost their homes, and still others their loved ones, the editors wondered whether South Florida would ever recover. "In a way, no," they said. "Those of us who have taken great losses will bear scars in our souls. Some of us now have financial burdens from which we may not fully recover. Nearly all of us carry the new and clear knowledge of our vulnerability." But, they continued, South Florida would come back. "The rubble will be cleared. The canopy of green will spread anew. Institutions will be reborn and rebuilt, and so will families. . . . Miami and all of South Florida have always emerged stronger [from catastrophes natural and human-made] and it will again." Indeed, all of that did come to pass, in time.

INIKI, 1992

Rampaging dinosaurs are nothing compared to a massive hurricane, at least when you have a movie to finish. Director Steven Spielberg had planned to wrap up the filming of *Jurassic Park* on September 11, 1992. He and his cast and crew of 130 had been working on the Hawaiian island of Kauai for weeks, bringing author Michael Crichton's book of the same name to life. The plot revolves around an island theme park in which cloned and genetically engineered dinosaurs are the main attraction. What could possibly go wrong? As it turns out, everything—and mayhem ensues. Although Spielberg had to overcome many obstacles to bring this story to the silver screen, he hadn't planned on a hurricane. But that's exactly what arrived on the eleventh, when Hurricane Iniki slammed into Kauai. It was, Spielberg later said, "a real zinger."

Spielberg and his entourage weren't the only ones caught off guard. Hurricanes are extremely rare in Hawaii; before Iniki, only two had made landfall there since 1871. A number of good reasons explain this scarcity.

First, the Hawaiian Islands are very small and located in the midst of the jaw-droppingly vast Pacific. Thus, even though quite a few hurricanes cross the Pacific, the odds of one hitting the Hawaiian Islands are statistically low. Second, the prevailing trade winds in this part of the world typically blow hurricanes, which originate off the coast of Mexico, to the west, past Hawaii and toward Asia. Third, there is considerable wind shear in the vicinity of Hawaii that tends to disrupt a hurricane. Finally, the waters to the east of Hawaii are normally relatively cool (less than 80 degrees) compared to the waters to the south and west, and therefore they don't provide as much of the thermal energy that powers hurricanes.

So, on September 8, when tropical storm Iniki (Hawaiian for "sharp and piercing wind") was far to the southeast of Hawaii, few people were alarmed. Just like virtually all tropical cyclones, it was expected to slide by the islands. Over the next few days, however, tensions rose. Iniki grew much stronger, feeding off the Pacific waters, which were 1–3 degrees warmer than usual because it was an El Niño year. More worrying, Iniki wasn't heading due west. Instead, it was moving to the north, toward Hawaii, because a trough of low pressure to the west of the islands was pushing it in that direction. By Thursday, September 10, Iniki was a Category 2 hurricane with winds of 100 mph. It was heading directly toward Kauai, gaining strength. When informed of Iniki's approach, Kauai mayor JoAnn Yukimara told the audience at an event where she was speaking, "We should all pray it turns away." It didn't.

On Friday morning, September 11, the oversize title of the main article on the front page of the *Honolulu Advertiser* warned its readers, "Get Ready for Iniki." It was now a Category 4 hurricane, with winds of 145 mph and gusts up to 175, and already Kauai was being pounded by heavy surf and strong winds. The paper urged people to gather emergency supplies and evacuate to safer locations or higher ground.

There would be no filming of *Jurassic Park* that day, and there was no time to haul down or protect the elaborate sets dotting the island. Survival was the goal, and everyone associated with the movie crammed into the ballroom at the Westin Kauai hotel to take shelter from the storm. Reflecting on the situation years later, actor Sam Neill, who played paleontologist Dr. Alan Grant, said, "This was going to be more of an adventure than any of us had actually signed up for. . . . you think that we might die."

Iniki made landfall as a Category 4 on the southwest coast of Kauai at

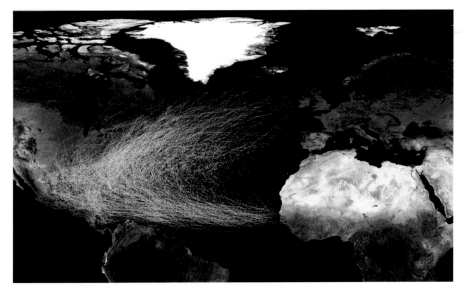

1. *Compilation showing the tracks of all Atlantic hurricanes from 1851 through 2012. Tracks are continued through the time that the hurricanes weaken into tropical storms and tropical depressions.*

2. *The wreck of the HMS* Deal Castle *off Puerto Rico during the Great Hurricane of 1780, as painted by John Thomas Serres, circa 1797. Near the left side of the painting, you can see some of the crew abandoning ship on a raft of wreckage.*

3. Oil on canvas painting titled The Great Gale of 1815, *by John Russell Bartlett, circa 1835–40.*

4. Fall foliage in Vermont. These wonderful colors are due, in part, to the destructive power of the Great Hurricane of 1938, which knocked down huge numbers of white pine trees and allowed a variety of deciduous trees to grow and show their dazzling fall displays.

5. *Winslow Homer's watercolor* After the Hurricane, Bahamas, *1899.*

6. Menemsha Hurricane, *by Thomas Hart Benton, 1954. This oil paint-ing depicts Menemsha Pond (an inlet of the ocean) on Martha's Vineyard, in the aftermath of Hurricane Carol, which pummeled the island with winds approaching 100 mph. Benton hurried down to the edge of the pond right as the hurricane was dying down and began making sketches of the scene. As this striking painting shows, the hurricane heavily damaged Dutcher Dock, knocked buildings off their foundations, and sank many vessels in the pond.*

7. When Hurricane Andrew came knocking, the staff at Miami MetroZoo (now Zoo Miami) herded a bunch of Caribbean flamingos into one of the men's bathrooms to shelter them from the storm.

8. View of the eyewall of Hurricane Katrina taken on August 28, 2005, as seen from a NOAA WP-3D Hurricane Hunter aircraft.

9. A young Hurricane Katrina survivor hugs her rescuer, Staff Sergeant Mike Maroney, after she was relocated to the Louis Armstrong New Orleans International Airport, Louisiana, on September 7. Sergeant Maroney is a pararescueman from the 58th Rescue Squadron at Nellis Air Force Base, Nevada.

10. Satellite image of Hurricane Sandy, off the Carolinas, taken at noon on Sunday, October 28, 2012.

11. The HMS Bounty II *shown partially submerged in the Atlantic Ocean during Hurricane Sandy, approximately 90 miles southeast of Cape Hatteras, North Carolina, October 29, 2012.*

*12. President Barack Obama hugs Donna Vanzant,
the owner of North Point Marina, as he tours damage
from Hurricane Sandy in Brigantine, New Jersey,
October 31, 2012.*

*13. Colorized infrared satellite image of Hurricane Maria approaching
Puerto Rico on September 20, 2017. This shot was taken three hours
before the hurricane slammed into the island.*

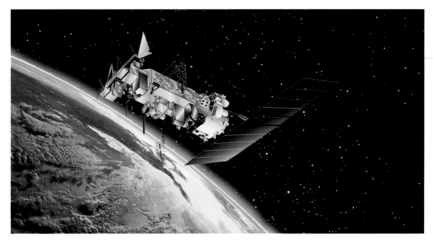

14. Artistic rendering of the Polar-orbiting Operational Environmental Satellite POES-18. POES can broadcast high-resolution, real-time data from instruments to local users around the world. Data are continuously recorded on board the satellites as they orbit the Earth. The data stream is downloaded once per orbit as the satellite passes over a command and data acquisition station.

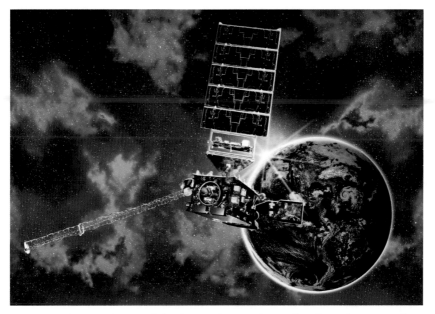

15. Artist's rendering of the Geostationary Operational Environmental Satellite GOES-17. Launched in March 2018, the GOES-R series is the next generation of geostationary weather satellites. It is a collaborative development and acquisition effort between NOAA and NASA. The advanced spacecraft and instrument technology used on the GOES-R series will result in more timely and accurate forecasts and warnings. Like the other satellites in the series, GOES-17 carries a suite of sophisticated Earth-sensing, lightning-detecting, solar-imaging, and space-weather-monitoring instruments.

16. *The author in August 1991, standing in front of a damaged summer house in Falmouth, Massachusetts, after Hurricane Bob.*

17. In the tradition of having my daughter, Lily Dolin, paint a small picture for each of my books, here is her rendition of palm trees bending in a hurricane's winds.

3:30 in the afternoon on the eleventh. The winds shook the walls of the Westin Kauai's ballroom, as water rushed in under the doors and came down through cracks in the ceiling. Spielberg tried to keep the younger cast members from worrying about the hurricane by playing games and telling ghost stories. Ever the director looking for a great shot, he also took advantage of the storm, leading cameramen down to the beach early on to film the enormous waves crashing on the shore, thinking that the footage could add a dramatic scene to the movie (ultimately, it did). But when conditions deteriorated, the hotel's security personnel told Spielberg it was too dangerous to be outside, and he and his cameramen returned to the ballroom.

By 6:00 p.m. the hurricane had moved well past the island, and the cast and crew of *Jurassic Park* had survived unscathed. The same couldn't be said for Kauai. Iniki is the strongest hurricane to have hit Hawaii in its recorded history. Damage on the island was deemed "mind boggling" by civil defense officials in Honolulu. Mayor Yukimara, who took to a helicopter to survey the scene from the air, said she saw such "total destruction—it broke my heart." Nearly 15,000 homes and businesses were damaged, roughly 5,000 of which were severely impacted, while 1,400 were obliterated. The island of Oahu had been hit with the outer bands of the hurricane and strong surf, sustaining widespread power outages, but relatively little damage. Iniki's price tag was $3.1 billion, and while more than 1,500 were injured, only six people died.

Although commercial airplanes were not allowed to leave Kauai, *Jurassic Park* producer Kathleen Kennedy managed to fly to Honolulu on a National Guard helicopter. There she chartered a private plane to bring emergency supplies and medical personnel to Kauai, and she used the empty plane to transport the cast and crew back to Honolulu. A couple of weeks later, Spielberg, a camera crew, and a few of the actors flew to Oahu to film one last scene. The movie hit theaters in June 1993, and to date it has grossed more than $1 billion worldwide.

Iniki crippled Kauai's economy, especially its vibrant tourist industry. Thousands of jobs were lost, and it was eight years before the annual number of visitors reached the levels enjoyed before the hurricane. Iniki also deeply affected those who lived through it. In the days after it blew through, three-year-old Davey Cook, whose family's house on Kauai was destroyed, had vivid dreams in which everything went back to the way it was before the hurricane. Over the next three years, Davey's teachers repeatedly told his parents that whenever he was asked to create a picture, "he would only draw dark circles—storm clouds."

KATRINA, 2005

Hurricane Katrina ravaged parts of Florida, Mississippi, Alabama, and Louisiana, costing $125 billion, making it the most expensive hurricane ever to strike the United States.* Estimates of the number of deaths (direct and indirect) vary, but most sources place it at about 1,800, with Louisiana claiming the lion's share. Ground zero for Katrina, however, was the city of New Orleans, which suffered the most devastating blow. Trying to describe Katrina, its impacts, and its immediate aftermath in a few pages, or even an entire chapter, is not a Herculean task but rather an impossible one. It is arguably the most complicated and controversial natural and human-made disaster in American history.

The single most comprehensive book on Katrina is Douglas Brinkley's *The Great Deluge*, which runs to more than 700 pages. Katrina's meteorological biography will be familiar to anyone who has reached this point in the book. Writ large, however, Katrina is an intricate tale of environmental degradation, intense human suffering, rapacious development, poor urban planning, faulty engineering, lawlessness and violence, and massive bureaucratic and political failures before, during, and after the storm. Katrina was also, contrastingly, characterized by many instances of heroism, human compassion, and charity. What follows, then, is not a complete portrait of Katrina, but rather the bones of the story.

On August 24, 1992, a tropical disturbance morphed into tropical storm Katrina while passing over the Bahamas. The following day, it became a Category 1 hurricane right before making landfall on Florida's southeastern coast, about 15 miles north of Miami. Katrina caused $630 million worth of damage and killed fourteen people, before exiting Florida and heading into the Gulf as a tropical storm. But the unusually warm waters of the Gulf gave Katrina a sustained burst of energy. By early Saturday, August 27, it

---

* It is the most expensive based on the 2019 Consumer Price Index Adjusted Cost. See Tables of Costliest Hurricanes at the end of the book.

had grown into a massive Category 3 hurricane that was heading straight toward New Orleans. For years people had talked about the "Big One" one day hitting the Big Easy, and now it appeared to be on the way.

There were plenty of reasons to be alarmed. Both Hurricane Betsy in 1965 and Hurricane Camille in 1969 had come close to New Orleans, but neither had hit it head-on. Still, Betsy in particular, which caused seventy-five deaths in Louisiana, laid bare the city's unique vulnerability to flooding in the wake of a hurricane. Roughly 50 percent of New Orleans is below sea level, and the city as a whole averages about 6 feet below sea level. Therefore, much of New Orleans is like a bowl, surrounded on three sides by bodies of water—Lake Pontchartrain, the Mississippi River, and Lake Borgne, a lagoon on the Gulf of Mexico—all of which would naturally flow into the low parts of the city. The only things preventing that from happening are the levees* surrounding the city like a suit of aquatic armor, and the drainage canals and pumps that keep the city dry.

Betsy's storm surge caused some of the levees to overtop, resulting in significant flooding. To address the problem, after Betsy the US Army Corps of Engineers reinforced, rebuilt, and extended the city's levee system. But on the eve of Katrina, there were considerable doubts about the system's reliability, especially given chronic underfunding and maintenance issues. Since Betsy, the city's vulnerability to flooding had also increased because of the continued destruction of Louisiana's coastal wetlands, which historically acted as buffers against storm surges by slowing them down and absorbing water. As the wetlands disappeared, the threat posed by storm surges worsened.

In many ways, Katrina was a disaster waiting to happen. Numerous reports and studies had predicted the potential catastrophe that would visit New Orleans when the Big One finally arrived. In 2002, New Orleans's *Times-Picayune* ran a series of articles exploring that possibility, titled "Washing Away." The authors concluded that a major hurricane, a Category 3 or higher, could result in a worst-case scenario, with hundreds of billions of gallons of water flowing over the levees. "That would turn the city and the east bank of Jefferson Parish into a lake as much as 30

---

* New Orleans's flood protection system was and is composed of both levees and floodwalls. However, to keep things simple, and the prose less cluttered, from here on the system will be referred to as just a levee system, as opposed to a levee and floodwall system.

feet deep, fouled with chemicals and waste from ruined septic systems, businesses and homes. Such a flood could trap hundreds of thousands of people in buildings and in vehicles. At the same time, high winds and tornadoes would tear at everything left standing." The series hinted that it could be far worse if the levees failed, which it held out as a distinct possibility.

Just a year before Katrina hit, FEMA had sponsored a week-long simulation exercise, evaluating what would happen if Pam, a hypothetical slow-moving Category 3 hurricane, brought 120-mph winds and 20 inches of rain to parts of southeastern Louisiana, and a storm surge overtopped the levees. The answer was sobering. In addition to killing roughly 60,000 people, injuring 175,000, making 200,000 sick from disease, forcing the evacuation of more than 1 million residents, and destroying 500,000–600,000 buildings, Pam would leave much of greater New Orleans under 10–20 feet of water, which the report described as a "HazMat gumbo," containing all sorts of chemicals, bacteria, and contaminants.

EVERYONE HAD PLENTY OF warning that Katrina was coming. The National Hurricane Center monitored and measured its every move, and the center's director, Max Mayfield, did an excellent job of communicating

Max Mayfield, director of the National Hurricane Center from 2000 to 2007.

the hurricane's trajectory and strength to local and national agencies and politicians, as well as to the press. With each report, concerns heightened.

Throughout Saturday, the National Hurricane Center's reports became more worrisome. The hurricane watch that it issued in the morning was upgraded to a warning that night, as Katrina ramped up from a weak to a very strong Category 3 storm. The center also said that the storm would likely continue to strengthen and could make landfall as a Category 5. Those reports precipitated a number of actions on the part of local, state, and federal authorities. Louisiana governor Kathleen Babineaux Blanco had already declared a state of emergency late Friday night, and on Saturday she urged people along the coast and in New Orleans to evacuate. To make that process easier, she initiated the state's "contraflow" evacuation plan for southeastern Louisiana, which opened all lanes of the interstate highways to northbound traffic only. At Blanco's request, President George W. Bush, who, while on vacation, was monitoring the situation from his ranch in Texas, declared a federal state of emergency for Louisiana, which triggered assistance through FEMA. St. Charles Parish, to the west of New Orleans, and Plaquemines Parish to the south ordered mandatory evacuations, while New Orleans mayor Ray C. Nagin declared a state of emergency in the city and also urged residents to evacuate.

Despite this flurry of activity at the city, state, and federal levels, Mayfield was concerned that people weren't taking Katrina seriously enough. On Saturday afternoon, he told the *Times-Picayune*, "The guidance we get and common sense and experience suggests this storm is not done strengthening. . . . This is really scary." He urged residents who were thinking of not evacuating to reconsider their decision, given what was headed their way. On Saturday night, Mayfield called Blanco and Nagin to personally warn them about the unprecedented threat that Katrina posed to their constituents. "The thing I remember telling" them, Mayfield later recalled, "is that when I walked out of the Hurricane Center that night I wanted to be able to sleep at night knowing that I had done everything that I could do."

Mayfield's comments forced Blanco and Nagin to consider whether to order mandatory evacuations. This is an extremely fraught decision for any politician to make, since urging people to evacuate is much easier than officially ordering them to do so. Evacuations are extremely expensive, whether they are voluntary or mandatory, with costs including travel expenses, lost wages, and missed vacations. While mandatory evacuations are necessarily more expensive than voluntary ones, given the greater number of people involved, exactly how expensive depends on the severity of the storm and the characteristics of the population ordered to evacuate. One study in 2003 estimated that the cost of a mandatory evacuation of North Carolina's coastal counties facing a Category 3 hurricane would be roughly $32 million; in contrast, a voluntary evacuation would cost about $6 million. A mandatory evacuation for New Orleans and coastal Louisiana would undoubtedly be much more expensive because of the much larger affected population.

The cost of a mandatory evacuation, however, is not the only thing that politicians have to weigh when deciding what to do. If they order an evacuation but then the storm doesn't hit, or it is much less severe than predicted, the political backlash can be severe. Not only does a "false alarm" entail political risks, but it also dilutes the impact of future evacuation orders, since many people will simply assume, "Hey, they were wrong the last time, so why should we believe them now?" What Mayfield and all of the National Hurricane Center reporting were telling Blanco and Nagin, however, was that Katrina would be no false alarm.

By 7:00 a.m. on Sunday, August 28, Katrina was, in the National Hurricane Center advisory's words, "A POTENTIALLY CATASTROPHIC CATEGORY FIVE HURRICANE," with winds of 175 mph, and still heading toward New Orleans. This new information, along with Mayfield's personal outreach, finally convinced Blanco and Nagin to take further action. A few hours later, Blanco ordered a mandatory evacuation for coastal Louisiana, and Nagin did the same for New Orleans, marking the first time in the city's history that such an order had been issued.* During a press conference Nagin said, "We're facing the storm most of us have feared. This is very serious . . . the first choice of every citizen should be to leave the city." Nagin told those who were not able to leave to take refuge at the Superdome, New Orleans's premier sporting venue, which can hold more than 75,000 spectators. President Bush issued an emergency declaration for Mississippi, and FEMA's director, Michael Brown, headed to Baton Rouge to oversee the federal response.

---

* A couple of coastal Mississippi counties ordered mandatory evacuations at the same time.

As people attempted to evacuate throughout the day, highways became jammed, creating major backups. Still, roughly 1.5 million people were able to leave, including about 80 percent of the 500,000 citizens of New Orleans. Most of the roughly 100,000 who remained in the city were relatively poor and predominantly black, and either didn't own a car or didn't have access to one. Many of them were too infirm to leave. At 6:00 p.m., as the outer bands of Katrina came ashore along the coast, Nagin ordered a curfew in the city, and by 9:00 that night, 10,000 people had gathered at the Superdome for shelter.

Katrina lost some power overnight. When it made landfall in the vicinity of Buras, Louisiana, at 6:00 a.m. on Monday, it was a strong Category 3. In a replay of Hurricane Camille, Buras was virtually wiped from the map, as was its sister community of Triumph. The more than 3,000 residents of the area heeded the evacuation orders, thereby saving their lives.

In addition to its vicious winds, Katrina was dropping an inch of rain or more per hour. Fortunately for New Orleans, it didn't suffer a direct hit. Instead, the storm's eye passed about 30 miles east of the city, near the

A view of inundated areas in New Orleans following the breaching of the levees surrounding the city as a result of Hurricane Katrina.

mouth of the Pearl River, at 10:00 a.m. Katrina continued moving through inland Mississippi, rapidly losing strength, and by 6:00 p.m. it had weakened to a tropical storm.

————

KATRINA LEFT A TRAIL of widespread destruction in Mississippi, killing 238 people and wiping out 60,000 housing units. But it was Louisiana, and New Orleans in particular, that suffered the most. Some early reports on Monday prematurely claimed that the city had "dodged a bullet." One example was an article in the *Chicago Tribune* that said, "Until nearly the last minute Monday, it looked like Hurricane Katrina might deal New Orleans the cataclysmic blow that scientists have long feared for the low-

Flooded roadways can be seen as the Coast Guard conducts
initial Hurricane Katrina damage assessment flights
on August 29, 2005.

lying city, which is uniquely vulnerable to the ravages of mighty storms from the sea. . . . What saved [it] from even worse damage was the storm's last-minute turn to the east." Such reports proved to be woefully wrong. Although the heart of Katrina missed New Orleans, the storm clobbered the city just the same, and what transpired in the coming days was nothing short of a catastrophe.

Katrina was a massive storm, and it produced an equally massive storm surge, reaching as high as 27.8 feet at Pass Christian, Mississippi, eclipsing the former record of 24.6 feet, which had been set at the same location during Hurricane Camille. The surge in the vicinity of New Orleans was closer to 20 feet, but it caused the Mississippi River, the Mississippi River–Gulf Outlet Canal, and Lake Pontchartrain to rise precipitously. As a result, levees overtopped in many parts of the city, leading to considerable flooding of low-lying areas. The real problems, however, began when various levees breached. The first identified failure was along the Seventeenth Street canal on Monday at about 5:00 a.m. Up to fifty other breaches followed, and by Wednesday, when the water finally stopped rushing into the city, 80 percent of New Orleans was submerged, with

The two fishing boats Sea Wolf *and* Sea Falcon
found themselves high and dry in Empire, Louisiana,
after Hurricane Katrina ripped through the area.

A Waffle House in Biloxi, Mississippi, stripped by
Hurricane Katrina of everything but its foundation,
sign, and some stools.

some areas covered to a depth of 10 feet or more. Hundreds of thousands of homes and businesses were inundated.

Had the levees held, New Orleans would still have sustained significant flooding, but the damage would likely not have been as catastrophic. When the levees broke, essentially allowing Lake Pontchartrain and the city to merge into one vast expanse of water, Katrina became a disaster of truly historic proportions.

The suffering and misery in New Orleans and the surrounding parishes in the days after Katrina's landfall are almost unimaginable. Tens of thousands of people were stranded in their homes, which were filled with or surrounded by the "HazMat gumbo" that the Hurricane Pam simulation had predicted. With temperatures in the nineties, and at times exceeding 100 degrees, the stagnant water became a fetid stew of dangerous chemicals and sewage that was hazardous to come in contact with, or even smell. Rashes, infections, rasping coughs, and other breathing problems were widespread. Dead and bloated bodies could be seen floating in the water, draped over cars and fences, or washed up where the floodwaters met dry land.

As the water rose, many people were forced into their attics, or had to break through to their roofs to escape. Some of those who couldn't break through ended up drowning in their own homes. Without electricity or running water, and low on food, many who were trapped experienced severe dehydration and hunger while waiting for help to arrive. Some didn't make it that long. The elderly and the frail were most at risk. Rescuers could often tell whether a house had dead people in it by the smell alone.

Looting was widespread, both for survival and for more selfish reasons. Although some looters were caught in the act and were either run off or arrested, that was the exception rather than the rule. The New Orleans police force, which had a troubled history of scandals and corruption investigations, was having a difficult time holding itself together, much less policing. Hundreds of officers had lost their homes in the storm, and a few hundred simply deserted their posts without permission. With stations flooded, cruisers damaged, communications compromised, and many officers not reporting for duty, the police struggled to coordinate their response to the crisis. Although they did, intermittently, try to stop looters and arsonists, much of their time was spent helping the victims

A warning sign to looters appears outside homes in Gulfport, Mississippi, in the aftermath of Hurricane Katrina.

of the hurricane and flood. The Louisiana National Guard and regular army forces also concentrated on victim aid and rescue, rather than on law enforcement.

The Superdome, where 10,000 people had sheltered, lost electricity early on Monday morning. The emergency generators powered only dim emergency lighting and not the air-conditioning, so the temperature quickly rose. Katrina's winds had ripped two sizable holes in the roof, letting the rain in. By Monday night, the Superdome's population had swelled to 25,000, but the building was stocked with only enough food and water to last 15,000 people three days. Fortunately, an additional 65,000 meals arrived on Tuesday evening. With no running water, the bathrooms didn't work. Recalling his experience at the Superdome, FEMA employee Marty Bahamonde said, "It was a shelter of last resort that cascaded into a cesspool of human waste and filth. Hallways and corridors were used as toilets, trash was everywhere, and among it all, [there were] children, thousands of them. It was sad, it was inhumane, it was wrong!" The city's Morial Convention Center also became a makeshift shelter, housing perhaps as many as 25,000 in equally horrific, if not worse, conditions.

Thousands of doctors and staff at area hospitals faced hellish choices in deciding how to treat the nearly 2,000 patients under their care. Most of the hospitals had no power and limited supplies of water and medicine. Many patients died before evacuations took place. At Memorial Medical Center, the fact that an unusually large number of its 260 patients didn't survive the unfolding disaster triggered extensive investigations into what happened to the 45 who died, which resulted in dramatic accusations that some of the deceased were pumped full of drugs to hasten their demise. The investigations and the ensuing trial are the basis of the Pulitzer Prize–winning book by Sheri Fink, *Five Days at Memorial*.

Rescue efforts were frustratingly slow. The delays were especially disturbing because those who couldn't leave the city before the hurricane hit—the poor and debilitated—were the most vulnerable and the most in need of help to survive. The Superdome and the convention center weren't completely evacuated until Sunday, September 4. The evacuees were sent to the Astrodome and the Reliant Center (now the NRG Center) in Houston, Texas, as well as other locations throughout the country, where they were given food, shelter, medical treatment, and the chance to take a breath and start making decisions about the next steps in their lives.

It took the better part of a week for a wide range of organizations and individuals to rescue or respond to the many thousands trapped in homes, hospitals, and businesses. Among those who participated in these efforts were the Louisiana National Guard, the Coast Guard, the army's 82nd Airborne Division, the marines, the New Orleans Police Department, and FEMA. In addition, many private individuals and organizations from around the country swooped in with personnel and supplies. Walmart sent an army of employees and essential goods, including food, clothes, and water, to the city, and American Airlines flew in emergency supplies and flew out evacuees. Perhaps the most famous example of this kind of generosity and support was provided by the so-called Cajun Navy, a volunteer group of small boat owners from around Louisiana who headed into New Orleans two days after Katrina hit and are credited with saving as many as 10,000 people, ferrying them to safety.

It wasn't until Monday, September 5, that the Army Corps finally closed all the levee breaches. At that point, the city's elaborate pumping system, hobbled by debris blockages and a lack of spare parts, started working again. The floodwaters were sent back into Lake Pontchartrain, and the city was finally drained by early October.

BEYOND THE SUFFERING AND misery in the aftermath of Katrina remained the question of why Katrina had become such a horrific disaster for New Orleans and why it had taken so long to supply relief to the city. Part of the blame lies with the enormous cast of private individuals, politicians, businesses, and other organizations who, over hundreds of years, had made development decisions that sacrificed Louisiana's coastal wetlands in the name of "progress." Since the mid-twentieth century alone, the state has lost more than 2,000 square miles of wetlands, an area slightly larger than the state of Delaware. While some of that loss is due to natural causes, including hurricanes, much of it is the direct result of human actions. Without the storm protection that wetlands provide, New Orleans, along with every other city and town along the coast, was made more vulnerable to hurricanes.

New Orleans's levees were built to withstand a Category 3 hurricane, but they clearly couldn't stand up to Katrina. That failure turned a very bad situation into a calamity. The breaching of the levees was due to a long history of underfunding, as well as serious flaws in their design and construction. Blame for those shortfalls should be laid squarely at the feet of the politicians who shortchanged the levee system; the Army Corps, which built it; and the Orleans Levee Board, which oversaw the system's operations and maintenance.

The response of local, state, and federal governments to the hurricane and its immediate aftermath was also severely lacking. Despite significant and very clear advance warning that a major hurricane was on the way, Blanco and Nagin waited until less than twenty-four hours before predicted landfall to issue mandatory evacuation orders, when the recommended time for calling evacuations of such large and heavily populated areas is at least 48, if not 72, hours prior to impact. Nagin later admitted that waiting so long was a mistake. "There's . . . things that I would do totally differently now," he told CNN's Anderson Cooper in early 2006. "I wish I had talked to Max Mayfield earlier, number one. . . . so the possibility of a mandatory evacuation would have been done 24 hours earlier."

But no matter how early the order was issued, a more complete evacuation of New Orleans would have been somewhat compromised because the city's evacuation plan was vague when it came to concrete details of how best to get people out of the city. Furthermore, the city government failed to make good use of some of the resources it did have for evacuating residents. For example, rather than 360 Regional Transit Authority buses being employed to ferry people out of the city, almost all of the buses sat in their lots. When Amtrak, which was driving its trains out of New Orleans in advance of the hurricane, offered 700 seats to transport people out of harm's way, the mayor's office ignored this invitation, and the "ghost train" left empty.

Much of the blame for the inadequate response goes to the federal government. President Bush, FEMA director Brown, and Brown's boss (Michael Chertoff, the secretary of homeland security) failed to quickly grasp the magnitude of the crisis, and even as the reality of it dawned on them, they were slow to react. Their response was often characterized by incompetence rather than effectiveness.

President Bush didn't visit the Gulf Coast until Friday, September 2, with stops at Mobile, Biloxi, Baton Rouge, and New Orleans. In Mobile, he spoke to the press, and during his remarks he turned to Brown and said, "Brownie, you're doing a heck of a job." As Douglas Brinkley cogently points out, nothing could have been further from the truth. "Michael

Brown was patently *not* doing a heck of a job, whether through his own failings or the lack of cooperation from others. The FEMA operation itself was an unmitigated disaster. The phrase became emblematic of the President's ignorance about the situation and his tendency to take a casual attitude toward it." The lack of cooperation that Brinkley alludes to was a serious problem with respect to Louisiana, since Nagin, Blanco, and the Feds often failed to communicate and work well with one another. But FEMA itself was arguably the biggest problem.

During President Bill Clinton's administration, FEMA was given a higher profile and more funding than it had under President George H. W. Bush. Clinton elevated FEMA to a cabinet-level agency and appointed James Lee Witt to lead it, making him the first FEMA director who actually had hands-on experience in emergency management, having led the Arkansas Office of Emergency Services. Witt was nicknamed "The Master of Disaster," and during his tenure he streamlined the bureaucracy. As a result, FEMA received consistently high marks for its professionalism and effectiveness.

Two years after President George W. Bush was elected, he revoked FEMA's cabinet-level status and folded the agency into the sprawling Department of Homeland Security, which was created in the aftermath of the terrorist attacks on September 11, 2001. Bush also slashed FEMA's budget and picked directors, as well as some of their underlings, who had no background in emergency management, and instead were chosen because of political connections. The first director under Bush was Joe Allbaugh, who had been Bush's gubernatorial chief of staff in Texas and was his campaign director in 2000. Michael Brown was FEMA's general counsel and deputy director under Allbaugh before he was tapped to become director. A lawyer by training, Brown also had no emergency management experience. Most recently before joining FEMA, he had been the judges and stewards commissioner for the International Arabian Horse Association, and his tenure there was marred by numerous lawsuits against the organization over disciplinary actions.

Although Brown had won praise, as well as some criticism, for FEMA's performance after a series of hurricanes hit Florida in 2004, Katrina was a different story. Simply put, Brown did a poor job leading the federal government response, and that response was further hobbled by inadequate decision-making and guidance on the part of his superiors. Among the agency's numerous shortcomings were its failures to know what was happening in real time on the ground; to strategically position federal personnel in advance of the hurricane; to get buses into the city in a timely fashion to evacuate survivors; to have emergency supplies ready to go; to deliver those supplies when they were available; to coordinate aid from outside organizations offering help; to facilitate communications among emergency responders and with the public; and to expeditiously remove dead bodies.*

The frustration and anger many felt with respect to FEMA's bungling was succinctly expressed by Terry Ebbert, chief of New Orleans homeland security, who remarked on Thursday, September 1, "This is a national disgrace. FEMA has been here three days, yet there is no command and control. We can send massive amounts of aid to tsunami victims [in Indonesia] but we can't bail out the city of New Orleans?" On September 4, the *Times-Picayune* published an "Open Letter to President George W. Bush," echoing Ebbert's complaints. Despite the fact that there were multiple ways to get into the city, the editors wrote, "our nation's bureaucrats spent days after last week's hurricane wringing their hands, lamenting the fact that they could neither rescue the city's stranded victims nor bring them food, water and medical supplies." The people who are trained and tasked with rapidly delivering relief during such emergencies were nowhere to be found. Instead of sending in the troops and supplies, the federal officials in charge of relief efforts claimed, amazingly enough, that getting into the city was not possible, even though journalists and Walmart personnel and trucks were able to get there on their own. "We're angry, Mr. President," the editors continued. "Our people deserved rescuing. . . . That's to the government's shame."

At a congressional hearing in December 2005, Patricia Thompson, a resident of New Orleans, gave a visceral account of how many in the city felt "abandoned" in the hurricane's aftermath. "City officials did nothing to protect us. We were told to go to the Superdome, the Convention Center, the interstate bridge for safety. We did this more than once. In fact, we

---

* In 2015, Brown wrote an article in which he said that he is tired of being blamed for the failed response and that most of the fault really lies with the governor of Louisiana and the mayor of New Orleans for failing to order evacuation earlier, as well as with his superiors who, he claimed, stripped him of decision-making ability during the height of the crisis. Michael Brown, "Stop Blaming Me for Hurricane Katrina," *Politico*, August 27, 2015, https://www.politico.com/magazine/story/2015/08/katrina-ten-years-later-michael-brown -121782?o=0.

tried them all for every day over a week. We saw buses, helicopters and FEMA trucks, but no one stopped to help us. We never felt so cut off in all our lives. When you feel like this you do one of two things, you either give up or go into survival mode. We chose the latter. This is how we made it. We slept next to dead bodies, we slept on streets at least four times next to human feces and urine. There was garbage everywhere in the city. Panic and fear had taken over."

As a result of his poor performance, Brown resigned on September 12. To his credit, Bush ultimately realized that the federal government's response to Katrina had been abysmal. On September 13, he responded to a reporter's question saying, "Katrina exposed serious problems in our response capability at all levels of government and to the extent the federal government didn't fully do its job right, I take responsibility."

Still, the hurricane left a permanent scar on Bush's reputation and legacy. As one Bush adviser commented, "He never recovered from Katrina. The unfolding disaster with the Iraq war [a conflict that Bush ordered] didn't help, but it's clear that after Katrina he never got back the popularity that he had." Some observers believe that the Katrina debacle contributed to the huge Democratic wave of victories during the 2006 midterm elections. Even today, when a president fails to respond to a crisis in an admirable way, and instead is pilloried for his inadequate actions, pundits are quick to label that event as being the president's "Katrina."

Many have argued that race was a factor in the federal government's response to the disaster. Actor Colin Farrell raised this issue when he was asked about the aftermath of Katrina during an interview on the television show *Access Hollywood*. "If it was a bunch of white people on roofs in the Hamptons, I don't have any f****** doubt there would have been every single helicopter, every plane, every single means that the government has to help these people." Writer and professor of sociology Michael Eric Dyson offered a less colorful assessment of the situation. "It is safe to say that race played a major role in the failure of the federal government—especially for Bush and FEMA head Michael Brown—to respond in a timely manner to the poor black folk of Louisiana because black grief and pain have been ignored throughout the nation's history."

Others, however, saw things differently. Right after Katrina, then-senator Barack Obama commented, "There has been a lot of attention in the media about the fact that those who were left behind in New Orleans were disproportionately poor and disproportionately African American. I have said publicly that I do not subscribe to the notion that the painfully slow response of FEMA and the Department of Homeland Security was somehow racially based. I do not agree with that. I think the ineptitude was colorblind." Whether it was pure ineptitude, or some combination of ineptitude and racism, is an incredibly difficult question to answer, though from a broader perspective, President Obama offered perhaps the best and most succinct postmortem for Katrina. While giving a speech in 2015 at a new community center in New Orleans's Lower Ninth Ward, one of the areas hit hardest by the hurricane, Obama said, "What started out as a natural disaster became a man-made disaster—a failure of government to look out for its citizens."

The hard work of recovery after Katrina began immediately. It was a monumental task, which, years later, is still ongoing. An enormous number of bridges, roads, and piers were out of commission. In New Orleans alone, 134,000, or roughly 70 percent, of the housing units were damaged, while the comparable number for the Gulf Coast was 1 million. Many of those units were rendered uninhabitable. Tens of thousands, if not hundreds of thousands, of people suddenly were unemployed, their livelihoods literally blown away or drowned into oblivion. The loss of so many units and jobs caused the homeless population to explode. At the same time, population levels took a major hit, with the starkest change occurring in New Orleans, where the number of residents contracted by more than 50 percent and has not yet fully rebounded.

Insurance claims covered tens of billions of dollars of losses due to Katrina, while generous philanthropic and individual donations added another $7 billion. But it was the federal government that provided the most, pumping well over $100 billion into hurricane relief and rebuilding.

Following Katrina, federal, state, and local governments spent roughly $20 billion to totally revamp the 350-mile ring of protection around New Orleans. Improvements included strengthening and extending levees, building storm surge gates, adding a concrete surge barrier (visible from space), and constructing more powerful pump stations, one of which is the world's largest. Whether such improvements will protect New Orleans in the event of another major hurricane is an open question. The new system, which was constrained by a lack of funding and engineering feasibility, was designed to withstand a so-called 100-year flood—in other words, a flood that would result from a storm that has a 1 percent chance of occurring in any given year. Unfortunately, Katrina created what was more like a one-in-200-to-250-year flood, so if another Katrina hits, there is likely, once again, to be a considerable deluge in the city.

But the situation is even more dire than that. In mid-2019, less than a year after the new and improved levee system was finally completed, the US Army Corps of Engineers admitted that the levees were sinking because of the immense weight of the engineered system, combined with the weakness of the soils that underlie it. The issue of sinking levees, along with recent rises in sea level, led the corps to predict that by 2023, the storm damage risk reduction system it built—one of the largest public works projects ever—will no longer be able to protect New Orleans against a 100-year flood. Thus, the corps concluded, "Absent future levee lifts to offset consolidation, settlement, subsidence, and sea level rise, risk to life and property in the Greater New Orleans area will progressively increase." What, if any, action will be taken to remedy this grave situation is currently being debated by government officials and the public alike.

SANDY, 2012

It wasn't much of a threat on Monday, October 22, 2012—just a newly formed tropical storm named Sandy, in the heart of the Caribbean Sea, slowly moving north. Meteorologists from Europe, Canada, and the United States ran their computer models to see what the storm might do in the coming days, and some of the results were surprising, even shocking. The main American model—the Global Forecast System Model—had the storm becoming a large hurricane and following a rather typical path, heading up the Eastern Seaboard parallel to the coast and far offshore, and then veering to the right, away from land and into the North Atlantic. The European and Canadian models, however, envisioned a startlingly different future. They, too, had Sandy becoming a large hurricane, but instead of ultimately veering away from the coast, they had it taking a sharp turn to the left, and coming ashore along the mid-Atlantic coast in the vicinity of southern New Jersey.

The European and Canadian models, many American meteorologists felt, couldn't be right. After all, since 1851 no hurricane coming up from the Caribbean had ever made such a dramatic left-hand turn, hitting New Jersey dead-on. The only hurricane known to have made landfall in New

Jersey during that time was the so-called Vagabond Hurricane of 1903, which struck near Atlantic City, but it didn't come up from the Caribbean; instead it barreled across the Atlantic at a much higher latitude. The odds of Sandy ultimately hitting the Garden State seemed to many of the Americans so remote as to be implausible. As it turned out, however, the European and Canadian models were correct. In the words of Columbia University professor and meteorologist Adam Sobel, on Thursday, October 25, the Global Forecast System Model "blinked" and "locked in on the left turn."

By the time the models aligned, Sandy had already proved deadly. On October 24, as a Category 1 hurricane, it rolled over the eastern tip of Jamaica, killing one and causing more than $15 million in damage. The following day, Sandy hit eastern Cuba as a Category 3, leaving eleven dead and $80 million worth of damage. While Sandy scored a direct hit on Cuba, the glancing blow it delivered to Haiti was even worse.

The poorest country in the Western Hemisphere, Haiti was still suffering mightily from the devastating magnitude 7 earthquake that had occurred on January 12, 2010, when the outer edges of Sandy arrived, bringing high winds and more than 20 inches of rain. Hundreds of thousands of displaced Haitians were living in tents and damaged houses, many of which were crushed or swept away by subsequent floods and mudslides. Fifty-four people died, roughly 18,000 were left homeless, and since nearly 70 percent of the country's crops had been destroyed, those who survived faced an even direr situation than the exceedingly bleak one they had been dealing with in the earthquake's aftermath. Soon after leaving Cuba and Haiti behind, Sandy, now a Category 2, hit the edge of the Bahamas, where it killed two people and then continued north as a Category 1 hurricane.

Sandy's history thus far was bad enough, but the models envisioned an even worse future—one in which the storm was likely to become a "whopper." They predicted that as Sandy headed north, it would be boxed in by highs to the east and north that would ultimately steer it toward the mid-Atlantic coast. Furthermore, the jet stream, which would normally be expected to push Sandy out to sea, was in a position that would encourage, not hinder, the storm's westward movement. But most concerning was the cold, low-pressure system over the eastern United States. The models had that system merging with Sandy, creating a huge hybrid and very powerful storm that meteorologists and the press dubbed "Frankenstorm."

The catchy name became internet catnip, and almost immediately it spawned an eponymous Twitter account, and both Frankenstorm and Sandy were soon trending on the social media platform. Adding to the drama were the press accounts comparing Sandy to the Perfect Storm of 1991, which had some similar characteristics and was made famous by Sebastian Junger's novel of the same name and the blockbuster movie it spawned. Even though the Perfect Storm didn't make landfall in the United States, it caused hundreds of millions of dollars' worth of damage and killed thirteen, including six men on board the Gloucester, Massachusetts, fishing boat *Andrea Gail*, whose tragic struggle with the storm forms the centerpiece of Junger's book.

The models had Sandy coming ashore in the beginning of the following week, right around Halloween. That juxtaposition was too much for some reporters to pass up. National Public Radio, for example, labeled Sandy the "Halloween Horror." As for precisely where Sandy would strike, it was still too far out to know for sure, but in a sense it didn't matter, because a landfall almost anywhere along the heavily populated mid-Atlantic coast could create a major disaster.

AS FEARFUL ANTICIPATION ENVELOPED coastal cities and towns, people started preparing for Sandy's arrival, and vessels of all types headed for port in search of a safe harbor. Robin Walbridge, however, decided to head out to sea. He was captain of the *Bounty*, a replica of HMS *Bounty*, the British vessel that Captain William Bligh sailed to Tahiti in 1787 to gather breadfruit trees and transport them to the British possessions in the West Indies to use as food for slaves. The ship became infamous when the first mate, Fletcher Christian, led a mutiny on April 28, 1789, setting Bligh and eighteen men who remained loyal to him adrift in a 23-foot launch, which they would use to sail back to civilization. The mutiny and its aftermath became the basis of numerous books and movies.

Walbridge's 108-foot *Bounty*, a fully operational ship that was slightly larger than the original, was built for the 1962 film titled *Mutiny on the Bounty*, starring Marlon Brando as Christian. After the movie wrapped, the *Bounty* went through several owners, and by the start of the twenty-first century it was being used as a tourist attraction and as a prop in pirate-themed movies. Over the years, the *Bounty* had more than its fair share of

Captain William Bligh and eighteen of his loyal men,
being set adrift from HMS Bounty *on April 28, 1789, as depicted*
in a colored engraving by Robert Dodd, circa 1790.

serious problems with rotting wood, leaks, and faulty equipment, casting considerable doubt on its seaworthiness. In late September 2012, it went to a shipyard in Boothbay, Maine, for repairs, but after a month's worth of work the ship was still not in the best of shape. Nevertheless, it sailed to New London, Connecticut, arriving on October 24.

The following afternoon, Walbridge, who turned sixty-three that day, called the fifteen crew members together for a meeting. While the core crew had considerable maritime experience, many on board did not. The majority had spent less than six months on the *Bounty* and had never worked on another tall ship. Walbridge wanted to discuss the *Bounty*'s imminent departure for St. Petersburg, Florida, where it was supposed to participate in a charity event on November 10. He said that he was well aware of Sandy's forecasted march up the coast, and that his plan was to go far out to sea, to the east of Sandy. Once it turned toward the coast, the *Bounty* would sail down to Florida, in effect skirting the hurricane.

Walbridge knew some of the crew were nervous about heading down the coast while Sandy was coming north, and he assured them that the *Bounty* would be safe. During his seventeen years at her helm, he had sailed through a lot of rough weather, and he assured them he wasn't worried about Sandy.

HMS Bounty II, *1960 tall ship.*

In fact, just before the ship went to Boothbay, Walbridge had told a television reporter that the *Bounty* "chased hurricanes," and that he used their terrific winds to his advantage. Still, Walbridge said that he understood if anyone wanted to leave the ship, and it wouldn't be held against them. They could meet up again with the ship in Florida, but would have to pay their own way to get there. Despite some misgivings about sailing with a hurricane in the offing, and being on board a ship that had questionable repairs and a less-than-stellar history of performance, none of the crew bailed. The *Bounty* weighed anchor in New London a little after sunset.

ON FRIDAY, OCTOBER 26, the National Hurricane Center forecast predicted that over the next few days, Sandy would merge with the cold, low-pressure system to the west and be transformed into an extratropical cyclone, with a cold core and asymmetrical shape, meaning that it would no longer technically be a hurricane, which has a warm core and is more symmetrical around the eye. That change in the label—going from hurricane to extratropical cyclone—didn't in any way lessen Sandy's potential impact.

With Sandy, there was every indication that it would retain Category 1–strength winds and cause a tremendous storm surge of 4–8 feet along the New Jersey and New York coasts, where it was expected to come ashore. Worse still, Sandy was huge, with tropical-storm-force winds extending out nearly 500 miles from its center, meaning that it was almost 1,000 miles wide, a distance equivalent to driving from Boston to Charleston, South Carolina. Those gigantic dimensions made Sandy the largest Atlantic hurricane ever recorded, although records of size go back only to 1988. Viewed from space, Sandy appeared poised to gobble up much of the Eastern Seaboard.

Preparations for Sandy moved into high gear. New York governor Andrew M. Cuomo declared a state of emergency on Friday, and the following morning, New Jersey governor Chris Christie did the same for his state. "We should not underestimate the impact of this storm," Christie said in his announcement, "and we should not assume the predictions will be wrong. I know, I've lived here all my life too, and everyone is saying, crap, this isn't going to happen, the weathermen always get it wrong, and we'll hang out and not pay attention to this. Please don't. We have to be prepared for the worst here." To that end, Christie ordered a mandatory evacuation of the barrier islands from Sandy Hook south to Cape May, and of the casinos in Atlantic City, effective at 4:00 p.m. on Sunday. President Barack Obama, wanting to avoid the mistakes that Bush had made during Katrina, and eager to do the right thing and show strong leadership during a crisis, ordered FEMA to prepare to offer any and all assistance necessary to state and local responders, and FEMA staff had already begun laying the groundwork to do just that.

At Saturday's 6:00 p.m. press conference, New York City mayor Michael Bloomberg decided against evacuations. "We're making that decision based on the nature of the storm," Bloomberg said. "Although we're expecting a large surge of water, it is not expected to be a tropical storm or hurricane-type surge. With this storm, we'll likely see a slow pileup of water rather than a sudden surge, which is what you would expect with a hurricane, and which we saw with Irene 14 months ago. So [Sandy] will be less dangerous."

The Irene he was talking about was Hurricane Irene, which struck the region in late August 2011. In advance of Irene, the state feared that the subways would flood, so it shut down the entire system for the first time ever. While Irene did cause a storm surge of a little over 4 feet, it didn't flood the subways, and the city avoided the widespread devastation that had been expected. Apparently, Bloomberg and his team assumed that Sandy would be "less dangerous" than Irene because Sandy was forecast to come ashore as *only* an extratropical storm, not a hurricane. That was a mistaken assumption, and throughout Saturday and into Sunday morning, meteorologists from the National Hurricane Center and other organizations tried to convince Bloomberg's team that flooding was going to be severe, and that evacuations were warranted. Making matters more urgent, during that time the forecast worsened and the storm surge was now predicted to be 6–11 feet, posing a much greater threat than Irene had.

The persuasion worked. Just before noon on Sunday, October 28, Bloomberg held another press conference, announcing mandatory evacuations of low-lying areas, where 375,000 people lived, as well as the closure of all city schools on Monday, giving 1.1 million kids a long weekend. About the same time, Governor Cuomo ordered that all mass transit service in the city be suspended beginning at 7:00 p.m., leaving roughly 8.5 million subway, bus, and train commuters without a ride home. Broadway theaters canceled shows for Sunday and Monday, as did Carnegie Hall. Diplomats and staff at the United Nations were told to take Monday off. And the New York Stock Exchange and Nasdaq announced that they would be closed on Monday. The last time weather had caused such a disruption was 1985, when Hurricane Gloria had struck.

It wasn't only New York and New Jersey that were worried. Given Sandy's massive size, much of the East Coast was battening down. President Obama declared a state of emergency in Connecticut, Washington, DC, Delaware, Maryland, Massachusetts, New York, New Jersey, and Rhode Island. Airlines up and down the coast canceled flights. Baltimore, Boston, and Washington canceled school for Monday, and in the nation's capitol, the Metro and federal agencies were also to be closed.

AS THE EAST COAST was preparing for Sandy's arrival, the captain and crew of the *Bounty* were struggling to survive. On Saturday, Walbridge decided to scrap his original plan to sail and motor around the hurricane by going to the east of it, and instead pursued a new course to the southwest. Apparently, he wanted to get on the west side of the hurricane, where the winds were less intense and were blowing to the southwest, which would, in effect, help speed the *Bounty* to its next destination in

Florida. This decision, however, set the *Bounty* on a collision course with the storm. By Sunday morning, 20- to 30-foot seas and wind gusts up to 100 mph were pummeling the *Bounty*. Straining under the pressure, the ship was taking on water faster than the pumps could spit it back into the ocean. Many crew members were seasick and fatigued, since sleep was nearly impossible in the violently rocking ship. The engineer, who had fractured his right hand during a fall the day before, fell again, injuring a leg and suffering a nasty gash on his arm.

In the midst of this desperate situation, forty-two-year-old Claudene Christian, who had joined the *Bounty*'s crew the previous May as a deckhand looking for adventure and had no prior experience sailing a tall ship, texted her mother. "I am ok and HAPPY TO BE HERE on Bounty doing what I love," she wrote. "And if I do go down with the ship & the worst happens . . . Just know that I AM TRULY GENUINELY HAPPY!! . . . I love you."

Throughout the day and into the evening, the captain and crew fought to keep the *Bounty* afloat and moving forward, but it was a losing battle against the furious onslaught of wind and waves. At 8:45 p.m., when the *Bounty* was about 100 miles southeast of Cape Hatteras, Walbridge reached out to the Coast Guard's Sector North Carolina. He wasn't requesting a rescue; rather, he wanted to alert them to the *Bounty*'s perilous situation and let them know they might need assistance in the morning. At the time, one of the ship's main sails had been shredded, water in the engine room had reached 4 feet, and only one of the two engines was still operating, just barely. Walbridge was also in serious pain, having earlier been hurled onto the edge of a bolted-down table when the ship was struck by a wave. Another crew member, who was similarly thrown across the deck, dislocated his shoulder and broke several ribs.

Soon after midnight, a Coast Guard C-130 plane reached the *Bounty* after a pulse-pounding ride contending with hurricane-force winds, limited visibility, and torrential rain. When copilot Mike Myers finally saw the *Bounty* through the gloom just 500 feet below, he said, "It looks like a big pirate ship in the middle of a hurricane."

The C-130's mission was to monitor the situation, maintain communication with the ship, and, if possible, drop emergency supplies and pumps onto the ship's deck. But by the time the plane arrived, things on the *Bounty* had gone from bad to worse. The only working engine had died, and the ship was now adrift. The water in the engine room was 6 feet deep, and it was rising fast. Conditions in the C-130 were so rough that some of crew were vomiting, and there was no way they could drop anything from the C-130 onto the *Bounty*'s deck. So the plane circled, kept in contact with the ship, and reported back to base what it was seeing and hearing.

Realizing that the *Bounty* was not going to make it, the crew began gathering gear and preparing to abandon ship. The plan was to do so around dawn, when Coast Guard Jayhawk rescue helicopters were expected to arrive. But Walbridge and his crew couldn't wait that long. At 3:30 a.m., with more than 10 feet of water sloshing around in the ship, they donned their immersion, or "Gumby," suits. About an hour later, the ship rolled heavily to starboard, and the bow was buried in a massive wave. The first mate sent a last-ditch distress call to the C-130, telling the pilot that the *Bounty* was going under and that they were abandoning ship. Next thing they were all in the water, fighting to swim clear of the ship and to keep from getting entangled in its rigging.

Two helicopters arrived on the scene around 7:00 a.m. on Monday. In 60-mph winds, their brave pilots, mechanics, and swimmers performed heroically, plucking thirteen survivors from two rafts and one from the water, and then ferrying them back to base on the mainland. Not everyone was so fortunate. Christian, who had sent her mother the joyful yet worrying text the day before, was found at 4:38 in the afternoon about 8 miles from where the crew had abandoned ship. The swimmers retrieved her lifeless body from the water and performed CPR in the helicopter, but there was no bringing her back. For two and a half days, the Coast Guard searched for Walbridge. Only when it was determined that, given the water temperature and the thermal performance of the Gumby suit, he could no longer have survived did they call off the operation. Walbridge's body was never found. As for the *Bounty*, it sank to the bottom, some 14,000 feet down.

Thorough investigations of the sinking by the National Transportation Safety Board and the Coast Guard came to the same basic conclusion, placing blame on Walbridge and the owner of the ship, the HMS Bounty Organization. The safety board put it best, finding "that the probable cause of the sinking of tall ship *Bounty* was the captain's reckless decision to sail the vessel into the well-forecasted path of Hurricane Sandy, which subjected the aging vessel and the inexperienced crew to conditions from which the vessel could not recover. Contributing to the sinking was the lack of effective safety oversight by the vessel organization."

———

MEANWHILE, BLOOMBERG'S AND Christie's mandatory evacuation orders were having mixed results. Many heeded the call to retreat from the coast, but others remained in place, either out of choice or because they had no way of leaving. Rosy memories of Irene complicated matters. A resident in New York's Battery Park City who refused to evacuate complained that with Irene, "they made such a big hype out of it and nothing happened." His friend added, "It's more painful to evacuate than stay."

Sunday's 5:00 p.m. advisory from the National Hurricane Center said Sandy would likely come ashore late Monday with hurricane-force winds, and it was "EXPECTED TO BRING LIFE-THREATENING STORM SURGE FLOODING TO THE MID-ATLANTIC COAST." The advisory also said that snow accumulations of anywhere from 1 to 3 feet were expected in the mountains of West Virginia, southwestern Virginia, and along the North Carolina–Tennessee border. That was the first, and is still the only, time that an advisory issued by the National Hurricane Center predicted snow, which was another indication of Sandy's unique nature.

On Monday, Sandy sped up and made the predicted turn to the left, racing toward the coast at 30 mph. Conditions worsened as Sandy's advance shock troops of water and wind assaulted the mid-Atlantic region. By the afternoon, the massive storm surge had inundated low-lying areas, and pounding waves were engulfing beaches, dunes, and houses along the coast.

At 2:30 p.m., wind gusts of more than 60 mph caused a crane atop a building under construction near the edge New York's Central Park to snap, leaving it dangling 1,000 feet above the street. Known as One57, the luxury tower was slated to be ninety stories high upon completion, while boasting penthouse apartments that were expected to go for a staggering $90 million apiece. As the waters rose, overtopping the banks of the Hudson and East Rivers, Governor Cuomo closed the Holland and Hugh L. Carey* Tunnels, and then the bridges into and out of the city, on account of the wind. Power outages were growing by the hour. Already, 40,000 people at the tip of Long Island were in the dark.

At 5:00 p.m., Hurricane Sandy became an extratropical cyclone, and the National Hurricane Center stopped referring to it as a hurricane. Many news outlets began calling her "Superstorm Sandy" instead. At 7:30 p.m.,

---

* Formerly the Brooklyn-Battery Tunnel.

Sandy made landfall just northeast of Atlantic City, with winds of 80 mph. Its waves pounded the shore and crashed into one another with such force that their vibrations were picked up by seismographs nearly 2,500 miles away in Seattle. Frankenstorm had arrived, and it would, indeed, prove to be a nightmare.

NEW YORK CITY WAS in the worst position imaginable, on the most dangerous side of the eye. Sandy's winds were pushing a massive storm surge before them, topped by towering waves, heading right toward Gotham. One wave measured by a buoy about 20 miles from New York Harbor was an astounding 32½ feet high, shattering the regional record set by Hurricane Irene by more than 6 feet. Geography only exacerbated the situation. The coastal contours of Long Island and northern New Jersey create a wedge, and the city is where the wedge comes together. So, as the surge of water approached, it was compressed like water rushing through a funnel, pushing it higher still. Add the fact that Sandy struck at a full-moon-generated high tide, which tacked on about a foot to the surge, and you have the makings of a flood of historic proportions.

On Monday night and into Tuesday morning, the city was under siege. Water rose to more than 14 feet above mean low tide, besting Irene by nearly 5 feet. Parts of Staten Island and Manhattan were awash in 4–9 feet of surge. Seven subway tunnels connecting lower Manhattan and Brooklyn flooded. Joseph J. Lhota, the chairman of the Metropolitan Transportation Authority, said that the 108-year-old subway system had "never faced a disaster as devastating as what we experienced" on Monday night. The Holland, Queens-Midtown, and Hugh L. Carey Tunnels were all inundated, with the last holding an incredible 43 million gallons of water.

The regional utility company Con Edison expected that Sandy would flood some of its equipment, and if that happened the equipment could short out and be destroyed. To avoid such destruction, Con Edison cut power to significant parts of the city on Monday afternoon. The deluge that came later took out even more of the electrical grid, as submerged substations failed. The most spectacular failure occurred around 8:30 p.m., when a substation at Fourteenth Street in Lower Manhattan experienced a dramatic arcing fault, creating pulsating, brilliant, bluish-white flashes that lit up the sky and were captured on amateur video and immediately

The Hugh L. Carey Tunnel, flooded after Hurricane Sandy.

uploaded to YouTube for the world to see. By 9:00, the combination of preemptive outages and Sandy-induced catastrophic failures had plunged all of Manhattan below Thirty-Ninth Street into darkness. At one point, close to a million Con Edison customers in and around the city had lost electricity.

Sandy devastated Breezy Point, Queens, a tight-knit community of about 4,000 at the western end of the Rockaway Peninsula. The surge flooded virtually every home, completely destroying 250 of them. After the water came the flames. Short-circuiting electrical equipment sparked a fire in one home, which the whipping winds quickly spread to other homes nearby. The Rockaway Point Volunteer Fire Department valiantly tried to get close enough to fight the fires, but was kept at bay by the floodwaters. By the time the fire burned out, it had destroyed another 111 homes and damaged 20 more, making it one of the worst residential fires in New York's history.

On Staten Island, which received an especially punishing blow, residents Pedro Correa and Robert Gavars had a harrowing time. Correa evacuated his family to Brooklyn early on Monday and then returned to his house with Gavars that evening to check on things. They began driving back to Brooklyn around 7:00 p.m., but the car stalled in the rising waters. They slogged back to Correa's two-story house, planning to shelter there until the storm passed, but water rushing into the house soon forced them to the second floor, and it kept rising toward the ceiling. When Correa saw a neighbor's house floating by, he and Gavars jumped onto its roof. For nearly forty-five minutes they sailed through the storm atop their unusual raft. Finally, when the house came to rest, they jumped off. Using planks as flotation devices, they made their way to relatively dry land, where they were welcomed into a nearby house. Recalling his ordeal, Correa commented, "I made it through Iraq, I made it through the World Trade Center, but I didn't think I'd make it through this." When he finally went back to his neighborhood after the water had subsided, he discovered that his house, too, had been ripped from its foundation and had floated a quarter mile away.

About the same time that Correa and Gavars were going through their ordeal, another Staten Islander, Glenda Moore, was taking her two boys— four-year-old Connor and two-year-old Brandon—to her sister's house in Brooklyn. As she drove on a boulevard near the outer edge of the island, the water surged inland, enveloping her car and causing it to stall. She frantically unbuckled her boys from their car seats and grabbed hold of them, hoping to take them to higher ground. But another massive surge swept the car and the boys away. In a reprehensible twist on an already truly tragic story, Glenda told authorities that after her boys were ripped from her arms, she knocked on the door of several houses looking for help and even unsuccessfully tried to break into one home by throwing a flowerpot through the window, but nobody offered assistance or would let her in. So, she spent the night huddled on the doorstep of an empty house. After two days of searching, the police found the boys' bodies in a nearby marsh.*

In Brooklyn, twenty-four-year-old friends Jessie Streich-Kest and Jacob Vogelman, went to walk Jessie's dog, Max, at around 8:00 p.m. A few old and majestic trees lining a quiet street could not withstand the gusty winds.

---

* Because Moore is black and the residents who turned her away were white, some have implied that racism was involved and that if Moore had been white, the outcome would have been different. See, for example, Makkada B. Selah, "White Staten Islanders Refuse to Help Black Mom Whose Sons Were Swept Away by Sandy," *Black Enterprise*, November 3, 2012; Jorge Rivas, "Staten Island Residents Refused to Help Black Mom as Sandy Swept Sons Away," *ColorLines*, November 2, 2012; and Jerome Reilly, "Storm Rages over Brothers' Death," *Independent.ie*, November 11, 2012.

Their roots, sitting in the rain-saturated soil, gave way and the trees thundered to the ground. One of them crushed the couple to death, and their bodies were found the next morning. Max was injured but survived.

As the winds died down, Lauren Abraham ventured out of her house in Queens to photograph a power line that had snapped and fallen to the ground nearby, and was jumping around sending out a shower of sparks. She got too close, and the tip of the frayed wire touched her body, igniting it. As the *New York Times* reported, "A half-dozen or so witnesses watched in utter horror. They said her body burned for about a half-hour before the police and firefighters arrived."

SANDY ALSO SAVAGED NEW JERSEY. Along most of the coast, barrier beaches were breached, cities and towns were flooded and covered in great drifts of sand, houses were destroyed, and communities were devastated. One of the most touching stories of survival involved twenty-eight-year-old Mike Iann. He was in his home in Toms River, New Jersey, when Sandy's surge and winds began ripping the place apart. When he opened the front door to see whether he could escape, a wave sucked him out of the house and about a half mile into Barnegat Bay. Using all of his energy to swim back to shore, he ended up just a short distance away from where his harrowing voyage had begun. With almost no clothes on, and shivering uncontrollably because of his lengthy immersion, Mike broke into a home in search of shelter (the owners had left before the storm). Fearing he would not survive the night, he wrote a final note and placed it on one of the tables.

> Who ever reads this, I'm DIEING—I'm 28 yrs old my name is Mike. I had to break in to your house. I took blankets off the couch. I have hypothermia. I didn't take any thing. A wave thru me out of my house down the block. I don't think I'm going to make it. The water outside is 10ft deep at least. There's no res[c]ue. Tell my dad I love him and I tryed get[t]ing out. His number is ###-###-#### his name is Tony. I hope u can read this I'm in the dark. I took a black jacket too. Goodbye. God all mighty help me.

But Mike didn't die. A man on a Jet Ski rescued him the next morning, and soon he was reunited with his father. When the owners of the house

Hurricane Sandy demolished the Funtown Pier in Seaside Heights,
New Jersey, sending the Star Jet roller coaster and other amusements
plunging into the surf.

returned the next day and saw the note, they had no idea who Mike was, or what had happened to him. Hoping to learn more, they called the number and, to their great relief, learned that Mike was safe.

AFTER LANDFALL, THE HEART of Sandy moved inland, gradually weakening, and over the next couple of days it traced a course through southern New Jersey, northern Delaware, southern Pennsylvania, and Ohio. By the end of the week, remnants of the storm were over eastern Canada. True to the forecast, Sandy dumped huge amounts of snow in West Virginia, Pennsylvania, and even North Carolina, where mountains in Wolf Laurel were blanketed in 36 inches. As a result, some started referring to Sandy as a "blizzacane" or "snor-eastercane."

On Tuesday, October 30, people confronted the destruction that Sandy had wrought—destroyed homes, downed trees, shattered windows, boardwalks broken apart, streets laminated in sand, and flooded cars. The loss of power below Thirty-Ninth Street in Manhattan temporarily split the city in two, as many who lived in the darkened areas went in search of electricity. Just north of Thirty-Ninth, the wandering New Yorkers, pilgrims of a sort, congregated wherever they could find outlets to charge their devices, hot meals to eat, and warm rooms to sit in.

All US financial markets remained closed on Tuesday, making it only the second time in the history of the New York Stock Exchange that weather had caused such a two-day disruption in trading—the first being the Great Blizzard of 1888. New York City schools were closed for the rest of the week. The New York City Marathon, scheduled for the following weekend, was canceled, since so much of the city was still suffering.

Dogs, many of them spooked by the storm, got another rude surprise when their owners took them for their regular stroll in Central Park. Heavily damaged, the park was closed on Tuesday, and gates barred the way. According to the *New York Times*, a white Labrador named Rollo, so upset over the disruption to his daily routine, "decided to engage in a sit-down strike in front of the 79th Street entrance on Fifth Avenue," and refused to budge. His owner had to drag him away.

While the flooding of the tunnels in the city was a disaster for commuters and businesses, there was a silver lining, depending on your point of view. New York is infamous for its rat population, which by some estimates runs into the tens of millions, though it is likely much smaller (nobody really knows, since rats are notoriously difficult subjects for census takers). Whatever the population size, the sudden deluge brought on by Sandy caught many of the rats by surprise, and even though they are excellent swimmers and can even dive for extended periods, a number of them drowned—though how many, again, is unknown. For those who disdain rats, such winnowing of the population was welcome. For the rat lovers, it was just another sign of Sandy's terrible wrath. Nevertheless, probably both sides of the debate can agree it was a good thing that massive hordes of rats didn't rush up and out of the tunnels to escape the flood, as many media outlets had alarmingly predicted would happen. A few days after the storm, *New York* magazine told its relieved readers, "The Ratpocalypse Has Been Canceled."

SANDY WAS RESPONSIBLE FOR seventy-two direct deaths in the United States, and eighty-seven indirect deaths. All told, 8.5 million people had their power knocked out for days, weeks, or even months in some places. Total damage from the storm added up to $65 billion. New York and New

Jersey were hardest hit. In New York, roughly 305,000 homes were damaged or destroyed, and there were forty-eight direct deaths. The respective numbers for New Jersey were 350,000 and twelve.

Given the magnitude of the damage, it took a while for things to return to normal. Con Edison, which had much of its equipment damaged or destroyed by contact with corrosive salt water, restored power to 95 percent of its customers within thirteen days, and in New Jersey the same level of service took eleven days to achieve. Eighty percent of subway service was running within five days, and within two weeks most of the system was back on track, with the exception of a few subway lines that required much more extensive repairs to make them operational. After massive dewatering operations, all of the flooded tunnels were reopened to traffic within seventeen days. But the long-term work of repairing and modernizing admittedly aging and, in some cases, decrepit infrastructure is still ongoing. Similarly, the surviving victims of Sandy, whose lives were turned upside down almost overnight, also have traveled a long road to recovery, and many have still not made it all the way back.

HARVEY, IRMA, MARIA, 2017

The 2017 hurricane season turned out to be one for the record books. As one government official noted, it was the "hurricane season that wouldn't quit," while the *Washington Post* labeled it "the Atlantic hurricane season from hell." Federal forecasters predicted that there could be as many as nine hurricanes, four of which could be major hurricanes with winds of 111 mph or higher. While that prediction turned out to be fairly accurate, it was not quite bold enough. In the end, there were ten hurricanes, six of which were major. Four of those hurricanes roared ashore, when, typically, only two hurricanes make landfall annually in the United States.

But what really set 2017 apart and burned it into the nation's collective consciousness was that three out of the four hurricanes that made landfall were major ones—a huge number for a single year.* By contrast, it usually

---

* The fourth hurricane, called Nate, greatly damaged Costa Rica, becoming the costliest natural disaster to visit that country, but by the time it reached the shores of the United States, in the vicinity of the Louisiana-Mississippi border, it was a very weak hurricane that was quickly downgraded to a tropical depression, which caused relatively minor damage.

takes about five years for the United States to be visited by three major hurricanes. Each of 2017's trio were beasts, making landfall at Category 4 intensity with winds of at least 130 mph. Since records have been kept, all the way back to 1851, the only other year that two Category 4+ hurricanes hit the US mainland or one of its territories was 1992, when Iniki, a Category 4, and Andrew, a Category 5, struck Hawaii and Florida, respectively. Never before had there been three Category 4's in a single year. The damage attributed to Harvey, Irma, and Maria is $125 billion, $50 billion, and $90 billion, respectively, adding up to $265 billion, making 2017 the most expensive hurricane season on record, by far.

For one month in 2017, the United States was gripped by hurricane fever. From late August through late September, Americans were transfixed by the nearly nonstop media coverage of Hurricanes Harvey, Irma, and Maria as they delivered misery to tens of millions. Each brought tremendous winds, towering storm surges, torrential rain, and death. Gutwrenching scenes of flooded homes, savaged landscapes, unimaginable anguish, and chilling desperation viscerally grabbed viewers' attention, creating a national community of tragedy. The only good news to come out of this bruising hurricane season was that the National Hurricane Center's track forecasts were the most accurate they had ever produced. So, people at least had a very good idea of where and when the hurricanes would strike.

The headline statistics for the three monster storms were sobering. Hurricane Harvey made landfall on August 26 near Rockport, Texas, about 160 miles southwest of Houston, thereby ending an astonishing almost-twelve-year "major hurricane drought" in the United States. Instead of moving on, Harvey stalled in that general area for days, looping on- and offshore, hemmed in by two high-pressure systems—one in the southeastern United States, and the other in the Southwest. Finally, on August 30, Harvey made landfall again near Cameron, Louisiana, and then marched inland, weakening along the way.

Harvey dumped more than 50 inches of rain in Houston within forty-eight hours, and it doused Nederland, Texas, with a shocking deluge of 60.58 inches, a new US record for a single storm, eclipsing the existing record by more than 8 inches. The 33 trillion gallons of water that fell over Texas, Louisiana, Tennessee, and Kentucky is enough to fill a cube 3 miles on a side. In the Houston area alone, the weight of the water caused

*A Texas National Guardsman carries a resident from her home
to safety after Hurricane Harvey.*

the crust of the Earth to sink nearly an inch. Harvey was directly responsible for sixty-eight deaths in the United States, all of which were in Texas,
and all but three of those were due to freshwater flooding as opposed to
storm surge. Another thirty-five people died of indirect causes.

While Hurricane Irma was still a Category 5, its eyewall hit the US
Virgin Islands on September 6, ripping apart much of St. Thomas and St.
John. "We're totally devastated," one resident of St. John said. "We've lost
homes, we've lost roofs. We've lost vehicles." Four days later, after skirting
Puerto Rico, Irma made landfall in the Florida Keys—at Cudjoe Key as
a Category 4—and then made a second landfall near Marco Island, Florida, as a Category 3. From there, it traveled up the southwestern side of
the state, gradually weakening to a tropical storm before dissipating over
Georgia, Alabama, Mississippi, and Tennessee.

Irma maintained winds of 185 mph for an astonishing thirty-five
hours over the open Atlantic, setting a world record for sustained wind
intensity during the satellite era. Since early forecasts had Irma zeroing in on southern Florida, many local officials ordered evacuations,
prompting more than 6 million residents to leave the area—the largest
mass exodus in American history. The vast majority of the ten direct
and eighty-two indirect deaths attributed to Irma in the United States

A Florida house, toppled as a result of erosion from Hurricane Irma.

were in Florida. Extreme and, in some cases, record-setting flooding was widespread. Strong winds decimated the state's agricultural sector. More than 50 percent of the orange crop was lost. Damage for Irma totaled $50 billion, but it could have been far worse. Before forecasters shifted the expected landfall to the western side of the state, it was thought Miami might take a direct hit. In that eventuality, insurers had predicted that losses could reach $200 billion.

On September 20, Category 5 Hurricane Maria just missed making a direct hit on the US Virgin island of St. Croix. Still, the island was raked by Category 4–level winds, causing considerable damage. Later that day, Maria made landfall on the southeastern edge of Puerto Rico as a strong Category 4, with winds of 155 mph. It passed diagonally over the island, dumping up to 3 feet of water in some areas, making it the most intense rainfall event there since 1956. Maria then exited near the island's northwest corner as a strong Category 2, before sailing off into the Atlantic. During its eight-hour transit across Puerto Rico, Maria damaged or obliterated virtually every human-made structure outside the capital of San Juan and many within the city's limits, leveled 80 percent of the crops, and knocked out power to the entire island, leaving its 3.4 million residents in the dark and without running water. As one Puerto Rican resident said, Maria "destroyed us."

Tragically, Puerto Rico was exceptionally vulnerable to such widespread destruction. The territory has long suffered from crushing debt, government inefficiency and corruption, and often second-class treatment by the federal government, even though Puerto Rico is a US territory, and has been ever since it was ceded to the United States after the Spanish-American War in 1898. As a result, Puerto Rico's economy was in shambles, its infrastructure was extremely frail and often failing, and nearly half of the population lived below the poverty line. Even a well-functioning and wealthy state would have been hobbled by the likes of Maria. Puerto Rico didn't stand a chance.

The death toll from Maria has spawned considerable controversy. In the immediate aftermath of the hurricane, Puerto Rico reported that the death toll was 64, a figure based on the number of death certificates that listed the hurricane as the cause. Numerous news organizations and experts doubted that it could be so low, given the widespread devastation. Facing criticism and lawsuits for suppressing or not accurately reporting the death toll, the Puerto Rican government commissioned a study into the matter. That study, completed in August 2018 by George Washington University, in cooperation with the University of Puerto Rico, concluded that 2,975 people died as a result of Maria in the six months after the hurricane (this figure was based on *excess mortality*, the extra deaths that occurred above what would have been expected during the same time period if there had been no hurricane).

However, that number is not the only one that has been put forth. A few months before the George Washington study, a Harvard-led study published in the *New England Journal of Medicine* concluded that the excess mortality from Maria in the three months after the hurricane was 4,645 and said that was a conservative estimate. There have been still more investigations. For example, a review of mortality data by the *New York Times* found that excess mortality in the forty-two days after the hurricane was 1,052. The Puerto Rico Health Department issued excess-mortality numbers for September–December 2017 that totaled 1,397.

It is always difficult to calculate a hurricane's death toll. Making such an estimate depends on the availability of data and how deaths are counted—specifically, the assumptions made and methods used. Be that as it may, the controversy over the death toll due to Maria has been much more heated than for any prior hurricane. Methodologies and conclusions of the various studies have been questioned, and the numbers have also become highly politicized. For example, in a series of tweets shortly after the George Washington study came out, President Donald J. Trump said,

> 3000 people did not die in . . . Puerto Rico. When I left the Island, AFTER the storm had hit, they had anywhere from 6 to 18 deaths. As time went by it did not go up by much. Then, a long time later, they started to report really large numbers, like 3000. . . . This was done by the Democrats in order to make me look as bad as possible when I was successfully raising Billions of Dollars to help rebuild Puerto Rico. If a person died for any reason, like old age, just add them onto the list.

While there are many legitimate reasons to question the death toll numbers that have been presented, none of the numbers are the result of a Democratic effort to make the president look bad. Nobody can, with certainty, give the actual number of direct and indirect deaths due to Maria, but there is no doubt that it is quite a bit higher than the original 64, and almost certainly in the range of 1,000 or more, depending on the time frame applied.

The controversy over the death toll is part of an even larger controversy over the federal response to Maria. Almost as soon as Maria had passed, two counternarratives began. Simply put, on the one side the Trump administration claimed it was doing a wonderful job dealing with the crisis in Puerto Rico, while on the other side, Puerto Rican officials vehemently disagreed. And, of course, each side had its own vocal group of supporters.

The escalating war of words between the Trump administration and Puerto Rican politicians only made matters worse. For example, in early 2019, when the Senate failed to approve a disaster relief package that the Democrats argued contained too little money for Puerto Rico, Trump lashed out, tweeting, "Puerto Rico got far more money than Texas & Florida combined, yet their government can't do anything right, the place is a mess—nothing works." In other tweets, he called Carmen Yulín Cruz, the mayor of San Juan, "crazed and incompetent," and said, "The people of Puerto Rico are GREAT, but the politicians are incompetent or corrupt." Cruz responded in a tweet, "Pres Trump continues to embarrass himself & the Office he holds. He is unhinged & thus lies about the $ received by PR. HE KNOWS HIS RESPONSE was inefficient at best. He can huff & puff all he wants but he cannot escape the death of 3,000 on his watch. SHAME ON YOU!" Puerto Rican governor Ricardo Rossello also chimed in, tweeting, "Mr. President, this 'place' you refer to, #PuertoRico, is home to over three million proud Americans that are still recovering from the storm and in need of federal assistance. We are not your adversaries, we are your citizens."

Beyond the accusations and rhetoric, there is evidence that, in fact, the short-term federal response—within the first six months—in Puerto Rico was lacking, relative to the response in Texas and Florida to Hurricanes Harvey and Irma over the same time period. There were disparities in terms of the number of federal and military personnel sent in, the quantity of supplies delivered, and the amount of relief claims approved and money provided to the victims. A fuller analysis of how the federal government responded to these three hurricanes over the long run, however, has yet to be done.

Each hurricane is unique, and each, therefore, poses unique problems to deal with and overcome in providing assistance. That was certainly the case with Maria. Although many people made fun of Trump when he pointed out that Puerto Rico was "an island surrounded by water, big water, ocean water," that is, of course, true, and that fact of geography did complicate relief efforts. In addition, even though each hurricane caused widespread disruption, Puerto Rico got the worst of it, with virtually its entire infrastructure destroyed or heavily damaged.

Other factors hindered the federal response to all three hurricanes. With Harvey, Irma, and Maria occurring one after another, FEMA and other federal agencies were stretched to their limits, hampering their ability to act. Making matters worse was the disconnect between the skills of responders and the needs identified. For example, a General Accountability Office study of the government's performance in 2017 found, "at the height of FEMA workforce deployments in October 2017, 54 percent of staff were serving in a capacity in which they" were not "Qualified," according to FEMA's own standards.

———

THE HISTORIC HURRICANE SEASON of 2017 has already spawned a number of books, and no doubt there are more on the way. Signature weather events, especially devastating hurricanes, generate an understandable and commendable impulse to capture in words what happened and why. When those tomes are written, they will join the growing library devoted to chronicling America's most memorable hurricanes.

Stormy Weather Ahead

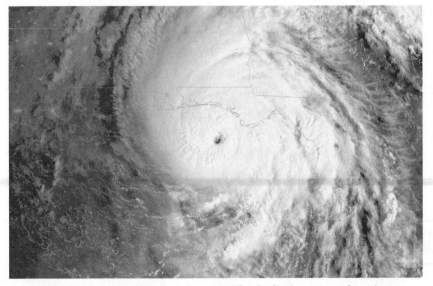

While this book was being written, Michael, the Category 5 hurricane pictured here, struck the Florida Panhandle on October 10, 2018, devastating Mexico Beach, killing seventy-two, and causing $25 billion in damage.

THE CYCLE CONTINUES. EVERY YEAR, A NEW HURRICANE SEA-son unfolds with the potential to break records, be average, or be relatively quiet. But no matter what an individual hurricane season brings, over time one thing is certain: the United States will continue to be pummeled by these tremendous storms. And because of global warming, hurricanes of the future will most likely be worse than those of the past.

Simply stated, *global warming* is the increase in the Earth's average surface temperature as a result of the buildup of greenhouse gases, such as carbon dioxide, methane, and nitrous oxide, created predominantly by anthropogenic sources, especially the burning of fossil fuels (natural sources for such gases also contribute to warming). In the atmosphere, these gases act like a blanket, trapping heat from the sun that otherwise would escape into space, and in the process they warm the planet. Over time, the anthropogenic emissions of greenhouse gases, especially carbon dioxide, have risen, and there is an overwhelming consensus among scientists that this escalation has already contributed to an increase in the average global temperature of about 1 degree Celsius, or roughly 2 degrees Fahrenheit, since preindustrial times (1850–1900).

In its last major assessment report, issued in 2014, the Intergovernmental Panel on Climate Change (IPCC) concluded, "Human influence on the climate system is clear, and recent anthropogenic emissions of greenhouse gases are the highest in history. . . . Warming of the climate system is unequivocal, and since the 1950s, many of the observed changes are unprecedented over decades to millennia. The atmosphere and ocean have warmed, the amounts of snow and ice have diminished, and sea level has risen." Climate models also predict that average global temperatures will keep rising if we continue to emit the same or higher levels of greenhouse gases in the future. An IPCC report in 2018 concluded that "global warming is likely to reach 1.5° C [above preindustrial levels] between 2030 and 2052 if it continues to increase at the current rate." But by reducing greenhouse gases over time, we can also reduce the amount of warming that will take place.*

Global warming has already made the impact of hurricanes worse. Because sea level has risen as a result of the thermal expansion of the oceans and the melting of glaciers, storm surges are higher and more destructive. As MIT professor Kerry Emanuel pointed out, "Had Sandy struck New York a century ago, there would have been substantially less flooding, as

---

* The terms *global warming* and *climate change* are often used interchangeably, but they refer to different things. Global warming is, as stated in the text, the warming of the Earth's surface temperature as a result of the buildup of greenhouse gases. *Climate change* is a broader term, referring to the manifold alterations to the climate that occur or might occur as a result of the warming of the planet, such as increased droughts and heat waves, more intense rainstorms, and changes in hurricane behavior.

sea level was then roughly a foot lower." Continued warming will only add to this problem.

A growing number of studies have found strong evidence linking global warming to increased precipitation during storms, including hurricanes. The reason is that warming leads to more evaporation, and warmer air is able to contain higher concentrations of moisture, which can come down as rain. One study concluded that "extreme precipitation, like that of Hurricane Maria, has become much more likely in recent years," and that increases in atmospheric and ocean temperatures have probably contributed to that result. Three other studies taken together found that global warming likely made the precipitation during Hurricane Harvey anywhere from 8 to 38 percent heavier than would have been the case in a world where warming had not taken place.

Considerable research also predicts that warmer oceans, which provide more heat energy to fuel hurricanes, will make the winds produced by these storms even more powerful (indeed, some observers believe that the uptick in the intensity of hurricanes over the past few decades, especially the greater-than-average number of severe Category 4 and 5 hurricanes, might be an indication that this is already happening). Other studies show that the speed at which tropical cyclones, including hurricanes, travel over the Earth has slowed a bit since the mid-twentieth century, and although the researchers cannot conclusively attribute that slowdown to global warming, such a link is a distinct possibility.

If the continued warming of the atmosphere causes future hurricanes to linger longer, affected areas will be subjected not only to more prolonged, damaging winds but also to significant periods of increased rain. Indeed, one simulation analyzed how twenty-two recent hurricanes might have been altered, had they formed under the warmer conditions that predictions say will be the norm toward the end of this century. It concluded that, on average, the hurricanes would have moved more slowly, had higher maximum winds, and dropped a lot more rain. Another study suggests that a warmer atmosphere might result in fewer hurricanes, but that those that do occur will be more intense. And one analysis raises the possibility that global warming will reduce vertical wind shear along the East Coast of the United States, which typically acts as a brake on hurricane intensification. If such a reduction takes place, hurricanes occurring in that region in the future "may be much stronger than what we've experienced in the past."

Despite the understandable desire to point to a clear, indisputable cause-and-effect link, at this moment nobody can say with absolute certainty exactly how hurricanes will change over time as a result of global warming. Scientists would be the first to admit that there are still many unknowns, as well as limitations in data and modeling, that make it exceedingly difficult to predict the impact of a warmer world on these massive storms. As Dr. Geert Jan van Oldenborgh of the Royal Netherlands Meteorological Institute noted, "The effect of climate change on hurricanes is horribly complicated. We're working on it, but it's very difficult." The mounting scientific consensus that an increase in global warming will likely make future hurricanes worse, however, is not encouraging.* But even if global warming causes no difference at all in hurricane behavior, society still has to grapple with a hurricane-filled future. And that poses many challenges, not the least of which has to do with changing demographics.

Recent trends in coastal population have gone in only one direction: up. That means more people, more buildings, and more infrastructure have been placed in the path of hurricanes, thereby increasing the risk of damage, injury, and death. How much risk there is obviously depends on where the hurricane goes, how strong its winds are, and how much rain it pours down. But one thing is certain: since coastal populations and development are expected to increase over time, so, too, will the risks presented by hurricanes.

Of course, society and individuals can take action to better prepare for hurricanes and create an added level of protection from their blows. Building codes can be strengthened and enforced so that structures are able to withstand more punishment. Zoning laws can be designed to minimize the placement of structures in areas highly vulnerable to hurricane damage, especially flooding, and the federal government can stop subsidizing flood insurance, thereby decreasing the incentive for people to build and rebuild in those very risky areas. Evacuation plans can be established or

---

* Since this book focuses on hurricanes, it does not consider the many other serious threats to our future posed by global warming and, more broadly, climate change—among them the increased frequency of droughts and heat waves, shifts in agricultural zones, coral bleaching, and an uptick in the number of "climate refugees." These and other threats make it imperative that society take serious action to reverse global warming. In addition, this is not the place to consider the broader debate over global warming and all the various ways in which society can address this critical issue. There are plenty of good policy books that do just that.

improved upon to give people a better chance of fleeing the storm. People can be more informed about the importance of heeding evacuation orders, instead of putting themselves at risk. Individuals can also take actions to make their homes and businesses more hurricane resistant, such as installing hurricane shutters and retrofitting or redesigning buildings to make them sturdier and less prone to flooding.

Moreover, local governments can better protect key infrastructure from potential storm damage, or move that infrastructure to safer locations. Particularly vulnerable cities can build hurricane protection barriers to reduce the impact of storm surges and flooding. Federal, state, and local governments can expand emergency preparedness programs, and also undertake efforts to reduce wetland loss and reestablish wetlands that have disappeared. The federal government can bolster investment in hurricane-related research so that we can learn more about the past, present, and future of hurricanes, and possibly improve the accuracy of hurricane forecasts, giving people better information on when and where storms will strike, and how powerful they will be.

Society and individuals can also take actions to better cope with hurricanes once they hit, and to deal with the immediate aftermath. FEMA, whose purpose is to provide relief and a coordinated response, can be given more resources and more qualified personnel to increase its effectiveness and speed of reaction in the wake of a disaster. In addition, the agency can better harmonize its efforts with state and local governments, as well as the many charitable organizations that step forward to help hurricane victims. Hurricane shelters can be designated and adequately provisioned well in advance of hurricane strikes. People can stock up on supplies, including food and water, and they can also plan ahead to know what they will do in the event of a hurricane.

Determining which of these actions, as well as many other worthy ones not mentioned, should be taken is well beyond the scope of this book, which seeks to present the history of American hurricanes, not to offer policy prescriptions or a guide to personal behavior. Nevertheless, it is clear that implementing such actions will take high levels of political, bureaucratic, and individual resolve, as well as vast amounts of money, all of which are too often in short supply. And if we as a society become convinced by the growing weight of scientific evidence that global warming will indeed make hurricanes of the future worse than those of the past, then it will be incumbent upon us to act even more expeditiously and more boldly to counter this threat in any way we can.

AS THIS BOOK WAS heading into the final stage of production, Hurricane Dorian riveted the nation. Beginning in late August 2019, Americans watched the round-the-clock coverage of this rapidly intensifying storm as it marched slowly across the Atlantic. Each day, reports became more alarming as Dorian not only grew into a monster Category 5 hurricane, but also appeared to be heading directly for the East Coast of the United States. Especially concerning were the forecast tracks that had Dorian plowing into heavily populated regions of Florida. As a result, people in the Sunshine State began worrying about and preparing for a potential cataclysm.

But first in line were the Bahamas. On September 1, Dorian made landfall on the Bahamian island of Abaco, slamming into it with sustained winds of 185 mph and gusts over 200 mph. Just hours later, the storm was over Grand Bahama Island. And there, Dorian essentially stalled in place for an excruciating forty hours, remaining stationary at times, or creeping along at less than 1.3 mph—about half the speed at which a typical human walks. For the first fifteen of those hours, Dorian maintained Category 5 intensity, and then it ratcheted down to a Category 2 before moving on.

The resulting devastation was truly apocalyptic. Nearly every vestige of civilization was gravely damaged or obliterated, leaving a wreckage-strewn landscape, and tens of thousands of Bahamians physically and emotionally shattered, without shelter, food, water, and, in many cases, hope. An estimated 70,000 people were left homeless. One Bahamian said that the hurricane "put everyone on square zero."

A few days after the hurricane struck, Dr. Duane Sands, the Bahamas' health minister, warned the public "to prepare for unimaginable information about the death toll and the human suffering." As of late October 2019, the number of dead was 67, and there is little doubt that it will go higher as the cleanup continues (at the same time, 282 people were still missing). Some monetary damage estimates approach $10 billion. It will take generations for the islands to rebound, and life will never be the same.

Dorian left the Bahamas on the morning of September 3, 2019, as a Category 2 storm, heading north-northwest. According to some models, a broad swath of the southeastern coast of United States was under threat of landfall, while other models had the storm staying just offshore. Anticipating Dorian's onslaught and bracing for disaster, local authorities ordered mandatory evacuations from Florida to Virginia. Millions of people raided local supermarkets and stocked up on food and supplies, topped off their cars' gas tanks, and boarded up windows. Some hunkered down to ride it out, while others heeded the warnings and left.

Over the next few days, Dorian hugged the coastline, briefly regaining Category 3 status as it moved over warmer waters, then dropping to Category 1 just before making its only landfall in the United States, at North Carolina's Cape Hatteras. After that, Dorian zoomed off in a northeasterly direction, making landfall for a second time in Nova Scotia, Canada, where it knocked out power to roughly 400,000.

Dorian caused considerable damage in the Southeast, with North Carolina, where it scored a direct hit, getting the worst of it. The storm was responsible for major beach erosion, serious flooding, fierce winds and tornadoes that toppled trees and mangled or destroyed buildings, and a loss of power to hundreds of thousands of people. At least four people died, all of them men in North Carolina or Florida who passed away while either preparing for the storm or cleaning up after it.

While Dorian's impact on the United States was significant, it was virtually nothing compared with what happened to the Bahamas, and what might have happened if the hurricane had plowed head-on into the coast, instead of skirting the mainland and clipping North Carolina before sailing off into the Atlantic. This time, America was lucky. But if the history of US hurricanes tells us anything, it is that such luck will not last.

Tables of Costliest Hurricanes

US HURRICANES THAT RESULTED IN
AT LEAST $1 BILLION IN DAMAGES IN
THE YEAR THEY OCCURRED

HURRICANE	YEAR	CATEGORY*	UNADJUSTED COST (BILLIONS OF DOLLARS)
Katrina	2005	3	125.0
Harvey	2017	4	125.0
Maria	2017	4	90.0
Sandy	2012	1	65.0
Irma	2017	4	50.0
Ike	2008	2	30.0
Andrew	1992	5	27.0
Michael	2018	5	25.0
Florence	2018	1	24.0
Ivan	2004	3	20.5
Wilma	2005	3	19.0
Rita	2005	3	18.5
Charley	2004	4	16.0
Irene	2011	1	13.5
Matthew	2016	1	10.0
Frances	2004	2	9.8
Hugo	1989	4	9.0
Allison	2001	TS	8.5
Jeanne	2004	3	7.5
Floyd	1999	2	6.5
Georges	1998	2	6.0
Gustav	2008	2	6.0

Isabel	2003	2	5.5
Fran	1996	3	5.0
Opal	1995	3	4.7
Iniki	1992	4	3.1
Alicia	1983	3	3.0
Isaac	2012	1	2.8
Dennis	2005	3	2.5
Lee	2011	TS	2.5
Agnes	1972	1	2.1
Marilyn	1995	2	2.1
Dorian	2019	1	TBD
Juan	1985	1	1.5
Bob	1991	2	1.5
Betsy	1965	3	1.4
Camille	1969	5	1.4
Elena	1985	3	1.3
Dolly	2008	2	1.3
Lili	2002	1	1.1
Alberto	1994	TS	1.0
Bonnie	1998	3	1.0
Imelda	2019	TS	TBD
Frederick	1979	3	1.7

*TS = tropical storm.

Source: Data from NOAA, National Centers for Environmental Information, "Costliest U.S. Tropical Cyclones," October 8, 2019, https://www.ncdc.noaa.gov/billions/dcmi.pdf.

COSTLIEST US HURRICANES, BASED ON THE 2019 CONSUMER PRICE INDEX ADJUSTED COST

HURRICANE	YEAR	CATEGORY*	ADJUSTED COST (BILLIONS OF DOLLARS)
Katrina	2005	3	168.8
Harvey	2017	4	130.0
Maria	2017	4	93.6
Sandy	2012	1	73.5

Irma	2017	4	52.0
Andrew	1992	5	50.2
Ike	2008	2	36.6
Ivan	2004	3	28.5
Wilma	2005	3	25.7
Michael	2018	5	25.2
Rita	2005	3	25.0
Florence	2018	1	24.5
Charley	2004	4	22.2
Hugo	1989	4	19.1
Irene	2011	1	15.7
Frances	2004	2	13.6
Agnes	1972	1	12.9
Allison	2001	TS	12.5
Betsy	1965	3	11.5
Matthew	2016	1	10.8
Jeanne	2004	3	10.4
Floyd	1999	2	10.1
Camille	1969	5	10.0
Georges	1998	2	9.5
Fran	1996	3	8.3
Opal	1995	3	8.0
Diane	1955	1	8.0
Alicia	1983	3	7.9
Isabel	2003	2	7.7
Gustav	2008	2	7.3
Celia	1970	3	6.1
Frederick	1979	3	6.0
Iniki	1992	4	5.8
Long Island Express	1938	3	5.6
Great Atlantic Hurricane	1944	3	5.1
Carol	1954	3	4.4
Marilyn	1995	2	3.6
Juan	1985	1	3.6
Dennis	2005	3	3.4

Donna	1960	4	3.4
Elena	1985	3	3.2
Isaac	2012	1	3.1

*TS = tropical storm.

Source: Data from NOAA, National Centers for Environmental Information, "Costliest U.S. Tropical Cyclones," October 8, 2019, https://www.ncdc.noaa.gov/billions/dcmi.pdf.

ACKNOWLEDGMENTS

It has been fascinating and sobering, once again, to wade into the rich history of the United States, focusing this time on hurricanes. I have gained a much deeper appreciation of these terrific tempests, and of the people over the centuries who have sought to unravel their mysteries and forecast their arrival. I also have been greatly pained by the stories of those who suffered through these storms, and those who died. If this book provides any comfort to survivors of hurricanes, and gives readers a fuller context for better understanding them and confronting them in the future, it will have been a success.

Most of all I would like to thank Bob Weil (the editor in chief at Liveright) and Bill Rusin for suggesting I undertake a history of America's hurricanes. Unbeknownst to them, I had long been thinking about writing a book on a single hurricane, but hadn't found the one I wanted to cover. So, when they approached my agent with the idea of writing a narrative history of all of America's hurricanes, I was primed to say yes, and I am glad I did.

I owe a special thanks to the reviewers of the manuscript, whose excellent feedback greatly improved the book. They included Bryan Norcross, meteorologist and hurricane specialist, WPLG-TV Miami; Lourdes B. Avilés, meteorology professor at Plymouth State University; Bethany Groff Dorau, North Shore regional site manager for Historic New England; David E. Kane, publisher and editor, American History Press; and Ruth Rooks. Any errors in the book, of course, are mine alone.

Other people who were quite helpful include Bernard Barris, Eric Blake, Jennifer John Block, George Butch, Joan Chrissos, Laurie Chronley, Richard Crossley, Bob Cullim, Dennis Feltgen, Kevin Kinney, Monika Leal, Ron Magill, Jaime Marland, Elizabeth Pisano, Scott Price, Jane Shambra, Sarah Jane Shangraw, Shep Smithline, Georgia Stylianides, Chris Tourgee, Peter Urkowitz, Thomas Warren, and the excellent staff at Harvard's Widener Library and the Abbot Public Library in Marblehead, Massachusetts. The names of the institutions and individuals that provided artwork, for which I am very grateful, are provided in the credits at the end of the book.

Marie Pantojan, former assistant editor at Liveright, did a wonderful job of editing the book, and being a soothing and supportive voice up until just after I handed in the manuscript, when she left for another position. Dan Gerstle, senior editor at Liveright, took over from Marie and skillfully guided the book through the production process. Stephanie Hiebert proved herself to be an excellent and very efficient copy editor, whose eye for detail greatly improved the text and captions. The rest of the crew at Liveright and W. W. Norton—Steve Attardo, Haley Bracken, Cordelia Calvert, Nick Curley, Rebecca Homiski, Gina Iaquinta, Gabriel Kachuck, Peter Miller, Anna Oler, Don Rifkin—did their typical, excellent job of creating a gorgeous book, and giving it a wonderful launch into the world.

Russell Galen, my longtime agent, continues to be indispensable in helping me build my writing career and navigate my way through the oftentimes bewildering world of publishing. His sage advice is invaluable. This is our sixth book together, and I hope there will be many more.

Of all who deserve thanks, none are more important than my immediate and extended family, whose unwavering support is the main reason I have had the amazing and much-appreciated opportunity to be a full-time writer, which is far and away the best and most difficult job I have ever had. My wife Jennifer, however, deserves the lion's share of the credit. The best thing that ever happened to me was marrying her some twenty-five years ago.

NOTES

ABBREVIATIONS USED IN THE NOTES

BAMS   *Bulletin of the American Meteorological Society*
HRD   Hurricane Research Division (NOAA)
MH   *The Miami Herald*
MWR   *Monthly Weather Report*
NHC   National Hurricane Center
NOAA   National Oceanic and Atmospheric Administration
NWS   National Weather Service
NYT   *The New York Times*

EXTRACTS (SUPPLIED BY A SUB-SUB-LIBRARIAN)

xi   **"Out of the south":** *The Holy Bible* (London: Printers to the Queen, 1851), 487.

xi   **"Good God!":** "From Alexander Hamilton to *The Royal Danish American Gazette* (September 6, 1772)," in *The Papers of Alexander Hamilton*, vol. 1, ed. Harold C. Syrett (New York: Columbia University Press, 1961), 34–38.

xi   **"Reader, persons who have never":** John James Audubon, *The Life of John James Audubon* (New York: G. P. Putnam's Sons, 1873), 246.

xii   **"There is probably no feature":** F. H. Bigelow, "Cyclones, Hurricanes, and Tornadoes," in *Yearbook of the United States, Department of Agriculture, 1898* (Washington, DC: Government Printing Office, 1899), 531.

xii   **"Remember to get the weather":** Ernest Hemingway to John Dos Passos (March 26, 1932), in *Ernest Hemingway, Selected Letters, 1917–1961*, ed. Carlos Baker (New York: Scribner Classics, 2003), 355.

xii   **"All the thousands of hurricane stories":** Marjory Stoneman Douglas, *Hurricane* (New York: Rinehart, 1958), 328.

INTRODUCTION

xv   **Throughout the day, television and radio:** Background material for this section on Audrey comes from Cathy C. Post, *Hurricane Audrey: The Deadly Storm of 1957* (Gretna, LA: Pelican, 2007); *All Over but to Cry: The Louisiana Tidal Wave*, directed by Jennifer John Block (New Orleans: Fresh Media, 2009), DVD; Nola Mae Wittler Ross and Susan McFillen Goodson, *Hurricane Audrey* (Sulphur, LA: Wise, 1996); Ernest Zebrowski and Judith A. Howard, *Category 5: The Story of Camille, Lessons Unlearned from America's Most Violent Hurricane* (Ann Arbor:

University of Michigan Press, 2005), 13–22; Robert B. Ross and Maurice D. Blum, "Hurricane Audrey, 1957," *MWR*, June 1957, 221–27; and HRD, "60th Anniversary of Hurricane Audrey," June 26, 2017, https://noaahrd.wordpress .com/2017/06/26/60th-anniversary-of-hurricane-audrey.

xvi **Early that morning, Dr. Cecil Clark:** Background for the Clarks' story comes from Post, *Hurricane Audrey*, 36–38, 53–54, 73–75, 88–91, 98–99, 145–49, 168–70, 173–78, 188–91, 221–22, 237–40, and 275–77; and Ross and Goodson, *Hurricane Audrey*, 87–91.

xvi **"Water is seeping into":** Ross and Goodson, *Hurricane Audrey*, 88.

xviii **"When I saw the water rising":** Ibid., 89.

xix **"It must be a mistake":** Post, *Hurricane Audrey*, 238.

xix **"I did what was necessary":** Ross and Goodson, *Hurricane Audrey*, 89.

xix **This harrowing and tragic story:** Years after the hurricane, more than a hundred families in Cameron Parish filed wrongful-death lawsuits against the federal Weather Bureau, which had the responsibility of issuing forecasts (the Weather Bureau was the predecessor of today's National Weather Service). In general, the lawsuits contended that the bureau was "negligent in failing to give adequate, clear, correct, and proper warning concerning the nature, intensity, location, path, velocity and speed, existence of tidal wave of Hurricane Audrey as well as the correct time it would strike the Louisiana Coast." When the first case was brought to trial, the judge ruled against the plaintiffs, finding the government not liable for the deaths. The judge agreed with the expert witness who stated that the forecasts were as accurate as could be expected, given the forecasting tools available to the bureau at the time. When the case was appealed, it was upheld, and at that point the rest of the pending lawsuits were dropped. See *Whitney Bartie v. United States of America*, US District Court W.D. Louisiana, Lake Charles Division, March 28, 1963, https://www.leagle.com/decision/1963226216fsupp101225.

xx **"Everything's gone":** Post, *Hurricane Audrey*, 204.

xx **If you are among the many:** Darryl T. Cohen, "60 Million Live in Path of Hurricanes," US Census Bureau, August 6, 2018, https://www.census.gov/library/stories/2018/08/coastal-county-population-rises.html.

xx **In an average year, six hurricanes:** Christopher W. Landsea, "Subject: E11) How Many Tropical Cyclones Have There Been Each Year in the Atlantic Basin? What Years Were the Greatest and Fewest Seen?" HRD, Frequently Asked Questions, last revised June 1, 2018, https://www.aoml.noaa.gov/hrd/tcfaq/E11.html.

xx **Typically, two hurricanes hit:** Christopher W. Landsea, "Subject: E19) How Many Direct Hits by Hurricanes of Various Categories Have Affected Each State?" HRD, Frequently Asked Questions, last revised June 19, 2019, https://www.aoml.noaa.gov/hrd/tcfaq/E19.html.

xxi **There have also been years:** Eric S. Blake, Christopher W. Landsea, and Ethan J. Gibney, "The Deadliest, Costliest, and Most Intense United States Tropical Cyclones from 1851 to 2010 (and Other Frequently Requested Hurricane Facts)," NOAA Technical Memorandum NWS NHC-6, August 2011, 17; Bob Sheets and Jack Williams, *Hurricane Watch: Forecasting the Deadliest Storms on Earth* (New York: Vintage Books, 2001), 194; and Christopher W. Landsea, "Subject: E23) What Is the Complete List of Continental U.S. Landfalling Hurricanes?" HRD, Frequently Asked Questions, last revised June 20, 2019, https://www.aoml.noaa .gov/hrd/tcfaq/E23.html.

xxi **"hurricane amnesia":** CNN, "6 to 8 U.S. Hurricanes Expected in 2002," May 21, 2002, http://www.cnn.com/2002/WEATHER/05/20/hurricane.outlook/index.html.

xxi **Residents of Florida, Texas:** Blake et al., "Deadliest, Costliest," 21; and Landsea, "Subject: E19) How Many Direct Hits."

xxi **roughly 50 percent of the cost:** Adam B. Smith and Richard W. Katz, "U.S. Billion-Dollar Weather and Climate Disasters: Data Sources, Trends, Accuracy and Biases," *Natural Hazards*, June 2013, 387–410; and NOAA, National Centers for Environmental Information (NCEI), "Billion-Dollar Disasters: Calculating the Costs," accessed May 2018, https://www.ncdc.noaa.gov/monitoring -references/dyk/billions-calculations.

xxi **have killed nearly 30,000 people:** Blake et al., "Deadliest, Costliest," 27; and data presented later in this book.

xxii **Given that there have been:** Ivan Ray Tannehill, *Hurricanes: Their Nature and History* (New York: Greenwood Press, 1938), 220–44; and Blake et al., "Deadliest, Costliest," 42–46.

xxii **Hurricanes also discharge:** Chris Landsea, "Subject: D7) How Much Energy Does a Hurricane Release?" HRD, Frequently Asked Questions, accessed April 2018, http://www.aoml.noaa.gov/hrd/tcfaq/D7.html.

xxiii **To put it another way:** Steve Graham and Holli Riebeck, "Hurricanes: The Greatest Storms on Earth," NASA Earth Observatory, November 1, 2006, https:// earthobservatory.nasa.gov/Features/Hurricanes.

xxiii **"number of huge watery cones":** Raphael Semmes, *My Adventures Afloat: A Personal Memoir of My Cruises and Services* (London: Richard Bentley, 1869), 476.

xxiv **While about 60 percent:** Christopher W. Landsea, "A Climatology of Intense (or Major) Atlantic Hurricanes," *MWR*, June 1993, 1703, 1712.

xxiv **Many other hurricanes:** Nick Stockton, "To See the Birth of an Atlantic Hurricane, Look to Africa," *Wired*, March 25, 2015, https://www.wired.com/2015/03/ see-birth-atlantic-hurricane-look-africa; Simon Winchester, *When the Sky Breaks: Hurricanes, Tornadoes, and the Worst Weather in the World* (New York: Viking, 2017), 35–38; Roger A. Pielke Jr. and Roger A. Pielke Sr., *Hurricanes: Their Nature and Impact on Society* (New York: John Wiley, 1997), 68–73; Neil L. Frank, "The Great Galveston Hurricane of 1900," in *Hurricanes: Coping with Disaster*, ed. Robert Simpson (Washington, DC: American Geophysical Union, 2003), 130; and "Hurricane Life Cycle," Hurricanes: Science and Society, accessed March 2018, http://hurricanescience.org/science/science/hurricanelifecycle.

xxiv **Whether they come from:** Neal Dorst, "Subject: G16) What Is the Average Forward Speed of a Hurricane?" HRD, Frequently Asked Questions, last updated May 29, 2014, http://www.aoml.noaa.gov/hrd/tcfaq/G16.html.

xxiv **Nevertheless, no two hurricanes:** Gordon E. Dunn and Banner I. Miller, *Atlantic Hurricanes* (Baton Rouge: Louisiana State University Press, 1964), 58.

xxiv **Hurricanes go by different names:** Frederick Hirth, "The Word 'Typhoon.' Its History and Origin," *Journal of the Royal Geographical Society* 50 (1880): 263; Patrick J. Fitzpatrick, *Hurricanes* (Santa Barbara, CA: ABC-CLIO, 2006), 85; and Robert H. Simpson, "Hurricanes," *Scientific American*, June 1954, 32.

xxv **"cockeyed Bobs" or "willy-willys":** W. Ernest Cooke, *The Climate of Western Australia from Meteorological Observations Made during the Years 1876–1899* (Perth, Australia: William Alfred Watson, 1901), 11; and Gary Barnes, "Severe Local Storms in the Tropics," in *Severe Convective Storms*, ed. Charles A. Doswell III, Meteorological Monograph no. 50 (Boston: American Meteorological Society, 2001), 405.

xxv **The Mayans named their god:** Julia Cresswell, "Hurricane," *Oxford Dictionary of Word Origins* (Oxford: Oxford University Press, 2002), 217; Stuart B. Schwartz,

Sea of Storms: A History of Hurricanes in the Greater Caribbean from Columbus to Katrina (Princeton, NJ: Princeton University Press, 2015), 6–7; Pielke and Pielke, *Hurricanes*, 16; and Dunn and Miller, *Atlantic Hurricanes*, 7.

xxv **As one climbs the hurricane:** Les Standiford, *Last Train to Paradise: Henry Flagler and the Spectacular Rise and Fall of the Railroad That Crossed an Ocean* (New York: Broadway Paperbacks, 2002), 229; and Carl H. Hobbs, *The Beach Book: Science of the Shore* (New York: Columbia University Press, 2012), 21.

xxvi **"no canvas could withstand them":** Richard Hamblyn, *The Invention of Clouds: How an Amateur Meteorologist Forged the Language of the Skies* (New York: Farrar, Straus and Giroux, 2001), 271.

xxvi **Together, these two elemental forces:** Edward N. Rappaport, "Fatalities in the United States from Atlantic Tropical Cyclones," *BAMS*, March 2014, 341–43.

xxvi **Each cubic yard of water:** Kenneth Chang, "The Destructive Power of Water," *NYT*, March 12, 2011.

xxvi **"hide from wind, run from the water":** Steve Roberts Jr., "NWS: 'Hide from the Wind, Run from the Water' for Cat 4 Hurricane Florence," *Virginia Gazette*, September 11, 2018.

CHAPTER 1—A NEW AND VIOLENT WORLD

1 **Christopher Columbus:** Background for Columbus's fourth voyage and his reception in Hispaniola comes from Ferdinand Columbus, *The Life of the Admiral Christopher Columbus by His Son Ferdinand*, trans. Benjamin Keen (London: Folio Society, 1960), 223–24; "Hernando Colón's Account of the Fourth Voyage," in *New Iberian World: A Documentary History of the Discovery and Settlement of Latin America to the Early 17th Century*, vol. 2, *The Caribbean* (New York: Times Books, 1984), 120–21; Samuel Eliot Morison, *Admiral of the Ocean Sea: A Life of Christopher Columbus* (Boston: Little, Brown, 1946), 570–71, 580–92; David Ludlum, *Early American Hurricanes: 1492–1870* (Boston: American Meteorological Society, 1963), 1–7; and Laurence Bergreen, *Columbus: The Four Voyages* (New York: Viking, 2011), 288–89, 298–303.

1 **"Grand Admiral of the Ocean Sea":** Christopher Columbus, *The Diario of Christopher Columbus's First Voyage to America, 1492–1493*, abstracted by Fray Bartolomé de las Casas, trans. Oliver Dunn and James E. Kelley Jr. (Norman: University of Oklahoma, 1989), 19.

3 **"for eight days because of the great danger":** Ibid.

3 **"as a prophet and soothsayer":** Morison, *Admiral of the Ocean Sea*, 590.

4 **While Europe certainly had terrific:** Mathew Mulcahy, *Hurricanes and Society in the British Greater Caribbean, 1624–1783* (Baltimore: Johns Hopkins University Press, 2006), 20–21.

4 **"In all the Indies, I have always found":** "Columbus Letter to Santangel," addendum, March 4, 1493, in *New Iberian World*, vol. 2, *The Caribbean*, 62.

4 **In 1493, during Columbus's second:** Morison, *Admiral of the Ocean Sea*, 490–91; and Ludlum, *Early American Hurricanes*, 3–6.

5 **One of those who perished:** Bergreen, *Columbus: The Four Voyages*, 274–86; and Ferdinand Columbus, *Life of the Admiral*, 225.

6 **"The storm was terrible":** Ferdinand Columbus, *Life of the Admiral*, 111–12; see also page 224.

6 **Columbus's "enemies":** Ibid., 225.

6 **Ever since Columbus's first voyage:** H. Michael Tarver and Emily Slape, "Over-

view Essay," in *The Spanish Empire: A Historical Encyclopedia*, vol. 1, ed. H. Michael Tarver and Emily Slape (Santa Barbara, CA: ABC-CLIO, 2016), 61–62.

7 **Don Tristán de Luna y Arellano:** Background for this section on Luna and the colonization effort at Pensacola Bay comes from *The Luna Papers, 1559–1561*, vol. 1, ed. Herbert Ingram Priestley (Tuscaloosa: University of Alabama Press, 2010), ix–lxvii; Charles Hudson, Marvin T. Smith, Chester B. DePratter, and Emilia Kelley, *Southeastern Archaeology*, Summer 1989, 31, 33–42; and Eugene Lyon, "Spain's Sixteenth-Century North American Settlement Attempts: A Neglected Aspect," *Florida Historical Quarterly*, January 1981, 279.

8 **Just a few years after the collapse:** Background for this section on the hurricane of 1565, the colonizing efforts of René Goulaine de Laudonnière and Jean Ribaut, and the conflict between the forces of Ribaut and Pedro Menéndez de Avilés comes from three letters by Pedro Menéndez de Avilés to His Royal Catholic Majesty published in *Proceedings of the Massachusetts Historical Society*, 2nd ser., 8 (1894): September 11, 1565 (pp. 419–25), October 15, 1565 (pp. 425–39); and December 5, 1565 (pp. 440–53); as well as John T. McGrath, *The French in Early Florida: In the Eye of the Hurricane* (Gainesville: University Press of Florida, 2000), 8–11, 67–72, 96–110, 132–55; Margaret Bransford, "A Hurricane That Made History," *French Review*, January 1950, 223–26; and René Goulaine de Laudonnière, "History of Jean Ribault's First and Second Voyage to Florida," *Historical Collections of Louisiana and Florida*, ed. B. F. French (New York: J. Sabin, 1869), 324–44.

9 **Ribaut arrived a few months later:** John Noble Wilford, "A French Fort, Long Lost, Is Found in South Carolina," *NYT*, June 6, 1996.

11 **"There rose so great a tempest":** Laudonnière, "History of Jean Ribault's First," 336.

13 **The first one, in the summer of 1609:** Background for the hurricane that struck the third supply mission in the summer of 1609, and the early years of the Jamestown settlement, comes from William Strachey, "A True Reportory of the Wreck and Redemption of Sir Thomas Gates, Knight, upon and from the Islands of the Bermudas: His Coming to Virginia and the Estate of That Colony Then and After, under the Government of the Lord La Warr, July 15, 1610," in *A Voyage to Virginia in 1609: Two Narratives, Strachey's "True Reportory" & Jourdain's Discovery of the Bermudas*, ed. Louis B. Wright (Charlottesville: University of Virginia Press, 2013), 1–77; Silvester Jourdain, "A Discovery of the Bermudas, Otherwise Called the Isle of Devils," in *Voyage to Virginia in 1609*, 105–15; George Somers, "Letter to Salisbury, 15 June 1610," in *Jamestown Narratives: Eyewitness Accounts of the Virginia Colony*, ed. Edward Wright Haile (Champlain, VA: RoundHouse, 1998), 445–46; Benjamin Wooley, *Savage Kingdom: The True Story of Jamestown, 1607, and the Settlement of America* (New York: Harper Collins, 2007), 100–14, 138–43, 168–70, 215–63; David A. Price, *Love and Hate in Jamestown: John Smith, Pocahontas, and the Heart of a New Nation* (New York: Alfred A. Knopf, 2003), 3–4, 11–12, 97–98, 130–44; Karen Ordahl Kupperman, *The Jamestown Project* (Cambridge, MA: Harvard University Press, 2007), 9–10, 174–82, 210–30, 234–42, 247–54; and Hobson Woodward, *A Brave Vessel: The True Tale of the Castaways Who Rescued Jamestown and Inspired Shakespeare's* The Tempest (New York: Viking, 2009), 24–51, 104–6, 154–56.

14 **"A dreadful and hideous storm":** Strachey, "True Reportory," 4.

15 **"some [of them] lost their masts":** John Smith, *The Generall Historie of Virginia, New England & The Summer Isles, Together with The True Travels, Adven-*

tures and Observations, and A Sea Grammar, vol. 1 (Glasgow: James MacLehose, 1907), 189.

15 **"fury added to fury":** Strachey, "True Reportory," 6.

15 **"It could not be said to rain":** Ibid., 7.

15 **"from stern to stem":** Ibid., 10.

15 **"yet all that I had ever suffered":** Ibid., 7–8.

15 **which were called the "Devil's Islands":** Ibid., 16.

16 **Far from being devil's islands:** Jourdain, "Discovery of the Bermudas," 110, 112.

16 **As the famine worsened:** George Percy, "A True Relation of the Proceedings and Occurrents of Moment Which Have Hap'ned in Virginia . . . ," in *Jamestown Narratives: Eyewitness Accounts of the Virginia Colony, the First Decade, 1607–1617*, ed. Edward Wright Haile (Champlain, VA: RoundHouse, 1998), 505.

17 **Then, clinging to the edge of life:** Dennis Montgomery, " 'Such a Dish as Powdered Wife I Never Heard Of,' " *Colonial Williamsburg Journal*, Winter 2007; and Joseph Stromberg, "Starving Settlers in Jamestown Colony Resorted to Cannibalism," *Smithsonian*, April 30, 2013, https://www.smithsonianmag .com/history/starving-settlers-in-jamestown-colony-resorted-to-cannibalism -46000815.

17 **"If God had not sent":** Smith, *Generall Historie of Virginia*, 206–7. See also Price, *Love and Hate in Jamestown*, 139, 144.

17 **William Shakespeare relied in part:** Alden T. Vaughan, foreword to *Voyage to Virginia in 1609*, xiii–xiv; and Woodward, *Brave Vessel*, 154–56.

18 **It must be added, though:** Mulcahy, *Hurricanes and Society*, 55–57; and Jonathan Mercantini, "The Great Carolina Hurricane of 1752," *South Carolina Historical Magazine*, October 2002, 353.

18 **"to a salubrious state":** Alexander Hewatt, *An Historical Account of the Rise and Progress of the Colonies of South Carolina and Georgia*, vol. 2 (London: Alexander Donaldson, 1779), 179.

19 **The list of colonial hurricanes:** For excellent background on these hurricanes, see Ludlum, *Early American Hurricanes*, 16–17, 24–25, 42–43.

19 **The Great Colonial Hurricane of 1635 struck:** Background for this hurricane comes from Increase Mather, *An Essay for the Recording of Illustrious Providences: Wherein, an Account Is Given of Many Remarkable and Very Memorable Events, Which Have Happened in This Last Age, Especially in New-England* (Boston: Samuel Green, 1684), 311–12; Richard Mather, *Journal of Richard Mather, 1635; His Life and Death, 1670* (Boston: David Clapp, 1850), 24–30; John Winthrop, *Winthrop's Journal, "History of New England," 1630–1649*, vol. 1, ed. James Kendall Hosmer (New York: Charles Scribner's Sons, 1908), 155–57; and Ludlum, *Early American Hurricanes*, 10–13.

19 **"flying from their wigwams":** Winthrop, *Winthrop's Journal*, 157.

19 **"was such a mighty storm":** William Bradford, *History of Plymouth Plantation*, ed. Charles Deane (Boston: Little, Brown, 1856), 33–38.

19 **the pinnace *Watch and Wait*:** The background and all the quotes relating to the *Watch and Wait* come from Anthony Thacher, "Anthony Thacher's Narrative of His Shipwreck," in *Chronicles of the First Planters of the Colony of Massachusetts Bay, from 1623 to 1636*, ed. Alexander Young (Boston: Charles C. Little and James Brown, 1846), 485–95.

20 **In September 1635:** John R. Totten, *Thacher Genealogy*, part 1 (New York: New York Genealogical and Biographical Society, 1910), 74.

21 **At the same time that Thacher:** Background for this section on the *James* comes

from Mather, *Journal of Richard Mather*, 27–28 (the quotes are all from this source); and Mather, *An Essay for the Recording*, 311.

21 **The ship was carrying a group:** David McCullough, *John Adams* (New York: Simon & Schuster, 2001), 29.

22 **The hurricane that struck off of Florida:** Background for this section on the 1715 hurricane comes from E. Lynne Wright, *Florida Disasters: True Stories of Tragedy and Survival* (Guilford: Globe Pequot, 2017), 7–11; David Cordingly, *Spanish Gold: Captain Woodes Rogers and the Pirates of the Caribbean* (London: Bloomsbury, 2011), 123–25; and Colin Woodard, *The Republic of Pirates: Being the True and Surprising Story of the Caribbean Pirates and the Man Who Brought Them Down* (New York: Harcourt, 2007), 103–6.

23 **"it was so violent that":** David Cordingly, *Under the Black Flag: The Romance and the Reality of Life among the Pirates* (Orlando, FL: Harvest Books, 1995), 125.

CHAPTER 2—THE LAW OF STORMS

25 **On the evening of October 21, 1743:** Background for Franklin's contribution to hurricane science comes from "From Benjamin Franklin to Jared Eliot, 13 February 1750," in *The Papers of Benjamin Franklin*, vol. 3, ed. Leonard W. Labaree (New Haven, CT: Yale University Press, 1961), 463–66; David Ludlum, *Early American Hurricanes: 1492–1870* (Boston: American Meteorological Society, 1963), 22–23; A. D. Bache, "Attempt to Fix the Date of Dr. Franklin's Observation, in Relation to the North-east Storms of the Atlantic States," *Journal of the Franklin Institute*, November 1833, 300–303; and Bob Sheets and Jack Williams, *Hurricane Watch: Forecasting the Deadliest Storms on Earth* (New York: Vintage Books, 2001), 12–14.

27 **On the day of the hurricane:** Background for this section on John Winthrop comes from Ludlum, *Early American Hurricanes*, 22; David M. Ludlum, "Part I, Four Centuries of Surprises," *American Heritage*, June/July 1986, https://www.americanheritage.com/content/part-i-four-centuries-surprises; and Frederick E. Brasch, "John Winthrop (1714–1779), America's First Astronomer, and the Science of His Period," *Publications of the Astronomical Society of the Pacific*, August–October 1916, 153–56.

27 **"Meteorologie Diary":** Ludlum, "Part I, Four Centuries of Surprises."

27 **Since a normal barometric reading:** C. Donald Ahrens, *Meteorology Today: An Introduction to Weather, Climate, and the Environment* (Boston: Brooks/Cole/Cengage Learning, 2013), 11.

28 **Aristotle's treatise *Meteorologica*:** H. Howard Frisinger, "Aristotle and His 'Meteorologica,'" *BAMS*, July 1972, 634–38.

28 **The most famous American practitioner:** Edwin T. Martin, *Thomas Jefferson: Scientist* (New York: Henry Schuman, 1952), 131; Susan Solomon, John S. Daniel, and Daniel L. Druckenbrod, "Revolutionary Minds: Thomas Jefferson and James Madison Participated in a Small 'Revolution' against British Weather-Monitoring Practices," *American Scientist*, September/October 2007, 430; and Lucia Stanton, "Monticello Weather Report," *Monticello Keepsakes*, Fall 1982.

28 **"the indexes of climate":** "From Thomas Jefferson to Lewis E. Beck, 16 July 1824," Founders Online, National Archives, http://founders.archives.gov/documents/Jefferson/98-01-02-4410; and Stanton, "Monticello Weather Report."

28 **His work was amplified:** Theodore S. Feldman, "Late Enlightenment Meteorology," in *The Quantifying Spirit in the Eighteenth Century*, ed. Tore Frang-

smyr, J. L. Heilbron, and Robin E. Rider (Berkeley: University of California Press, 1990), 143–58.

28 **"invention of clouds":** Richard Hamblyn, *The Invention of Clouds: How an Amateur Meteorologist Forged the Language of the Skies* (New York: Farrar, Straus and Giroux, 2001).

29 **"On the Modification of Clouds":** Luke Howard, *Essay on the Modifications of Clouds* (1803; repr., London: John Churchill, 1865). See also Hamblyn, *Invention of Clouds*, 3–6.

29 **"language of the skies":** Hamblyn, *Invention of Clouds*.

29 **"Of all the departments of science":** Thomas Jefferson to George F. Hopkins (September 5, 1822), in *The Writings of Thomas Jefferson: Being His Autobiography, Correspondence, Reports, Messages, Addresses, and Other Writings, Official and Private*, vol. 7, ed. H. A. Washington (New York: Derby & Jackson, 1859), 259.

29 **The first struck at the beginning:** Background for this hurricane comes from William Reid, *An Attempt to Develop the Law of Storms by Means of Facts, Arranged According to Place and Time; and Hence to Point Out a Cause for the Variable Winds, with the View to Practical Use in Navigation* (London: John Weale, 1838), 276–310; "Short Account of the Desolation Made in Several of the West India Islands by the Late Hurricanes," in *The Annual Register, or a View of the History, Politics, and Literature, for the Year 1780* (London: J. Dodsley, 1781), 292–94; and Wayne Neely, *The Great Hurricane of 1780* (Bloomington, IN: IUniverse, 2012).

29 **"The sea broke suddenly in":** John Dalling to Lord George Germain (October 20, 1780), in *The New Annual Register, or General Repository of History, Politics, and Literature, for the Year 1781* (London: G. Robinson, 1782), appdx. 3.

29 **"will be ever acknowledged":** William Beckford, *A Descriptive Account of the Island of Jamaica*, vol. 1 (London: T. and J. Egerton, 1790), 90.

29 **As the storm transited the island:** Reid, *Attempt to Develop the Law of Storms*, 277.

30 **The terrifying ordeal of one:** Lieutenant Archer, "Account of the Loss of His Majesty's Ship Phoenix, Off Cuba, in the Year 1780," in *The Mariner's Chronicle*, vol. 2, ed. Archibald Duncan (London: James Cundee, 1804), 281–99. All the quotes in this section come from this source.

31 **Meanwhile, after leaving Cuba:** Reid, *Attempt to Develop the Law of Storms*, 307; and Ludlum, *Early American Hurricanes*, 68–69.

32 **But it had its most devastating:** Bryan Edwards, *The History Civil and Commercial, of the British Colonies in the West Indies* (London: B. Crosby, 1798), 90; Reid, *Attempt to Develop the Law of Storms*, 313; and Élisée Reclus, *The Ocean, Atmosphere, and Life* (New York: Harper & Brothers, 1874), 256.

32 **"It is impossible to describe":** Godfrey Basil Mundy, "Lord Rodney to Philip Stephens (December 10, 1780)," in *The Life and Correspondence of the Late Admiral Lord Rodney*, vol. 1 (London: John Murray, 1830), 449–50.

32 **The hurricane also gravely damaged:** William Laird Clowes, *The Royal Navy: A History from Earliest Times to the Present*, vol. 3 (London: Sampson Low, Marston, 1898), 479; Reclus, *Ocean, Atmosphere, and Life*, 256; and Reid, *Attempt to Develop the Law of Storms*, 311–13.

32 **The overall death toll:** Neely, *Great Hurricane of 1780*, 122.

32 **"The lesson [of the hurricanes]":** Nathaniel Philbrick, *In the Hurricane's Eye: The Genius of George Washington and the Victory at Yorktown* (New York: Viking, 2018), 18; see also pp. xii–xv.

32 **Thus, by following this course:** Ibid., 179–238.

33 **"Oh God, it is all over!":** Benjamin Terry, *A History of England from the Earliest Times to the Death of Queen Victoria*, 4th ed. (Chicago: Scott, Foresman, 1908), 939.

34 **Twin hurricanes hit North Carolina:** Ludlum, *Early American Hurricanes*, 34–35.

34 **Great Louisiana Hurricane of 1812:** Ibid., 75–76; and George Pabis, "Subduing Nature through Engineering: Caleb G. Forshey and the Levees-Only Policy, 1851–1881," in *Transforming New Orleans and Its Environs: Centuries of Change*, ed. Craig E. Colten (Pittsburgh, PA: University of Pittsburgh Press, 2000), 64.

34 **Great September Gale of 1815:** Background for this hurricane comes from Moses Brown, "Official Record of the Great Gale of 1815," in *Proceedings of the Rhode Island Historical Society, 1893–1894* (Providence, RI: Printed for the Society, 1894), 232–35; Ludlum, *Early American Hurricanes*, 77–81; John Farrar, "An Account of the Violent and Destructive Storm of the 23rd of September, 1815," *Quarterly Journal of Literature, Science, and the Arts*, April 1819, 102–6; Richard Miller Devens, *American Progress: Or the Great Events of the Greatest Century* (Chicago: C. A. Nichols, 1883), 178–85; and Esther Hoppin E. Lardner, "The Great Gale of Sept. 23, 1815," in *Proceedings of the Rhode Island Historical Society, 1893–1894*, 202–5.

34 **"a proper hurricane, like those":** Noah Webster, *The Autobiographies of Noah Webster: From the Letters and Essays, Memoir, and Diary*, ed. Richard M. Rollins (Columbia: University of South Carolina Press, 1989), 343.

34 **"Destruction and desolation were everywhere":** Lardner, "Great Gale of Sept. 23, 1815," 204.

35 **"The wind caught up the waters":** Oliver Wendell Holmes, *Pages from an Old Volume of Life: A Collection of Essays, 1857–1881* (Boston: Houghton, Mifflin, 1891), 163.

35 **"It chanced to be our washing-day":** Oliver Wendell Holmes, "The September Gale," in *The Poetical Works of Oliver Wendell Holmes*, vol. 1 (Boston: Houghton, Mifflin, 1892), 29–31.

35 **William C. Redfield:** Background on Redfield, his early life, and his work on hurricanes comes from John Howard Redfield, *Recollections of John Howard Redfield* (Philadelphia: Morris Press, 1900), 9–47; Denison Olmstead, *Address on the Scientific Life and Labors of William C. Redfield, A. M.* (New Haven, CT: E. Hayes, 1857), 3–12; and Diana Ross McCain, "Middletown Native Was in Forefront of Hurricane Research," *Hartford Courant*, September 9, 1998.

37 **"These facts at first seemed":** John Howard Redfield, *Recollections*, 46.

37 **While pursuing self-directed:** Olmstead, *Address on the Scientific Life*, 8–10.

38 **"Remarks on the Prevailing Storms":** William C. Redfield, "Remarks on the Prevailing Storms of the Atlantic Coast, of the North American States," *American Journal of Science and Arts*, July 1831, 17–51.

38 **But Redfield was not the first . . . that preceded his observations:** Reid, *Attempt to Develop the Law of Storms*, 2; "Theory of Storms," *North American Review*, April 1844, 336–37; Ludlum, *Early American Hurricanes*, ix; Henry Piddington, *The Sailor's Horn-Book for the Law of Storms* (London: Smith, Elder, 1848), 1–3; Ivan Ray Tannehill, *The Hurricane Hunters* (New York: Dodd, Mead, 1956), 27–28; and John D. Cox, *Storm Watchers: The Turbulent History of Weather Prediction from Franklin's Kite to El Niño* (New York: John Wiley, 2002), 31.

38 **"a sort of violent whirlwind":** Piddington, *Sailor's Horn-Book*, 233.

38 **In subsequent years, Redfield:** William C. Redfield, "Observations on the Hur-

ricanes and Storms of the West Indies and the Coast of the United States," in *The American Coast Pilot* (New York: Edmund and George W. Blunt, 1833), 626–29; William C. Redfield, "Summary Statements of Some of the Leading Facts in Meteorology," *American Journal of Science and Arts*, January 1834, 122–35; and William C. Redfield, "Observations on the Storm of December 15, 1839," *Transactions of the American Philosophical Society*, 1843, 77–82.

38 **Besides characterizing hurricanes:** Olmstead, *Address on the Scientific Life*, 14.

39 **His name was James P. Espy:** Background for Espy and his theory comes from Peter Moore, *Weather Experiment: The Pioneers Who Sought to See the Future* (New York: Farrar, Straus and Giroux, 2015), 119–26; L. M. Morehead, *A Few Incidents in the Life of Professor James P. Espy, by His Niece* (Cincinnati, OH: Robert Clarke, 1888); and Sheets and Williams, *Hurricane Watch*, 35–36.

41 **"American Storm Controversy":** Background for this controversy comes from Moore, *Weather Experiment*, 112–40; "Theory of Storms," *North American Review*, 335–71; Cox, *Storm Watchers*, 33–39; James Rodger Fleming, *Meteorology in America, 1800–1870* (Baltimore: Johns Hopkins University Press, 1990), 23–54; "Mr. Espy's Theory of Centripetal Storms," *Knickerbocker*, September 1839, 379; and Sheets and Williams, *Hurricane Watch*, 36–40.

41 **"Storm King":** Morehead, *Few Incidents in the Life*, 12, 15, 22; and Lee Sandlin, *Storm Kings: The Untold History of America's First Tornado Chasers* (New York: Pantheon Books, 2003), 55.

41 **"Meteorology has ever been":** Joseph Henry, "Meteorology," in *Report of the Commissioner of Patents for the Year 1858, Agriculture*, US Senate, ex. doc. no. 47 (Washington, DC: William A. Harris, 1859), 429.

41 **Colonel William Reid:** Background for Reid and his role in the hurricane debate comes from Reid, *Attempt to Develop the Law of Storms*; *Account of the Fatal Hurricane by Which Barbados Suffered in August 1831* (Bridgetown, Barbados: Samuel Hyde, 1831); Moore, *Weather Experiment*, 99–100, 109–12, 130–33; and "Colonel Reid's Law of Storms," *Spectator*, October 13, 1838, 973–74.

41 **a powerful hurricane devastated Barbados:** For background on this hurricane, see *Account of the Fatal Hurricane*; and Frederic William Naylor Bayley, *Four Years' Residence in the West Indies, during the Years 1826, 7, 8, and 9, by the Son of a Military Officer* (London: William Kidd, 1833), 710–11.

41 **"the agonizing shrieks of millions":** Andrew Halliday, *The West Indies: The Natural and Physical History of the Windward and Leeward Colonies* (London: John William Parker, 1837), 35.

41 **"their causes and mode of action":** Reid, *Attempt to Develop the Law of Storms*, 2.

42 **After reviewing the work:** "Statistics and Philosophy of Storms," *Edinburgh Review*, January 1839, 228.

42 **Englishman Henry Piddington:** A. K. Sen Sarma, "Henry Piddington (1797–1858): A Bicentennial Tribute," *Weather* 52, no. 6 (1997), 187–93.

43 **Piddington's intellectual meanderings:** Henry Piddington, "Researches on the Gale and Hurricane in the Bay of Bengal on the 3rd, 4th, and 5th of June, 1839; Being a First Memoir with Reference to the Theory of the Law of Storms in India," *Journal of the Asiatic Society*, July 1839, 559.

43 **he coined the word *cyclone*:** Piddington, *Sailor's Horn-Book*, 8.

43 **"to explain to the seaman":** Ibid., i.

44 **"are navigators mainly indebted":** Mathew C. Perry, "Introductory Note," in William C. Redfield, "Observations in Relation to the Cyclones of the Western Pacific: Embraced in a Communication to Commodore Perry," in *Narrative of*

the Expedition of an American Squadron to the China Seas and Japan, Performed in the Years 1852, 1853, and 1854, vol. 2, House of Representatives, doc. 97, 33d Congress, 2d Session (Washington, DC: A. O. P. Nicholson, 1856), 335.

44 **"should be remembered by seamen":** A. B. Becher, *The Storm Compass or, Seaman's Hurricane Companion* (London: J. D. Potter, 1853), 3.

44 **Espy launched his own tour:** Background for Espy's travels in Europe comes from Fleming, *Meteorology in America*, 49–50; and Moore, *Weather Experiment*, 138–39.

44 **"I hear from England":** Fleming, *Meteorology in America*, 50.

44 **France's Academy of Sciences:** Morehead, *Few Incidents in the Life*, 17; and James P. Espy, *Philosophy of Storms* (Boston: Charles C. Little and James Brown, 1841), xxxi–xxxix.

44 **"France has its Cuvier":** "Memoir of Professor Espy," *Dial*, April 1860, 259.

44 ***The Philosophy of Storms:*** Espy, *Philosophy of Storms*.

45 **"The earnest and deep convictions":** Alexander D. Bache, "Remarks," in *Annual Report of the Board of Regents of the Smithsonian Institution, Showing the Operations, Expenditures, and Condition of the Institution for the Year 1859*, US Senate, misc. doc. (Washington, DC: Thomas H. Ford, 1860), 110.

45 **"methodically monomaniac[al]":** John Quincy Adams, Entry for January 6, 1842, in *Memoirs of John Quincy Adams, Comprising Portions of His Diary from 1795 to 1848*, vol. 11, ed. Charles Francis Adams (Philadelphia: J. B. Lippincott, 1876), 52–53.

45 **Redfield died in 1857:** Moore, *Weather Experiment*, 224–25; and Sheets and Williams, *Hurricane Watch*, 37.

45 **William Ferrel:** Background for Ferrel and his insights into hurricanes comes from Cleveland Abbe, "Memoir of William Ferrel, 1817–1891," in *Biographical Memoirs*, vol. 3 (Washington, DC: National Academy of Sciences, 1895), 265–96; Fleming, *Meteorology in America*, 136–39; and Cox, *Storm Watchers*, 65–69.

46 **"If a body is moving in any direction":** William Ferrel, "The Influence of the Earth's Rotation upon the Relative Motion of Bodies near Its Surface," *Astronomical Journal*, January 20, 1858, 99. See also "An Essay on the Winds and the Currents of the Ocean," *Nashville Journal of Medicine and Surgery* 11 (1856), reprinted in "Popular Essay on the Movements of the Atmosphere," in *Professional Papers of the Signal Service* (Washington, DC: Office of the Chief Signal Officer, 1882), 7–19.

CHAPTER 3—SEEING INTO THE FUTURE

48 **"present state of the science of meteorology":** John Ruskin, "Remarks on the Present State of Meteorological Science," in *Transactions of the Meteorological Society*, vol. 1 (London: Smith, Elder, 1839), 56–59.

49 **"to trace the path of the tempest":** Ibid., 58.

49 **"The meteorologist is impotent":** Ibid.

49 **Samuel Finley Breese Morse:** Background for the following section about Morse's early life and the invention, reception, and growth of the electric telegraph comes from Kenneth Silverman, *Lightning Man: The Accursed Life of Samuel F. B. Morse* (New York: Alfred A. Knopf, 2003), 3–4, 8–13, 16–21, 29–32, 40–42, 58–59, 67, 73–74, 79–80, 97–128, 143–44, 147–273; Daniel Walker Howe, *What Hath God Wrought: The Transformation of America, 1815–1848* (New York: Oxford University Press, 2007), 690–94; Tom Standage, *The Victorian Internet: The*

Remarkable Story of the Telegraph and the Nineteenth Century's On-line Pioneers (New York: Walker, 1998), 25–66; and Mark Lloyd, *Prologue to a Farce: Communication and Democracy in America* (Urbana: University of Illinois Press, 2006), 46–49.

50 **"to promote the fine arts":** Steven Lubar, *Inside the Lost Museum: Curating, Past and Present* (Cambridge, MA: Harvard University Press, 2017), 287.

52 **"3 cheers" for Polk:** Silverman, *Lightning Man*, 238.

52 **"Highway of Thought":** Andrew Delap, "The Electro-Magnetic Telegraph," in *The People's Journal*, vol. 2, ed. John Saunders (London: People's Journal Office, 1847), 210.

52 **"annihilated space and time":** Silverman, *Lightning Man*, 240; and William Robertson, *The History of America: Including the United States*, vol. 2 (New York: Blakeman and Mason, 1859), 1127.

52 **"with *lightning speed*":** "Morse's Electro-Magnetic Telegraph," *Pittsfield Sun*, June 6, 1844.

53 **"Lightning Man":** Silverman, *Lightning Man*, 244.

53 **"In the Atlantic ports":** William C. Redfield, "On Three Several Hurricanes of the American Seas and Their Relations to the Northers, So Called, of the Gulf of Mexico and the Bay of Honduras, with Charts Illustrating the Same," *American Journal of Science and Arts*, November 1846, 344.

53 **"The citizens of the United States":** Joseph Henry, "Explanations and Illustrations of the Plan of the Smithsonian Institution," *American Journal of Science and Arts*, 2nd series, November 1848, 316; and Cleveland Abbe, "Historical Notes on the Systems of Weather Telegraphy, and Especially Their Development in the United States," *American Journal of Science and Arts*, August 1871, 84.

54 **He soon reached out:** Joseph Henry, "Annual Report of the Secretary," in *Fourth Annual Report of the Board of Regents of the Smithsonian Institution to the Senate and House of Representatives*, 31st Congress, 1st Session (Washington, DC: Printer to the Senate, 1850), 15; and Samuel Pierpont Langley, "The Meteorological Work of the Smithsonian Institution," *American Meteorological Journal*, January 1894, 374–75.

54 **With this rudimentary system:** James Rodger Fleming, *Meteorology in America, 1800–1870* (Baltimore: Johns Hopkins University Press, 1990), 143–45; and Joseph Henry, "Report of the Secretary for 1858," in *Annual Report of the Board of Regents of the Smithsonian Institution*, 35th Congress, 2d Session, misc. doc. 57 (Washington, DC: James B. Steedman, 1859), 32.

55 **"Yesterday, there was a severe storm":** "The Weather," *Washington Evening Star*, May 7, 1857.

55 **Henry's interest was not only:** Fleming, *Meteorology in America*, 75–93; and David Laskin, *Braving the Elements: The Stormy History of American Weather* (New York: Anchor, 1997), 141–42.

55 **Henry's ultimate goal—to marry . . . not only weather reporting but also forecasting:** Fleming, *Meteorology in America*, 141–50.

56 **That finally happened on February 9:** Ibid., 150–56; Donald R. Whitnah, *A History of the United States Weather Bureau* (Urbana: University of Illinois Press, 1965), 15–19; Bob Sheets and Jack Williams, *Hurricane Watch: Forecasting the Deadliest Storms on Earth* (New York: Vintage Books, 2001), 44–46; and W. J. Humphreys, *Biographical Memoir of Cleveland Abbe, 1838–1916* (Washington, DC: National Academy of Sciences, 1919), 474–77.

57 **The corps issued its first:** Sheets and Williams, *Hurricane Watch*, 45; Laskin,

Braving the Elements, 142–43; Mark Monmonier, *Air Apparent: How Meteorologists Learned to Map, Predict, and Dramatize the Weather* (Chicago: University of Chicago Press, 1999), 50–52; and Ivan Ray Tannehill, *Hurricanes: Their Nature and History* (New York: Greenwood Press, 1938), 7–8.

58 **Despite the high hopes:** Whitnah, *History of the United States Weather Bureau*, 23–29.

58 **The army's most embarrassing:** Jamie L. Pietruska, "US Weather Bureau Chief Willis Moore and the Reimagination of Uncertainty in Long-Range Forecasting," *Environment and History*, February 2011, 82.

58 **"Fresh to brisk easterly winds":** "U.S. Daily Weather Maps," March 11, 1888—7 A.M., NOAA Central Library, accessed June 2018, https://library.noaa.gov/Collections/Digital-Collections/US-Daily-Weather-Maps.

58 **Instead of fair weather:** Mary Cable, *The Blizzard of '88* (New York: Atheneum, 1988); and Judd Caplovich, *Blizzard: The Great Storm of 88* (Vernon, CT: Vero, 1987).

58 **Beyond these highly publicized:** Isaac Monroe Cline, *Storms, Floods and Sunshine: A Book of Memoirs* (New Orleans: Pelican, 1945), 65–66.

58 **But the most serious:** Whitnah, *History of the United States Weather Bureau*, 43–58.

58 **Throughout this period:** Sheets and Williams, *Hurricane Watch*, 46–47; Whitnah, *A History of the United States*, 31–32; and Raymond Arsenault, "The Public Storm: Hurricanes and the State in Twentieth-Century America," in *American Public Life and the Historical Imagination*, ed. Wendy Gamber, Michael Grossberg, and Hendrik Hartog (Notre Dame, IN: University of Notre Dame Press, 2003), 267.

59 **Nevertheless, the corps did issue:** Jack Williams, "When Storms Were a Surprise: A History of Hurricane Warnings," *Washington Post*, August 16, 2013; Tannehill, *Hurricanes*, 112; and Robert C. Sheets, "The National Hurricane Center—Past, Present, and Future," *Weather and Forecasting*, June 1990, 190.

60 **Viñes was born in 1837:** Background for this section on Viñes, including the quotes attributed to him, comes from Luis E. Ramos Guadalupe, *Father Benito Viñes: The 19th-Century Life and Contributions of a Cuban Hurricane Observer and Scientist*, trans. Oswaldo Garcia (Boston: American Meteorological Society, 2014), 1–7, 55–64.

60 **As a man of the cloth:** Jefferson B. Browne, *Key West: The Old and the New* (St. Augustine, FL: Record Company, 1912), 156.

60 **When Viñes took over:** Guadalupe, *Father Benito Viñes*, 6–21.

61 **"cat's tails," "cock's plumes":** Ralph Abercromby, "On the Relation between Tropical and Extra-tropical Cyclones," *Proceedings of the Royal Society of London*, November 17, 1887–April 12, 1888, 20; and Marjory Stoneman Douglas, *Hurricane* (New York: Rinehart, 1958), 236.

61 **Like a maestro:** Guadalupe, *Father Benito Viñes*, 71–105; Benito Viñes, *Practical Hints in Regard to West Indian Hurricanes*, trans. George L. Dyer (Washington, DC: Government Printing Office, 1885); and Sheets and Williams, *Hurricane Watch*, 47–51.

62 **"successful forecasts were almost certainly":** Sheets and Williams, *Hurricane Watch*, 48.

62 **Two years later, Adolphus Greely:** Guadalupe, *Father Benito Viñes*, 126–27.

62 **Early in 1893, Viñes received:** Ibid., 144–47.

63 **During the third week of August 1893:** Cleveland Abbe, ed., *Monthly Weather Review*, vol. 21, no. 8 (August 1893): 205–7.

63 **"The Midnight Storm":** Eric S. Blake, Christopher W. Landsea, and Ethan J. Gibney, "The Deadliest, Costliest, and Most Intense United States Tropical Cyclones from 1851 to 2010 (and Other Frequently Requested Hurricane Facts)," NOAA Technical Memorandum NWS NHC-6, August 2011, 43. See also Abbe, *Monthly Weather Review*, 207.

63 **For several days prior:** "U.S. Daily Weather Maps," August 23, 1893—Forecast till 8 P.M. Thursday, accessed June 2018.

63 **"northwesterly winds" and "light rain":** "U.S. Daily Weather Maps," August 23, 1893—8 P.M., accessed June 2018; and Abbe, *Monthly Weather Review*, 205–7.

63 **"almost unexampled fury":** "Swept by Wind and Rain," *NYT*, August 25, 1893.

63 **Hundreds of chimneys:** "Storm on Long Island," *NYT*, August 25, 1893; "Great Loss at Coney Island," *NYT*, August 25, 1893; and "Swept by Wind and Rain," *NYT*.

63 **In Central Park, "more than":** "Swept by Wind and Rain," *NYT*.

64 **"dashed upon the shore":** "Storm on Long Island," *NYT*. See also "Many Sailors' Lives Lost," *NYT*, August 25, 1893.

64 **Thirty-four sailors died:** "Many Sailors' Lives Lost," *NYT*.

64 **The hurricane nearly obliterated:** Background for what transpired on Hog Island during the hurricane, and thereafter, comes from Alfred H. Bellot, *History of the Rockaways from the Year 1685 to 1917* (Far Rockaway, NY: Bellot's Histories, 1917), 94–95; "Damage on Long Island," *NYT*, August 26, 1893; Norimitsu Onishi, "Queens Spit Tried to Be a Resort but Sank in a Hurricane," *NYT*, March 18, 1997; and "What Really Happened to Hog Island?" *From the Stacks* (blog), New York Historical Society, August 31, 2011, http://blog.nyhistory.org/what -really-happened-to-hog-island.

64 **With no vessel in sight:** "Damage on Long Island," *NYT*.

65 **"forensic hurricanologist":** Onishi, "Queens Spit Tried to Be a Resort."

65 **While the people of New York City:** Background for this section on the Sea Islands Hurricane of 1893 comes from Joel Chandler Harris, "The Sea Island Hurricanes, the Devastation," *Scribner's Magazine*, February 1894, 229–47; Joel Chandler Harris, "The Sea Island Hurricanes, the Relief," *Scribner's Magazine*, March 1894, 267–84; William Marscher and Fran Marscher, *The Great Sea Island Storm of 1893* (Macon, GA: Mercer University Press, 2004), 1–19; Clara Barton, *A Story of the Red Cross: Glimpses of Field Work* (New York: D. Appleton, 1917), 77–93; Blake et al., "Deadliest, Costliest," 7; Marian Moser Jones, "Race, Class and Gender in Clara Barton's Late Nineteenth-Century Disaster Relief," *Environment and History*, February 2001, 107–31; Tom Rubillo, *Hurricane Destruction in South Carolina* (Charleston, SC: History Press, 2006), 99–103; "Sea Islands Overwhelmed," *NYT*, September 3, 1893; "Gov. Tillman's Anxiety," *NYT*, September 3, 1893; "In a Death-Dealing Wind," *NYT*, August 29, 1893; "Georgia Resort in Ruins," *NYT*, September 5, 1893; and Joey Holleman, "1893 Storm Killed Hundreds in S.C.," *State*, September 14, 1999.

65 **On Friday morning, August 25:** "U.S. Daily Weather Maps," August 25, 1893—8 A.M., and August 25, 1893—8 P.M., both accessed June 2018.

65 **The following day, the bureau:** "U.S. Daily Weather Maps," August 26, 1893—8 P.M., accessed June 2018; Abbe, *Monthly Weather Review*, 207–8; and Sheets and Williams, *Hurricane Watch*, 53.

65 **On Sunday morning, the bureau:** "U.S. Daily Weather Maps," August 27, 1893, 8 A.M., and August 27, 1893, 8 P.M., both accessed June 2018; and "Forecast by the Weather Men," *NYT*, August 30, 1893.

65 **Although a few brief notices:** Marscher and Marscher, *Great Sea Island Storm of 1893*, 16–18.

66 **"seemed to revel in the destruction":** Rubillo, *Hurricane Destruction*, 99.

66 **The profile of the islands:** W. C. Gannett, "The August Storm at the Sea Islands," *Unity*, November 16, 1893, 163.

66 **They also provided most:** Shepherd W. McKinley, "Phosphate: 1870–1925," *South Carolina Encyclopedia*, June 20, 2016, http://www.scencyclopedia.org/sce /entries/phosphate.

67 **"When the tide rose on the 27th":** Gannett, "August Storm at the Sea Islands," 163.

67 **As historian Marian Moser Jones:** Jones, "Race, Class and Gender," 119–26.

67 **"The Angel of the Battlefield":** Lucy Larcom, "Clara Barton," in *Our Famous Women: An Authorized Record of the Lives and Deeds of Distinguished American Women of Our Times* (Hartford, CT: A. D. Worthington, 1884), 104.

68 **"It is a great undertaking":** Clara Barton, Diary Entry for Friday, September 29, 1893, in *Clara Barton Papers: Diaries and Journals: 1893, May–1894, May*, Library of Congress, Manuscript/Mixed Material, https://www.loc.gov/item/mss119730041.

69 **"I had desired to do more":** Barton, *Story of the Red Cross*, 92.

69 **Thus, the Red Cross's intervention:** Elizabeth Brown Pryor, *Clara Barton: Professional Angel* (Philadelphia: University of Pennsylvania Press, 1987), 279.

69 **Dunbar Davis:** Background for Dunbar Davis comes from David Stick, *Graveyard of the Atlantic: Shipwrecks of the North Carolina Coast* (Chapel Hill: University of North Carolina Press, 1952), 133–43; and "Dunbar Davis Did His Duty: The Incredible Achievement of One Man in the Historic Hurricane of 1893," *State*, October 14, 1961, 9.

70 **"By this time I was getting":** Stick, *Graveyard of the Atlantic*, 142.

71 **Eight of them sank:** Ibid., 135–36.

71 **After a particularly active August:** Mark W. Harrington, ed., *Monthly Weather Review*, vol. 21, no. 9 (September 1893).

71 **The first blow was a sneak attack:** Background for this section on the hurricane that hit the Louisiana, Mississippi, and Alabama coast comes from Blake et al., "Deadliest, Costliest," 7, 43; Rose C. Falls, *Cheniere Caminada, or The Wind of Death: The Story of the Storm in Louisiana* (New Orleans: Hopkins Printing, 1893); "Swept by an Ocean Wave," *NYT*, October 5, 1893; E. Charles Plaisance, "Chénière: The Destruction of a Community," *Louisiana History*, Spring 1973, 179–85; Donald W. Davis, "Cheniere Caminada and the Hurricane of 1893," in *Coastal Zone '93: Proceedings of the Eighth Symposium on Coastal and Ocean Management*, vol. 2, ed. Orville T. Magoon, W. Stanley Wilson, Hugh Converse, and L. Thomas Tobin (New York: American Society of Civil Engineers, 1993), 2256–69; Barbara C. Ewell and Pamela Glenn Menke, "'The Awakening' and the Great October Storm of 1893," *Southern Literary Journal*, Spring 2010, 1–5; Christie Mathern Hall, "Cheniere Caminada's Great October Storm," *Country Roads*, September 27, 2016, https:// countryroadsmagazine.com/art-and-culture/history/chenier-caminadas-great -october-storm; and "The Storm of Death," *Colfax Chronicle*, October 7, 1893.

71 **"fair, preceded by light showers":** "U.S. Daily Weather Maps," September 30, 1893, 8 P.M., accessed September 26, 2018.

71 **"This will be the last time":** Falls, *Cheniere Caminada*, 5.

72 **"hurricane advanced suddenly and unexpectedly":** Mark W. Harrington, ed., *Monthly Weather Review*, vol. 21, no. 10 (October 1893): 272. See also Sheets and Williams, *Hurricane Watch*, 57.

72 **"holding onto the sill":** Falls, *Cheniere Caminada*, 8.

72 **"brave and sturdy men":** Ibid., 9.

73 **"696 only are now living":** Ibid., 8.

74 **The final hurricane of the 1893:** Harrington, *Monthly Weather Review*, October 1893, 274–75; Sheets and Williams, *Hurricane Watch*, 57; and Walter J. Fraser, *Hurricanes: Three Centuries of Storms at Sea and Ashore* (Athens: University of Georgia Press, 2006), 184–87.

74 **Although more reporting stations:** Sheets, "National Hurricane Center," 190, 194; and Edgar B. Calvert, "The Hurricane Warning Service and Its Reorganization," *MWR*, March 1935, 86.

75 **In the months leading up:** Background for this section on Moore and the president, as well as the two quotes, comes from Willis Luther Moore, "I Am Thinking of Hurricanes," *American Mercury*, September 1927, 81–86.

75 **In addition, other observation:** Ivan Ray Tannehill, *The Hurricane Hunters* (New York: Dodd, Mead, 1956), 57–58; and Calvert, "Hurricane Warning Service," 86.

CHAPTER 4—OBLITERATED

78 **"The sky seemed to be made":** Herbert Molloy Mason Jr., *Death from the Sea: The Galveston Hurricane of 1900* (New York: Dial Press, 1972), 78–79.

78 **The storm that would hit:** Background for this section on the Galveston Hurricane comes from Erik Larson, *Isaac's Storm: A Man, a Time, and the Deadliest Hurricane in History* (New York: Vintage Books, 1999); Mason, *Death from the Sea*; Isaac Monroe Cline, *Storms, Floods and Sunshine: A Book of Memoirs* (New Orleans: Pelican, 1945); Clarence Ousley, *Galveston in Nineteen Hundred* (Atlanta: William C. Chase, 1900); Murat Halstead, *Galveston: The Horrors of a Stricken City* ([Chicago]: American Publishers Association, 1900); John Edward Weems, "The Galveston Storm of 1900," *Southwestern Historical Quarterly*, April 1958, 494–507; Kerry Emanuel, *Divine Wind: The History and Science of Hurricanes* (New York: Oxford University Press, 2005), 83–90; and William H. Thiesen, "Saving Lives during America's Deadliest Disaster," *Naval History*, December 2012, 46–52.

78 **In the wake of the hurricane:** Isaac M. Cline, "West India Hurricanes," *Galveston Daily News*, July 16, 1891.

78 **Cline was born in Monroe County:** Background for Cline's early years and stationing in Galveston comes from Larson, *Isaac's Storm*, 28–31, 57–69; and Mason, *Death from the Sea*, 61–63.

80 **Upon this rather unimpressive:** Background for this section about Galveston's beginnings up through the time of Jean Lafitte comes from Donald Willett, "Cannibals and Pirates: The First Inhabitants of Galveston," in *Galveston Chronicles: The Queen City of the Gulf*, ed. Donald Willett (Charleston, SC: History Press, 2013), 1–10; Mason, *Death from the Sea*, 22–29, 89; David Roth, *Texas Hurricane History* (Camp Springs, MD: NWS, last updated January 17, 2010), 13–14; and W. T. Block, "Texas Hurricanes of the 19th Century: Killer Storms Devastated Coastline," *Beaumont Enterprise*, February 19, 1978.

81 **In 1842, Galveston was hit:** Mason, *Death from the Sea*, 38–39; and Roth, *Texas Hurricane History*, 15.

81 **"The tremendous hurricane":** Mrs. Houstoun, "Texas and the Gulf of Mexico;

or, Yachting in the New World," *Smith's Weekly Volume for Town & Country*, February 12, 1845, 127. See also Mason, *Death from the Sea*, 36–38.

81 **In 1845 the Republic of Texas:** Edward Coyle Sealy, "Galveston Wharves," *Handbook of Texas Online*, accessed August 2018, http://www.tshaonline.org /handbook/online/articles/etg01; L. Tuffy Ellis, "The Revolutionizing of the Texas Cotton Trade, 1865–1885," *Southwestern Historical Quarterly*, April 1970, 478; and Mason, *Death from the Sea*, 52–54.

81 **When readers of the *Galveston Daily News*:** Cline, "West India Hurricanes."

82 **Nothing in the current:** John D. Cox, *Storm Watchers: The Turbulent History of Weather Prediction from Franklin's Kite to El Nino* (New York: John Wiley, 2002), 118–21.

82 **Furthermore, when it came to:** "Western Gulf of Mexico Tropical Cyclones from 1851 to 2014," NWS, accessed August 2018, https://www.weather.gov/crp /tropical_cyclone_tracks.

82 **Had Cline looked further back:** Mason, *Death from the Sea*, 27, 38–39, 66–67; Eric S. Blake, Christopher W. Landsea, and Ethan J. Gibney, "The Deadliest, Costliest, and Most Intense United States Tropical Cyclones from 1851 to 2010 (and Other Frequently Requested Hurricane Facts)," NOAA Technical Memorandum NWS NHC-6, August 2011, 42–43; and Roth, *Texas Hurricane History*, 8–9.

82 **In addition to the hurricanes:** David Ludlum, *Early American Hurricanes: 1492–1870* (Boston: American Meteorological Society, 1963), 179–82; and Roth, *Texas Hurricane History*, 18–19.

83 **"What would happen," he asked:** Roth, *Texas Hurricane History*, 19.

83 **A hurricane that destroyed Isle Dernière:** Abby Sallenger, *Island in a Storm: A Rising Sea, a Vanishing Coast, and a Nineteenth-Century Disaster That Warns of a Warmer World* (New York: Public Affairs, 2009).

83 **"In each of these two cases":** Cline, "West India Hurricanes."

83 **Both of these so-called accidental:** General background for the two hurricanes to hit Indianola comes from Larson, *Isaac's Storm*, 81–83; Mason, *Death from the Sea*, 71–72; A. W. Greeley, "Hurricanes on the Coast of Texas," *National Geographic Magazine*, November 1900; and Ivan Ray Tannehill, *Hurricanes: Their Nature and History* (New York: Greenwood Press, 1938), 34–36.

83 **on September 16, 1875:** "Telegraphic, the Equinoctal Storm," *Dallas Daily Herald*, September 22, 1875; "Texas Coast Disasters," *NYT*, September 22, 1875; "The Texas Cyclone," *NYT*, September 23, 1875; and "Galveston under Water," *NYT*, September 21, 1875.

84 **"We are destitute," he wrote:** "Texas Coast Disasters," *NYT*.

84 **Indianola partially rose:** "State News," *Brenham Weekly Banner*, August 26, 1886; "Indianola and Galveston," *Austin Weekly Statesman*, August 26, 1886; "A Gale from the Gulf," *Fort Worth Daily Gazette*, August 21, 1886; "Indianola," *Austin Weekly Statesman*, August 26, 1886; and Joe Holley, "A Texas Ghost Town Yields Hard Hurricane Lessons," *Houston Chronicle*, September 22, 2017.

84 **"Take it all in all":** "Indianola and Galveston," *Austin Weekly Statesman*.

85 **"When men such as these" . . . "and they didn't build":** Mason, *Death from the Sea*, 74.

85 **"If Galveston had any":** Larson, *Isaac's Storm*, 84.

85 **"The opinion held by some":** Cline, "West India Hurricanes."

85 **Confident in their future . . . souvenirs were always for sale:** Larson, *Isaac's Storm*, 12–13; Mason, *Death from the Sea*, 16–17, 21, 52–58, 81–82; Ousley, *Gal-*

veston in Nineteen Hundred, 63, 151, 158–63; Halstead, *Galveston: The Horrors*, 39–49; and Denise Alexander, *Galveston's Historic Downtown and Strand District* (Charleston, SC: Arcadia, 2010), 123.

86 **It boasted more millionaires:** Larson, *Isaac's Storm*, 13.

86 **"Wall Street of the Southwest":** Paul Burka, "Grande Dame of the Gulf," *Texas Monthly*, December 1983, https://www.texasmonthly.com/articles/grande-dame-of-the-gulf. See also Larson, *Isaac's Storm*, 12.

87 **The first notice of the disturbance . . . north of Cuba:** Larson, *Isaac's Storm*, 36, 56, 78, 87–89, 108; "U.S. Daily Weather Maps," September 5, 1900—8 A. M., NOAA Central Library, accessed August 2018, https://library.noaa.gov/Collections/Digital-Collections/US-Daily-Weather-Maps; and Anya Krugovoy Silver, *Hurricanes of the Gulf of Mexico* (Baton Rouge: Louisiana State University, 2010), 4–5.

87 **"moderate breeze":** Larson, *Isaac's Storm*, 36.

87 **The bureau claimed that the storm:** Larson, *Isaac's Storm*, 111–14, 122; and "U.S. Daily Weather Maps," September 6, 1900—8 A. M., accessed August 2018.

87 **Still, the bureau felt:** Larson, *Isaac's Storm*, 9–10, 127, 132–34; "U.S. Daily Weather Maps," September 7, 1900—8 A. M., accessed August 2018; and Silver, *Hurricanes of the Gulf*, 5–6.

87 **In his 1899 report to Congress:** Willis L. Moore, *Report of the Chief of the Weather Bureau, 1898–99*, vol. 1 (Washington, DC: Government Printing Office, 1900), 8. See also Walter M. Drum, "The Pioneer Forecasters of Hurricanes," *Messenger*, June 1905, 613–14.

88 **This was simply not true:** Larson, *Isaac's Storm*, 102–6; and Stuart B. Schwartz, *Sea of Storms: A History of Hurricanes in the Greater Caribbean from Columbus to Katrina* (Princeton, NJ: Princeton University Press, 2015), 216–17.

88 **To put an end to Cuba's:** Larson, *Isaac's Storm*, 102–6; and Cox, *Storm Watchers*, 120.

88 **"an extraordinary contempt for the public":** Larson, *Isaac's Storm*, 106.

88 **Had the Americans listened:** Ibid., 107–8, 111, 133.

89 **The following day, Father Lorenzo Gangoite:** Marjory Stoneman Douglas, *Hurricane* (New York: Rinehart, 1958), 244, 254.

89 **He was right about Texas:** Larson, *Isaac's Storm*, 134.

89 **On Friday morning at 9:35:** Ibid., 9, 15, 127.

89 **"In some obscure way":** Joseph L. Cline, *When the Heavens Frowned* (1946; repr., Gretna, LA: Pelican, 2000), 48.

90 **"Unusually heavy swells":** E. B. Garriott, "Forecasts and Warnings," *MWR*, September 1900, 373. See also Larson, *Isaac's Storm*, 5–15.

90 **"usual signs which herald":** Garriott, "Forecasts and Warnings," 372.

90 **According to Isaac's own account:** Cline, *Storms, Floods and Sunshine*, 93.

90 **"I assumed authority":** Ibid., 98.

90 **"some 6,000 lives":** Ibid., 93–94.

90 **In Larson's convincing history:** Larson, *Isaac's Storm*, 167–68.

90 **The scene at the beach:** Ibid., 141–42; and Silver, *Hurricanes of the Gulf*, 1, 8.

91 **"advising him of the terrible situation":** Cline, *Storms, Floods and Sunshine*, 93–94.

91 **Wading through fast-surging water:** "Houston, Texas, Sept. 8," *NYT*, September 9, 1900; and Cline, *When the Heavens Frowned*, 50–51.

91 **"already covered the island":** Cline, *Storms, Floods and Sunshine*, 95.

92 **In his 1891 article, Isaac:** Cline, "West India Hurricanes."

92 **He and his fellow meteorologists . . . to the north, across the bay:** For back-

ground on these hurricane-ocean dynamics, see Bob Sheets and Jack Williams, *Hurricane Watch: Forecasting the Deadliest Storms on Earth* (New York: Vintage Books, 2001), 71–77; and Gordon E. Dunn and Banner I. Miller, *Atlantic Hurricanes* (Baton Rouge: Louisiana State University Press, 1964), 206–22.

93 **In deeper water, gravity:** Sheets and Williams, *Hurricane Watch*, 73.

93 **it crashed into the Texas coast:** Larson, *Isaac's Storm*, 197.

93 **Certain other factors unknown:** Emanuel, *Divine Wind*, 88–89; and Bryan Norcross, personal communication, May 23, 2019.

94 **"The people of Galveston were like rats":** Halstead, *Galveston: The Horrors*, 77–78.

94 **When Isaac got home:** Background for this section on the travails of Isaac and his family during the hurricane comes from Cline, *Storms, Floods and Sunshine*, 95–97; Cline, *When the Heavens Frowned*, 52–62; Larson, *Isaac's Storm*, 171–72, 188–92, 204–5, 210, 217–20; and Mason, *Death from the Sea*, 132–34.

94 **its lowest barometric reading being 27.64:** Blake et al., "Deadliest, Costliest," 13.

94 **"suicidal to attempt to journey":** Garriott, "Forecasts and Warnings," 373.

94 **Furthermore, Cora was pregnant:** Cline, *When the Heavens Frowned*, 52.

94 **At its peak that evening:** "The Galveston Hurricane of 1900," National Ocean Service, accessed August 2018, https://oceanservice.noaa.gov/news/features/sep13/galveston.html; Sheets and Williams, *Hurricane Watch*, 64; and Norcross, personal communication.

95 **"useless to fight for life":** Cline, *Storms, Floods and Sunshine*, 96.

96 **"While being carried forward":** Ibid., 97.

97 **"Even in death":** Ibid., 98.

97 **The crowd at Ritter's Café:** Background for this section comes from Mason, *Death from the Sea*, 108–9; Larson, *Isaac's Storm*, 158–59; and Halstead, *Galveston: The Horrors*, 87.

97 **"You can't frighten me":** Mason, *Death from the Sea*, 108.

97 **St. Mary's Orphanage was almost:** Background for this section on what happened at the orphanage comes from Mason, *Death from the Sea*, 148–51; Larson, *Isaac's Storm*, 212–13; and Paul Lester, *The Great Galveston Disaster* (Philadelphia: Globe Bible, 1900), 355–56.

98 **Finally, the elements won:** Lester, *Great Galveston Disaster*, 355–56.

98 **After the hurricane had passed:** Larson, *Isaac's Storm*, 213.

98 **"a most beautiful day":** Cline, *Storms, Floods and Sunshine*, 97–98.

98 **"revealed one of the most horrible":** Garriott, "Forecasts and Warnings," 374.

99 **The cost of the damage was pegged:** Ousley, *Galveston in Nineteen Hundred*, 17, 32; and Garriott, "Forecasts and Warnings," 371.

99 **Dead and mangled bodies:** Larson, *Isaac's Storm*, 264–65; Mason, *Death from the Sea*, 221; Garriott, "Forecasts and Warnings," 374; "Many Towns Wrecked," *NYT*, September 10, 1900; "Number of Dead May Reach 10,000," *NYT*, September 11, 1900; "The Wrecking of Galveston," *NYT*, September 11, 1900; "Houston, Texas, Sept. 11," *NYT*, September 12, 1900; and Ousley, *Galveston in Nineteen Hundred*, 291.

99 **Martial law was declared:** "Martial Law in Galveston," *NYT*, September 12, 1900.

101 **"Thousands of dead in the streets":** Halstead, *Galveston: The Horrors*, 142–44.

102 **"ghouls [who] were holding":** See, for example, "Ghouls Shot on Sight," *NYT*, September 13, 1900; "Ghoulish," *Lexington Dispatch*, September 19, 1900;

"Storm's Victims Number 10,000," *Virginian–Pilot*, September 13, 1900; and Halstead, *Galveston: The Horrors*, 96–99.

103 **"Diligent inquiry fails to discover":** Ousley, *Galveston in Nineteen Hundred*, 37.

103 **"The tale is too dreadful to recall":** Clara Barton, *A Story of the Red Cross: Glimpses of Field Work* (New York: D. Appleton, 1917), 166.

103 **"sincerely hope[d] that Galveston":** "Kaiser Sends Condolences," *NYT*, September 18, 1900.

103 **It took ten years, but they did it:** "Galveston Seawall and Grade Raising Project," American Society of Civil Engineers, accessed August 2018, https://www .asce.org/project/galveston-seawall-and-grade-raising-project.

104 **The first major test of Galveston's:** H. C. Frankenfield, "The Tropical Storm of August 10, 1915," *MWR*, August 1915, 405–12; "Galveston's Problem," *NYT*, August 21, 1915; and Henry M. Robert, "A Sea Wall's Efficiency," *NYT*, August 24, 1915.

105 **"nothing more could have been done":** Cline, *Storms, Floods and Sunshine*, 99. See also Larson, *Isaac's Storm*, 267–71.

105 **"The practical utility of":** "The Weather and Its Prophets," *Houston Daily Post*, September 14, 1900.

105 **He lied and said that warnings:** Willis L. Moore, "The Late Hurricane," *Houston Post*, September 28, 1900.

106 **"the excellent service rendered":** Garriott, "Forecasts and Warnings," 376.

106 **"The value of the Weather Bureau's":** Ibid.

CHAPTER 5—DEATH AND DESTRUCTION IN THE SUNSHINE STATE

107 **The first three and a half decades ... even that was of mixed value:** Bob Sheets and Jack Williams, *Hurricane Watch: Forecasting the Deadliest Storms on Earth* (New York: Vintage Books, 2001), 74–84; Robert C. Sheets, "The National Hurricane Center—Past, Present, and Future," *Weather and Forecasting*, June 1990, 194–95; Science Advisory Board, *Report of the Science Advisory Board, July 31, 1933 to September 1, 1934* (Washington, DC: Government Printing Office, 1934), 54; Edgar B. Calvert, "The Hurricane Warning Service and Its Reorganization," *MWR*, March 1935, 86; Donald R. Whitnah, *A History of the United States Weather Bureau* (Urbana: University of Illinois Press, 1965), 95, 133–35; Lourdes B. Avilés, *Taken by Storm 1938: A Social and Meteorological History of the Great New England Hurricane* (Boston: American Meteorological Society, 2013), 74; Edward N. Rappaport and Robert H. Simpson, "Impact of Technologies from Two World Wars," in *Hurricanes: Coping with Disaster*, ed. Robert Simpson (Washington, DC: American Geophysical Union, 2003), 39, 41, 45–48; and Raymond Arsenault, "The Public Storm: Hurricanes and the State in Twentieth-Century America," in *American Public Life and the Historical Imagination*, ed. Wendy Gamber, Michael Grossberg, and Hendrik Hartog (Notre Dame, IN: University of Notre Dame Press, 2003), 270.

109 **"In taking advantage of the wonderful":** "Wireless Telegraph Message from President to King," *Electrical World and Engineer*, January 24, 1903, 161.

109 **the steamship *Cartago*:** E. B. Garriott, "Weather, Forecasts, and Warnings for the Month," *MWR*, August 1909, 539. See also Ivan Ray Tannehill, *Hurricanes: Their Nature and History* (New York: Greenwood Press, 1938), 8–9.

109 **"Had it not been for the warnings":** Garriott, "Weather, Forecasts, and Warnings," 539.

109 **indeed, many ships were spared:** "Radios from Arctic to Help American Business," *BAMS*, June 1922.

109 **That very reasonable urge:** Ivan Ray Tannehill, *The Hurricane Hunters* (New York: Dodd, Mead, 1956), 59–60, 67–69.

110 **"Vessel masters soon learned":** Ibid., 69–70.

110 **the United States was pummeled:** Christopher R. Landsea, "Subject: E23) What Is the Complete List of Continental U.S. Landfalling Hurricanes?" HRD, Frequently Asked Questions, last revised July 31, 2018, https://www.aoml.noaa.gov/hrd/tcfaq/E23.html.

110 **Henry Morrison Flagler:** Background for this section on Flagler and his role in the creation of Miami comes from Les Standiford, *Last Train to Paradise: Henry Flagler and the Spectacular Rise and Fall of the Railroad That Crossed an Ocean* (New York: Broadway Paperbacks, 2002), 35–68, 201–2; Ida M. Tarbell, *The History of the Standard Oil Company*, vol. 1 (New York: McClure, Phillips, 1904), 44; Learning Network, "May 15, 1911/Supreme Court Orders Standard Oil to be Broken Up," *NYT*, May 15, 2012, https://learning.blogs.nytimes.com/2012/05/15/may-15-1911-supreme-court-orders-standard-oil-to-be-broken-up; Arva Moore Parks, *Miami: The Magic City* (Miami: Centennial Press, 1991), 60–65, 106–20; and Polly Redford, *Billion-Dollar Sandbar: A Biography of Miami Beach* (New York: E. P. Dutton, 1970), 27–32.

112 **"Mayaimi," the name:** Marjory Stoneman Douglas, *The Everglades: River of Grass* (1947; repr., Sarasota, FL: Pineapple Press, 1997), 68.

112 **Between 1900 and 1910:** James J. Carney, "Population Growth in Miami and Dade County, Florida," *Tequesta*, 1946, 54; and Redford, *Billion-Dollar Sandbar*, 33–165.

112 **In 1925 alone, $60 million's worth:** Jay Barnes, *Florida's Hurricane History* (Chapel Hill: University of North Carolina Press, 2007), 111; and Frederick Lewis Allen, *Only Yesterday: An Informal History of the Nineteen-Twenties* (New York: Harper & Brothers, 1931), 271.

112 **Properties changed hands at lightning speed:** Paul S. George, "Brokers, Binders, and Builders: Greater Miami's Boom of the Mid-1920s," *Florida Historical Quarterly*, July 1986, 27–51.

112 **Miami's prosperity bubbled over:** Ted Steinberg, *Acts of God: The Unnatural History of Natural Disaster in America* (New York: Oxford University Press, 2000), 50; Seth Bramson, *Images of America: Miami Beach* (Charleston, SC: Arcadia, 2005), 7–8; Kyle Munzenreider, "100 Years: The Dark and Dirty History of Miami Beach," *Miami New Times*, March 26, 2015; and Allen, *Only Yesterday*, 270–79.

113 **"a real estate theme park":** Steinberg, *Acts of God*, 50.

113 **"the world's playground":** Allen, *Only Yesterday*, 278.

113 **"Magic City":** Connie Ogle, "Why Is Miami Called the Magic City? Here's the Real Story," *MH*, December 5, 2017.

113 **It weighed a hefty 7½ pounds:** Ibid., 278; and Eliot Kleinberg, *Black Cloud: The Great Florida Hurricane of 1928* (New York: Carroll & Graf, 2003), 26.

113 **"The Florida boom was the first":** John Kenneth Galbraith, *The Great Crash 1929* (1954; repr., Boston: Mariner Books, 2009), 6.

113 **The last hurricane to impact:** Standiford, *Last Train to Paradise*, 120–29.

114 **Since 1906, other hurricanes:** Barnes, *Florida's Hurricane History*, 90–109; and John M. Williams and Iver W. Duedall, *Florida Hurricanes and Tropical Storms, 1871–2001* (Gainesville: University Press of Florida, 2002), 11–14.

114 **Even when a hurricane came ashore:** Williams and Duedall, *Florida Hurricanes*, 14; and Redford, *Billion-Dollar Sandbar*, 166–67.

114 **"need not fear serious damage":** "City Well Protected," *MH*, July 31, 1926.

114 **On Tuesday, September 14, 1926:** Background for this section on the Great Miami Hurricane of 1926 comes from "Great Miami Hurricane of 1926," NWS, accessed August 2018, https://www.weather.gov/mfl/miami_hurricane; Leo Francis Reardon, *The Florida Hurricane & Disaster, 1926* (1926; repr., Miami: Centennial Press, 1992); Barnes, *Florida's Hurricane History*, 111–26; Charles L. Mitchell, "The West Indian Hurricane of September 14–22, 1926," *MWR*, October 1926, 410–12; Robert Mykle, *Killer 'Cane: The Deadly Hurricane of 1928* (New York: Cooper Square Press, 2002), 83–91; Marjory Stoneman Douglas, *Hurricane* (New York: Rinehart, 1958), 258–67; and Williams and Duedall, *Florida Hurricanes*, 16–17.

114 **the *Miami Herald* informed its readers:** "Hurricane Reported," *MH*, September 17, 1926.

114 **Gray's sudden fear:** "Warnings Sent Late," *MH*, September 28, 1926.

116 **"The storm is not over!":** Barnes, *Florida's Hurricane History*, 113; and "Storm Path Traced," *MH*, September 21, 1926.

116 **When the eye passed by:** C. F. Talman, "Tropical Hurricanes Are a World Scourge," *NYT*, September 23, 1928; and "Survivors Picture Hurricane Horrors," *NYT*, September 22, 1926.

116 **In these two communities alone:** "Fury of Hurricane Told by Witnesses," *NYT*, September 21, 1926; and "75 Are Dead in Miami Storm, 60 Lives Are Taken in Hollywood," *MH*, September 20, 1926.

116 **"The Floridana Club, the once brilliant":** "Miami Dead Put at 250," *NYT*, September 22, 1926.

116 **"The intensity of the storm":** "Great Miami Hurricane of 1926," NWS.

117 **"The city built on wild promises":** Douglas, *Hurricane*, 266.

117 **Leo Francis Reardon's account:** This account, including all the quotes, comes from Reardon, *Florida Hurricane*, 4–11.

119 **Many people there had poignant stories . . . then fled to safety:** Ibid., 71.

120 **The hurricane tracked northwest:** Background for this section comes from Reardon, *Florida Hurricane*, 93, 96; Barnes, *Florida's Hurricane History*, 120–21; Mykle, *Killer 'Cane*, 84–91; Douglas, *Everglades*, 9–14, 186, 314–48; and Kleinberg, *Black Cloud*, 5, 15, 29–31.

121 **To keep this from happening again:** Lawrence E. Will, *Okeechobee Hurricane and the Hoover Dike* (St. Petersburg, FL: Great Outdoors Publishing, 1961), 16.

122 **Fred A. Flanders, the state engineer:** Mykle, *Killer 'Cane*, 85–86; and James D. Snyder, *Black Gold and Silver Sands: A Pictorial History of Agriculture in Palm Beach County* (Palm Beach, FL: Historical Society of Palm Beach, 2004), 80–82.

123 **Although contemporary accounts:** Russell L. Pfost, "Reassessing the Impact of Two Historical Florida Hurricanes," *BAMS*, October 2003, 1367–72. See also Reardon, *Florida Hurricane*, 107; L. L. Tyler, *A Pictorial History of the Florida Hurricane, September 18, 1926* (Miami: Tyler, 1926), 4; "Miami Puts Dead at 325," *NYT*, September 21, 1926; Reese Amis, "Hurricane Rages 9 Hours," *NYT*, September 20, 1926; and "Injured in Florida Estimated at 4,000," *NYT*, September 29, 1926.

123 **$105 million:** "Great Miami Hurricane of 1926," NWS. See also Barnes, *Florida's Hurricane History*, 126.

123 **"A lot of people who'd come"**: Barnes, *Florida's Hurricane History*, 126.

123 **"Chicago had her fire"**: "Miami's Unconquerable Soul," *Miami Tribune*, September 19, 1926; and Reardon, *Florida Hurricane*, 14.

124 **In the near term, the University of Miami**: Kleinberg, *Black Cloud*, 29; and Wikipedia, s.v. "Sebastian the Ibis," accessed August 2018, https://en.wikipedia.org/wiki/Sebastian_the_Ibis.

124 **"tropical disturbance of considerable intensity"**: Mykle, *Killer 'Cane*, 113–15.

124 **On September 12, having progressed**: Kleinberg, *Black Cloud*, 35–46; "Homeless Face Famine," *NYT*, September 16, 1928; Charles L. Mitchell, "The West Indian Hurricane of September 10–20, 1928," *MWR*, September 1928, 347–48; and Mykle, *Killer 'Cane*, 113–22.

125 **On September 13 the hurricane**: Oliver L. Fassig, "San Felipe—The Hurricane of September 13, 1928, at San Juan, P.R." *MWR*, September 1928, 350–52; Kleinberg, *Black Cloud*, 47–56; Mykle, *Killer 'Cane*, 124–25; "San Juan Area in Ruins," *NYT*, September 15, 1928; "Porto Ricans Are Starving," *NYT*, September 17, 1928; Mitchell, "West Indian Hurricane of 1928," 348; and Barnes, *Florida's Hurricane History*, 128.

125 **After the hurricane left Puerto Rico**: "West Indies Storm Strikes Porto Rico; Damage Is Reported," *MH*, September 14, 1928; "Latest Storm Warning Interpreted by Gray," *MH*, September 15, 1928; and Kleinberg, *Black Cloud*, 57–71.

125 **New analysis indicated**: "Florida Battered by 100-Mile Wind," *NYT*, September 17, 1928; and "Storm Casualties Mount," *MH*, September 17, 1928.

126 **Station managers did their best . . . had already arrived**: Kleinberg, *Black Cloud*, 69–72.

126 **so very few Floridians had one**: Robert Henson, *Weather on the Air: A History of Broadcast Meteorology* (Boston: American Meteorological Society, 2010), 148.

126 **That was 0.18 inch lower**: Mitchell, "West Indian Hurricane of 1928," 349.

126 **The storm was many hundreds**: Kleinberg, *Black Cloud*, 82; "Storm Casualties Mount," *MH*; and Bryan Norcross, personal communication, May 23, 2019.

126 **The devastation in Moore Haven**: Mykle, *Killer 'Cane*, 92; John L. Hackney, "Revolutionary Drain Plans Asked at Okeechobee Meet," *Tampa Bay Daily Times*, October 25, 1926; and "Storm Protection Works," *Miami Daily News*, August 20, 1927.

127 **Although anemometers at two**: Mitchell, "West Indian Hurricane of 1928," 349; HRD, "Continental United States Hurricane Impacts/Landfalls, 1851-2017," accessed May 2018, https://www.aoml.noaa.gov/hrd/hurdat/All_U.S._Hurricanes.html; and Norcross, personal communication.

127 **Fortunately, some people around the lake**: Will, *Okeechobee Hurricane*, 17, 21, 50.

127 **Just as with the 1926 hurricane**: "335 Believed to be Dead in Storm Sector," *MH*, September 19, 1928; Kleinberg, *Black Cloud*, 99; and Will, *Okeechobee Hurricane*, 7–67.

127 **"The monstropolous beast"**: Zora Neale Hurston, *Their Eyes Were Watching God* (New York: HarperPerennial, 2006), 161–62.

127 **Even before the dike gave way**: Background for this section on Torry Island, as well as the quote, comes from Will, *Okeechobee Hurricane*, 21–24.

128 **"I could hear the women"**: Eric L. Gross, *Somebody Got Drowned, Lord: Florida and the Great Okeechobee Hurricane Disaster of 1928* (PhD diss., Florida State University, 1995), 463.

129   **about $75 million:** Kleinberg, *Black Cloud*, 245.

129   **The Red Cross's number was 1,836:** Will, *Okeechobee*, 70–71; Mykle, *Killer 'Cane*, 212–13; and Pfost, "Reassessing the Impact," 1369–72.

129   **"Ugly death was simply everywhere":** Kleinberg, *Black Cloud*, 141.

129   **"for the purpose of collecting":** Mitchell, "West Indian Hurricane of 1928," 349 (emphasis added).

129   **One of them, Coot Simpson:** Kleinberg, *Black Cloud*, 183–90.

130   **Most of the dead were either:** Ibid., 214–15, 227–30; and Mykle, *Killer 'Cane*, 208–9, 212–13.

130   **On September 30, 1928:** Vincent Oaksmith, "Proclamation," *Palm Beach Post*, September 30, 1928.

131   **"Our hearts were torn":** Mary McLeod Bethune, "Thousands White and Colored, at Memorial Services for Hurricane Victims in West Palm Beach, Fla.," *New York Age*, October 13, 1928.

131   **The breaching of the Lake Okeechobee:** Kleinberg, *Black Cloud*, 191–204.

132   **What would happen if such:** Katrina Elsken, "Herbert Hoover Dike Protects All of South Florida," *Lake Okeechobee News*, January 28, 2018.

132   **"Brother, Can You Spare a Dime?":** National Public Radio, "A Depression-Era Anthem for Our Times," *Weekend Edition Saturday*, November 15, 2008, https:// www.npr.org/2008/11/15/96654742/a-depression-era-anthem-for-our-times.

132   **The board's analysis found:** National Research Council, *Report of the Science Advisory Board, July 31, 1933 to September 1, 1934* (Washington, DC: Government Printing Office, 1934), 17, 45–57.

133   **"sadly sketchy":** Whitnah, *History of the United States Weather Bureau*, 135.

133   **The impetus for change received:** Ibid., 135; Eric S. Blake, Christopher W. Landsea, and Ethan J. Gibney, "The Deadliest, Costliest, and Most Intense United States Tropical Cyclones from 1851 to 2010 (and Other Frequently Requested Hurricane Facts)," NOAA Technical Memorandum NWS NHC-6, August 2011, 44; and Tannehill, *Hurricane Hunters*, 70–71.

134   **"Forecaster on golf course":** Sheets, "National Hurricane Center," 195; and Robert W. Burpee, "Grady Norton: Hurricane Forecaster and Communicator Extraordinaire," *Forecaster Biography*, September 1988, 250.

134   **"In Galveston, the weather remained":** Sheets, "National Hurricane Center," 195.

134   **By the time the Science Advisory Board . . . located throughout the West Indies:** Sheets, "National Hurricane Center," 195–96; Calvert, "Hurricane Warning Service," 86; Whitnah, *History of the United States Weather Bureau*, 135; HRD, "80th Anniversary of the Establishment of the Hurricane Warning Network," March 31, 2015, https://noaahrd.wordpress.com/2015/03/31 /80th-anniversary-of-the-establishment-of-the-hurricane-warning-network; and Thomas Neil Knowles, *Category 5: The 1935 Labor Day Hurricane* (Gainesville: University Press of Florida, 2009), 16–17.

135   **"Uncle Sam has perfected":** Willie Drye, "The True Story of the Most Intense Hurricane You've Never Heard Of," *National Geographic*, September 8, 2017; and John L. Frazier, "Storm Warnings: Hurricane Coming," *Index-Journal Magazine*, July 3, 1935.

135   **The first began as a minor:** Background for this section on the Labor Day Hurricane of 1935 comes from Knowles, *Category 5*; Phil Scott, *Hemingway's Hurricane: The Great Florida Keys Storm of 1935* (New York: International Marine, 2006); Willie Drye, *Storm of the Century: The Labor Day Hurricane of 1935*

(Washington, DC: National Geographic, 2002); and US House of Representatives, *Florida Hurricane Disaster: Hearings before the Committee on World War Veterans' Legislation, House of Representatives, Seventy-Fourth Congress, Second Session, on H. R. 9486, a Bill for the Relief of Widows, Children and Dependent Parents of World War Veterans Who Died as the Result of the Florida Hurricane at Windley Island and Matecumbe Keys, September 2, 1935* (Washington, DC: Government Printing Office, 1936).

135 **The next day, the bureau grew:** Scott, *Hemingway's Hurricane*, 43, 65; W. F. McDonald, "The Hurricane of August 31 to September 6, 1935," *MWR*, September 1935, 269; and Knowles, *Category 5*, 80–81, 87.

136 **"like no other place in Florida":** Mary V. Dearborn, *Ernest Hemingway: A Biography* (New York: Alfred A. Knopf, 2017), 252.

136 **"It's the best place I've ever been":** Jeffrey Meyers, *Hemingway: A Biography* (New York: Harper & Row, 1985), 206.

137 **"Work is off until it is past":** Ernest Hemingway, "Who Murdered the Vets? A First-Hand Account on the Florida Hurricane," *New Masses*, September 17, 1935, 9.

137 **The veterans were at three:** Background for the veterans, the Bonus Army, and the veterans' ultimate arrival in the Florida Keys comes from Paul Dickson and Thomas B. Allen, *The Bonus Army: An American Epic* (New York: Walker, 2004); Phil Scott, *Hemingway's Hurricane*, 12–18, 31–33; John D. Weaver, "Bonus March," *American Heritage* 14, no. 4 (June 1963), https://www.americanheritage.com/content/bonus-march; and Rexford G. Tugwell, "Roosevelt and the Bonus Marchers of 1932," *Political Science Quarterly*, September 1972, 363–76.

138 **Hoover viewed the Bonus Army . . . and their shantytown set ablaze:** Michael A. Bellesiles, *A People's History of the U.S. Military: Ordinary Soldiers Reflect on Their Experience of War, from the American Revolution to Afghanistan* (New York: New Press, 2012), 219; and Dickson and Allen, *Bonus Army*, 7, 120–25, 142–45, 159–83.

138 **"use all humanity consistent with":** Charles Rappleye, *Herbert Hoover in the White House: The Ordeal of the Presidency* (New York: Simon & Schuster, 2016), 374.

139 **"Well, Felix, this will elect me":** Donald J. Lisio, *The President and Protest: Hoover, MacArthur and the Bonus Riot* (New York: Fordham University Press, 1994), 285.

139 **"Give a man a dole":** James T. Patterson, *America's Struggle against Poverty in the Twentieth Century* (Cambridge, MA: Harvard University Press, 2000), 58.

140 **When Henry Flagler stepped off:** Standiford, *Last Train to Paradise*, 201–6.

140 **"railroad across the ocean":** William Mayo Venable, "Importance of the Railway to Key West," *Engineering Magazine*, October 1908, 51.

140 **"Flagler's Folly":** Frederick A. Talbot, *The Railway Conquest of the World* (Philadelphia: J. B. Lippincott, 1911), 242.

140 **"The Eighth Wonder of the World":** L. E. St. John, "Miami, FL," *Railway Conductor*, April 1912, 274.

140 **The increasingly decrepit:** Scott, *Hemingway's Hurricane*, 30–31.

140 **Much of the highway was already:** Ibid., 32–33; Knowles, *Category 5*, 32–33; and Jerry Wilkinson, "History of the Overseas Highway," General Keys History, accessed August 2018, http://www.keyshistory.org/osh.html.

140 **The 700 or so veterans:** Fred C. Painton, "Rendezvous with Death," *American*

Legion Monthly, November 1935, 28–29; Drye, *Storm of the Century*, 7–9; and US House, *Florida Hurricane Disaster*, 257.

141 **"some were hard, useless characters":** Douglas, *Hurricane*, 272.

141 **"Sure, there were a few":** Knowles, *Category 5*, 46.

141 **The camps themselves were shoddy:** US House, *Florida Hurricane Disaster*, 174.

141 **Between Key West and mainland Florida:** Ibid., 459.

141 **Ray Sheldon, the camps' director:** Ibid., 303; and Scott, *Hemingway's Hurricane*, 56–70.

142 **On Sunday morning, the sun shone:** Scott, *Hemingway's Hurricane*, 72–91; and Knowles, *Category 5*, 89–90, 92, 98, 103.

142 **"Naturally we were all interested":** Scott, *Hemingway's Hurricane*, 78.

142 **It was up to him, in conjunction:** Ibid., 58, 91–95.

142 **which were an unusually warm 86 degrees:** Drye, *Storm of the Century*, 80.

143 **On Monday morning, Labor Day:** US House, *Florida Hurricane Disaster*, 184.

143 **Sheldon could see that the barometer . . . with the Lower Matecumbe and Windley Keys:** Ibid., 160, 303, 335, 354; Scott, *Hemingway's Hurricane*, 105–6, 110–11; and Knowles, *Category 5*, 121–25.

144 **In the midafternoon, the Weather Bureau:** Background for Cuba's actions and Povey's flight comes from Drye, *Storm of the Century*, 129–30; HRD, "80th Anniversary of the Labor Day Hurricane and First Hurricane Reconnaissance," September 2, 2015, https://noaahrd.wordpress.com/2015/09/02/80th-anniversary-of-the-labor-day-hurricane-and-first-hurricane-reconnaissance; and Paul A. Oelkrug, "Guide to the Leonard J. Povey Papers, 1904–1984," History of Aviation Collection, Special Collections Department, McDermott Library, University of Texas at Dallas, January 2004, 3.

144 **"I was unable to fly close":** "Cubans Plan Aerial Hurricane Patrols," *MH*, September 23, 1935.

144 **Sheldon and Ghent thought . . . it was already there:** US House, *Florida Hurricane Disaster*, 160, 303–5, 354, 439; Scott, *Hemingway's Hurricane*, 92; Drye, *Storm of the Century*, 66–67, 106, 120, 122, 131–34, 141–45; and Knowles, *Category 5*, 104, 127–29, 134–35, 140–42.

145 **"You're the man we've been looking for":** Drye, *Storm of the Century*, 149.

145 **Sheldon then asked Haycraft:** Ibid., 149; "Engineer Describes Wreck of Veterans' Relief Train," *Tampa Tribune*, September 6, 1935; Knowles, *Category 5*, 172–74; and US House, *Florida Hurricane Disaster*, 439.

146 **"A wall of water from 15 to 20":** Drye, *Storm of the Century*, 150.

146 **Amazingly, all of the people:** HRD, "80th Anniversary of the Labor Day Hurricane."

147 **J. E. Duane was a cooperative:** Information found in Duane's diary comes from McDonald, "Hurricane of August 31," 269–70.

147 **"stars [were] shining brightly":** Drye, *Storm of the Century*, 244.

147 **At the diminutive Craig Key:** W. F. McDonald, "Lowest Barometer Reading in the Florida Keys Storm of September 2, 1935," *MWR*, October 1935, 295; and Blake et al., "Deadliest, Costliest," 13.

148 **Maximum sustained winds were 185 mph:** McDonald, "Hurricane of August 31," 269; Drye, *Storm of the Century*, 311; Barnes, *Florida's Hurricane History*, 145; Landsea, "Subject: E23) What Is the Complete List"; and Fassig, "San Felipe."

148 **It was also an incredibly compact:** McDonald, "Hurricane of August 31," 270.

148 **In subsequent days, as relief:** Associated Press, "Veterans Lead Fatalities," *NYT*,

September 5, 1935; Associated Press, "Hurricane's Toll 100," *NYT*, September 4, 1935; and Associated Press, "Veterans' Camp Wrecked by Storm," *NYT*, September 4, 1935.

149 **When word of the disaster reached:** Meyers, *Hemingway*, 288.

149 **"The brush was all brown":** Hemingway, "Who Murdered the Vets?" 10.

149 **"We were the first into Camp Five":** Ernest Hemingway to Maxwell Perkins (September 7, 1935), in *Ernest Hemingway: Selected Letters 1917–1961*, ed. Carlos Baker (New York: Scribner Classics, 2003), 421–22.

149 **Other stories were equally horrific:** Douglas, *Hurricane*, 277; and Scott, *Hemingway's Hurricane*, 195–96.

150 **Clifton and John Russell, both part:** Barnes, *Florida's Hurricane History*, 152–53.

150 **"When the buildings began to crack":** Drye, *Storm of the Century*, 155.

150 **"I would rather face":** Associated Press, "Veterans' Camp Wrecked."

150 **"I could take out the bodies":** Knowles, *Category 5*, 269–70.

150 **The most comprehensive accounting:** US House, *Florida Hurricane Disaster*, 332.

151 **Although President Roosevelt originally:** Knowles, *Category 5*, 291; Scott, *Hemingway's Hurricane*, 203–4; and "Mass Burial of 116 Storm Victims Set," *MH*, September 8, 1928.

151 **Almost all of the surviving veterans . . . all along the archipelago:** Knowles, *Category 5*, 303, 311; and US House, *Florida Hurricane Disaster*, 105.

152 **"to live in frame shacks":** Hemingway, "Who Murdered the Vets?" 10.

152 **"The veterans in those camps":** Hemingway to Perkins (September 7, 1935), 421.

152 **There were multiple investigations:** Knowles, *Category 5*, 291–302; Drye, *Storm of the Century*, 199–257; Scott, *Hemingway's Hurricane*, 206–11, 217–22; "Worley Absolves Railroad of Delay of Train to Camps," *MH*, September 7, 1928; and "Storm Death Called Unavoidable," *MH*, September 9, 1928.

153 **"To our mind, the catastrophe":** US House, *Florida Hurricane Disaster*, 441.

153 **A second investigation launched:** Scott, *Hemingway's Hurricane*, 211–17; and Drye, *Storm of the Century*, 235–57.

153 **"During the developing stage":** McDonald, "Hurricane of August 31," 271.

153 **"We maintain that if the storm":** Knowles, *Category 5*, 295.

CHAPTER 6—THE GREAT HURRICANE OF 1938

155 **It had been exceptionally rainy:** William Elliott Minsinger, ed., *The 1938 Hurricane: An Historical and Pictorial Summary* (Boston: Blue Hill Observatory, 1988), 9.

156 **"The entire civilized world":** William Manchester, *The Glory and the Dream: A Narrative of America, 1932–1972*, vol. 1 (Boston: Little, Brown, 1973), 217.

156 **"peace for our time":** David Faber, *Munich, 1938: Appeasement and World War II* (New York: Simon & Schuster, 2008), 7.

156 **After wading through twenty-six:** Minsinger, *1938 Hurricane*, 9–11; and "Storm Moves on Jersey," *NYT*, September 21, 1938.

157 **"There's something wrong":** John Kolber, "Big Wind Man," *Life*, October 4, 1948, 111.

157 **Norton got his big chance:** Robert W. Burpee, "Grady Norton: Hurricane Forecaster and Communicator Extraordinaire," *Forecaster Biography*, September 1988, 247–50.

157 **the SS *Alegrete*:** Ivan R. Tannehill, "Hurricane of September 16 to 22, 1938," *MWR*, September 1938, 287.

157 **In subsequent days, additional:** C. C. Clark to Office of the Chief, Weather Bureau (October 3, 1938), in Lourdes B. Avilés, *Taken by Storm 1938: A Social and Meteorological History of the Great New England Hurricane* (Boston: American Meteorological Society, 2013), 213–24; and Charles H. Pierce, "The Meteorological History of the New England Hurricane of Sept. 21, 1938," *MWR*, August 1939, 237.

157 **As the hurricane moved up the coast:** Background for this section on predictions about the hurricane and the disagreement between Mitchell and Pierce comes from Avilés, *Taken by Storm 1938*, 83–97, 213–24; Pierce, "Meteorological History," 237–85; R. A. Scotti, *Sudden Sea: The Great Hurricane of 1938* (Boston: Little, Brown, 2003), 71–78; and Ernest S. Clowes, *The Hurricane of 1938 on Eastern Long Island* (Bridgehampton, NY: Hampton Press, 1939), 5–6.

159 **The *New York Times* article:** "Storm Moves on Jersey," *NYT*.

159 **One of the only ships to report:** Tannehill, "Hurricane of September 16"; and Scotti, *Sudden Sea*, 54–56.

160 **"The Long Island Express":** Patricia Kitchen, "80 Years Later, Vivid Memories of Historic Long Island Express Hurricane," *Newsday*, September 21, 2018.

160 **The disagreement between Mitchell:** Avilés, *Taken by Storm 1938*, 89–96; Scotti, *Sudden Sea*, 71–78; and Cherie Burns, *The Great Hurricane: 1938* (New York: Atlantic Monthly Press, 2005), 52–54. See also the documentary *Violent Earth: New England's Killer Hurricane*, directed by Paul Jacobson and Robert Long (History Channel, 2006).

160 **"most of the time," Avilés contends:** Avilés, *Taken by Storm*, 95.

161 **The devastating New England hurricanes:** Tannehill, "Hurricane of September 16," 286.

161 **"a thick and high bank of fog":** Joe McCarthy, "The '38 Hurricane," *American Heritage*, August 1969, https://www.americanheritage.com/content/%E2%80%9938-hurricane.

161 **Ever since he was a boy:** K. E. Parks and Russell Maloney, "Hurricane, the Talk of the Town," *The New Yorker*, November 12, 1938, 16–17.

162 **The actress Katharine Hepburn:** Background for this section, and the quotes, comes from Katharine Hepburn, *Me: Stories of My Life* (New York: Alfred A. Knopf, 1991), 211–13.

164 **Napatree Point, a long, narrow spit:** Background for this section on Napatree Point and the Moore family ordeal during the hurricane comes from Everett S. Allen, *A Wind to Shake the World: The Story of the 1938 Hurricane* (Boston: Little, Brown, 1976), 158–65 (all of the quotes come from this source); Scotti, *Sudden Sea*, 20–22, 67, 90, 153, 175–79, 191–94, 207–8; and Gregory Pettys, "How Napatree Point Got Its Name," *Westerly Life*, February 9, 2016, https://westerlylife.com/how-napatree-point-got-its-name.

168 **bus driver Norman Caswell:** Background for this story about Caswell, the bus, and the people on board comes from Allen, *Wind to Shake the World*, 220–24; and Scotti, *Sudden Sea*, 8–16, 173–75, 180–82, 184–87, 218–24, 232–33.

168 **"We'd better get out":** Scotti, *Sudden Sea*, 220.

169 **"Please let me die":** Allen, *Wind to Shake the World*, 222.

169 **"He died from the shock of this thing":** Ibid., 223.

169 **"Clayton, don't let the water":** Ibid.

169 **Tragically and ironically:** Scotti, *Sudden Sea*, 233.

169 **"series of waves, each higher":** David Ludlum, *The Country Journal, New England Weather Book* (Boston: Houghton Mifflin, 1976), 42.

170 **Not so David Cornel De Jong:** All of the background and quotes for this section come from David Cornel De Jong, "Coming through the Storm," *Yankee Magazine*, September 1939, 13–15, 28–29.

173 **"I think I've done enough damage":** Clowes, *Hurricane of 1938*, 40.

173 **"was not greatly disturbed":** Vincent McHugh, "It Huffed and It Puffed," *The New Yorker*, November 5, 1938, 68–69.

173 **As the hurricane moved inland:** Avilés, *Taken by Storm*, 125–30; Kerry Emanuel, *Divine Wind: The History and Science of Hurricanes* (New York: Oxford University Press, 2005), 109–10, 159–60; and Ludlum, *Country Journal*, 42.

174 **By the time it was over . . . of any kind in American history:** Allen, *Wind to Shake the World*, 349; Avilés, *Taken by Storm*, 16–17, 112–46; Tannehill, "Hurricane of September 16," 286–88; McCarthy, "'38 Hurricane"; Pierce, "Meteorological History," 237; Stephen Long, *Thirty-Eight: The Hurricane That Transformed New England* (New Haven, CT: Yale University Press, 2016), 9–10, 90–111, 133; Clowes, *Hurricane of 1938*, 12–15; John R. Winterich, "Hurricane," *The New Yorker*, December 17, 1938, 42–44; Bruce Fellman, "The Elm City: Then and Now," *Yale Alumni Magazine*, September/October 2006, http://archives.yalealumnimagazine.com/issues/2006_09/elms.html; Minsinger, *1938 Hurricane*, 10–13, 34; and Ludlum, *Country Journal*, 44.

175 **"The wind was oh so very bold":** Avilés, *Taken by Storm*, 146.

176 **"For twenty-five cents, I'll listen":** McCarthy, "'38 Hurricane."

177 **"In the long and laudable annals":** Allen, *Wind to Shake the World*, 351.

177 **"On the basis of the data":** Ibid., 347–48.

177 **"Had the storm not moved":** Scotti, *Sudden Sea*, 215.

CHAPTER 7—INTO, OVER, AND UNDER THE MAELSTROM

180 **the air force asked pilot Joseph B. Duckworth:** Background for this section on Duckworth and his groundbreaking flight comes from Ivan Ray Tannehill, *The Hurricane Hunters* (New York: Dodd, Mead, 1956), 91–100; Lew Fincher and Bill Read, "The 1943 'Surprise' Hurricane," NOAA History, accessed September 2018, http://www.history.noaa.gov/stories_tales/surprise.html; Sheets and Williams, *Hurricane Watch*, 96–100; David Toomey, *Stormchasers: The Hurricane Hunters and Their Fateful Flight into Hurricane Janet* (New York: W. W. Norton, 2002), 149–52; and C. V. Glines, "Duckworth's Legacy," *Air Force Magazine*, May 1990, http://www.airforcemag.com/MagazineArchive/Pages/1990/May%201990/0590duckworth.aspx.

182 **"the respect he had for Duckworth's":** Fincher and Read, "1943 'Surprise' Hurricane."

182 **"experimental instrument flight":** Bob Sheets and Jack Williams, *Hurricane Watch: Forecasting the Deadliest Storms on Earth* (New York: Vintage Books, 2001), 98.

182 **"Yes, we do," O'Hair responded . . . like a stick in a dog's mouth":** Tannehill, *Hurricane Hunters*, 98.

182 **"a shower curtain of darker clouds":** Fincher and Read, "1943 'Surprise' Hurricane."

183 **News of the historic flights . . . Grady Norton, the bureau's chief hurricane forecaster:** Sheets and Williams, *Hurricane Watch*, 99–100, 105–7; Tannehill, *Hurricane Hunters*, 75–78.

183 **Despite lobbying for such flights:** Tannehill, *Hurricane Hunters*, 75.

184 **The value of so-called Hurricane Hunter:** Background for this section on the flights into the Great Atlantic Hurricane of 1944, and the hurricane itself, comes from H. C. Summer, "The North Atlantic Hurricane of September 8-16, 1944," *MWR*, September 1944, 187–89; Tannehill, *Hurricane Hunters*, 121–29; and "The Great Atlantic Hurricane of 1944 Shows Forewarned Is Forearmed," New England Historical Society, accessed September 2018, http://www.newenglandhistoricalsociety.com/how-the-1st-storm-chasers-saved-new-england-from-the-1944-great-atlantic-hurricane.

185 **"Hour after hour, radio stations":** "The Great Whirlwind," *Time*, September 25, 1944, 16.

185 **The officers on the *Warrington*:** Robert A. Dawes Jr., *The Dragon's Breath: Hurricane at Sea* (Annapolis, MD: Naval Institute Press, 1996), 32–33, 101–2.

187 **One of the key instruments:** Kerry Emanuel, *Divine Wind: The History and Science of Hurricanes* (New York: Oxford University Press, 2005), 9–12.

187 **There have been thousands:** Background on Hurricane Hunter flights comes from Sheets and Williams, *Hurricane Watch*, 96–124; Tannehill, *Hurricane Hunters*, 167–223; Emanuel, *Divine Wind*, 193–202; and H. J. "Walt" Walter, *The Wind Chasers: A History of the U.S. Navy's Atlantic Fleet Hurricane Hunters* (Dallas, TX: Taylor, 1992).

187 **"the most dangerous part of his day":** Alexandra Potenza, "A Hurricane Hunter Explains What It's Like to Fly through the Eye of the Storm: A Conversation with Ian Sears, a Flight Meteorologist at NOAA," *Verge*, October 17, 2015.

188 **"hairy hops":** Tannehill, *Hurricane Hunters*, 185.

188 **"One minute this plane":** Ibid., 135–38.

188 **As the NOAA plane *Kermit*:** The quotes from Dr. Masters and the background material for this section come from Jeffrey Masters, "Hunting Hugo," Weather Underground, accessed September 2018, https://www.wunderground.com/resources/education/hugo1.asp; and HRD, "25th Anniversary of a 'Hairy Hop' into Hurricane Hugo," September 15, 2014, https://noaahrd.wordpress.com/2014/09/15/25th-anniversary-of-a-hairy-hop-into-hurricane-hugo.

189 **"beginning penetration":** Toomey, *Stormchasers*, 259; and Sean Breslin, "60 Years Ago, the Only Hurricane Hunter Plane to Go Down in an Atlantic Basin Storm Crashed in Hurricane Janet," Weather Channel, September 26, 2015, https://weather.com/storms/hurricane/news/hurricane-hunter-plane-crash-janet.

190 **In 1960, a radically new:** Background for this section on weather satellites comes from NASA Science, "The Television Infrared Observation Satellite Program (TIROS)," accessed September 2018, https://science.nasa.gov/missions/tiros; NWS, "Satellites," accessed September 2018, https://www.weather.gov/about/satellites; NOAA, "Geostationary Satellites," accessed September 2018, https://sos.noaa.gov/datasets/geostationary-satellites; NOAA, "Polar Orbiting: NOAA-17 Satellite Coverage," accessed September 2018, https://sos.noaa.gov/datasets/polar-orbiting-noaa-17-satellite-coverage; NASA, "GOES Overview and History," accessed September 2018, https://www.nasa.gov/content/goes-ovrreview/index.html; NOAA Satellite Information System, "NOAA's Geostationary and Polar-Orbiting Weather Satellites," accessed September 2018, https://noaasis.noaa.gov/NOAASIS/ml/genlsatl.html; and Gordon E. Dunn and Banner I. Miller, *Atlantic Hurricanes* (Baton Rouge: Louisiana State University Press, 1964), 172–73, 291–94.

190 **"Never before had so small":** Daniel J. Boorstin, *The Americans: The Democratic Experience* (New York: Random House, 1973).

190 **On November 3 it launched Sputnik 2:** Paul Dickson, *Sputnik: Shock of the Century* (New York: Walker, 2001), 1–7, 140–41.

191 **"the greatest single achievement":** Robert C. Sheets, "The National Hurricane Center—Past, Present, and Future," *Weather and Forecasting,* June 1990, 201.

192 **The data gathered by Hurricane Hunters:** Sheets and Williams, *Hurricane Watch,* 148–51; Dunn and Miller, *Atlantic Hurricanes,* 182–86; Mark DeMaria, "A History of Hurricane Forecasting for the Atlantic Basin, 1920–1995," in *Historical Essays on Meteorology 1919–1995,* ed. James Rodger Fleming (Boston: American Meteorological Society, 1996), 274, 279.

192 **"no natural phenomenon poses":** Emanuel, *Divine Wind,* 227.

192 **The most valuable hurricane forecasting:** Background for this section on computer modeling and hurricane forecasting comes from Sheets and Williams, *Hurricane Watch,* 203–10; Emanuel, *Divine Wind,* 14–15, 227–38; NHC, "NHC Track and Intensity Models," accessed September 2018, https://www .nhc.noaa.gov/modelsummary.shtml; Samantha Durbin, "What Are Weather Models, Exactly, and How Do They Work?" *Washington Post,* May 18, 2018, https://www.washingtonpost.com/news/capital-weather-gang/wp/2018/05/18/what -exactly-are-weather-models-and-how-do-they-work/?utm_term=.481ae8ad5cff; Scott Neuman, "Computers, Pinch of Art Aid Hurricane Forecasters," Special Series: Superstorm Sandy: Before, During, and Beyond, NPR, October 26, 2012, https://www.npr.org/2012/10/26/163725684/computers-pinch-of-art-aid -hurricane-forecasters; Jeff Masters, "Hurricane Forecast Computer Models," Weather Underground, accessed September 2018, https://www.wunderground .com/hurricane/models.asp; Sarah N. Collins, Robert S. James, Pallav Ray, Katherine Chen, Angie Lassman, and James Brownlee, "Grids in Numerical Weather and Climate Models," in *Climate Change and Regional/Local Responses,* ed. Pallav Ray and Yuanzhi Zhang (Intech, 2013), https://www.intechopen.com/books/ climate-change-and-regional-local-responses/grids-in-numerical-weather-and -climate-models; John D. Cox, *Storm Watchers: The Turbulent History of Weather Prediction from Franklin's Kite to El Nino,* 199; and Edward Norton Lorenz, "A Scientist by Choice," Kyoto Prize Lecture, 1991, http://www.kyotoprize.org/en/ laureates/commemorative_lectures, 8–9.

194 **"significantly increase[s] forecast accuracy":** NHC, "National Weather Service Director Cautions: Don't Chase Single Model Runs This Hurricane Season," June 15, 2018, https://www.weather.gov/news/181406-director-cautions. See also Edward N. Rappaport, James L. Franklin, Lixion A. Avila, Stephen R. Baig, John L. Beven II, Eric S. Blake, Christopher A. Burr, et al., "Advances and Challenges at the National Hurricane Center," *Weather and Forecasting,* April 2009, 405–6.

194 **That is why forecasters employ:** For background on the cone of uncertainty, see NHC, "Definition of the NHC Track Forecast Cone," accessed September 2018, https://www.nhc.noaa.gov/aboutcone.shtml; and Marshall Shepherd, "The Hurricane Forecast 'Cone of Uncertainty' May Not Mean What You Think," *Forbes,* April 17, 2017, https://www.forbes.com/sites/marshallshepherd/2017/04/17/the -hurricane-forecast-cone-of-uncertainty-may-not-mean-what-you-think/#593ec 33960a0.

194 **"two-thirds of historical official":** NHC, "Definition of the NHC Track Forecast Cone."

194 **The good news is that over time:** John Cangialosi, "The State of Hurricane Forecasting: A Look at Model and NHC Accuracy," WeatherNation, April 25,

2018, http://www.weathernationtv.com/news/state-hurricane-forecasting-look -model-nhc-accuracy.

194 **"Modern 72-hour predictions":** Richard B. Alley, Kerry A. Emanuel, and Fuqing Zhang, "Advances in Weather Prediction," *Science*, January 25, 2019, 342. See also Robinson Meyer, "Modern Weather Forecasts Are Stunningly Accurate," *Atlantic*, January 30, 2019, https://www.theatlantic.com/science/ archive/2019/01/polar-vortex-weather-forecasting-good-now/581605.

195 **Edward N. Lorenz's groundbreaking:** Background for this section on Lorenz comes from Lorenz, "Scientist by Choice"; James Gleick, *Chaos: Making a New Science* (New York: Penguin Books, 1987), 11–23; Cox, *Storm Watchers*, 220–25; Peter Dizikes, "When the Butterfly Effect Took Flight," *MIT Technology Review*, February 22, 2011, https://www.technologyreview.com/s/422809/when-the-butterfly -effect-took-flight; Peter Dizikes, "The Meaning of the Butterfly," *Boston Globe*, June 8, 2008, http://archive.boston.com/bostonglobe/ideas/articles/2008/06/08 /the_meaning_of_the_butterfly; Jamie L. Vernon, "Understanding the Butterfly Effect," *American Scientist*, May–June 2017, https://www.americanscientist .org/article/understanding-the-butterfly-effect; and Sam Kean, *Caesar's Last Breath: Decoding the Secrets of the Air around Us* (New York: Little, Brown, 2017), 287–92.

195 **"As a boy I was always":** "Edward Lorenz, Father of Chaos Theory and Butterfly Effect, Dies at 90," *MIT News*, April 16, 2008, http://news.mit.edu/2008/obit -lorenz-0416.

197 **"[weather] prediction of the sufficiently":** Edward N. Lorenz, "Deterministic Nonperiodic Flow," *Journal of the Atmospheric Sciences*, March 1963, 141.

197 **"sensitive dependence on initial conditions":** Edward N. Lorenz, *The Essence of Chaos* (Seattle: University of Washington Press, 1995), 8; and Stephen H. Kellert, *In the Wake of Chaos* (Chicago: University of Chicago Press, 1993), 12.

197 **"Does the flap of a butterfly's wings":** Edward N. Lorenz, "Predictability: Does the Flap of a Butterfly's Wings in Brazil Set Off a Tornado in Texas?" (address to the American Association for the Advancement of Science, December 29, 1972).

198 **"The fifties and sixties were years":** Gleick, *Chaos*, 18.

198 **"Experiments with sophisticated weather":** Emanuel, *Divine Wind*, 234.

198 **"By generating a range":** European Centre for Medium-Range Weather Forecasts, "Fact Sheet: Ensemble Weather Forecasting," accessed November 2018, https:// www.ecmwf.int/en/about/media-centre/fact-sheet-ensemble-weather-forecasting.

198 **"Despite incredible improvements":** Christopher W. Landsea and John P. Cangialosi, "Have We Reached the Limits of Predictability for Tropical Cyclone Forecasting?" *Bureau of the American Meteorological Association*, November 2018, 2242.

199 **This latter activity, called seasonal:** Background for seasonal hurricane forecasting comes from Philip J. Klotzbach and William Gray, "Twenty-Five Years of Atlantic Basin Seasonal Hurricane Forecasts (1984–2008)," *Geophysical Research Letters*, May 2009, L09711; Philip J. Klotzbach, Johnny C. L. Chan, Patrick J. Fitzpatrick, William M. Frank, Christopher W. Landsea, and John L. McBride, "The Science of William M. Gray: His Contributions to the Knowledge of Tropical Meteorology and Tropical Cyclones," *BAMS*, November 2017; and NOAA, "Forecasters Predict a Near- or Above-Normal 2018 Atlantic Hurricane Season," May 24, 2018, https://www.noaa.gov/media-release/forecasters-predict-near-or -above-normal-2018-atlantic-hurricane-season.

199 **Since Gray blazed the path:** Seasonal Hurricane Predictions, "Forecast-

ers," accessed November 2018, http://seasonalhurricanepredictions.bsc
.es/predictions; and Phil Klotzbach, "In Memory of Dr. William (Bill) Gray,"
accessed November 2018, https://tropical.colostate.edu/personnel.

199 **One analysis of twenty-five:** Klotzbach and Gray, "Twenty-Five Years of Atlantic
Basin."

200 **In the mid-1800s, James Espy:** Peter Moore, *Weather Experiment: The Pioneers
Who Sought to See the Future* (New York: Farrar, Straus and Giroux, 2015), 136–
39.

200 **This audacious experiment grew:** Background for Project Cirrus comes from
Barrington S. Havens, *History of Project Cirrus*, Report no. RL-756 (Schenect-
ady, NY: General Electric Research Laboratory, July 1952); Vincent J. Schaefer,
"The Early History of Weather Modification," *BAMS*, April 4, 1968, 337–42;
HRD, "70th Anniversary of the First Hurricane Seeding Experiment," October 12, 2017, https://noaahrd.wordpress.com/2017/10/12/70th-anniversary-of
-the-first-hurricane-seeding-experiment; Sheet and Williams, *Hurricane Watch*,
159–61; "Project Cirrus," *BAMS*, October 1950, 286–87; and Kean, *Caesar's Last
Breath*, 270–80.

201 **"In Savannah last week":** "Science: Yankee Meddling?" *Time*, November 10,
1947, 87; and Sheets and Williams, *Hurricane Watch*, 161.

201 **"99% sure":** HRD, "70th Anniversary."

202 **at the inception of Project Stormfury:** Background for Project Stormfury comes
from H. E. Willoughby, D. P. Jorgensen, R. A. Black, and S. L. Rosenthal, "Project Stormfury: A Scientific Chronicle, 1962–1983," *BAMS*, May 1985; Sheets and
Williams, *Hurricane Watch*, 166–77; and James Rodger Fleming, *Fixing the Sky:
The Checkered History of Weather and Climate Control* (New York: Columbia University Press, 2012), 177–79.

202 **it had a "kickass" name:** Kean, *Caesar's Last Breath*, 280.

203 **"two fatal flaws":** Willoughby et al., "Project Stormfury," 513.

203 **"It was disappointing to concede":** Kean, *Caesar's Last Breath*, 284.

203 **Since the mid- to late 1900s:** Sheets and Williams, *Hurricane Watch*, 157–59;
Charlie Jane Anders, "Why Can't We Stop a Hurricane Before It Hits Us?" *Popular Science*, November 8, 2012, https://www.popsci.com/science/article/2012
-11/why-can%E2%80%99t-we-stop-hurricane-it-hits-us; Mark Strauss, "Nuking
Hurricanes: The Surprising History of a Really Bad Idea," *National Geographic*,
November 30, 2016, https://news.nationalgeographic.com/2016/11/hurricanes
-weather-history-nuclear-weapons/#close; and *How to Stop a Hurricane* (video
documentary), directed by Robin Benger (Cogent/Benger, 2007), http://cogent
benger.com/documentaries/how-to-stop-a-hurricane.

203 **to "unwind" the storm:** Sheets and Williams, *Hurricane Watch*, 158.

204 **Every year, the National Hurricane Center:** Chris Landsea, "Subject: C5c) Why
Don't We Try to Destroy Tropical Cyclones by Nuking Them?" HRD, Frequently
Asked Questions, accessed November 2018, http://www.aoml.noaa.gov/hrd/tcfaq
/C5c.html. According to multiple sources, President Donald J. Trump suggested
that national security officials explore the option of dropping nuclear bombs on hurricanes to keep them from hitting the United States, although Trump later denied
having raised this possibility, labeling the reporting as "fake news." See Jonathan
Swan and Margaret Talev, "Scoop: Trump Suggested Nuking Hurricanes to Stop
Them from Hitting U.S.," Axios, August 25, 2019, https://www.axios.com/trump
-nuclear-bombs-hurricanes-97231f38-2394-4120-a3fa-8c9cf0e3f51c.html?utm
_source=twitter&utm_medium=social&utm_campaign=organic.

204 **This confluence of events:** Bryan Norcross, *Hurricane Almanac: The Essential Guide to Storms Past, Present, and Future* (New York: St. Martin's Griffin, 2007), 139; and Tannehill, *Hurricane Hunters*, 245.

205 **During the late 1940s and early 1950s . . . and start naming hurricanes after women:** Elizabeth Skilton, *Camille Was No Lady but Katrina Was a Bitch: Gender, Hurricanes & Popular Culture* (PhD diss., Tulane University, October 11, 2013), 79–84; Tannehill, *Hurricane Hunters*, 246–48; and Peter T. White, "Why Gales Are Gals," *NYT*, September 26, 1954.

205 **Clement Lindley Wragge:** Background for Wragge comes from Peter Adamson, "Clement Lindley Wragge and the Naming of Weather Disturbances," *Weather*, September 2003, 359–63; and Paul D. Wilson, "Wragge, Clement Lindley (1852–1922)," in *Australian Dictionary of Biography*, vol. 12 (1990), http://adb.anu.edu .au/biography/wragge-clement-lindley-9193/text16237.

205 **"mop of flaming red hair":** Wilson, "Wragge."

205 **Tropical storm Elina was . . . "remember him for many a long day":** Ibid., 359–61.

207 **The notion of naming storms after women:** George R. Stewart, *Storm* (New York: Random House, 1941).

207 **In doing the research for the book:** Skilton, *Camille Was No Lady*, 73–74.

207 **each storm is "an individual":** Stewart, *Storm*, 6, 12.

207 **"incipient little whorl":** Ibid., 18.

207 **But instead of women:** Ibid., 234.

207 ***Storm* became a bestseller:** Skilton, *Camille Was No Lady*, 78–79.

208 **Those who have heard this:** Stewart, *Storm*, ix.

208 **"tragedy and havoc created":** "She Blows," *Raleigh News & Observer*, August 16, 1955. See also "Weather Bureau Doubts Hurricanes Are Girls," *NYT*, October 21, 1954.

208 **"She would rather have":** Alvin Shuster, "Storms over the Weather Bureau," *NYT*, September 19, 1954.

208 **"founding mother of Florida's":** Howard Cohen, Margaria Fichtner, and Elinor Brecher, "Civic Activist, Feminist, Trailblazer Roxcy Bolton Dies at 90," *MH*, May 17, 2017. See also Sam Roberts, "Roxcy Bolton, Feminist Crusader for Equality, Including in Naming Hurricanes, Dies at 90," *NYT*, May 21, 2017.

208 **"all incensed at the practice":** Betty Friedan, *Life So Far* (New York: Simon & Schuster, 2000), 185.

208 **"witches," "capricious," "furious":** Skilton, *Camille Was No Lady*, 146–50, 226; Meyer Berger, "Eccentric Edna Grazed the City with a Wet, but Vicious, Left Jab," *NYT*, September 12, 1954; and "The Weather: Vicious Lady," *Time*, September 5, 1949.

209 **"cease and desist" order:** Skilton, *Camille Was No Lady*, 175–76, 184.

209 **"delight in having streets":** Ibid., 185–86.

209 **"Can't you just see":** United Press International, "Weather Men Insist Storms are Feminine," *NYT*, April 23, 1972.

209 **"himicanes":** Roberts, "Roxcy Bolton."

209 **Appointed by President Jimmy Carter:** Skilton, *Camille Was No Lady*, 211–20; and "Hurricane Names," *BAMS*, June 1979, 695.

210 **In the end the United States proved:** NHC, "Tropical Cyclone Names," accessed December 2018, https://www.nhc.noaa.gov/aboutnames.shtml; and NHC, "Tropical Cyclone Naming History and Retired Names," accessed November 2018, https://www.nhc.noaa.gov/aboutnames_history.shtml.

210 **Coming at a time when sexism:** Skilton, *Camille Was No Lady*, 215–20; World Meteorological Association, "Tropical Cyclone Naming," accessed November 2018, https://public.wmo.int/en/About-us/FAQs/faqs-tropical-cyclones/tropical -cyclone-naming; and Richard D. Lyons, "Another Sexist Bastion Falls: Hurricanes Renamed," *NYT*, May 13, 1978.

210 **This juxtaposition was followed:** Jonah Engel Bromwich, "Harvey and Irma, Married 75 Years, Marvel at the Storms Bearing Their Names," *NYT*, September 8, 2017; and Mary Bowerman, "Washington Couple Harvey and Irma Amazed by Hurricanes Bearing Their Names," *USA Today*, September 8, 2017.

211 **both names were retired:** NHC, "Tropical Cyclone Naming History."

211 **Herbert S. Saffir:** Background for this section on the Saffir-Simpson Hurricane Wind Scale comes from NHC, "Saffir-Simpson Hurricane Wind Scale," accessed September 2018, https://www.nhc.noaa.gov/aboutsshws.php; Debi Iacovelli, "The Saffir/Simpson Hurricane Scale: An Interview with Dr. Robert Simpson," *Mariner's Weather Log*, April 1999; Robert H. Simpson (with Neal M. Dorst), *Hurricane Pioneer: Memoirs of Bob Simpson* (Boston: American Meteorological Society, 2015), 114; and Ann Carter, "Q & A with Herbert Saffir," *Sun-Sentinel*, June 24, 2001.

212 **Born in Corpus Christi:** Background for Simpson's early life comes from Simpson, *Hurricane Pioneer*, 1–9.

213 **"What a dreadful experience":** Ibid., 8–9.

213 **"I once heard the financial meltdown":** Emily Langer, "Robert Simpson, Co-creator of 1-to-5 Hurricane Model, Dies at 102," *Washington Post*, December 20, 2014.

215 **On September 10, the forty-six-year-old:** Background for this flight and Hurricane Edna comes from HRD, "60th Anniversary of Hurricane Edna," September 10, 2014, https://noaahrd.wordpress.com/2014/09/10/60th-anniversary -of-hurricane-edna; "Edward R. Murrow—The Best of See It Now 7—Eye of a Hurricane," YouTube, June 18, 2017, https://www.youtube.com/watch?v =1c12MrQ2Y48 (all of the quotes come from a transcription of this episode); and William Malkin and George C. Holzworth, "Hurricane Edna, 1954," *MWR*, September 1954, 267–79.

216 **In 1961, television reporting:** Background for Hurricane Carla and Dan Rather's role in reporting on it come from Dan Rather (with Mickey Herskowitz), *The Camera Never Blinks: Adventures of a TV Journalist* (New York: William Morrow, 1977), 44–57 (all the quotes in this section come from this book); Dan Rather, *Rather Outspoken: My Life in the News* (New York: Grand Central, 2012), 87–88; NWS, "Hurricane Carla—50th Anniversary," accessed October 2018, https://www.weather.gov/crp/hurricanecarla; Mediabistro, "Dan Rather: My First Big Break," YouTube, February 23, 2012, https://www.youtube.com/watch ?v=vmJnbeRr0vc; and Millicent Huff and H. Bailey Carroll, "Hurricane Carla at Galveston, 1961," *Southwestern Historical Quarterly*, January 1962, 293–94.

219 **In the 1960s, as more satellites:** David Laskin, *Braving the Elements: The Stormy History of American Weather* (New York: Anchor, 1997), 183–84; and Robert Henson, *Weather on the Air: A History of Broadcast Meteorology* (Boston: American Meteorological Society, 2010), 153–57.

220 **"In Cantore you have science":** Ed Dwyer, "America's Weather Obsession," *Saturday Evening Post*, April 18, 2014, https://www.saturdayeveningpost.com /2014/04/americas-weather-obsession.

220 **During Hurricane Isabel in 2003:** Weather Channel, "Jim Cantore's Top

Three Hurricanes," YouTube, August 6, 2013, https://www.youtube.com/watch ?v=h0mLHLc1reM.

220 **"People want to see what's going on":** Dwyer, "America's Weather Obsession."

221 **"social mediarologists":** Nicholas Bogel-Burroughs and Patricia Mazzei, "For Forecasters, Hurricane Dorian Has Already Been a Handful," *NYT*, August 31, 2019.

221 **"People are bombarded with":** Nancy Dahlberg, "When the Next Hurricane Strikes, Much More Technology Will Be on Our Side," *Government Technology*, August 22, 2017, https://www.govtech.com/em/disaster/When-the-Next -Hurricane-Strikes-Much-More-Technology-Will-be-on-Our-Side.html.

221 **"Hurricanes are the latest discovery"** . . . **"*for* hurricanes or *against* them":** E. B. White, "The Eye of Edna," in *Essays of E. B. White* (New York: Harper & Row, 1977), 25–27.

CHAPTER 8—A ROGUES' GALLERY

225 **Hurricane Carol was first identified:** Background for Hurricane Carol comes from Walter R. Davis, "Hurricanes of 1954," *MWR*, December 1954, 370–73; NHC, "Hurricanes in History," accessed November 2018, https://www.nhc .noaa.gov/outreach/history/#carol; Charles Grutzner, "Storm Lashes City—New England Hit, Old North Church Spire Falls," *NYT*, September 1, 1954; "Carol and Her Sisters," *NYT*, September 2, 1954; "The Terrible Twins," *NYT*, September 12, 1954; and "By Those Who Were There, What It's Like to Be in the Middle of a Hurricane," *Life*, September 13, 1954, 35–40.

225 **"couldn't get that in the papers":** Alvin Shuster, "Storms over the Weather Bureau," *NYT*, September 19, 1954.

225 **Edna, the hurricane that Murrow:** Background for Hurricane Edna comes from Davis, "Hurricanes of 1954"; NHC, "Hurricanes in History"; Grutzner, "Storm Lashes City"; "Carol and Her Sisters," *NYT*; "Terrible Twins," *NYT*; and Shuster, "Storms over the Weather Bureau."

225 **Normally, New England could expect:** Davis, "Hurricanes of 1954," 370.

227 **Newspaper articles raised the possibility:** "The Hurricane Challenge," *NYT*, August 19, 1955; and "Hurricane Warnings," *NYT*, September 9, 1954.

227 **"one of those coincidences in nature":** "2 Hurricanes in 11 Days Held 'Just Coincidence,'" *NYT*, September 12, 1954.

227 **Enter Hazel, the most devastating:** Background for Hurricane Hazel comes from NWS, "Hurricane Hazel, October 15, 1954," accessed November 2018, https:// www.weather.gov/mhx/Oct151954EventReview; Davis, "Hurricanes of 1954"; Jay Barnes, *North Carolina's Hurricane History* (Chapel Hill: University of North Carolina Press, 2013), 17, 78–107; and NHC, "Hurricanes in History."

227 **One other notable death occurred:** Robert W. Burpee, "Grady Norton: Hurricane Forecaster and Communicator Extraordinaire," *Forecaster Biography*, September 1988, 253.

228 **Robert H. Simpson:** Background for this section on Robert Simpson comes from Sheets and Williams, *Hurricane Watch*, 134–36.

229 **On August 12, 1955:** Gordon E. Dunn, Walter R. Davis, and Paul L. Moore, "Hurricanes of 1955," *MWR*, December 1955, 315–26; HRD, "60th Anniversary of Hurricanes Connie and Diane and NHRP Funding Authorization," August 17, 2015, https://noaahrd.wordpress.com/2015/08/17/60th-anniversary -of-hurricanes-connie-and-diane-and-nhrp-funding-authorization; and NHC, "Hurricanes in History."

229 **Consideration of Simpson's plan:** Sheets and Williams, *Hurricane Watch*, 135–36; Durst, "National Hurricane Research Project," 1568; and Simpson, *Hurricane Pioneer*, 81.

229 **If Congress needed any reassurance:** HRD, "60th Anniversary of Hurricanes Connie and Diane"; and NHC, "Hurricanes in History."

229 **Coming on the heels of Connie:** Dunn et al., "Hurricanes of 1955."

229 **Simpson's plan came into being:** H. E. Willoughby, D. P. Jorgensen, R. A. Black, and S. L. Rosenthal, "Project Stormfury: A Scientific Chronicle, 1962–1983," *BAMS*, May 1985, 505.

229 **Although it was slated for only:** Neal M. Dorst, "The National Hurricane Research Project: 50 Years of Research, Rough Rides, and Name Changes," *BAMS*, October 2007, 1568–73.

230 **In recognition of their tremendously:** NHC, "Tropical Cyclone Naming History and Retired Names," accessed November 2018, https://www.nhc.noaa.gov/about names_history.shtml.

231 **Hurricane Camille, a relatively small:** Background for Hurricane Camille up through its landfall and immediate aftermath comes from Stefan Bechtel, *Roar of the Heavens* (New York: Citadel Press, 2006), 7–116; US Department of Commerce, "Hurricane Camille: A Report to the Administrator," September 1969; Ernest Zebrowski and Judith A. Howard, *Category 5: The Story of Camille, Lessons Unlearned from America's Most Violent Hurricane* (Ann Arbor: University of Michigan Press, 2005), 2–158; Sheets and Williams, *Hurricane Watch*, 150–56; Philip D. Hearn, *Hurricane Camille: Monster Storm of the Gulf Coast* (Jackson: University of Mississippi Press, 2004), 1–135; NWS, "Hurricane Camille— August 17, 1969," accessed December 2018, https://www.weather.gov/mob /camille; R. H. Simpson, Arnold L. Sugg, and Staff, "The Atlantic Hurricane Season of 1969," *MWR*, April 1970, 297–301; "Hurricane Camille," *Weatherwise*, July/August 1999, 28–31; and Roger A. Pielke Jr., Chantal Simonpietri, and Jennifer Oxelson, *Thirty Years after Hurricane Camille: Lessons Learned, Lessons Lost*, Hurricane Camille Project Report, July 12, 1999, https://sciencepolicy .colorado.edu/about_us/meet_us/roger_pielke/camille/report.html#pielkes.

231 **"the most wicked eyewall I have ever seen":** Bechtel, *Roar of the Heavens*, 39.

232 **Police officers stopped by:** Hearn, *Hurricane Camille*, 26–27; and "20 Out of 23 Revelers Died," *Delta Democrat-Times*, August 20, 1969.

233 **At 10:00 p.m. the electricity . . . who helped her reach shelter:** Bechtel, *Roar of the Heavens*, 70–72, 88–90, 99–100.

233 **Not long after Mary Ann's escape . . . relief workers took care of him:** Zebrowski and Howard, *Category 5*, 115–16, 123–27, 130.

234 **"The first thing that popped":** Ibid., 6–7.

234 **"most trusted man in America":** Douglas Brinkley, *Cronkite* (New York: Harper Collins, 2012), 52, 479.

234 **"This is the former site":** Zebrowski and Howard, *Category 5*, 4.

236 **There were, however, serious . . . occasionally in stories about Camille:** Ibid., 6–8, 238–39; Bechtel, *Roar of the Heavens*, 262–63, 266–68; Dan Ellis, "Hurricane Party," accessed December 2018, http://camille.passchristian.net /hurricane_party.htm; Philip D. Carter, "Writing It All Down at Pass Christian," *Delta Democrat-Times*, August 21, 1969; Ken Kaye, "Experts: Mythical Camille Hurricane Party Never Happened," *Sun-Sentinel*, March 12, 2015; John Pope, "That Infamous Hurricane Camille Party on Aug. 17, 1969? It Never Happened," *Times-Picayune*, August 17, 2014; Hearn, *Hurricane Camille*, 173–74; Ron Har-

rist, "Memories of Camille Still Haunt Gulf Coast," *Washington Post*, August 17, 1989; and "Veteran of Betsy Avoided Tragic 'Hurricane Party,'" *Times-Picayune*, August 23, 1969.

236 **"Get yourself a bottle":** Roy Reed, "Hurricanes: The Grim Lessons of Camille," *NYT*, August 24, 1969.

236 **Of the many people who suffered:** Background for this section on Paul Williams comes from Bechtel, *Roar of the Heavens*, 80–84, 100–102; and "Giving Thanks, Even Though," *St. Petersburg Times*, August 25, 1969.

238 **"I look at their pictures":** Hearn, *Hurricane Camille*, 173.

238 **The number of people killed:** Zebrowski and Howard, *Category 5*, 150; "1969: Hurricane Camille Was a Category 5 Killer Storm," *Times-Picayune*, December 13, 2011; and Associated Press, "Storm Toll 170; A Luxury Project Yields 23 Bodies," *NYT*, August 20, 1969.

238 **According to the Red Cross:** Simpson et al., "Atlantic Hurricane Season of 1969," 300.

238 **In Buras, Louisiana:** US Department of Commerce, "Hurricane Camille," 3; US Army Engineer District, Mobile, "Hurricane Camille: 14–22 August 1969," May 1970, 3; and Clarence Doucet, "Storm Devastates Coast," *Times-Picayune*, August 19, 1969.

238 **Nearly 100 boats were sunk:** US Department of Commerce, "Hurricane Camille," 64; and Roy Reed, "Two Oil Slicks from After Hurricane," *NYT*, August 22, 1969.

238 **"The Gulf Coast looks like":** Hearn, *Hurricane Camille*, 148.

238 **"of the meat chopper action":** "Hurricane Expert Calls Storm Biggest in U.S.," *NYT*, August 22, 1969.

239 **Damage along the coast:** NOAA, National Centers for Environmental Information (NCEI), "Costliest U.S. Tropical Cyclones," October 8, 2019, https://www.ncdc.noaa.gov/billions/dcmi.pdf.

239 **As Camille traveled north:** Background for how the remnants of Hurricane Camille affected Nelson County, Virginia, comes from Bechtel, *Roar of the Heavens*, 119–254; Zebrowski and Howard, *Category 5*, 9–11, 159–236; Encyclopedia Virginia, s.v. "Hurricane Camille (August 1969)," by Lisa Romano, last modified September 9, 2010, http://www.EncyclopediaVirginia.org/Hurricane_Camille_August_1969; Simpson et al., "Atlantic Hurricane Season of 1969," 299–300; Robert M. Smith, "Virginia Town Washed Out," *NYT*, August 23, 1969; and Paige Shoaf Simpson and Jerry H. Simpson Jr., *Torn Land* (Lynchburg, VA: J. P. Bell, 1970).

239 **"a hornet's nest":** Simpson and Simpson, *Torn Land*, 2.

240 **The Raines family would suffer:** Background for the story of the Raines family comes from Bechtel, *Roar of the Heavens*, 119–25, 133–34, 151–56, 163–66, 184–86, 195, 207–9, 213–17, 241–42, 270–71; Zebrowski and Howard, *Category 5*, 10–11, 162–64, 186–87, 201–2; and Simpson and Simpson, *Torn Land*, 155–56.

241 **"Let go, we'll catch you":** Bechtel, *Roar of the Heavens*, 155. See also Zebrowski and Howard, *Category 5*, 163.

241 **The hardest-hit family:** Emily Brown, "Nelson County Remembers Camille's Impact on Davis Creek," *Roanoke Times*, August 20, 2016, https://www.roanoke.com/news/virginia/nelson-county-remembers-camille-s-impact-on-davis-creek/article_3beee9f8-023c-5942-baaf-d4a403456eb5.html.

241 **In the end, roughly 120 people:** Zebrowski and Howard, *Category 5*, 226; Ency-

clopedia Virginia, "Hurricane Camille"; Simpson et al., "Atlantic Season of 1969," 299–300; and Simpson and Simpson, *Torn Land*, 32.

242 **Since there were no official:** Zebrowski and Howard, *Category 5*, 174–75; Bechtel, *Roar of the Heavens*, 5, 161; Encyclopedia Virginia, "Hurricane Camille"; and Simpson et al., "Atlantic Hurricane Season of 1969," 299–300.

242 **Bryan Norcross wasn't even:** Bryan Norcross, *My Hurricane Andrew Story* (self-pub., 2017), iii–iv.

242 **Andrew wasn't all that impressive:** Background for this section on Hurricane Andrew comes from NOAA, *Hurricane Andrew: South Florida and Louisiana, August 23–26, 1992* (Silver Spring, MD: US Department of Commerce, 1993); Norcross, *My Hurricane Andrew Story*; Rick Gore, "Andrew Aftermath," *National Geographic*, April 1993, 2–37; Sheets and Williams, *Hurricane Watch*, 222–64; Howard Kleinberg, *The Florida Hurricane & Disaster 1992* (Miami: Centennial Press, 1992); HRD, "25th Anniversary of Hurricane Andrew Striking South Florida," August 23, 2017, https://noaahrd.wordpress.com/2017/08/23/25th-anniversary-of-hurricane-andrew; and NOAA, "Hurricane Andrew: What It Was Like to Work in a Category 5 Storm," August 24, 2017, https://www.noaa.gov/stories/hurricane-andrew-what-it-was-like-to-work-in-category-5-storm.

243 **The last hit had come from:** John M. Williams and Iver W. Duedall, *Florida Hurricanes and Tropical Storms, 1871–2001* (Gainesville: University Press of Florida, 2002), 30–31; and Arnold L. Sugg, "The Hurricane Season of 1965," *MWR*, March 1966, 185–87.

243 **Since Betsy, the population:** "Miami-Dade County Facts—2009: A Compendium of Selected Statistics," Miami-Dade County Department of Planning and Zoning, April 2009, 5.

243 **At 5:00 p.m., the National Hurricane Center:** NOAA, *Hurricane Andrew: South Florida and Louisiana*, 29.

244 **"Throughout south Florida":** Martin Merzer, Ronnie Green, and Manny Garcia, "The Realization Hits Home: This One Really Could Be It," *MH*, August 23, 1992.

244 **"Everywhere we went":** Dave Barry, "Hurricane Andrew May Be History, but Watch Out for Those Baboons!" *Baltimore Sun*, September 2, 1992.

244 **"Today was like a Christmas day":** Merzer et al., "Realization Hits Home."

244 **"I'm going to go home now":** Norcross, *My Hurricane Andrew Story*, 34.

245 **"Bigger, Stronger, Closer":** David Hancock and Anthony Faiola, "Bigger, Stronger, Closer," *MH*, August 23, 1992.

245 **Andrew had reached Category 3:** NOAA, *Hurricane Andrew: South Florida and Louisiana*, 29.

245 **"DANGEROUS CATEGORY FOUR HURRICANE":** Sheets and Williams, *Hurricane Watch*, 237.

245 **At 5:00 p.m., Andrew made landfall:** Christopher W. Landsea, James L. Franklin, Colin J. McAdie, John L. Beven II, James M. Gross, Brian R. Jarvinen, Richard J. Pasch, Edward N. Rappaport, Jason P. Dunnon, and Peter P. Dodge, "A Reanalysis of Hurricane Andrew's Intensity," *BAMS*, November 2004, 1708.

246 **"almost sounded like a brick wall":** Norcross, *My Hurricane Andrew Story*, 88.

246 **"the bunker":** Ibid., 77.

247 **"If we move off this desk":** Ibid., 73.

248 **"Friends," Norcross recalled saying:** Ibid., 71.

248 **Andrew raced across southeastern:** NOAA, *Hurricane Andrew: South Florida and Louisiana*, xv, 8, D-1, D-3; Sheets and Williams, *Hurricane Watch*, 256–59. For more on the concept of direct and indirect deaths due to hurricanes, please see Edward N. Rappaport and B. Wayne Blanchard, "Fatalities in the United States Indirectly Associated with Atlantic Tropical Cyclones," *BAMS*, July 2016, 1139–48.

248 **Andrew tore a 30-mile-wide swath . . . clean off the face of the Earth:** NOAA, *Hurricane Andrew: South Florida and Louisiana*, xv, 10; Gore, "Andrew Aftermath," 2–37, 264; and Jay Barnes, *Florida's Hurricane History* (Chapel Hill: University of North Carolina Press, 2007), 264.

249 **More than 160,000 people:** Larry Rother, "After Homes Are Ruined, Hopes Are Dashed," *NYT*, August 28, 1992.

250 **"look as if they have been drenched":** Gore, "Andrew Aftermath," 33.

250 **"The devastation is unbelievable":** Donna Gehrke, "Zoo, 'Unbelievable' Devastation," *MH*, August 26, 1992.

250 **Scores, perhaps hundreds, of monkeys:** Ibid.; and Dan Fesperman, "In Andrew's Wake, a New Wild Kingdom Monkeys, Cougars Still Running Loose Weeks after Storm," *Baltimore Sun*, September 20, 1992; and Associated Press, "Hurricane Lets Loose Dozens of Research Monkeys on Streets with AM-Hurricane Aftermath," AP News, August 26, 1992.

250 **Parrots, capybaras:** Abby Goodnough, "Forget the Gators: Exotic Pets Run Wild in Florida," *NYT*, February 29, 2004.

251 **The most dramatic example:** M. Mayfield, Lixion Avila, and Edward N. Rappaport, "Atlantic Hurricane Season of 1992," *MWR*, March 1994, 517–38.

251 **Total damage in Florida:** NOAA, *Hurricane Andrew: South Florida and Louisiana*, xv, B-1; and NOAA, NCEI, "Costliest U.S. Tropical Cyclones."

251 **Bryan Norcross continued broadcasting:** Norcross, *My Hurricane Andrew Story*, 116–17.

251 **"the man who talked south Florida through":** Hal Boedeker, "The Man Who Talked South Florida Through," *MH*, August 25, 1992.

251 **"distinguished himself as local television's":** Hal Boedeker, "Channel 4, Norcross Excel," *MH*, August 25, 1992.

251 **Instead, they offered to renew:** Norcross, *My Hurricane Andrew Story*, 179.

251 **More than 3 million cubic yards:** Kleinberg, *Florida Hurricane*, 72.

252 **"Richard and I have been married":** John Dorschner, "The Hurricane That Changed Everything," in *Hurricane Andrew: The Big One* (Miami: Miami Herald Publishing, 1992), 18. See also Kleinberg, *Florida Hurricane*, 14.

252 **At the Keg South burger and beer:** Dorschner, "Hurricane That Changed Everything," 15. See also Lisa Getter and Grace Lim, "Looters Add Insult to Andrew's Injury," *MH*, August 26, 1992.

252 **On the afternoon of August 24:** FEMA, "Florida Hurricane Andrew (DR-955)," accessed November 2019, https://www.fema.gov/disaster/955.

252 **Created in 1979 by President Jimmy Carter:** Douglas Brinkley, *The Great Deluge: Hurricane Katrina, New Orleans, and the Mississippi Gulf Coast* (New York: William Morrow, 2006), 247; Reuters, "After the Storm; House Report Cites Appointees as Part of Relief Problems," *NYT*, September 2, 1992; and Kevin Drum, "Like Father, Like Son?" *Washington Monthly*, August 31, 2005, https://washingtonmonthly.com/2005/08/31/like-father-like-son.

253 **"the sorriest bunch of bureaucratic":** Michael Wines, "Congress Votes Sharp Increase in Storm Relief," *NYT*, September 29, 1989.

253　**The same day that Bush declared . . . little evidence of any federal response:** Dorschner, "Hurricane That Changed Everything," 16.

253　**"Enough is enough":** Kleinberg, *Florida Hurricane*, 40. See also Ronnie Greene, "Bottlenecks Thwart Aid Efforts," *MH*, August 29, 1992.

254　**Hale's emotional plea:** David Lyons and Martin Merzer, "Answering an Urgent Cry: Soldiers Shocked by Panorama of Ruin," *MH*, August 29, 1992; and Larry Rother, "Troops Arrive with Food for Florida's Storm Victims," *NYT*, August 29, 1992.

254　**There would be considerable:** Robert Pear, "Breakdown Seen in U.S. Storm Aid," *NYT*, August 29, 1992; and Kartik Krishnaiyer, "Part IV: Bush, Chiles, FEMA and the Botched Response," *Florida Squeeze*, August 11, 2017, https:// thefloridasqueeze.com/hurricane-andrew-25-years-later/part-iv-bush-chiles-fema -and-the-botched-response.

254　**"responded properly":** Pear, "Breakdown Seen."

254　**"going to participate in the blame game":** Adam Howard, "How Hurricanes Have Disrupted and Defined Past Elections," NBC News, October 6, 2016, https://www.nbcnews.com/storyline/hurricane-matthew/how-hurricanes-have -disrupted-defined-past-elections-n660796.

254　**"FEMA was prepared to do":** Ivor van Heerden and Mike Bryan, *The Storm: What Went Wrong and Why during Hurricane Katrina—The Inside Story from One Louisiana Scientist* (New York: Viking, 2006), 138.

254　**"pitch in, any way you can":** Kleinberg, *Florida Hurricane*, 86.

254　**Still, some have argued:** Meredith McGraw, "A Look Back at How Hurricanes Affect Presidential Elections," October 7, 2016, ABC News, https://abcnews.go .com/Politics/back-hurricanes-affect-presidential-elections/story?id=42643749; Howard, "How Hurricanes Have Disrupted"; Ed O'Keefe, "One Bush Gets Praise for His Handling of Hurricanes—including Katrina," *Washington Post*, August 25, 2015; and van Heerden and Bryan, *Storm*, 138.

255　**"Thousands of South Floridians":** "We Shall Overcome," *MH*, August 26, 1992.

255　**Director Steven Spielberg had planned:** Background for the *Jurassic Park* connection to Hurricane Iniki comes from Jurassic Time Official Channel, "Iniki Jurassic," YouTube, July 25, 2014, https://www.youtube.com/watch?v=DP_ drlbBpRM; and Susan Essoyan and Jim Newton, "Hurricane Damage in Hawaii Expected to Top $1 Billion," *Los Angeles Times*, September 13, 1992.

255　**when Hurricane Iniki slammed:** Background for Hurricane Iniki comes from *Hurricane Iniki, September 6–13, 1992*, Natural Disaster Survey Report (Silver Spring, MD: US Department of Commerce, NOAA, NWS, 1993); Makena Coffman and Ilan Noy, "A Hurricane Hits Hawaii: A Tale of Vulnerability to Natural Disasters," *CESifo Forum*, February 2010, 67–72; HRD, "25th Anniversary of Hurricane Iniki," September 20, 2017, https://noaahrd.wordpress .com/2017/09/20/25th-anniversary-of-hurricane-iniki; Central Pacific Hurricane Center, "The 1992 Central Pacific Tropical Cyclone Season," accessed December 2018, https://www.prh.noaa.gov/cphc/summaries/1992.php#Iniki; Honolulu Advertiser, *Hurricane Iniki* (Honolulu: Mutual Publishing, 1992), compilation of coverage from the newspaper; and "Hurricane Iniki: Quick Facts about Hawaii's Most Powerful Storm," Hawaii News Now, September 7, 2017 (updated August 15, [2019]), http://www.hawaiinewsnow.com/story/36315106/hurricane-iniki -quick-facts-about-hawaiis-most-powerful-storm.

255　**"a real zinger":** Al Kamen, "Hawaii Hurricane Devastates Kauai," *Washington Post*, September 13, 1992.

255 **Hurricanes are extremely rare:** Jason Daley, "Why Hawaiian Hurricanes Are So Rare," Smithsonian.com, August 23, 2018, https://www.smithsonianmag .com/smart-news/why-are-hawaiian-hurricanes-so-rare-180970116; Jonathan Belles, "Hawaii Hurricanes: How Unusual Are They?" Weather Channel, August 21, 2018, https://weather.com/storms/hurricane/news/2018-08-03 -hawaii-hurricane-tropical-typical-track-history; Rafi Letzter, "Hawaii Faces Huge Hurricane: Why That's So Rare," Live Science, August 22, 2018, https:// www.livescience.com/63402-hurricane-lane-hawaii-rare.html; and Mary Beth Griggs, "Hurricanes like Lane Rarely Hit Hawaii. Here's Why," *Popular Science*, August 22, 2018.

256 **Iniki grew much stronger:** Jim Borg, "The Power behind Hurricane Iniki," *Honolulu Advertiser*, September 12, 1992.

256 **"We should all pray it turns away":** Walter Wright, "Get Ready for Iniki," *Honolulu Advertiser*, September 11, 1992.

256 **"This was going to be more":** Jurassic Time Official Channel, "Iniki Jurassic."

257 **Damage on the island was deemed "mind boggling":** "Iniki's Madness," *Honolulu Advertiser*, September 12, 1992.

257 **such "total destruction—it broke":** David Waite and Jan TenBruggencate, "Kauai Mayor: Hurricane Left 'Total Destruction,'" *Star Bulletin & Advertiser*, September 13, 1992.

257 **Nearly 15,000 homes:** Central Pacific Hurricane Center, "1992 Central Pacific Tropical Cyclone Season"; NOAA, NCEI, "Costliest U.S. Tropical Cyclones"; James Dooley, "Oahu Storm Damage Confined," *Honolulu Advertiser*, September 13, 1992; and L. A. Hendrickson, R. L. Vogt, D. Goebert, and E. Pon, "Morbidity on Kauai before and after Hurricane Iniki," *Preventive Medicine*, September–October, 1997.

257 **Thousands of jobs were lost:** Coffman and Noy, "Hurricane Hits Hawaii," 69, 71; and Jan TenBruggencate, "Kauai's Unemployment at 25% in Iniki's Wake," *Honolulu Advertiser*, October 6, 1992.

258 **"he would only draw dark circles":** Anthony Sommer, "Iniki: A Decade after the Disaster," *Star Bulletin*, September 8, 2002.

258 **Hurricane Katrina ravaged parts:** Background for this section on Hurricane Katrina comes from Richard D. Knabb, Jamie R. Rhome, and Daniel P. Brown, "Hurricane Katrina, 23–30 August 2005," Tropical Cyclone Report, NHC, December 20, 2005 (with later updates in 2006 and 2011); Brinkley, *Great Deluge*; Time Magazine, *Hurricane Katrina: The Storm That Changed America* (New York: Time Books, 2005); Robert Ricks Jr., "In the Shoes of Katrina's Forecasters," *Weatherwise*, July/August 2007, 36–41; Eric S. Blake, Christopher W. Landsea, and Ethan J. Gibney, "The Deadliest, Costliest, and Most Intense United States Tropical Cyclones from 1851 to 2010 (and Other Frequently Requested Hurricane Facts)," NOAA Technical Memorandum NWS NHC-6, August 2011, 5, 7; NOAA, NCEI, "Costliest U.S. Tropical Cyclones"; and American Society of Civil Engineers, *The New Orleans Hurricane Protection System: What Went Wrong and Why* (Reston, VA: ASCE, 2007).

258 **Estimates of the number:** Knabb et al., "Hurricane Katrina," 11; Carl Bialik, "We Still Don't Know How Many People Died Because of Katrina," FiveThirtyEight, August 26, 2015, https://fivethirtyeight.com/features/we-still-dont-know -how-many-people-died-because-of-katrina; and Rappaport and Blanchard, "Fatalities in the United States," 1142.

258 **On August 24, 1992:** CNN, "Hurricane Katrina Statistics Fast Facts," August

30, 2018, https://www.cnn.com/2013/08/23/us/hurricane-katrina-statistics-fast -facts/index.html; Ken Kaye, "Hurricane Katrina Hit South Florida 10 Years Ago Today," *Sun Sentinel*, August 25, 2015, https://www.sun-sentinel.com/news /weather/sfl-blog-208-katrina-anniversary-20150814-story.html.

259 **There were plenty of reasons . . . underfunding and maintenance issues:** Mike Scott, "Remembering Hurricane Betsy, a New Orleans Nightmare," NOLA .com, May 31, 2017, https://www.nola.com/300/2017/05/hurricane_betsy_new_ orleans_05312017.html; David Remnick, "Under Water," *The New Yorker*, September 12, 2005; and Richard Campanella, "How Humans Sank New Orleans," *Atlantic*, February 6, 2018, https://www.theatlantic.com/technology/archive /2018/02/how-humans-sank-new-orleans/552323.

259 **Since Betsy, the city's vulnerability:** J. Tibbetts, "Louisiana's Wetlands: A Lesson in Nature Appreciation," *Environmental Health Perspectives*, January 2006, A40–43; and Brinkley, *Great Deluge*, 13.

259 **Numerous reports and studies:** Brinkley, *Great Deluge*, 14–15.

259 **"That would turn the city":** John McQuaid and Mark Schleifstein, "The Big One," *Times-Picayune*, June 24, 2002.

260 **The series hinted that:** John McQuaid and Mark Schleifstein, "Washing Away: Worst-Case Scenarios if a Hurricane Hits Louisiana (2002)," NOLA.com, https:// www.nola.com/environment/page/washing_away_2002.html.

260 **Just a year before Katrina hit:** John McQuaid, "'Hurricane Pam' Exercise Offered Glimpse of Katrina Misery," NOLA.com, September 9, 2005, https:// www.nola.com/environment/page/washing_away_2002.html (the quoted phrase "HazMat gumbo" comes from this source); *A Failure of Initiative*, Final Report of the Select Bipartisan Committee to Investigate the Preparation for and Response to Hurricane Katrina, US House of Representatives (Washington, DC: Government Printing Office, 2006), 81; Brinkley, *Great Deluge*, 18–19; and FEMA, "Hurricane Pam Exercise Concludes," July 23, 2004, https://www.fema.gov/news -release/2004/07/23/hurricane-pam-exercise-concludes.

261 **"The guidance we get":** Mark Schleifstein, "Hurricane Center Director Warns New Orleans: This Is Really Scary," *Times-Picayune*, August 27, 2005.

261 **"The thing I remember telling":** "FEMA Chief Taken Off Hurricane Relief Efforts," Fox News, September 9, 2005.

262 **One study in 2003 estimated:** John C. Whitehead, "One Million Dollars per Mile? The Opportunity Costs of Hurricane Evacuation," *Ocean & Coastal Management* 46, nos. 11–12 (2003): 1069–83.

262 **"A POTENTIALLY CATASTROPHIC":** NHC, "Hurricane Katrina," Special Advisory no. 22, August 28, 2005, https://www.nhc.noaa.gov/archive/2005/pub/ al122005.public.022.shtml?.

262 **"We're facing the storm":** Brinkley, *Great Deluge*, 87.

263 **In a replay of Hurricane Camille:** Ibid., 133.

264 **Katrina left a trail:** Haley Barbour and Jere Nash, *Katrina Left a Trail: America's Great Storm* (Jackson: University Press of Mississippi, 2015), 28–29.

264 **"dodged a bullet":** Brian Williams, "Brian Williams: We Were Witnesses," NBC News, August 28, 2006, http://www.nbcnews.com/id/14518359/ns/nbc_nightly _news_with_brian_williams-after_katrina/t/brian-williams-we-were-witnesses /#.XIesQ1NJEkg; and Brian Montopoli, "A Matter of Time," CBS News, September 12, 2005, https://www.cbsnews.com/news/a-matter-of-time.

264 **"Until nearly the last minute":** Jeremy Manier and Michael Hawthorne, "Path Puts Off City's Day of Reckoning," *Chicago Tribune*, August 30, 2005.

267 **Looting was widespread:** Dan Baum, "Deluged," *The New Yorker*, January 9, 2006; and Brinkley, *Great Deluge*, 48–54, 199–208, 511–13, 599–600.

268 **"It was a shelter of last resort":** Brinkley, *Great Deluge*, 239.

268 **Thousands of doctors and staff:** Ibid., 631; Bradford H. Gray and Kathy Hebert, *After Katrina: Hospitals in Hurricane Katrina, Challenges Facing Custodial Institutions in a Disaster* (Washington, DC: Urban Institute, 2006); and Denise Danna and Sandra E. Cordray, *Nursing in the Storm: Voices from Hurricane Katrina* (New York: Springer, 2010).

268 *Five Days at Memorial*: Sheri Fink, *Five Days at Memorial* (New York: Crown, 2013).

269 **the so-called Cajun Navy:** Brinkley, *Great Deluge*, 372–81, 423, 447, 614–15; and "How Citizens Turned into Saviors after Katrina Struck," CBS News, August 29, 2015, https://www.cbsnews.com/news/remembering-the-cajun-navy-10-years -after-hurricane-katrina.

269 **Since the mid-twentieth century:** Elizabeth Kolbert, "The Control of Nature: Under Water," *The New Yorker*, April 1, 2019, 34.

269 **While some of that loss:** Monica Palaseanu-Lovejoy, "How Hurricanes Shape Wetlands in Southern Louisiana," Smithsonian Ocean, November 2013, https:// ocean.si.edu/ecosystems/coasts-shallow-water/how-hurricanes-shape-wetlands -southern-louisiana.

269 **New Orleans's levees were built:** Brinkley, *Great Deluge*, 7–9, 12, 194–97, 279– 80; G. L. Sills, N. D. Vroman, R. E. Wahl, and N. T. Schwantz, "Overview of New Orleans Levee Failures: Lessons Learned and Their Impact on National Levee Design and Assessment," *Journal of Geotechnical and Geoenvironmental Engineering*, May 2008, 556–65; and American Society of Civil Engineers, *New Orleans Hurricane Protection System*.

270 **Despite significant and very clear . . . and the "ghost train" left empty:** Susan B. Glasser and Michael Grunwald, "The Steady Buildup to a City's Chaos," *Washington Post*, September 11, 2005 (the quoted phrase "ghost train" comes from this source). See also Brinkley, *Great Deluge*, 19–20, 90–92, 250.

270 **"There's . . . things that I would":** *Anderson Cooper 360 Degrees*, January 20, 2006, transcript, CNN.com, http://transcripts.cnn.com/TRANSCRIPTS/0601/ 20/acd.01.html.

270 **"Brownie, you're doing":** "Bush: 'Brownie, You're Doing a Heck of a Job,'" video, CNN Politics, accessed December 2018, https://www.cnn.com/videos/ politics/2017/10/26/george-w-bush-hurricane-katrina-fema-michael-brown.cnn /video/playlists/president-george-w-bush; and Scott Shane, Eric Lipton, and Christopher Drew, "After Failures, Government Officials Play Blame Game," *NYT*, September 5, 2005.

270 **"Michael Brown was patently":** Brinkley, *Great Deluge*, 549.

271 **During President Bill Clinton's . . . over disciplinary actions:** Brinkley, *Great Deluge*, 245–50; Jon Elliston, "FEMA: Confederacy of Dunces," *Nation*, September 8, 2005; Alan C. Miller and Carla Rivera, "A True Master of Disaster," *Los Angeles Times*, April 8, 1994; *Frontline*, "A Short History of FEMA," PBS, November 22, 2005, https://www.pbs.org/wgbh/pages/frontline/storm/ etc/femahist.html; Ken Silverstein, "FEMA Steeped in Politics," *Seattle Times*, September 9, 2005; Daren Fonda and Rita Healy, "How Reliable Is Brown's Resume?" *Time*, September 8, 2005; Peter G. Gosselin and Alan C. Miller, "Why FEMA Was Missing in Action," *Los Angeles Times*, September 5, 2005; and Seth

Borenstein and Matt Stearns, "FEMA Leader's Background Was in Law, Horses," *Seattle Times*, September 4, 2005.

271 **"The Master of Disaster":** Leslie Wayne and Glen Justice, "FEMA Director under Clinton Profits from Experience," *NYT*, October 10, 2005.

271 **Among the agency's numerous:** Brinkley, *Great Deluge*, 162–63, 208–9, 268–69, 278, 290–91, 334–36, 356, 396, 410–12, 509, 535–36, 563, 580–83, 610–11; Time Magazine, *Hurricane Katrina*, 92–93; Glasser and Grunwald, "Steady Buildup to a City's Chaos"; and Eric Lipton, "Republicans' Report on Katrina Assails Administration Response," *NYT*, February 13, 2006; "Actually It Was FEMA's Job," editorial, *NYT*, October 2, 2005.

272 **"This is a national disgrace":** Brinkley, *Great Deluge*, 452.

272 **"Open Letter to President":** "Open Letter to President George W. Bush," *Times-Picayune*, September 4, 2005.

272 **At a congressional hearing in December 2005:** Romain Huret, "Explaining the Unexplainable: Hurricane Katrina, FEMA, and the Bush Administration," in *Hurricane Katrina in Transatlantic Perspective*, ed. Romain Huret and Randy J. Sparks (Baton Rouge: Louisiana State University Press, 2014), 47.

273 **As a result of his poor performance:** CNN, "FEMA Director Brown Resigns," September 12, 2005, http://www.cnn.com/2005/POLITICS/09/12/brown.resigns.

273 **"Katrina exposed serious problems":** CNN, "Bush: 'I Take Responsibility' for Federal Failures after Katrina," September 13, 2005, http://www.cnn.com/2005/POLITICS/09/13/katrina.washington/index.html.

273 **"He never recovered from Katrina":** Kenneth T. Walsh, "The Undoing of George W. Bush," *U.S. News & World Report*, August 28, 2015, https://www.usnews.com/news/the-report/articles/2015/08/28/hurricane-katrina-was-the-beginning-of-the-end-for-george-w-bush. See also Richard T. Sylves, "President Bush and Hurricane Katrina: A Presidential Leadership Study," *Annals of the American Academy of Political and Social Science*, March 2006, 26–56.

273 **Some observers believe:** Howard, "How Hurricanes Have Disrupted."

273 **"If it was a bunch of white people":** Michael Eric Dyson, *Come Hell or High Water: Hurricane Katrina and the Color of Disaster* (New York: Basic Books, 2006), 17.

273 **"It is safe to say that race":** Ibid., 24.

273 **"There has been a lot of attention":** Rebecca Nelson, "Will President Obama Reverse Course on Race and Katrina?" *Atlantic*, August 27, 2015, https://www.theatlantic.com/politics/archive/2015/08/will-president-obama-reverse-course-on-race-and-katrina/451284. See also Brinkley, *Great Deluge*, 618.

274 **"What started out as a natural disaster":** Scott Neuman, "Obama: Katrina a 'Man-Made' Disaster Caused by Government Failure," *The Two-Way* (blog), NPR, August 27, 2015, https://www.npr.org/sections/thetwo-way/2015/08/27/435258344/obama-katrina-a-man-made-disaster-caused-by-government-failure.

274 **The hard work of recovery . . . hurricane relief and rebuilding:** CNN, "Hurricane Katrina Statistics Fast Facts"; Jeremy Hobson, "How New Orleans Reduced Its Homeless Population by 90 Percent," WBUR, February 19, 2019, https://www.wbur.org/hereandnow/2019/02/19/new-orleans-reducing-homeless-hurricane-katrina; Allison Plyer, "Facts for Features: Katrina Impact," Data Center, August 26, 2016, https://www.datacenterresearch.org/data-resources/katrina/facts-for-impact; Campbell Robertson and Richard Fausset, "10 Years after Katrina," *NYT*, August 26, 2015; and Michael L. Dolfman, Solidelle Fortier Wasser, and

Bruce Bergman, "The Effects of Hurricane Katrina on the New Orleans Economy," *Monthly Labor Review*, June 2007, 3–18.

274 **Following Katrina, federal, state:** John Schwartz and Mark Schleifstein, "Fortified but Still in Peril, New Orleans Braces for Its Future," *NYT*, February 24, 2018; Mark Schleifstein, "With New Massive Pumps Online, New Orleans Levee System Faces 2018 Hurricane Season," NOLA.com, *Times-Picayune*, May 27, 2018, https://expo.nola.com/erry-2018/05/df6c9a722a7295/new_orleans_area _levees_under.html; "New Orleans Area Levee System 'High Risk,' and 'Minimally Acceptable,' Corps Says," *Times-Picayune*, May 22, 2018; "Our Levees and Pumps Aren't Enough to Keep New Orleans Dry," *Times-Picayune*, May 27, 2018; and Andy Horowitz, "When the Levees Break Again," *NYT*, May 31, 2019.

275 **But the situation is even more:** US Army Corps of Engineers, "Notice of Intent to Prepare a Draft Environmental Impact Statement for the Lake Pontchartrain and Vicinity General Re-evaluation Report, Louisiana," *Federal Register*, April 2, 2019, 12598–99; and Thomas Frank, "After a $14-Billion Upgrade, New Orleans' Levees Are Sinking," *Scientific American* (reprinted from *E&E News*, April 11, 2019), https://www.scientificamerican.com/article/after-a-14-billion-upgrade -new-orleans-levees-are-sinking/?redirect=1.

275 **"Absent future levee lifts":** US Army Corps of Engineers, "Notice of Intent to Prepare a Draft," 12598.

275 **It wasn't much of a threat . . . hitting New Jersey dead-on:** Adam Sobel, *Storm Surge: Hurricane Sandy, Our Changing Climate, and Extreme Weather of the Past and Future* (New York: HarperWave, 2014), xv, 25–70; Kathryn Miles, *Superstorm: Nine Days inside Hurricane Sandy* (New York: Dutton, 2014), 9–11; Eric S. Blake, Todd B. Kimberlain, Robert J. Berg, John P. Cangialosi, and John L. Beven II, "Hurricane Sandy, 22–29 October 2012," Tropical Cyclone Report AL182012, NHC, February 12, 2013; and Nick Wiltgen, "Superstorm Sandy: Triumph of the Forecasting Models," Weather Channel, October 30, 2013, https://weather.com/ storms/hurricane/news/sandy-triumph-of-the-models-20121102#/1.

275 **The only hurricane known:** Tom Karmel, "New Jersey Hurricane Hunting: A Brief Recap of a Small State's Big Hurricane History," Rutgers NJ Weather Network, August 21, 2014, https://www.njweather.org/content/new-jersey -hurricane-hunting-brief-recap-small-state%E2%80%99s-big-hurricane-history; and Miles, *Superstorm*, 11.

276 **the Global Forecast System Model "blinked":** Sobel, *Storm Surge*, 70.

276 **By the time the models aligned . . . continued north as a Category 1 hurricane:** Richard Knox, "Before Sandy Hit U.S., Storm Was a Killer in Haiti," NPR, October 31, 2012, https://www.npr.org/sections/health-shots/2012/10/31/164045691/ before-sandy-hit-u-s-storm-was-a-killer-in-haiti; Blake et al., "Hurricane Sandy," 1–5, 120; and Karl Tate, "Timeline of Hurricane Sandy's Week of Destruction (Infographic)," Live Science, November 1, 2012, https://www.livescience.com /24473-timeline-of-hurricane-sandy-s-week-of-destruction-infographic.html.

276 **likely to become a "whopper":** John Schwartz, "Early Worries That Hurricane Sandy Could Be a 'Perfect Storm,'" *NYT*, October 25, 2012.

276 **"Frankenstorm":** Andy Newman, "Cloudy with a Chance of Hybrid Vortices," *NYT*, October 25, 2012; and Jason Hanna and Mariano Castillo, "How Sandy Was Dubbed 'Frankenstorm,'" *This Just In* (blog), CNN, October 26, 2012, http://news.blogs.cnn.com/2012/10/26/how-sandy-was-dubbed-frankenstorm.

277 **The catchy name became:** Doyle Rice, "What's in a Name? Frankenstorm vs. Sandy," *USA Today*, October 26, 2012.

277 **The models had Sandy ... could create a major disaster:** Sobel, *Storm Surge*, 55–74; Miles, *Superstorm*, 151–52; Newman, "Cloudy with a Chance"; Jennifer Preston, "Tracking Hurricane Sandy up the East Coast," *NYT*, October 25, 2012; and Adam Taylor, "Frankenstorm: The Mother of All Snowicanes Is Barreling toward New York City," *Business Insider*, October 25, 2012.

277 **"Halloween Horror":** Mark Memmott, "Halloween Horror: Hurricane Sandy Could Be 'Billion-Dollar Storm,'" *The Two-Way* (blog), NPR, October 25, 2012, https://www.npr.org/sections/thetwo-way/2012/10/25/163607781/halloween -horror-hurricane-sandy-could-be-billion-dollar-storm.

277 **Robin Walbridge, however ... in New London a little after sunset:** Gregory A. Freeman, *The Gathering Wind: Hurricane Sandy, the Sailing Ship* Bounty, *and a Courageous Rescue at Sea* (New York: New American Library, 2013), 15–31, 47–73; Miles, *Superstorm*, 12–20, 85–91, 171–74, 182–84; and National Transportation Safety Board, *Marine Accident Brief: Sinking of Tall Ship* Bounty (Washington, DC: NTSB, March 2014), 1–5 (the quoted phrase "chased hurricanes" comes from this source).

279 **On Friday, October 26 ... much of the Eastern Seaboard:** Sobel, *Storm Surge*, 73, 95–101, 111–14, 127–28; and Blake et al., "Hurricane Sandy," 6.

280 **That change in the label:** Sobel, *Storm Surge*, 99.

280 **New York governor Andrew M. Cuomo:** "Governor Cuomo Declares State of Emergency in New York in Preparation for Potential Impact of Hurricane Sandy," New York State, October 26, 2012, https://www.governor.ny.gov/news /governor-cuomo-declares-state-emergency-new-york-preparation-potential-impact -hurricane-sandy.

280 **"We should not underestimate":** "New Jersey Governor on Hurricane Sandy," Times Video, October 27, 2012, https://www.nytimes.com/video/multimedia /100000001870409/gov-chris-christie-on-hurricane-sandy.html.

280 **President Barack Obama, wanting:** Miles, *Superstorm*, 244.

280 **"We're making that decision":** Sobel, *Storm Surge*, 124; and Eric Holthaus and Jason Samenow, "Department of Homeland Security May Review Superstorm Sandy Warnings," *Washington Post*, November 28, 2012.

280 **The Irene he was talking about:** Sam Dolnick, "Recovery Is Slower in New York Suburbs," *NYT*, August 28, 2011; and Sobel, *Storm Surge*, 122–23.

281 **Just before noon on Sunday:** Ben Yakas, "Bloomberg Orders Mandatory Evacuation of All NYers in Zone A," Gothamist, October 28, 2012, http://gothamist .com/2012/10/28/watch_live_now_bloomberg_updates_ci_1.php; Miles, *Superstorm*, 275–76; and James Baron, "Sharp Warnings as Hurricane Churns In," *NYT*, October 28, 2012.

281 **About the same time, Governor Cuomo:** Ted Mann, "New York City Subways to Shut Down as Sandy Nears," *Wall Street Journal*, October 28, 2012.

281 **It wasn't only New York:** Baron, "Sharp Warnings"; CNN, "Hurricane Sandy Fast Facts," October 29, 2018, https://www.cnn.com/2013/07/13/world/americas/ hurricane-sandy-fast-facts/index.html; and Michael J. De La Merced, "Bracing for Storm, U.S. Stock Markets to Close," *NYT*, October 28, 2012.

281 **As the East Coast was preparing:** Background for this section on the *Bounty*, its sinking, and the rescues of the crew comes from National Transportation Safety Board, *Marine Accident Brief*; US Coast Guard, "Investigation into the Circumstances Surrounding the Sinking of the Tall Ship Bounty," MISLE Activity no. 4474566, May 2, 2014; Freeman, *Gathering Wind*, 92–226; Miles, *Superstorm*, 291–306, 310–14; Kathryn Miles, "Sunk: The Incredible Truth about a Ship That

Never Should Have Sailed," *Outside*, February 11, 2013, https://www.outside online.com/1913636/sunk-incredible-truth-about-ship-never-should-have-sailed; and Thom Patterson, "Family of Killed Bounty Deckhand Sues Shipowners," CNN, May 12, 2013, https://www.cnn.com/2013/05/10/us/bounty-shipwreck-lawsuit /index.html.

282 **"I am ok and HAPPY TO BE HERE":** Freeman, *Gathering Wind*, 93.

282 **"It looks like a big pirate ship":** Ibid., 136.

283 **"that the probable cause":** National Transportation Safety Board, *Marine Accident Brief*, 15.

284 **"they made such a big hype":** Cara Buckley, "Panicked Evacuations Mix with Nonchalance in Hurricane Sandy's Path," *NYT*, October 28, 2012.

284 **"EXPECTED TO BRING LIFE-THREATENING":** NHC, "Hurricane Sandy," Advisory no. 26, October 28, 2012, https://www.nhc.noaa.gov/archive/2012/ al18/al182012.public.026.shtml?.

284 **That was the first, and is still:** Sobel, *Storm Surge*, 141.

284 **At 2:30 p.m., wind gusts:** Marc Santora, "Crane Is Dangling off Luxury High-Rise," *NYT*, October 29, 2012.

284 **As the waters rose, overtopping:** Matt Chaban, "Hurricane Sandy Shuts Down Transportation, Nearly Every Bridge, Tunnel and Major Roadway Closed," *New York Daily News*, October 29, 2012.

284 **Already, 40,000 people:** Sarah Maslin, "A Road Disappears, and a Body Is Discovered," *NYT*, October 29, 2012.

284 **At 5:00 p.m., Hurricane Sandy became:** Miles, *Superstorm*, 321; and Tim Sharp, "Superstorm Sandy: Facts about the Frankenstorm," Live Science, November 27, 2012, https://www.livescience.com/24380-hurricane-sandy-status-data.html.

284 **At 7:30 p.m., Sandy made landfall:** Blake et al., "Hurricane Sandy," 4, 6.

285 **Its waves pounded the shore:** Joseph Stromberg, "Hurricane Sandy Generated Seismic Shaking as Far Away as Seattle," Smithsonian.com, April 18, 2013, https://www.smithsonianmag.com/science-nature/hurricane-sandy-generated -seismic-shaking-as-far-away-as-seattle-25993081.

285 **One wave measured by a buoy:** "Hurricane Sandy Smashes Ocean Wave Records," Live Science, November 14, 2012, https://www.livescience.com/24790 -hurricane-sandy-wave-record.html.

285 **The coastal contours of Long Island:** Sobel, *Storm Surge*, 150.

285 **Add the fact that Sandy struck:** Sharp, "Superstorm Sandy."

285 **"never faced a disaster as devastating":** Matt Flegenheimer, "Flooded Tunnels May Keep City's Subway Network Closed for Several Days," *NYT*, October 30, 2012.

285 **The Holland, Queens-Midtown:** Peter Kenyon, "Superstorm Devastates New York Region," *TunnelTalk*, October 2012, https://www.tunneltalk.com/New -York-Nov12-Hurricane-Sandy-inundates-subway-and-traffic-tunnels.php.

285 **The regional utility company:** Dave Carpenter, Jeff Donn, and Jonathan Fahey, "ConEd Prepared for Big Storm, Got an Even Bigger One," NBC News, October 30, 2012, https://www.nbcnewyork.com/news/local/ConEd-Outages-Blackout -Flood-Equipment-Manhattan-NYC-Sandy-Storm-Surge-176525591.html; Sobel, *Storm Surge*, 148–49; and Scott DiSavino and David Sheppard, "ConEd Cuts Power to Part of Lower Manhattan due to Sandy," Reuters, October 29, 2012, https://www.reuters.com/article/us-storm-sandy-conedison/coned-cuts-power-to -part-of-lower-manhattan-due-to-sandy-idUSBRE89S1CP20121030.

286 **Sandy devastated Breezy Point:** Sam Dolnick and Corey Kilgannon, "Wind-

Driven Flames Reduce Scores of Homes to Embers in Queens Enclave," *NYT*, October 30, 2012; and "Cause of Breezy Point Fire during Sandy Determined," NBC News 4, December 24, 2012, https://www.nbcnewyork.com/news/local/Cause -Breezy-Point-Queens-Rockaway-Fires-During-Sandy-Determined-184715051.html.

286 **On Staten Island, which received:** Kirk Semple, "With No Choice, Taking Leap from Roof to Floating Roof," *NYT*, October 30, 2012. The quote is from this source.

287 **About the same that Correa:** Jorge Rivas, "Staten Island Residents Refused to Help Black Mom as Sandy Swept Sons Away," *ColorLines*, November 2, 2012, https://www.colorlines.com/articles/staten-island-residents-refused-help-black-mom -sandy-swept-sons-away; Doug Auer, "Flood of Tears: Bodies of SI Boys Found after Being Swept Away by Sandy," *New York Post*, November 2, 2012; Stephen Maguire, "New Yorkers Shut Mother Out as Her Sons Drowned," *Irish Examiner*, November 6, 2012, https://www.irishexaminer.com/ireland/new-yorkers -shut-mother-out-as-her-sons-drowned-213076.html; Mathew Katz, Nicholas Rizzi, Tom Liddy, and Murray Weiss, "Mom Whose Kids Were Swept Away by Sandy Confronted Neighbor the Next Day," DNAinfo, November 5, 2012, https://www.dnainfo.com/new-york/20121105/arrochar/mom-whose-kids-were -swept-away-by-sandy-confronted-neighbor-next-day; and CNN, "Young Brothers, 'Denied Refuge,' Swept to Death by Sandy," November 4, 2012.

287 **In Brooklyn, twenty-four-year-old:** N. R. Kleinfield and Michael Powell, "In Storm Deaths, Mystery, Fate and Bad Timing," *NYT*, October 30, 2012.

288 **"A half-dozen or so witnesses":** Ibid.

288 **One of the most touching stories:** Justin Louis, "A Sandy Survivor Leaves Behind a Heartbreaking Goodbye Note at the Jersey Shore" (interview of Mike Iann on 92.7 WOBM), November 1, 2012, https://wobm.com/an-amazing-story -of-survival-from-toms-river-audio; Rob Spahr, "Man Swept Away during Hurricane Sandy Writes 'Goodbye' Letter, and Lives to Tell about It,"NJ.com, November 8, 2012, https://www.nj.com/monmouth/2012/11/man_swept_away_during _hurricane_sandy_writes_goodbye_note_and_lives_to_tell_about_it.html; and Sarah Medina, "The Most Incredible Hurricane Sandy Survival Story," HuffPost, December 6, 2012, https://www.huffpost.com/entry/a-hurricane-sandy -victim-_n_2066776.

288 **"Who ever reads this, I'm D I E I N G ":** Louis, "Sandy Survivor Leaves Behind."

289 **After landfall, the heart of Sandy:** Blake et al., "Hurricane Sandy," 4, 14.

289 **"blizzacane" or "snor-eastercane":** Douglas Main, "Frankenstorm! Forecaster's Frightful Name for Sandy Sticks," NBC News, October 26, 2012, http://www .nbcnews.com/id/49573698/ns/technology_and_science-science/t/frankenstorm -forecasters-frightful-name-sandy-sticks/#.XJuB8kRJEkg.

289 **The loss of power below:** Sharon Otterman, "Above 40th Street, the Powerless Go to Recharge," *NYT*, November 1, 2012; and Alex Koppelman, "After Sandy, a Dark Downtown," *The New Yorker*, October 30, 2012.

290 **All US financial markets remained:** Eric Savitz, "NYSE Confirms U.S. Markets to Close Again on Tuesday," *Forbes*, October 29, 2012; and Michael J. De La Merced, "Storm Forces Markets to Remain Closed," *NYT*, October 29, 2012.

290 **New York City schools were closed:** Garth Johnson, "Hurricane Sandy Closes NYC Schools for 5 Days, Most Since 'Asbestos Week' of 1993," Gothamist, October 31, 2012, http://gothamist.com/2012/10/31/public_school_closings_a _brief_hist.php.

290 **The New York City Marathon:** Alex Koppelman, "The Marathon Is Cancelled— Finally," *The New Yorker*, November 2, 2012.

290 **"decided to engage in a sit-down":** Liz Robbins, "A Closed Central Park Leaves Dogs at a Loss," *NYT*, October 30, 2012.

290 **While the flooding of the tunnels:** Bora Zivkovic, "Did NYC Rats Survive Hurricane Sandy?" *A Blog around the Clock*, Scientific American, October 31, 2012, https://blogs.scientificamerican.com/a-blog-around-the-clock/did-nyc-rats -survive-hurricane-sandy; and Bruce Upbin, "No Rat Exodus Reported from NYC Tunnels. Millions of Them Likely Drowned," *Forbes*, October 31, 2012, https://www.forbes.com/sites/bruceupbin/2012/10/31/no-rat-exodus-reported -from-nyc-tunnels-they-probably-all-drowned/#2d95e0b46bfb.

290 **"The Ratpocalypse":** Dan Amira, "The Ratpocalypse Has Been Canceled," *New York*, October 31, 2012, http://nymag.com/intelligencer/2012/10/subway -rats-sandy-hurricane-disease.html.

290 **Sandy was responsible for:** Blake et al., "Hurricane Sandy," 14–15, 120; and NOAA, NCEI, "Costliest U.S. Tropical Cyclones."

291 **Con Edison, which had much:** Associated Press, "Restoring Power to Hurricane Sandy Victims Takes Days to Weeks; 'It's Hard, Grueling Work,'" PennLive, January 5, 2019, https://www.pennlive.com/midstate/2012/11/restoring_power_to _hurricane_s.html.

291 **Eighty percent of subway service:** Sarah Kaufman, Carson Qing, Nolan Levenson, and Melinda Hanson, *Transportation during and after Hurricane Sandy* (New York: Rudin Center for Transportation, New York University, 2012), 8–16; Alex Davies, "One Year Later: Here's How New York City's Subways Have Improved since Hurricane Sandy," *Business Insider*, October 29, 2013; and Vincent Barone, "Superstorm Sandy NYC: MTA Continues to Rebuild Four Years Later," amNewYork, October 27, 2016, https://www.amny.com/transit/super storm-sandy-nyc-mta-continues-to-rebuild-four-years-later-1.12516779.

291 **"hurricane season that wouldn't quit":** NOAA, "Extremely Active 2017 Atlantic Hurricane Season Finally Ends," November 30, 2017, http://www.noaa.gov /media-release/extremely-active-2017-atlantic-hurricane-season-finally-ends.

291 **"the Atlantic hurricane season from hell":** Brian McNoldy, Phil Klotzbach, and Jason Samenow, "The Atlantic Hurricane Season from Hell Is Finally Over," *Washington Post*, November 30, 2017.

291 **Federal forecasters predicted:** NWS, "NOAA 2017 Atlantic Hurricane Season Outlook," May 25, 2017, https://www.cpc.ncep.noaa.gov/products/outlooks /hurricane2017/May/hurricane.shtml.

291 **By contrast, it usually takes:** Blake et al., "Deadliest, Costliest," 15; and Christopher W. Landsea, "Subject: E19) How Many Direct Hits by Hurricanes of Various Categories Have Affected Each State?" HRD, Frequently Asked Questions, last revised August 1, 2018, https://www.aoml.noaa.gov/hrd/tcfaq/E19.html.

292 **Since records have been kept:** Christopher W. Landsea, "Subject: E23) What Is the Complete List of Continental U.S. Landfalling Hurricanes?" HRD, Frequently Asked Questions, last revised July 31, 2018, https://www.aoml.noaa.gov/hrd/tcfaq/ E23.html; Tom McKay, "Hurricane Nate Sets Record for Most Consecutive Atlantic Hurricanes since At Least 1893," Gizmodo, October 8, 2017, https://gizmodo .com/hurricane-nate-sets-record-for-most-consecutive-atlanti-1819264248; Chris Dolce, "Three Category 4 Hurricanes Have Made a U.S. Landfall in 2017," Weather Channel, September 20, 2017, https://weather.com/storms/hurricane /news/hurricane-maria-irma-harvey-three-united-states-category-4-landfalls; and Chris Dolce, "Hurricanes Irma and Harvey Mark the First Time Two Atlantic Category 4 U.S. Landfalls Have Occurred in the Same Year," Weather Channel,

September 10, 2017, https://weather.com/storms/hurricane/news/hurricane-irma
-harvey-landfall-category-4-united-states-history.

292 **The damage attributed to Harvey:** NOAA, NCEI, "Costliest U.S. Tropical
Cyclones"; NOAA, National Centers for Environmental Information (NCEI),
"Hurricanes and Tropical Storms—Annual 2017," accessed December 2018,
https://www.ncdc.noaa.gov/sotc/tropical-cyclones/201713.

292 **The only good news:** Brian McNoldy and Angela Fritz, "National Hurricane
Center Issued Its Best Forecasts on Record This Year," *Washington Post*, Novem-
ber 14, 2017; and Dennis Feltgen (Communications & Public Affairs Officer,
NHC), personal communication, May 15, 2019.

292 **"major hurricane drought":** McNoldy et al., "Atlantic Hurricane Season from Hell."

292 **Instead of moving on:** Background for Hurricane Harvey comes from Eric S.
Blake and David Zelinsky, "Hurricane Harvey, 17 August–1 September 2017,"
Tropical Cyclone Report AL092017, NHC, May 9, 2018; and NWS, "Major Hurricane Harvey—August 25–29, 2017," accessed December 2018, https://www
.weather.gov/crp/hurricane_harvey.

292 **Harvey dumped more than 50 inches:** NWS, "Major Hurricane Harvey"; Blake
and Zelinsky, "Hurricane Harvey," 6.

292 **The 33 trillion gallons:** Angela Fritz and Jason Samenow, "Harvey Unloaded 33
Trillion Gallons of Water in the U.S.," *Washington Post*, September 2, 2017.

292 **In the Houston area alone:** Alexis C. Madrigal, "The Houston Flooding Pushed
the Earth's Crust Down 2 Centimeters," *Atlantic*, September 5, 2017, https://
www.theatlantic.com/technology/archive/2017/09/hurricane-harvey-deformed
-the-earths-crust-around-houston/538866.

293 **While Hurricane Irma was still:** Background for Hurricane Irma comes from
John P. Cangialosi, Andrew S. Latto, and Robbie Berg, "Hurricane Irma, 30
August–12 September 2017," Tropical Cyclone Report AL112017, NHC, June 30,
2018; and Amy O'Connor, "Florida's Hurricane Irma Recovery: The Cost, the
Challenges, the Lessons," *Insurance Journal*, November 30, 2017, https://www
.insurancejournal.com/news/southeast/2017/11/30/472582.htm.

293 **"We're totally devastated":** "American Living on St. John: 'We're Totally Devastated' after Irma," CBS News, September, 13, 2017, https://www.cbsnews.com/
news/hurricane-irma-damage-st-john-us-virgin-islands.

293 **Irma maintained winds of 185 mph:** NWS, "Hurricane Irma 2017," accessed
December 2018, https://www.weather.gov/tae/Irma2017.

293 **Since early forecasts had Irma:** Ralph Ellis, Joe Sterling, and Dakin Andone,
"Florida Gov. Rick Scott Tells Residents: 'You Need to Go Right Now,'" CNN,
September 9, 2017, https://www.cnn.com/2017/09/08/us/hurricane-irma
-evacuation-florida/index.html; and Greg Allen, "Lessons from Hurricane Irma:
When to Evacuate and When to Shelter in Place," *Morning Edition*, NPR, June 1,
2018, https://www.npr.org/2018/06/01/615293318/lessons-from-hurricane-irma
-when-to-evacuate-and-when-to-shelter-in-place.

294 **In that eventuality:** Brian K. Sullivan, "Powerful Hurricane Irma, on Path to
Slam Caribbean Then Florida, Could Surpass Katrina," *Insurance Journal*,
September 5, 2017, https://www.insurancejournal.com/news/southeast/2017
/09/05/463398.htm.

294 **On September 20, Category 5:** Background for Hurricane Maria comes from
Richard J. Pasch, Andrew B. Penny, and Robbie Berg, "Hurricane Maria, 16–
30 September 2017," Tropical Cyclone Report AL152017, NHC, April 10, 2018;
FEMA, "2017 Hurricane Season: FEMA After-Action Report," July 12, 2018.

294 **It passed diagonally over the island:** David Keellings and José J. Hernández Ayala, "Extreme Rainfall Associated with Hurricane Maria over Puerto Rico and Its Connections to Climate Variability and Change," *Geophysical Research Letters*, March 12, 2019, 2964.

295 **Maria "destroyed us":** "Hurricane Maria Updates: In Puerto Rico, the Storm 'Destroyed Us'" *NYT*, September 21, 2017.

295 **The death toll from Maria:** *Ascertainment of the Estimated Excess Mortality from Hurricane Maria in Puerto Rico*, Project Report (Washington, DC: Milken Institute School of Public Health, George Washington University, 2018); Amy B. Wang, "Sorry, Mr. President: The Hurricane Maria Death Toll in Puerto Rico Didn't Grow by 'Magic,'" *Washington Post*, September 15, 2018; and Sheri Fink, "Nearly a Year after Hurricane Maria, Puerto Rico Revises Death Toll to 2,975," *NYT*, August 28, 2018.

295 **A few months before:** Nishant Kishore, Domingo Marqués, Ayesha Mahmud, Mathew V. Kiang, Irmary Rodriguez, Arlan Fuller, Peggy Ebner, et al., "Mortality in Puerto Rico after Hurricane Maria," *New England Journal of Medicine*, July 12, 2018, 162–70, https://www.nejm.org/doi/full/10.1056/NEJMsa1803972.

295 **For example, a review of mortality:** Frances Robles, Kenan Davis, Sheri Fink, and Sarah Almukhtar, "Official Toll in Puerto Rico: 64. Actual Deaths May Be 1,052," *NYT*, December 9, 2017. See also Glenn Kessler, "President Trump's Four-Pinocchio Complaint about the Maria Death Toll Figures," *Washington Post*, September 13, 2018.

295 **The Puerto Rico Health Department:** Kessler, "President Trump's Four-Pinocchio Complaint"; and Danica Coto, "Puerto Rico Agency Sues Government to Obtain Death Data," Associated Press, June 1, 2018, https://apnews.com/7d19 e956de344d7188c79b455c0315f6.

296 **Methodologies and conclusions:** Amy Sherman, "Fact-Checking the Death Toll Estimates from Hurricane Maria in Puerto Rico," PolitiFact, June 5, 2018, https://www.politifact.com/truth-o-meter/article/2018/jun/05/fact-checking-death-toll-estimates-hurricane-maria; John Morales, "Why Hurricane Maria's Death Toll Is Misunderstood and Incomparable to Other Disasters," *Washington Post*, August 29, 2018; Eugene Kiely, Robert Farley, Lori Robertson, and D'Angelo Gore, "Trump's False Tweets on Hurricane Maria's Death Toll," FactCheck.org, September 13, 2018, https://www.factcheck.org/2018/09/trumps-false-tweets-on-hurricane-marias-death-toll.

296 **"3000 people did not die":** Kessler, "President Trump's Four-Pinocchio Complaint."

296 **Simply put, on the one side:** Mark Landler, "Trump Rates His Hurricane Relief: 'Great.' 'Amazing.' 'Tremendous,'" *NYT*, September 26, 2017; Frances Robles, Lizette Alvarez, and Nicholas Fandos, "In Battered Puerto Rico, Governor Warns of a Humanitarian Crisis," *NYT*, September 25, 2017; Chantal Da Silva, "Trump Condemned over 'Blatantly False' Claim Hurricane Maria Response Was 'Incredible Success,'" *Time*, September 12, 2018; and David A. Graham, "Trump's Dubious Revisionist History of Hurricane Maria," *Atlantic*, September 12, 2018.

296 **For example, in early 2019:** Tim Elfrink, "Trump Hits Out at 'Crazed and Incompetent' Puerto Rican Leaders after Disaster Bill Fails," *Washington Post*, April 2, 2019; David Jackson, "'Unhinged': President Trump and San Juan Mayor Carmen Yulin Cruz Trade Insults over Puerto Rico Relief," *USA Today*, April 2, 2019; Erica Werner and Jeff Stein, "Massive Disaster Relief Bill Stalls in Senate over Puerto Rico Dispute," *Washington Post*, April 1, 2019; and Cait-

lyn Oprysko, "Trump Accuses 'Grossly Incompetent' Puerto Rican Politicians of Misusing Federal Hurricane Aid," *Politico*, April 2, 2019, https://www.politico.com/story/2019/04/02/trump-puerto-rico-hurricane-aid-1247759.

296 **"Puerto Rico got far more":** Anni Karni and Patricia Mazzei, "Trump Lashes Out Again at Puerto Rico, Bewildering the Island," *NYT*, April 2, 2019.

297 **"crazed and incompetent":** Elfrink, "Trump Hits Out."

297 **"The people of Puerto Rico":** Aaron Rupar, "Trump's Latest Outburst against Puerto Rico, Explained," Vox, April 2, 2019, https://www.vox.com/2019/4/2/18291975/trump-puerto-rico-disaster-relief-funding-bill-explained.

297 **"Pres Trump continues to embarrass":** Elfrink, "Trump Hits Out."

297 **"Mr. President, this 'place' you refer to":** Ibid.

297 **Beyond the accusations and rhetoric:** Charley E. Willison, Phillip M. Singer, Melissa S. Creary, and Scott L. Greer, "Quantifying Inequities in US Federal Response to Hurricane Disaster in Texas and Florida Compared with Puerto Rico," *BMJ Global Health*, April 2019; Ron Nixon and Matt Stevens, "Harvey, Irma, Maria: Trump Administration's Response Compared," *NYT*, September 27, 2017; Danny Vinik, "How Trump Favored Texas over Puerto Rico," *Politico*, March 27, 2018; Landler, "Trump Rates His Hurricane Relief"; Nicole Einbinder, "How the Response to Hurricane Maria Compared to Harvey and Irma," *Frontline*, PBS, May 1, 2018, https://www.pbs.org/wgbh/frontline/article/how-the-response-to-hurricane-maria-compared-to-harvey-and-irma; Patricia Mazzei, "Hunger and an 'Abandoned' Hospital: Puerto Rico Waits as Washington Bickers," *NYT*, April 7, 2019; and Errin Haines Whack, "Hurricane Maria a Reminder of 'Second-Class' Status for Some," Associated Press, September 30, 2017, https://www.apnews.com/e651f0c7072646698126dcfdffeebd80.

297 **"an island surrounded by water":** Eliza Relman, "Trump on Puerto Rican Crisis: 'This Is an Island Surrounded by Water, Big Water, Ocean Water,'" *Business Insider*, September 29, 2017.

297 **"at the height of FEMA":** Government Accountability Office, *2017 Hurricanes and Wildfires: Initial Observations on the Federal Response and Key Recovery Challenges*, Report to Congressional Addressees, GAO-18-472 (Washington, DC: GAO, 2018), ii.

EPILOGUE—STORMY WEATHER AHEAD

300 **Over time, the anthropogenic emissions:** Intergovernmental Panel on Climate Change (IPCC), *Climate Change 2014: Synthesis Report. Contribution of Working Groups I, II and III to the Fifth Assessment Report of the Intergovernmental Panel on Climate Change* (Geneva: IPCC, 2015), 2; NASA, "Scientific Consensus: Earth's Climate Is Warming," Global Climate Change: Vital Signs of the Planet, accessed March 2019, https://climate.nasa.gov/scientific-consensus; John Cook, Naomi Oreskes, Peter T. Doran, William R. L. Anderegg, Bart Verheggen, Ed W. Maibach, J. Stuart Carlton, et al., "Consensus on Consensus: A Synthesis of Consensus Estimates on Human-Caused Global Warming," *Environmental Research Letters*, April 13, 2016, https://iopscience.iop.org/article/10.1088/1748-9326/11/4/048002; Intergovernmental Panel on Climate Change (IPCC), "Summary for Policymakers," in *Global Warming of 1.5°C*, IPCC Special Report (Geneva: IPCC, 2018), 4; NASA, "2018 Fourth Warmest Year in Continued Warming Trend, According to NASA, NOAA," Global Climate Change: Vital Signs of the Planet, February 6, 2019, https://climate.nasa.gov/news/2841/2018

-fourth-warmest-year-in-continued-warming-trend-according-to-nasa-noaa; and IPCC, "Framing and Context," in *Global Warming of 1.5°C*, 51.

300 **"Human influence on the climate":** IPCC, *Climate Change 2014*, 2.

300 **"global warming is likely to reach":** IPCC, "Summary for Policymakers." See also Jeff Tollefson, "Limiting Warming to 1.5° Celsius Will Require Drastic Action, IPCC Says," *Nature*, October 8, 2018.

300 **"Had Sandy struck New York":** Kerry Emanuel, "Climate Change and Hurricane Katrina: What Have We Learned?" The Conversation, August 24, 2015, https://theconversation.com/climate-change-and-hurricane-katrina-what-have -we-learned-46297. See also Jonathan D. Woodruff, Jennifer L. Irish, and Suzana J. Camargo, "Coastal Flooding by Tropical Cyclones and Sea-Level Rise," *Nature*, December 5, 2013, 44–52; and Michael E. Mann, "What We Know about the Climate Change–Hurricane Connection," *Observations* (blog), Scientific American, September 8, 2017, https://blogs.scientificamerican.com/observations/what-we -know-about-the-climate-change-hurricane-connection.

301 **A growing number of studies:** Geophysical Fluid Dynamics Laboratory, "Global Warming and Hurricanes: An Overview of Current Research Results," last revised August 15, 2019, https://www.gfdl.noaa.gov/global-warming-and -hurricanes; US Global Change Research Program, "Our Changing Climate," in *Impacts, Risks, and Adaptation in the United States: Fourth National Climate Assessment* (2018), vol. 2, chap. 2, https://nca2018.globalchange.gov/chapter/2; Stefan Rahmstorf, Kerry Emanuel, Mike Mann, and Jim Kossin, "Does Global Warming Make Tropical Cyclones Stronger?" RealClimate, May 30, 2018, http:// www.realclimate.org/index.php/archives/2018/05/does-global-warming-make -tropical-cyclones-stronger; and M. Liu, G. A. Vecchi, J. A. Smith, and Thomas R. Knutson, "Causes of Large Projected Increases in Hurricane Precipitation Rates with Global Warming," *npj Climate and Atmospheric Science* 2, art. 38 (2019), https://www.nature.com/articles/s41612-019-0095-3.

301 **"extreme precipitation, like that of":** David Keellings and José J. Hernández Ayala, "Extreme Rainfall Associated with Hurricane Maria over Puerto Rico and Its Connections to Climate Variability and Change," *Geophysical Research Letters*, March 12, 2019, 2964–73. See also Guiling Wang, Dagang Wang, Kevin E. Trenberth, Amir Erfanian, Miao Yu, Michael G. Bosilovich, and Dana T. Parr, "The Peak Structure and Future Changes of the Relationships between Extreme Precipitation and Temperature," *Nature Climate Change* 7 (2017): 268–74. See also Christina M. Patricola and Michael F. Wehner, "Anthropogenic Influences on Major Tropical Cyclone Events," *Nature*, 2018, https://www.nature.com/articles /s41586-018-0673-2.

301 **Three other studies:** Geert Jan van Oldenborgh, Karen van der Wiel, Antonia Sebastian, Roop Singh, Julie Arrighi, Frederike Otto, Karsten Haustein, Sihan Li, Gabriel Vecchi, and Heidi Cullen, "Attribution of Extreme Rainfall from Hurricane Harvey, August 2017," *Environmental Research Letters*, December 13, 2017, 12409; Mark D. Risser and Michael F. Wehner, "Attributable Human-Induced Changes in the Likelihood and Magnitude of the Observed Extreme Precipitation during Hurricane Harvey," *Geophysical Research Letters*, December 23, 2017, 12457–64; and Simon Wang, Lin Zhao, Jin-Ho Yoon, Phil Klotzback, and Robert R. Gillies, "Quantitative Attribution of Climate Effects on Hurricane Harvey's Extreme Rainfall in Texas," *Environmental Research Letters*, April 30, 2018, 1–10. See also Kerry Emanuel, "Assessing the Present and Future Prob-

ability of Hurricane Harvey's Rainfall," *Proceedings of the National Academy of Sciences*, November 13, 2017, https://www.pnas.org/content/114/48/12681; and Henry Fountain, "Scientists Link Hurricane Harvey's Record Rainfall to Climate Change," *NYT*, December 13, 2017.

301 **Considerable research also predicts:** Rahmstorf et al., "Does Global Warming Make"; Kerry Emanuel, "Increasing Destructiveness of Tropical Cyclones over the Past 30 Years," *Nature*, July 31, 2005, 686–88; Emanuel, "Climate Change and Hurricane Katrina"; James B. Elsner, James P. Kossin, and Thomas H. Jagger, "The Increasing Intensity of the Strongest Tropical Cyclones," *Nature*, September 2008, 92–95; Kerry Emanuel, *What We Know about Climate Change* (Cambridge, MA: MIT Press, 2018), 38–40; Geophysical Fluid Dynamics Laboratory, "Global Warming and Hurricanes"; and US Global Change Research Program, "Our Changing Climate."

301 **indeed, some observers believe:** US Global Change Research Program, "Our Changing Climate"; Kieran T. Bhatia, Gabriel A. Vecchi, Thomas R. Knutson, Hiroyuki Murakami, James Kossin, Keith W. Dixon, and Carolyn E. Whitlock, "Recent Increases in Tropical Cyclone Intensification Rates," *Nature Communications*, February 7, 2019, https://www.nature.com/articles/s41467-019-08471-z; US Global Change Research Program, "Extreme Weather," accessed March 2019, https://nca2014.globalchange.gov/highlights/report-findings/extreme-weather; Annie Sneed, "Was the Extreme 2017 Hurricane Season Driven by Climate Change?" *Scientific American*, October 26, 2017, https://www.scientificamerican .com/article/was-the-extreme-2017-hurricane-season-driven-by-climate-change; David Leonhardt, "Hurricanes Are Getting Worse," *NYT*, September 3, 2019; and Mann, "What We Know." Just as this book was going into the final stage of production, another study came out with the following conclusion: "We find that hurricanes are indeed becoming more damaging. The frequency of the very most damaging hurricanes has increased at a rate of 330% per century." Aslak Grinsted, Peter Ditlevsen, and Jess Hesselbjerg Christensen, "Normalized US Hurricane Damage Estimates Using Area of Total Destruction, 1900−2018," *Proceedings of the National Academy of Sciences*, November 11, 2019, https://www.pnas.org/ content/early/2019/11/05/1912277116. However, other climate scientists have cast doubt on such conclusions. See, for example, Associated Press, "Hurricanes That Cause Major Destruction Are Becoming More Frequent, Study Says," *Los Angeles Times*, November 11, 2019; and Geophysical Fluid Dynamics Laboratory, "Global Warming and Hurricanes."

301 **Other studies show that:** James P. Kossin, "A Global Slowdown of Tropical-Cyclone Translation Speed," *Nature*, 2018, 104–7; Timothy M. Hall and James P. Kossin, "Hurricane Stalling along the North American Coast and Implications for Rainfall," *npj Climate and Atmospheric Science*, June 3, 2019, https://www .nature.com/articles/s41612-019-0074-8; Craig Welch, "Hurricanes Are Moving Slower—And That's a Huge Problem," *National Geographic*, June 6, 2018, https://news.nationalgeographic.com/2018/06/hurricanes-cyclones-move-slower -drop-more-rain-climate-change-science; and Giorgia Guglielmi, "Hurricanes Slow Their Roll around the World," *Nature*, June 6, 2018, https://www.nature .com/articles/d41586-018-05324-5#ref-CR4.

301 **Indeed, one simulation analyzed:** Ethan D. Guttman, Roy M. Rasmussen, Cha-ghai Liu, and Kyoko Ikeda, "Changes in Hurricanes from a 13-Yr Convection-Permitting Pseudo–Global Warming Simulation," *Journal of Climate*, May 1,

2008, 3643–57; National Science Foundation, "Hurricanes: Stronger, Slower, Wetter in the Future?" News Release 18-034, May 21, 2018, https://www.nsf.gov /news/news_summ.jsp?cntn_id=245396.

301 **Another study suggests:** Nam-Young Kang and James B. Elsner, "Trade-off between Intensity and Frequency of Global Tropical Cyclones," *Nature Climate Change*, 2015, 661–64; and Angela Fritz, "Global Warming Fueling Fewer but Stronger Hurricanes, Study Says," *Washington Post*, May 18, 2015, https://www .washingtonpost.com/news/capital-weather-gang/wp/2015/05/18/global-warming -fueling-fewer-but-stronger-hurricanes-study-says/?utm_term=.455734ed41fb.

301 **"may be much stronger":** Mingfan Ting, James P. Kossin, Suzana J. Camargo, and Cuichua Li, "Past and Future Hurricane Intensity Change along the U.S. East Coast," *Scientific Reports* 9, art. 7795 (2019): 4; and Rebecca Lindsey, "Warming May Increase Risk of Rapidly Intensifying Hurricanes along U.S. East Coast," Climate.gov, May 24, 2019, https://www.climate.gov/news-features/featured-images /warming-may-increase-risk-rapidly-intensifying-hurricanes-along-us.

302 **"The effect of climate change":** Fountain, "Scientists Link Hurricane Harvey's Record Rainfall." See also Kimberly Miller, "What Does Climate Science Tell Us about Monster Storms like Hurricane Michael?" Phys.org, October 10, 2019, https://phys.org/news/2019-10-climate-science-monster-storms-hurricane.html; and Geophysical Fluid Dynamics Laboratory, "Global Warming and Hurricanes." The latter source contains the following statement: "In the Atlantic, it is premature to conclude with high confidence that human activities—and particularly greenhouse gas emissions that cause global warming—have already had a detectable impact on hurricane activity."

302 **Recent trends in coastal population:** Darryl T. Cohen, "60 Million People Live in the Path of Hurricanes," US Census Bureau, August 6, 2018, https://www .census.gov/library/stories/2018/08/coastal-county-population-rises.html.

304 **As this book was heading:** Background for Hurricane Dorian comes from Matthew Cappucci, "Dorian's Horrific Eyewall Slammed Grand Bahama Island for 40 Hours Straight," *Washington Post*, September 3, 2019; Fernando Alfonso III, Mike Hayes, Braden Goyette, and Meg Wagner, "Hurricane Dorian's Path and Destruction," CNN, September 8, 2019, https://www.cnn.com/us/live-news/hurricane-dorian -bahamas-aftermath/h_7c8eec3e294355d16965d0e2b55359a0; Bay Area News Group, "Map: Hurricane Dorian Mandatory Evacuations in Florida, Georgia, South Carolina," *Mercury News*, September 3, 2019; NWS, "Hurricane Dorian, September 6, 2019," accessed October 2019, https://www.weather.gov/mhx/Dorian2019; Phil Helsel, Saphora Smith, and Minyvonne Burke, "As Hurricane Dorian Begins Lashing Florida, Southeast Braces for Disaster," NBC News, September 3, 2019; Associated Press, "Dorian Strikes Canada After Leaving at Least 43 Dead in Bahamas and Wreaking Havoc in North Carolina," *Los Angeles Times*, September 7, 2019, https://www.latimes.com/world-nation/story/2019-09-07/hurricane-dorian -north-carolina-damage-bahamas-death-toll; Sloane Heffernan, "Dorian Claims Third Life in NC; Weather Service Confirms Hurricane-Spawned Tornado Hit Emerald Isle," WRAL.com, September 9, 2019, https://www.wral.com/dorian -claims-third-life-in-nc-weather-service-confirms-hurricane-spawned-tornado-hit -emerald-isle/18622549; Ian Austen, "While No Longer a Hurricane, Dorian Still Inflicts Damage on Canada," *NYT*, September 7, 2019; Campbell Robertson, Richard Fausset, and Nicholas Bogel-Burroughs, " 'I'll Just Have to Restart Everything': Ocracoke Island Is Hit Hard by Dorian," *NYT*, September 6, 2019; Richard Fausset and Nicholas Bogel-Burroughs, "Hurricane Dorian Becomes a Carolina Problem

with a Fierce Lashing of the Coast," *NYT*, September 5, 2019; and Reuters, "Four Deaths—Hurricane Dorian Floods Island as It Swipes North Carolina Then Heads North," *NYT*, September 7, 2019.

304 **"put everyone on square zero"**: Kirk Semple, "On Dorian-Battered Island, What's Left? Virtually Nothing," *NYT*, September 6, 2019.

304 **"to prepare for unimaginable"**: Helena de Moura, "Bahamas Death Toll Is Likely to Soar, Health Minister Warns," CNN, September 5, 2019, https://www.cnn.com /us/live-news/hurricane-dorian-bahamas-aftermath/h_7c8eec3e294355d169 65d0e2b55359a0.

304 **As of late October 2019:** Riel Major, "Dorian Death Toll Rises to 67 as Two More Bodies Found," *Tribune*, October 28, 2019.

SELECT BIBLIOGRAPHY

This bibliography contains but a small fraction of the sources cited in this book. It is intended as a starting point for the general reader who wants to learn more about the history of America's hurricanes. For additional information about specific topics and particular hurricanes covered in the text, please refer to the endnotes.

Allen, Everett S. *A Wind to Shake the World: The Story of the 1938 Hurricane*. Boston: Little, Brown, 1976.

Avilés, Lourdes B. *Taken by Storm 1938: A Social and Meteorological History of the Great New England Hurricane*. Boston: American Meteorological Society, 2013.

Barnes, Jay. *Florida's Hurricane History*. Chapel Hill: University of North Carolina Press, 2007.

Bechtel, Stefan. *Roar of the Heavens*. New York: Citadel Press, 2006.

Brinkley, Douglas. *The Great Deluge: Hurricane Katrina, New Orleans, and the Mississippi Gulf Coast*. New York: William Morrow, 2006.

Burns, Cherie. *The Great Hurricane: 1938*. New York: Atlantic Monthly Press, 2005.

Cox, John D. *Storm Watchers: The Turbulent History of Weather Prediction from Franklin's Kite to El Niño*. New York: John Wiley, 2002.

Douglas, Marjory Stoneman. *Hurricane*. New York: Rinehart, 1958.

Drye, Willie. *Storm of the Century: The Labor Day Hurricane of 1935*. Washington, DC: National Geographic, 2002.

Emanuel, Kerry. *Divine Wind: The History and Science of Hurricanes*. New York: Oxford University Press, 2005.

Falls, Rose C. *Cheniere Caminada, or The Wind of Death: The Story of the Storm in Louisiana*. New Orleans: Hopkins Printing, 1893.

Fleming, James Rodger. *Fixing the Sky: The Checkered History of Weather and Climate Control*. New York: Columbia University Press, 2012.

———. *Meteorology in America, 1800–1870*. Baltimore: Johns Hopkins University Press, 1990.

Freeman, Gregory A. *The Gathering Wind: Hurricane Sandy, the Sailing Ship* Bounty, *and a Courageous Rescue at Sea*. New York: New American Library, 2013.

Guadalupe, Luis E. Ramos. *Father Benito Viñes: The 19th-Century Life and Contributions of a Cuban Hurricane Observer and Scientist*. Translated by Oswaldo Garcia. Boston: American Meteorological Society, 2014.

Hearn, Philip D. *Hurricane Camille: Monster Storm of the Gulf Coast*. Jackson: University of Mississippi Press, 2004.

Henson, Robert. *Weather on the Air: A History of Broadcast Meteorology.* Boston: American Meteorological Society, 2010.

Kean, Sam. *Caesar's Last Breath: Decoding the Secrets of the Air around Us.* New York: Little, Brown, 2017.

Kleinberg, Eliot. *Black Cloud: The Great Florida Hurricane of 1928.* New York: Carroll & Graf, 2003.

Knowles, Thomas Neil. *Category 5: The 1935 Labor Day Hurricane.* Gainesville: University Press of Florida, 2009.

Larson, Erik. *Isaac's Storm: A Man, a Time, and the Deadliest Hurricane in History.* New York: Vintage Books, 1999.

Long, Stephen. *Thirty-Eight: The Hurricane That Transformed New England.* New Haven, CT: Yale University Press, 2016.

Ludlum, David. *Early American Hurricanes: 1492–1870.* Boston: American Meteorological Society, 1963.

Mason, Herbert Molloy Jr. *Death from the Sea: The Galveston Hurricane of 1900.* New York: Dial Press, 1972.

Miles, Kathryn. *Superstorm: Nine Days inside Hurricane Sandy.* New York: Dutton, 2014.

Moore, Peter. *Weather Experiment: The Pioneers Who Sought to See the Future.* New York: Farrar, Straus and Giroux, 2015.

Mykle, Robert. *Killer 'Cane: The Deadly Hurricane of 1928.* New York: Cooper Square Press, 2002.

Norcross, Bryan. *My Hurricane Andrew Story.* Self-published, 2017.

Rubillo, Tom. *Hurricane Destruction in South Carolina.* Charleston, SC: History Press, 2006.

Sallenger, Abby. *Island in a Storm: A Rising Sea, a Vanishing Coast, and a Nineteenth-Century Disaster That Warns of a Warmer World.* New York: Public Affairs, 2009.

Scott, Phil. *Hemingway's Hurricane: The Great Florida Keys Storm of 1935.* New York: International Marine, 2006.

Scotti, R. A. *Sudden Sea: The Great Hurricane of 1938.* Boston: Little, Brown, 2003.

Sheets, Bob, and Jack Williams. *Hurricane Watch: Forecasting the Deadliest Storms on Earth.* New York: Vintage Books, 2001.

Simpson, Robert H. (with Neal M. Dorst). *Hurricane Pioneer: Memoirs of Bob Simpson.* Boston: American Meteorological Society, 2015.

Sobel, Adam. *Storm Surge: Hurricane Sandy, Our Changing Climate, and Extreme Weather of the Past and Future.* New York: Harper Wave, 2014.

Standiford, Les. *Last Train to Paradise: Henry Flagler and the Spectacular Rise and Fall of the Railroad That Crossed an Ocean.* New York: Broadway Paperbacks, 2002.

Steinberg, Ted. *Acts of God: The Unnatural History of Natural Disaster in America.* New York: Oxford University Press, 2000.

Tannehill, Ivan Ray. *The Hurricane Hunters.* New York: Dodd, Mead, 1956.

———. *Hurricanes: Their Nature and History.* New York: Greenwood Press, 1938.

Time Magazine. *Hurricane Katrina: The Storm That Changed America.* New York: Time Books, 2005.

Toomey, David. *Stormchasers: The Hurricane Hunters and Their Fateful Flight into Hurricane Janet.* New York: W. W. Norton, 2002.

Walter, H. J. "Walt." *The Wind Chasers: A History of the U.S. Navy's Atlantic Fleet Hurricane Hunters.* Dallas, TX: Taylor, 1992.

Will, Lawrence E. *Okeechobee Hurricane and the Hoover Dike.* St. Petersburg, FL: Great Outdoors Publishing, 1961.

Woodward, Hobson. *A Brave Vessel: The True Tale of the Castaways Who Rescued James-town and Inspired Shakespeare's* The Tempest. New York: Viking, 2009.

Zebrowski, Ernest, and Judith A. Howard. *Category 5: The Story of Camille, Lessons Unlearned from America's Most Violent Hurricane.* Ann Arbor: University of Michigan Press, 2005.

ILLUSTRATION CREDITS

page xv: Courtesy Library of Congress

page 1: Courtesy John Carter Brown Library at Brown University

page 3: Courtesy John Carter Brown Library at Brown University

page 5: Courtesy Metropolitan Museum of Art

page 8: Courtesy Library of Congress

page 9: Courtesy John Carter Brown Library at Brown University

page 10: Courtesy Library of Congress

page 13: Courtesy John Carter Brown Library at Brown University

page 16: Courtesy Library of Congress

page 18: *The Works of Mr. William Shakespear; in Six Volumes*, ed. Nicholas Rowe (London: Jacob Tonson, 1709)

page 21: Courtesy Houghton Library, Harvard University

page 25: Courtesy Library of Congress

page 26: Courtesy Library of Congress

page 31: Archibald Duncan, *The Mariner's Chronicle: Being a Collection of the Most Interesting Narratives of Shipwrecks, Fires, Famines*, etc. vol. II (London: James Cundee, 1804)

page 33: Courtesy Library of Congress

page 35: Courtesy Library of Congress

page 40: Courtesy Library of Congress

page 48: Courtesy Library of Congress

page 54: Courtesy Library of Congress

page 56: Courtesy Library of Congress

page 57: Courtesy NOAA

page 59: Courtesy NOAA

page 68: Courtesy Library of Congress

page 77: Courtesy Sherry Hightower, Pixabay

page 79: Courtesy National Archives, Washington, DC

page 84: Courtesy Library of Congress

page 96: Courtesy Library of Congress

page 99: Courtesy Library of Congress

page 100: Courtesy Library of Congress

page 101: Courtesy Library of Congress

page 104: Courtesy Library of Congress

page 107: Courtesy Florida Memory, State Library & Archives of Florida

page 111: Courtesy Florida Memory, State Library & Archives of Florida

page 115: Courtesy Florida Memory, State Library & Archives of Florida

page 117: Courtesy Florida Memory, State Library & Archives of Florida

page 120: Courtesy Library of Congress

page 129: Courtesy Florida Memory, State Library & Archives of Florida

page 131: Courtesy Florida Memory, State Library & Archives of Florida

page 133: Courtesy Library of Congress

page 136: Courtesy Library of Congress

page 138: Courtesy Library of Congress

page 146: Courtesy Florida Memory, State Library & Archives of Florida

page 148: Courtesy NOAA

page 151: Courtesy Library of Congress

page 155: Courtesy NOAA

page 158: Courtesy NOAA

page 163: Courtesy Connecticut Historical Society

page 165: Courtesy *The Westerly Sun*

page 165: Courtesy *The Westerly Sun*

page 166: Courtesy Collection of the New Haven Railroad Historical & Technical Association Inc.

page 167: Courtesy National Archives, Waltham, MA

page 167: Courtesy National Archives, Waltham, MA

page 172: Courtesy Rhode Island School of Design

page 174: Courtesy NOAA

page 176: Courtesy Crossley Books/*The Crossley ID Guide: Eastern Birds.*

page 179: Courtesy NOAA

page 181: Courtesy US Air Force

page 184: Courtesy US Navy

page 186: Courtesy US Air Force

page 191: Courtesy NASA

page 195: Courtesy NOAA

page 196: Courtesy MIT Museum

page 197: Courtesy www.CartoonCollections.com

page 202: Courtesy NOAA

page 209: Courtesy Florida Memory, State Library & Archives of Florida

page 211: Courtesy www.CartoonCollections.com

page 212: Courtesy Neal M. Dorst

page 216: Courtesy NOAA

page 218: Courtesy NOAA

page 223: Courtesy NOAA

page 224: Courtesy US Air Force

page 226: Courtesy Boston Public Library, Leslie Jones Collection

page 228: Courtesy NOAA

page 230: Courtesy National Archives, Waltham, MA

page 232: Courtesy NOAA

page 235: Courtesy Local History and Genealogy Department Image Collection/Biloxi Public Library/Harrison County Library System. Photograph by Chauncey Hinman.

page 235: Courtesy Local History and Genealogy Department Image Collection/Biloxi Public Library/Harrison County Library System. Photograph by Chauncey Hinman.

page 237: Courtesy Local History and Genealogy Department Image Collection/Biloxi Public Library/Harrison County Library System. Photograph by Chauncey Hinman.

page 237: Courtesy Local History and Genealogy Department Image Collection/Biloxi Public Library/Harrison County Library System. Photograph by Chauncey Hinman.

page 247: Courtesy George Butch

page 249: Courtesy NOAA

page 250: Courtesy NOAA

page 260: Courtesy NOAA

page 263: Courtesy NOAA, Lieutenant Commander Mark Moran, NOAA Corps

page 264: Courtesy Petty Officer 2nd Class Kyle Niemi, US Coast Guard

page 265: Courtesy Petty Officer 2nd Class, Jennifer Johnson, US Coast Guard

page 266: Courtesy Carol M. Highsmith's America, Library of Congress

page 267: Courtesy Specialist Brendan Mackie, US Coast Guard

page 279: Courtesy Shutterstock.com; photograph by James Steidl

page 286: Courtesy Patrick Cashin, New York Metropolitan Transportation Authority

page 289: Courtesy Master Sergent Mark C. Olsen, US Air Force

page 293: Courtesy Lieutenant Zachary West, US Department of Defense

page 294: Courtesy Paul Brennan, Pixabay

page 299: Courtesy NOAA

INSERT

1. Courtesy Nilfanion

3. Courtesy Rhode Island Historical Society

4. Courtesy Michelle Maria, Pixabay

6. Private Collection. Photograph courtesy Sotheby's Inc. © 2019.

7. Courtesy Ron Magill

8. Courtesy NOAA

9. Courtesy US Air Force

10. Courtesy NASA

11. Courtesy Petty Officer 2nd Class Tim Kuklewski, US Coast Guard

12. Courtesy Pete Souza, White House Photo

13. Courtesy NOAA

14. Courtesy NOAA

15. Courtesy NASA

16. Courtesy Jennifer Dolin

17. Courtesy Lily Dolin

INDEX

Note: Page numbers in *italics* refer to illustrations.

ABOUT THE

AUTHOR

ERIC JAY DOLIN is the author of *Leviathan: The History of Whaling in America*, which was chosen as one of the best nonfiction books of 2007 by the *Los Angeles Times, Boston Globe*, and *Providence Journal*, and also won the 2007 John Lyman Award for US Maritime History; and *Fur, Fortune, and Empire: The Epic History of the Fur Trade in America*, which was chosen by the *Seattle Times* as one of the best nonfiction books of 2010, and also won the James P. Hanlan Book Award, given by the New England Historical Association. He also wrote *When America First Met China: An Exotic History of Tea, Drugs, and Money in the Age of Sail*, which was chosen by *Kirkus Reviews* as one of the 100 best nonfiction books of 2012; and *Brilliant Beacons: A History of the American Lighthouse*, which was chosen by the website gCaptain and by *Classic Boat* magazine as one of the best nautical books of 2016, and was selected as a "must-read" book for 2017 by the Massachusetts Center for the Book. His last book before *A Furious Sky* is *Black Flags, Blue Waters: The Epic History of America's Most Notorious Pirates*, which was chosen as a "must-read" book for 2019, and was a finalist for the 2019 Julia Ward Howe Award given by the Boston Author's Club. A graduate of Brown, Yale, and MIT, where he received his PhD in environmental policy, Dolin lives in Marblehead, Massachusetts, with his family. For more information on his background and books, visit his website, ericjaydolin.com. You can also follow Dolin's posts on his professional Facebook page, @ericjaydolin, or on Twitter, @EricJayDolin.